THE SACRED BOOKS OF
CONFUCIUS
AND OTHER CONFUCIAN CLASSICS

THE SACRED BOOKS OF
CONFUCIUS
AND OTHER CONFUCIAN CLASSICS

**Edited and Translated by
Ch'u Chai and Winberg Chai**

INTRODUCTION BY CH'U CHAI

UNIVERSITY BOOKS *New Hyde Park, New York*

To Dr. Alvin Johnson

with the high respect of
Ch'u Chai and Winberg Chai

CONTENTS

I. Confucianism as Humanism

1

Confucianism has dominated Chinese thought for the last twenty-five centuries. It had its beginning in the teachings of Confucius, but in the work of building its foundation, Mencius and Hsün Tzu took the lead. In its prominent characteristics Confucian philosophy is humanistic, occupying itself mainly with human relations and virtues, studiously shunning all questions that enter into ontological subtleties or partake of the supernatural. The doctrine of *jen,* or humanity, stands out from the mass of thought that Confucius developed as the central thesis of the whole system. His ethics, his politics, his life ideal, all flow from the supreme virtue—*jen.* It is the cardinal principle of the humanism that has been displayed in Chinese cultural achievement for thousands of years.

Jen, in the *Analects,* expresses the Confucian ideal of cultivating human relations, developing human faculties, sublimating one's personality, and upholding human rights. For *chün-tzu*[1] it is the supreme virtue. "Not even for the space of a single meal, should *chün-tzu* act contrary to *jen.*" "*Jen* should never be abandoned even though one goes to live amid the *yi-ti* [barbarians]." Thus it is defined as "perfect virtue," which transcends the barriers of race, creed, and time.

A composite of "two" and "man," *jen* stresses a correct procedure on human relations, a proper way for men to meet each other, leading to positive efforts for the good of others. Its basis is to be found first in one's duties toward one's parents and brothers. In the *Analects,* two important concepts, *hsiao,* filial piety, and *ti,* fraternal love, express the idea of *jen.* These two concepts express the same unselfish human feeling —*hsiao* signifying a state of spiritual communion with the eternity of time, and *ti* signifying a state of spiritual communion in the infinity of space. Hence these virtues have become the cornerstones of the social structure. By extending

1. *Chün-tzu,* meaning originally the "lord's son," now has a connotation of "noble man."

them in time and in space, and diffusing their influence
through all other related virtues, Confucius made them both
the bond of social solidarity and the connection between succeeding generations. In their broader extensions, they become
the rational basis for the love due to men.

In the *Analects,* there are two other similar concepts;
namely, *chung* (faithfulness) and *shu* (altruism). The former
means the state of mind when one is completely honest with
oneself, while the latter is the state of mind when one is in
complete understanding and sympathy with the outside
world. The concepts of *chung* and *shu* are the same as those
of *hsiao* and *ti,* only the latter refer principally to the relations
within the family, while the former have a wider, less specific
import, referring to what we may describe as true and unselfish love or singleness of mind. This is what Confucius
meant by saying that *jen* consists in "loving others."

Another outstanding feature of Confucianism is *yi,* or righteousness, which is attributable to Mencius. Mencius was born
more than a hundred years after the death of Confucius, but
to his genius and devotion may be traced the final triumph
of Confucianism. *Yi* means the appropriateness of an action
to a situation; it is a categorical imperative. That which is
appropriate or imperative is said to conform to *yi.* That is to
say, *yi* implies an obligation which is unconditional and absolute. In our community life there are certain things that
should be done for their own sake, because they are morally
appropriate or obligatory in themselves. If one does these
things only because of other, nonmoral, considerations—say,
as the means to achieve one's personal ends—one's action is
no longer appropriate or righteous, because one is then acting
for profit (*li*) and not for *yi. Yi* and profit in Confucianism are
diametrically opposed terms. Confucius himself said: "The
noble-minded man comprehends *yi;* the low-minded man
comprehends *li.*" Mencius called this "the distinction between
appropriateness and profit," a distinction greatly emphasized
in Confucianism.

In the Confucian scheme of virtues, *jen* stands supreme and
overshadows all others. But Mencius claimed that, for the
cultivation of virtues, *jen* should be coupled with *yi.* "What
one upholds in one's heart is *jen;* what one upholds in one's
conduct is *yi.*" From this short passage it may be inferred that
jen is the proper basis for inner feelings, while *yi* is the proper
way of guiding external conduct. Thus Mencius said: "The
sense of compassion is beginning of *jen;* the sense of shame

and dislike is the beginning of *yi*." One who has the sense of compassion and the sense of shame and dislike will naturally refrain from doing things that are not in conformity with the principles of *jen* and *yi*. These virtures are inherent in the traditional spirit of the nation.

The third excellent feature of Confucianism is the word *li*, a code of ritual, in which is embodied the essence of ancient culture. Hsün Tzu, another great champion of Confucianism, went further by recommending *li* as the norm of social conduct. The English language and Occidental thought seem alike incapable of supplying a term that can express its full meaning. To consider it as referring to politeness, or to the rules of etiquette, is to take much too superficial a view. Although we translate it as "a code of ritual," it really means much more than that. Etymologically, *li* is religious in nature, the word being a combination of two elements that denote worship with a sacrificial vessel. In the time of Confucius, it came to include all forms of rituals, especially in connection with the proper conduct of the noble lords (*chün-tzu*). And in the course of its evolution, *li* was later transformed into a set of general rules of propriety, the regulating principle in a well-ordered society. Instead of being a mere pattern for a nobleman's conduct, it became a great ethical system that governed the conduct of all men. In many instances it may mean "social order," "social institutions and conventions," or "all regulations that arise from the man-to-man relations." In this interpretation of *li*, Hsün Tzu made a great contribution to Confucianism.

While Confucius advocated *jen* as the prime virtue of life and Mencius gave *yi* the position of a cardinal virtue to that of *jen*, Hsün Tzu stressed *li* as a principal virtue for upholding *jen* and practicing *yi*. "Whence does *li* arise? In reply, I [Hsün Tzu] say: Man by birth has desires. When these desires are not satisfied, he cannot but pursue their satisfaction. When the pursuit is carried on without restraint or limit, there cannot but be contention. When there is contention, there is chaos. When there is chaos, there is dissolution. The ancient kings were disgusted by this chaos, and instituted *li* and *yi* for its delimitation, so that man's desires might be nourished and their pursuit be gratified."

Indeed, *li* is a unique element in the teachings of Hsün Tzu. In society, as he long ago recognized, men are interrelated and united so that order may be maintained. But if man acts in accordance with his hereditary nature and sentiment, he will follow his own desires and impulse without regard to those of other men. Hence Hsün Tzu emphasized that the conduct of men living in a group must be governed by a code of tested and accepted rituals (*li*) rather than by the *jen* in the individual, the natural compassion of the human heart. *Li*, so conceived, denotes something very important and fundamental in social life. It is not merely an outgrowth of the inner spirit of *jen*, as it was regarded by Confucius and Mencius, but the most effective means of counteracting what he alleged to be the inherent baseness of human nature. It is a rule of conduct, one of the means of social control in accordance with which society seems always to have been erected.

In short, *jen*, *yi*, and *li* are the three cardinal virtues that underlie Confucianism. They are the norms of conduct that have been followed by the Chinese people for thousands of years. Each has served a useful purpose in the achievement of Chinese culture, and each is essential to the other two as a necessary complement. *Jen*, as the prime virtue of life, leads the way in prompting us to positive efforts for the good of others; *yi* follows, as the highest principle embodied in the activities of mankind; *li*, as the outward expression of moral sentiment and the standard of conduct, sheds light on *jen* and *yi* by bringing the whole conduct into harmony with reason and order, thus completing the foundation of Confucianism, to which all the humanistic principles and values are attributed.

2

Toward the end of the Warring States period and the beginning of the Han dynasty, about the time of Christ, the humanistic ideas, especially those of Mencius and Hsün, were further elaborated in an important book known as the *Li Chi* (The Book of Rites). One of its sections, called the *Ta Hsüeh* (The Great Learning), largely follows the ideas of Hsün Tzu, and its unique feature is the logical reasoning it shows in support of a general thesis. Here we have a good illustration of the unity of ethics and politics characteristic of humanism. According to its teachings, no matter how much the world has fallen into chaos, moral cultivation is the panacea for all social and political diseases. It is the root of everything—a well-balanced individual, a well-ordered family, a well-governed state, and a happy and harmonious world. The eight items as enumerated in this book represent a continuing process, and therein are to be found the basic principles of government. This short treatise is indeed a concise résumé of the humanistic political philosophy. It should be noted that its author was thinking in terms of world politics and world peace, also the subject of that section of the work entitled *Li Yün*. In the *Li Chi* there is another important section entitled *Chung Yung* (Doctrine of the Mean), which largely follows the ideas of Mencius. The concepts of *chung* (the mean) and *yung* (normality), may be characterized as the moral ideal of Chinese Humanism. This treatise, as shown by its title, is a systematic exposition of the mean in the normality (*chung yung*). To secure *chung yung* is not to pursue a middle course; it means rather the harmony of the universe. Thus the way of *chung yung* is a sense of justice and fairness, a spirit of tolerance, a state of harmony, and a doctrine of equity. To speak plainly, *chung yung* is a way of action which avoids going to extremes, or a state of mind in which human reasoning and feeling reach a perfect harmony. In devising a way to achieve *chung yung*, the humanists turned to *li* and music. *Li* is to direct man's desires, and music to harmonize man's sentiment, two of the most natural and common aspects of human nature. In the *Li Chi* there are several passages which elaborate the theories about *li* and music.

These two short treatises—the *Ta Hsüeh* and the *Chung Yung*—have exercised a great influence on later Chinese philosophy. They, together with the *Lun Yü* and the *Mencius,* comprise the Four Books which have formed the basic classics of Chinese Humanism.

Finally, there is another Confucian work of about the same period known as the *Hsiao Ching* (Classic of Filial Piety), which presents the most elemental social and religious concept of the Chinese people—family loyalty, which has been regarded as "the basis of virtue and source of instruction." The Chinese word for "culture" or "religion," *chiao*, is composed of *hsiao*, filial piety, and *chih*, meaning "to support [filial piety]." So filial piety, as taught in Confucianism, is not merely a domestic virtue, but diffuses its influence through all actions of life; it originates with the bonds of common parentage and extends to other relationships until it reaches the stage of *jen*. With a keen sense of reality and practicality, the Humanists made the virtue of filial piety the chief cornerstone of social structure. This is beautifully elaborated in the *Hsiao Ching*.

Before the Ch'in dynasty (255-206 B.C.) there was much intellectual freedom and progress, and there were a hundred schools of thought. In the new age that followed, there was need of unity both in the intellectual and political spheres. For this purpose, the Ch'in emperor Shih Huang Ti decreed in 213 B.C. that all writings of the various schools of thought in public circulation, and all other literature except works on medicine, divination, and agriculture, be delivered to the government and burned. This decree effectively put an end to all freedom of thought, and, as a result, Chinese philosophy, more particularly Confucianism, suffered a decline and lost much of its vitality and appeal.

The Han dynasty (205 B.C.-A.D. 220) was marked by the resurrection of Confucian classics and revival of letters. Though they disapproved of the drastic methods of the Ch'in, the Han rulers also attempted to unify the thought of the empire in order to maintain political unity. This new attempt was made by the Han emperor Wu (140-87 B.C.), who, instead of rejecting all schools of philosophy indiscriminately, selected Confucianism and gave it pre-eminence as the state orthodoxy. This innovation was attributed to Tung Chung-shu (c. 179-104 B.C.), the greatest of the early Han scholars. In a memorial presented to the emperor Wu in the year 136 B.C., he advocated a system of education based on Confucian classics. Thus it was he who created the institutional basis for Confucian orthodoxy, the famed Chinese examination system, which lasted until the beginning of the present century. However, it should be noted that Confucianism expounded by Tung Chung-shu and adopted in the early Han period was something quite different from that originally set forth by the Sage and his immediate followers. Han Confucianism was tinged by ideas of the rival schools, especially of Taoism. What Tung Chung-shu tried to do was, on the one hand, to work out a new philosophical interpretation and justification for the Han imperial institution, and, on the other hand, to devise a formula of "subjecting the people to the ruler and the ruler to Heaven," to check the absolute sway of the monarch. His work is one of the great achievements of Chinese thought.

After the collapse of Han there followed a long period of moral and political chaos in China, in which Buddhism of Indian origin, in collaboration with Chinese Taoism, flourished and overshadowed Confucianism. However, Chinese philosophy blossomed afresh during the ensuing period, which was noted for the rise of *Li Hsüeh Chia,* or the School of Study of *Li* (Reason), usually known in the West as Neo-Confucianism. This was a kind of summing up or revision of the ethics, morals, and beliefs of the past, but its principles of Confucianism were thoroughly tinged with Buddhism—just as Buddhism had interacted with Taoism and emerged as Ch'anism, so Confucianism interacted with Buddhism and emerged as Li-ism or Neo-Confucianism.

II. Confucianism as a Religion

1

As early as the time of Mencius, there was already a tendency among Confucius' followers to take an interest in supernaturalism. Hsün Tzu, the positivist among the early Confucians, raised a strong protest against the superstitious belief in magic, omens, and portents that dominated his age, arguing for a completely rational and naturalistic view of heaven and men. The tendency, however, persisted. The Han Confucians generally divided themselves into two groups: one known as the New-Text school, so-called because its version of the Confucian classics was written in the current script, and the other as the Old-Text school, so-called because it claimed to possess the ancient texts that existed before the time of "the Ch'in fire." The controversy between these two schools turned out to be one of the greatest in the history of Chinese scholarship. Their textual disagreement was accentuated by a difference in their views about the true significance of Confucius and Confucianism. The New-Text school considered Confucius as a "throneless king" and a savior of the world, thus elevating the Sage to a position approaching divinity, as described in apocryphal literature. In opposition to this view, the Old-Text school maintained that Confucius was simply a sage who had given new interpretation to the cultural heritage of the past before transmitting it to posterity. Although the views of the New-Text school now seem absurd and vain, they became popular in the Han period.

A good illustration of the apotheosis of Confucius is found in the following passage from the *Ch'un-ch'iu-wei Yen-K'ung-t'u* (Apocryphal Treatise on the Spring and Autumn Annals: Expository Chart on Confucius):

> Confucius' mother, Cheng-tsai, once while taking a walk happened upon the mound of a large tomb, where she fell

asleep and dreamed that she received an invitation from a Black Emperor. She went to him and in her dream had intercourse with him. He spoke to her, saying: "Your confinement will take place within a hollow mulberry tree." When she awoke she seemed to fall [pregnant] and [later] gave birth to Confucius within a hollow mulberry. This is why he is called the Black Sage [Hsüan (not Yüan) sheng]. . . . .

On Confucius' breast there was writing which said, "The act of instituting [a new dynasty] has been decided and the rule of the world has been transferred.". . .

After the unicorn was caught [in the fourteenth year of Duke Ai of Lu; i.e., 481 B.C.], Heaven rained blood which formed writing on the main gate [of the capital] of Lu and said: "Quickly prepare laws, for the Sage Confucius will die; the Chou [the ruling house], Chi will be destroyed; a comet will appear from the east. The government of the Ch'in [dynasty] will arise and will suddenly destroy the literary arts. But though the written records will then be dispersed, [the teachings of] Confucius will not be interrupted."

[Confucius' disciple] Tsu Hsia next day went to look at this, whereupon this writing of blood flew away as a red bird. This then changed itself into white writing, the composition of which is called the Yen-k'ung-tu [Expository Chart on Confucius]. In it are delineated charts for instituting laws.

While Confucius was discoursing on the classics, there was a bird which [came and] transformed itself into writing. Confucius accepted it and with it made an announcement to Heaven. A small red bird which settled on this writing became a piece of yellow jade, carved with an inscription which said: "Confucius, holding [Heaven's] Mandate to act, has created these governmental institutions in accordance with the laws. A small red bird came and settled on them."[1]

On the basis of the apocryphal literature which grew up within the Confucian school, the attempt to deify Confucius went on uninterrupted for many centuries in and after the Han dynasty. As early as A.D. 59, a beginning was made in the Confucius cult when Emperor Ming (A.D. 58-75) of the

1. Fung Yu-lan: *A History of Chinese Philosophy*, vol. II, pp. 129-130 (translated by Derk Bodde).

Later Han dynasty ordered sacrifices, hitherto confined to Confucius' temple in Lu, to be made in all the schools in the cities. This clearly established the Sage as the patron saint of education. Since then the effort to accelerate the canonization of Confucius had been made on the part of Confucian scholars. Confucius' temples had been built in almost every prefectural city throughout the empire. A complete code of sacrificial ritual had been drawn up for the worship of Confucius. The Confucian cult was already well established in the T'ang dynasty (618-907).

Inspired by the example of Christianity as a state religion in many Western countries, a group of Confucians, under the leadership of K'ang Yu-wei (1858-1927)—the dominant figure of the Reform Movement (1898)—renewed their efforts to promote the Confucian-religion movement, in the early twentieth century. They demanded that Confucianism be established as *kuo-chiao* (state-religion), Confucius be recognized as *chiao-chu* (founder of religion) and the year 551 B.C. (the date of birth of the Sage) be taken as Year One of China's national history. As a result of their propaganda K'ung-chiao hui (Confucian Association) for the study and exaltation of Confucius' teachings was organized on a nation-wide basis. When the Constitutional Convention met in 1915, these Confucians demanded a clause be included in the new constitution to establish Confucianism as a state religion. But this proposal was strongly opposed by groups of university-trained intellectuals and members of Catholic, Protestant, Moslem, Buddhist, and Taoist organizations. The latter also formed a "Society for Religious Freedom" to the Confucian state-religion movement. Consequently, the Draft Convention adopted a compromise resolution endorsing the moral superiority of Confucianism, but not hailing it a national religion. The constitution, however, was never adopted, and when it was finally dropped, gone with it was the last effort of the Confucian scholars to deify Confucius.

2

We are not in a position to review the pros and cons of the Confucian-religion movement. The important question is whether Confucianism can be considered a religion. Confucianism, as is generally asserted, is not a religion, for it has no religious ritual or sanction. It presents lofty intellectual ideals, but there is nothing to be feared by one who fails

to live up to them. In competing with a religion that preaches
the assurance of immortality, Confucianism suffers from its
silence on the realm beyond life. For instance, when Confucius was questioned on this, he replied evasively: "If you do
not know life, how can you know about death?" (*Analects*,
XI, 11). And, finally, Confucianism attaches great importance
to humanity. As Confucius said: "If you are not able to serve
men, how can you worship the gods?" (*ibid*). For all these
reasons, Confucianism is not a religion, but a philosophy and
a system of ethics. The greatness of Confucianism, however,
is that, without being a religion, it has taken the place of a
religion.[2] This requires some explanation.

Man is a being with a soul, and that soul, which looks into
the past and the future as well as the present, feels the need
of understanding the mystery of the universe in which he
lives. Religion lightens the burden of the mystery of the universe by giving him a sense of security and permanence.
Religion gives him a belief in a divine power that can control
the natural forces that threaten him, and a belief in a future
state of being the condition of which is determined by his
conduct in the present life. Jesus Christ says, "Peace I give
unto you, peace which the world cannot take away from you."
This is how religion gives man a sense of security and permanence.

It is possible for the Chinese people to derive religious
comfort from Confucianism. Ancestor worship, which forms
the leading element in the religion of the Chinese people, and
filial piety, are the two main props of Confucianism. It is to
Confucius and his followers that China is indebted for the
strictness with which the ceremonial rules and rites of ancestor worship are universally observed. These ceremonies
contain much of superstition and mythology. In justifying
them, Confucius and his followers gave them new interpreta-
tions and read new ideas into them. These we find in the
Confucian classics, especially the *Hsün-tzu* and the *Li Chi*.
In their defense of mourning and sacrificial ceremonies, de-
nounced by the Mohists[3] as extravagant, the Confucians made
their appeal to man's emotion. These ceremonial practices,
they argued, were originally the expression of man's affec-

2. When we say "religion" here, we mean religion in its broad and universal sense.

3. In ancient times, the fame of Mo Tzu, or Mo Ti, founder of the school
known as Mohism, was as great as that of Confucius. As he came from a
low stratum of society, he opposed all the elaborate feudal rites so dear to
Confucius.

tionate yearning for the dead, "the calling up of memories and intentions, of thoughts and longings." In their opinion, all these sacramental acts, therefore, should be performed in their proper form so as "to beautify death and thereby lessen its ugliness, to beautify sorrow and thereby heal its wounds, to beautify the feeling of reverence by serving the dead as if serving the living."[4] Seen in this light, the mourning and sacrificial ceremonies, which lie at the foundation of the Chinese religious belief, are acknowledged to be binding by the Chinese people as the religious elements in the Christian system, for which they serve as a substitute. Martin Luther said in his commentary on the *Book of Daniel:* "A God is simply that whereon the human heart rests with trust, faith, hope, and love." Similarly, the cult of ancestor worship, together with filial piety, as taught in Confucianism, is not dead form, but a living faith—a "resting," or "peace," in which one finds the same sense of security and permanence that the mass of mankind finds in the belief in God in Christianity.

There is, however, an important difference of Christianity and Confucianism as religions in the sense of systems of conduct which are accepted by the mass of population. In this sense, Confucianism, like Christianity, might be considered a religion; its teachings have been acknowledged to be true and its rules of conduct to be binding by the Chinese people. The difference is this: Christianity is a church religion, whereas Confucianism is a family religion. The church of Christianity says, "Glorify God and obey Him," whereas the family religion of Confucianism says, "Honor your forefather and worship him." The church religion of Christianity says, "If you want to glorify God and obey Him, you must first love Jesus Christ," whereas the family religion of Confucianism says, "If you want to honor your forefather and worship him, you must first be filial to your parents." The essence of Christianity, the love due to Jesus Christ, makes a man good in his individual life. The essence of Confucianism, the filial piety due to parents, makes a man good in his relations with his fellow men.

In the *Chung Yung,* we read: "The Master [Confucius] said: 'Filial piety is the force that continues the purposes and completes the affairs of our forefathers. . . . To gather in the same place where they earlier have gathered; to perform the same ceremonies which they earlier have performed; to play

4. Liu Wu-chi, *A Short History of Confucian Philosophy,* p. 100.

the same music which they earlier have played; to pay respect to those whom they honored; to love those who were dear to them; in fact, to serve those now dead as if they were living, and those now departed as if they were with us still. This is the highest achievement of filial piety'" (ch. XIX). This passage makes explicit the influence of filial piety as a religious force in awakening and kindling in men the sentiment necessary to make them continue the purpose and activities of ancestors. The sentiment of filial piety so permeated the ceremonies of ancestor worship that the two were really synchronized into one and operated together in the transmission of accumulated culture from one generation to another.

III. The Spirit of Confucianism

1

The spirit of Confucianism has become a major force in unifying China and has helped mold the mentality and temperament of the Chinese people. All the principles and values of Confucianism may be attributed to the doctrine of *jen*. *Jen* means seeds—the seeds in the stones of peaches and apricots, which, after being sown in the soil, will shoot and grow —showing that all things spring into life. This concept of *jen* has deeply permeated Chinese thought, and the Chinese evince a disposition to appreciate and enjoy life.

China is a land where the great mass of the people have to toil and struggle unceasingly in order to obtain even the bare necessities of daily existence. Although they cannot enjoy an abundance of food, they are contented with whatever Heaven may give them. The Chinese are profoundly thankful when they and their families can be sure of three meals a day to stave off the pangs of hunger. Whatever may be their innermost thoughts, they bear their hardships and privations with admirable heroism. The wonderful characteristic of the Chinese people—one that has been an important factor in steadying the nation, and the great ideal that touches their lives in every direction—is that every man, rich or poor, educated or illiterate, has a profound respect for life. They may lament their many ills, but they never curse life. What they insist upon is simply that in order to live well, one must try to get the best out of life and enjoy what one has. The passionate love of life is a national characteristic, and serves to distinguish the Chinese from the Hindus, who conceive the present world as "a sea of bitterness," and to whom "life is like a dream, like a bubble, like a shadow, like the morning dew, like lightning."

This profound respect for life is coupled with a corresponding notion of rational happiness. The Chinese are well-known as a cheerful and easily contented people; they have always been jealous of their right to happiness, which no poverty or disgrace can take away from them. As Confucius said, "The wise are free from doubts; the virtuous, from concerns; the courageous, from fear." And, again, "The noble man is completely at ease; the common man is always on edge." Indeed, Confucius' own life is certainly a very good example of this aspect of teaching. Disapproving of the degeneracy of his own times, he turned at an early age to the vocation of reformer. He traveled everywhere and talked with everybody. Although his efforts were in vain, he was not disappointed. Hence he made happiness the chief requisite of the way of the noble man.

While the Chinese have always been interested in the problem of happiness, their approach to it is very rational or philosophical. A Chinese depends for his happiness not on external circumstances but on his own virtue. He wants only what leads to happiness, and does not insist on having what is beyond his reach. The Chinese have much to offer to counteract our modern ills, particularly by showing the folly of self-seeking and the virtue of contentment. "One who is contented is always happy" is a saying that contains much of human wisdom and affords a key to the secret of the Chinese way of life. In the *Analects*, we read, "Tzu Kung asked: 'Poor without flattery; rich without arrogance—what would you say of that?' 'That will do,' said the Master, 'but it is still better to be poor and yet happy; rich and yet fond of *li.*'" As for himself, Confucius said: "To eat only vegetables and drink only water, with bent arms for a pillow, I am still happy in such a life. But ill-gotten wealth and honors are to me as wandering clouds." Confucius did not intend poverty to be synonymous with happiness, but he did intend that one's happiness should not be marred by poverty. This is exactly what Mencius taught when he said: "One must not let wealth and honor corrupt, not let poverty and low position defect one from one's principles, nor let power and duress beat into submission." This spirit of happiness—to be happy in poverty

—is found in both the educated and illiterate classes, for such is the penetration of the Chinese racial tradition.

This ideal of rational happiness tends toward a positive rather than a negative concept. In their teachings, Confucius and his followers aimed not merely at absence of pain, but also at conscious enjoyment; they aimed not merely at tranquility of mind, but also at the good of activity. What man hopes for is not merely to avoid pain, but also to utilize his ability and consciously to do something. Confucius taught that "noble man seeks to improve himself without rest." He engaged in carrying forward the eternal quest of mankind for ways to "pacify the world" and sought far and wide for the key to the accomplishment of this great task. The fruits of his labors are a priceless heritage. Although in the end he had to confess the futility of his quest, his persistence in carrying it on was in itself a great contribution. Virtue consists in activity; hence happiness is associated with virtue. The fundamental principle underlying the combination of happiness and virtue has been deeply impressed on the Chinese mind.

Confucianism also emphasizes human relationship and teaches men how to live in harmony with one another. A sense of justice and fairness, a spirit of tolerance, a readiness to compromise, coupled with a firm determination to enforce the observance of these virtues against the teachings of egoists and altruists alike—these are the true foundations of human relations. *Jen* must play its part in the relations among different kinds of people. Exaggeration, or total absence of *jen*, would upset the social order equally. Both altruism and egoism are too onesided and extreme and can only lead to calamities. Confucianism offers a standard for rectifying such fallacies; this is the way of *chung-yung*—that is, the doctrine of the mean. As we have noted above, the way of *chung-yung* is a way of action that avoids going to extremes, a state of mind in which human reasoning and feeling reach perfect harmony. Only harmony can bring about balance, and only balance can lead to progress. Hence, harmony, balance, and progress are the essential characteristics of the doctrine of the mean. This doctrine has had a great influence on the Chinese people; they remain cautious even in times of prosperity, and hopeful even in times of danger. This doctrine has contributed much in their efforts to overcome the many difficulties they have encountered in history.

2

In the manner by which Confucianism has been affirmed and emphasized we perceive a mighty factor in the continuity and perpetuity of Chinese culture and national existence. Now the question arises: how do the subtleties of this philosophy, long dominant in the intellectual and moral life of the nation, work down to the masses at the base? The answer lies in the fact that its roots originate in the family. In the course of centuries, the Chinese people have developed many institutions and customs to preserve and perpetuate society, to give joint protection to individuals, and to strengthen proper relationships among the people. The basic and most characteristic Chinese institution has been the family. As a matter of fact, a great deal of Confucianism, with its great stress on proper relations among human beings, is the rational justification or theoretical expression of this social institution.

In the Confucian conception, man's personality reflects itself in his actions and behavior in the five relationships: governmental, parental, conjugal, fraternal, and friendship. Of these five relationships, three concern the family; the remaining two, though not familial relationships, can be conceived in terms of it. But these are only the major ones; there were many more in ancient times. In the *Erh Yah*, the oldest dictionary of the Chinese language, dating from about the second century before Christ, there are more than one hundred terms for various family relationships, most of which have no equivalent in the English language. These stress the Confucian idea of the position of man among men, that every man must be in his proper place and with his proper responsibilities and duties. This is what is known as the theory of *ming feng*,[1] or "the doctrine of social status": *ming* means "name," and *feng* means "duty"; every man in the social relationship has certain responsibilities and duties. The Confucian doctrine is that if every man knows his duty and acts according to his duty, social order will be secured. In other words, one who follows the Confucian doctrine will fulfill his duty in his relationships (1) with himself, (2) with his family, (3) with the community, (4) with the nation, and (5) with the world. Among these, the relationship with the family is foremost.

1. This theory Confucius called the Rectification of Names (*cheng ming*), a doctrine which recognized as being of the utmost importance, as he said: "Let the ruler be ruler, the minister be minister; let the father be father, and the son son."

Mutual affection first arises out of the family and then extends to the community. Affection manifests itself with different degrees of intensity. From affection arises an appropriate attitude in a given moral situation, which one person assumes as a reciprocal duty to the other. Thus for the parents the appropriate attitude is kindness; for the children, filial piety; for the brothers, fraternity; and for the married couples, fidelity. The ethical relationship is indeed a relationship of affection and other appropriate attitudes. It is through the genuine fulfillment of the ethical relationships that exist in the family that the fulfillment of other relationships in the community is brought about. In other words, family affection binds together all social relations, and hence is the basic unit of all social institutions.

This is what we know as the Confucian ethical principle, or what can be called the Chinese social norm. This concept of the social norm is indeed the significant contribution made by Confucianism to Chinese civilization. It stresses that when every man is encouraged to practice filial piety (*hsiao*) and fraternal love, his resulting proper conduct, when extended to the larger social groups of which he becomes a member as his relationship expands, would mean not only the regulation of the family but also the good government of the state; this would eventually bring about peace in the world. What is called filial piety and fraternal love in the family is known as loyalty (*chung*) and altruism (*shu*) in the wider sphere of social relations. The great virtues embraced in the ideal of the social norm comprise the whole duty of man toward Heaven, toward himself, and toward his relations; and they are fostered in the family—the center of life.

In this connection, a passage from the *Hsun-tzu* is worth quoting: "*Li* rests on three bases: Heaven and earth, which are the source of all life; forefathers and ancestors, who are the source of the human race; sovereigns and teachers, who are the source of government. Without Heaven and earth, from where would life come? Without forefathers and ancestors, from where would the offspring come? Without sovereigns and teachers, from where would government come? If any of the three were lacking, there would be no man, or men would be without peace. Therefore, *li* is to serve Heaven above and earth below and to honor forefathers and ancestors and to exalt sovereigns and teachers. Herein lies the threefold basis of *li*" (Ch. 19).

This threefold basis of *li-ism* (ritualism) was probably symbolized in the five characters—Heaven, Earth, Emperor, Ancestors, and Tutors—inscribed on the tablet which was once installed in the shrine of almost every household. This symbolic observation signifies the true sources in the formation of the Confucian social norm, and also helps toward an understanding of the significance of the traditional Confucian ideologies concerning the principal relations of the individual to the world, which contain the entire structure of the social fabric.

And again, in the *Li Chi*, we read: "High in Heaven and below on earth, all things are scattered and diverse in kinds. In accordance with this pattern, *li* is instituted. These things flow forth unceasingly; they act in unison and yet are transformed. In accordance with this pattern, music arises. In spring all things burst forth, and in summer all things grow; this is *jen*. In autumn all things consummate, and in winter all things repose; this is *yi*. *Jen* is akin to music, and *yi* is akin to *li*. Music establishes union and harmony, and so it accords with *shen* [spirits] and follows the pattern of Heaven. *Li* maintains difference and distinction, and so it accords with *kuei* [ghosts] and follows the pattern of earth. Therefore the sage creates music in response to Heaven, and institutes *li* to match earth. When *li* and music are distinct and complete, Heaven and earth function in perfect order" (Ch. 19). This is the great principle—harmony and orderliness—which underlies the spirit of Confucianism.

In ethics, Confucianism upholds the five "constant virtues" of *jen, yi, li, chih* (wisdom), and *hsin* (sincerity); in politics it stresses the moral importance of human relationships. In the last analysis, virtue alone constitutes the ultimate goal of man. These Confucian principles and values, in which we can still find an inexhaustible store of wisdom as well as a useful set of rules for good living, could readily lead to the modern concepts of human rights and political democracy. However, in the course of time, they suffered much pandering in the hands of politicians and emperors, who gave prominence to that aspect of Confucianism which supports the autocratic rule.[2] Thus for two thousand years Confucianism had been closely affiliated with the imperial system, not as an immanent principle, but as an ideological tool of imperial rulers. There is some justification, therefore, for the contention of Chu Hsi (1130-1200) that "the way of Confucius had not been put

2. It preaches the right of the superior to rule and the duty of the inferior to obey and be content with their lot.

into practice for a single day" during the centuries of imperial rule.[3]

With the entire fabric of Chinese society shaken to the ground and the shape of things to come so uncertain, it is still premature to write the final chapter of the history of Confucianism. For the last twenty-five centuries, Confucianism has dominated Chinese thought and moulded the national character. It has also given continuity to the old civilization of China which, far from becoming extinct in its development, showed a vitality in its struggle for survival and supremacy. The significance of Confucianism lies in its power of adaptation. It has been constantly reborn and reoriented. There may still be hope that the best in Confucianism will find its place in a new cultural synthesis, thus saving it from exhaustion. In Confucianism there is at least a measure of truth, and philosophical truth remains forever. This explains in part why we translated and compiled these materials. Because of the limitation in its space, as well as the richness of the materials, this volume has to be terminated at the Han dynasty. However, it is our hope that the essential writings of Neo-Confucianism will be translated and compiled in the very near future so as to complete our study of Confucianism.

3. Chu Hsi, *Chu Wen-kung wen-chi* (Works of Master Chu), ch. 36, p. 579, "Reply to Ch'en T'ung-fu."

ONE: CONFUCIUS

CONTENTS

⋘§ INTRODUCTION

Confucius is the Latinized name of K'ung Tzu or Master K'ung. His family name was K'ung, and his given name was Ch'iu because of the peculiar shape of his cranium which looked like a *ch'iu* or a mound. Later he was called Chung-ni (Ni the Younger). Confucius was born in 551 B.C. in the state of Lu, the cultural center of ancient China.

Not much is known of the Sage's boyhood. After his father died when he was only three years old, he was brought up under the care and instruction of his widowed mother. Because of the death of his father, the family was poor, and he was at first unable to follow the path of pure scholarship. Later he told his disciples that because the fortunes of his family had been low when he was young, he had acquired skill in many things. He must have been a solemn child, for it is said that when he was six years old, he began to play "sage-king" with other children, performing the ancient rites, arranging sacrificial vessels and assuming ceremonial postures. At the age of fifteen, he devoted himself to learning and gained a reputation for knowledge and propriety. He began his career as a granary overseer in his native district, and eventually was placed in charge of the public fields.

In 528 B.C. K'ung abandoned his public employment to mourn the loss of his mother. During the three years' mourning he refrained from sensual indulgences and activities and devoted himself to the study of ancient history, literature, and institutions. It is not known exactly what position he took after the period of mourning was over, but it is assumed he began his career as a public teacher, for he had already commanded public attention and the respect of the great. In 518 B.C. the Duke of Lu sent him to Lo, the Royal Capital of Chou, to observe the relics of lost imperial greatness. The visit to the imperial court led him to a deeper understanding of the cultural past and opened up new vistas for his future pursuit. At the same time, it convinced him of the greatness of the Chou House, which he venerated. Upon returning to Lu, he continued teaching, and his fame increased greatly. He attracted a great variety of aspiring young men eager to be instructed in the classics, in conduct, and in government.

At age of fifty-two, Confucius entered the court of Lu, and soon he reached high official rank. As a result of political intrigue, however, he was forced to resign his post. He spent some fourteen years abroad with a handful of students, traveling, teaching, and visiting the feudal lords of his time. When he returned to his native state, he was already an old man of sixty-eight, unable to influence the government. Thwarted by royal pride and official jealousy, he endeavored to attain his noble ends by less direct but more certain means. He devoted himself more than ever to the instruction of youths and to the editing and recording of the ancient documents that formed the basis of his teaching.

Although he sought political success, his great achievement was in education. Master K'ung rescued ancient culture, now preserved in the Five Classics (the *Wu Ching*), from its degeneration in the hands of court officials and removed all branches of learning from official custody. He paved the way for equality in education by opening his door to all young men with a thirst for knowledge. He was the first teacher in the intellectual history of China to make education available to the great mass of common people.

Master K'ung died in 479 B.C., at the age of seventy-three. He was buried near his native town, and many of his students built houses near his tomb. Until recently there were temples honoring him in nearly every city. His followers visit at every festival and perform the music and rites which he taught. All the temples built to Master K'ung contain a central inscription reading: "He forms a triad with Heaven and Earth." In the person of Master K'ung, the dual powers of Heaven and Earth found their harmony completed. It was as much as to say: "He speaks, and his word is law to the world; he acts, and his conduct is an unerring example." This statement, although exaggeration, serves to mark the reverence in which he was held by the Chinese people.

His greatness can be measured by the extent, intensity, and duration of his influence on Chinese life. He dominated China's intellectual life for almost twenty-five centuries. His doctrines were accepted as state teachings; his works were regarded as the Canonical Books to be studied by students in schools; his cardinal virtues were regarded as the norms of the society. The teachings of Master K'ung, replete with wisdom and common sense, moulded the national character and touched every corner of human society.

The following passage from the *Chung Yung,* the *Doctrine of the Mean,* offers a good illustration of this influence:

"Only a man who, like this, is possessed of the absolute sincerity can expound the basic principles of society's complex make-up, establish great foundations of the world, and understand the transforming and nurturing operations of Heaven and Earth. What does he expect to rely on beyond his own sagacity? His humanity, how pervading! His depth, how unfathomable! His heavenliness, how overwhelming! Who can comprehend this unless he is possessed of perceptivity, discernment, sagacity, and wisdom and understands the heavenly virtue."

⇜ The Confucian Analects, or Lun Yü

The Confucian Analects furnishes source materials for the study of the teachings and personality of Confucius. The work is a collection of sayings by Confucius and some of his disciples, recorded by the disciples of the Confucian school. The Chinese characters for the title are *Lun Yü-Yü* meaning "sayings" and *Lun* meaning systematic compilation of the bamboo sheets. When the bamboo manuscripts were first edited, the title *Lun Yü* was not yet used. The first reference to *Lun Yü* was found in the writings of K'ung An-kuo (c. 160-120 B.C.), a descendant of Confucius, and since then the title came into general usage through adoptation by other commentators.

When the scholars of the Han dynasty began to collect and edit ancient writings, three different versions of *Lun Yü* came to light. One of these, from the state of Lu, was known as the "Lu Version"; another, from the state of Ch'i, as the "Ch'i Version"; and the third version, found in the walls of the house that had been occupied by Confucius and his descendants and written in the ancient script, was known as the "Ancient Script Version." These three versions do not wholly agree in scope and content, especially in the arrangement of the text. The version current today is the "Lu Version," divided into twenty chapters, with the first words of the chapters chosen as the chapter headings. Each paragraph consists of only a few words, and there is no connection between one paragraph and the next. We have rearranged the entire text into four parts: the teachings of Confucius, the personality of Confucius, the disciples of Confucius, and the miscellaneous records. In this way, this book will give some logical coherence and make it easy reading for those who are unfamiliar with Chinese philosophical writings. The numbers of the chapters and sections within the brackets at the end of each paragraph correspond to those in the original text.

Part One: The Teachings of Confucius

Chapter I. Humanity (Jen) and Cardinal Virtues

The doctrine of *jen* is the central thesis of the whole system that Confucius developed. All else is deduced from this governing doctrine; his ethics, his politics, his life ideal, all flow from it. *Jen,* in the *Analects,* expresses the Confucian ideal of cultivating humanity, developing human faculties, sublimating one's personality, and upholding human rights. Chu Hsi (1130-1200), a famous Confucian scholar of the Sung dynasty, defined *jen* as "the virtue of the soul," "the principle of love," and "the center of heaven and earth." In reading this chapter, bear in mind what we have already said of *jen.* Its ideograph is composed of two characters—"man" and "two"—signifying that there should be a correct procedure in human relationships, a proper way for men to meet each other. Confucius maintained that human relations should be based on the moral sentiment of *jen,* leading to positive efforts for the good of others. In fact, Confucius regarded *jen* not merely as a special kind of virtue, but all the virtues combined, and *jen* may thus be defined as "perfect virtue."

The idea of *jen* may be expressed in the conception of *hsiao,* or filial piety, and *ti,* or fraternal love. These two concepts express the same unselfish human feeling, filial piety signifying a state of spiritual communion in the eternity of time and fraternal love signifying a state of spiritual communion in the infinity of space. Confucius, with a keen sense of reality and practicality, made the virtues of filial piety and fraternal love the cornerstones of the social structure. By extending the cardinal virtues in time and space and diffusing their influence through all the other relationship virtues, he made them both the bond of social solidarity and the connection between succeeding generations. In their broader extensions, filial piety and fraternal love become the rational basis for the love due to men—that is, *jen,* or humanity.

In the *Analects* two other similar concepts are introduced—namely, *chung* or loyalty and *shu* or altruism, the former meaning the state of mind when one is completely honest with oneself and the latter meaning the state of mind when one is in complete understanding and sympathy with the outside world. These two concepts are the same as those of *hsiao* and *ti,* only the latter refer to the relations within the family, while the former have a wider significance. Such a state of mind, which we describe also as true and unselfish love or singleness of mind, is in fact what Confucius meant by *jen* or humanity, "loving others."

✧

1. The Master said: "Clever words and flattering looks seldom speak of *jen* (humanity)." [I-3]

2. The Master said: "It is best to live in the company of *jen.* If a man chooses not to live where *jen* prevails, how can he be considered wise?" [IV-1]

3. The Master said: "Without *jen,* a man cannot long endure adversity, nor can he long endure prosperity. A man of *jen* rests in *jen;* a man of wisdom finds it beneficial." [IV-2]

4. The Master said: "It is only a man of *jen* who knows how to love people and how to hate people." [IV-3]

5. The Master said: "If a man is devoted to *jen,* he will be free from evil." [IV-4]

6. The Master said: "Riches and honor are what one likes, but if they come contrary to the *Tao,*[1] they should not be retained. Poverty and lowliness are what one detests, but if they come contrary to the *Tao,* they should not be evaded. If a *chün-tzu* departs from *jen,* he is unworthy of such a name. Not even for the space of a single meal, should a *chün-tzu* act contrary to *jen.* In moments of haste, he cleaves to it; in times of difficulty, he cleaves to it." [IV-5]

7. The Master said: "I have not yet seen a man who loves *jen* nor a man who detests what is contrary to *jen.* He who loves *jen* esteems nothing else above it. He who detests what is contrary to *jen* seeks to be *jen*-minded so that he will not let anything contrary to *jen* appear in his person. Is there anyone who is able even for a single day to apply his energy to *jen?* Well, I have not seen a man whose energy was not equal to it. Should there be any such man, I have never met him." [IV-6]

1. *Tao*—a way of life—as used here, is ethical in meaning, denoting the principle of truth.

8. The Master said: "A man's faults are measured by his associates. Observe his faults and you may know whether he is *jen*-minded." [IV-7]

9. The Master said: "The wise delight in water; the *jen*-minded delight in mountains. The wise are active; the *jen*-minded are placid. The wise are happy; the *jen*-minded endure." [VI-21]

10. The Master said: "Is *jen* really so far away? I desire *jen*, and, see, it is by." [VII-29]

11. The Master said: "The wise man is free from perplexity; the *jen*-minded man is free from anxiety; the brave man is free from fear." [IX-28]

12. The Master said: "One who is firm of spirit, resolute in character, simple in manner, and slow of speech is near to *jen*." [XIII-27]

13. The Master said: "A man of virtue is sure to be good in speech, but one who is good in speech may not be virtuous. A man of *jen* is sure to be brave, but one who is brave may not be *jen*-minded." [XIV-5]

14. The Master said: "The strong-willed scholars and *jen*-minded men will not seek life at the expense of *jen,* but rather sacrifice their lives to preserve their *jen*." [XV-8]

15. The Master said: "*Jen* is more essential to man than fire and water. I have seen men die from stepping into fire and water, but I have never seen a man die from stepping into *jen*." [XV-34]

16. The Master said: "In attaining *jen,* a man need not defer to his teacher." [XV-35]

17. Fan Ch'ih asked about wisdom, and the Master said: "Devote yourself to the proper duty due to man, and respect the ghosts and spirits, but keep away from them; this may be called wisdom." Then he asked about *jen,* and the Master said: "A man of *jen* first concentrates on what is difficult and then on rewards; this may be called *jen*." [VI-20]

18. Tsai Wo asked: "Suppose a man of *jen* were told, 'There is a man down in the well,' would he go down after the man?" "Why should he do so?" said the Master. "A *chün-tzu* might be induced [to go to the well] but not be trapped [in it]. He might be deceived, but not led astray." [VI-24]

19. Tzu Kung said: "Suppose there were a prince who conferred benefits far and wide upon the people and who was able to succor the multitude, what might you say of him? Could he be called *jen*-minded?" "Would it be merely a matter of *jen?*" said the Master. "Would he be also a sage?

Even Yao and Shun fell short of it. A man of *jen* is one who, in seeking to establish himself, finds a foothold for others and who, desiring attainment for himself, helps others to attain. To be able from one's own self to draw a parallel in dealing with others is indeed the way of achieving *jen*." [VI-28]

20. Yen Yuen asked about *jen,* and the Master said: "*Jen* consists in submitting oneself to *li.* Submit yourself to *li* for one day and everybody will accord you *jen.* For is *jen* to begin in one's self, or is it to begin in others?" "May I beg for details?" asked Yen Yuen. The Master said: "Look not at what is contrary to *li,* listen not to what is contrary to *li,* speak not what is contrary to *li,* and make no movement that is contrary to *li.*" "Though I am slow-witted," said Yen Yuen, "I shall try to live up to the lesson taught by this saying." [XII-1]

21. Chung Kung asked about *jen,* and the Master said: "When abroad, behave as if you were meeting an honored guest; in employing the people, act as if you were officiating in the grand sacrifice. What you do not wish to yourself, do not do to others. Then neither in the country nor in the family, will there be any resentment against you." "Though I am slow-witted," said Chung Kung, "I shall try to live up to the lesson taught by this saying." [XII-2]

22. Szu-ma Niu asked about *jen,* and the Master said: "A man of *jen* is wary of speech." "Wary of speech?" echoed Szu-ma Niu, "is this what is meant by *jen?*" The Master said: "When a man feels the difficulty of achievement, can he help but be wary in speaking about it?" [XII-3]

23. Fan Chi asked about *jen,* and the Master said: "Love men." Then he asked about wisdom, and the Master said: "Know men." Fan Chi did not understand. The Master said: "Employ the upright and set aside the crooked, so can the crooked be made upright." Fan Chi, after leaving the Master, met Tzu Hsia and said: "Just now I was with the Master and asked him about wisdom. He said, 'Employ the upright and set aside the crooked, so can the crooked be made upright.' What did he mean?" "Truly rich is this saying!" said Tzu Hsia. "When Shun [sage king] ruled the world, choosing from among the multitude, he employed Kao Yao and those devoid of *jen* disappeared. When T'ang [founder of the Shang dynasty] ruled the world, choosing from among the multitude, he employed Yin Yi and those devoid of *jen* disappeared." [XII-22]

24. Fan Chi asked about *jen,* and the Master said: "It is, in private life, to be courteous; in business, to be attentive; in all human relations, to be honest. And it should never be abandoned, even though one goes to live amid the barbaric tribes of the east or north." [xiv-19]

25. Hsien asked: ". . . If a man refrains from domineering, boasting, resentment, and desire, this may be counted to him as *jen?*" "This may be counted as difficult," said the Master, "but whether as *jen,* I do not know." [xiv-2]

26. Tzu Kung asked how to achieve *jen,* and the Master said: "When a workman wishes to do a good job, he must first sharpen his tools. So when you stay in a state, serve only the worthy among its ministers, and make friends with those scholars who are *jen*-hearted." [xv-9]

27. Tzu Chang asked Master K'ung about *jen,* and Master K'ung said: "To be able to practice the five virtues in the world constitutes *jen.*" Upon being asked what they were, the Master said: "They are respect, magnanimity, sincerity, earnestness, and kindness. With respect, you will avoid insult; with magnanimity, you will win over the multitude; with sincerity, men will trust you; with earnestness, you will have achievements; and with kindness, you will be fitted to command others." [xvii-6]

28. The Master said: "When a man's father is alive, observe his purpose. When his father is dead, observe his conduct. If for the three years of mourning he does not change from the ways of his father, he is indeed deemed to be filial." [I-11]

29. Meng I-tzu asked about filial piety, and the Master said: "Never disobey." When Fan Chi was driving him in his carriage, the Master told him, saying: "Meng-sun asked me about filial piety, and I said, 'Never disobey.'" "What did you mean?" asked Fan Chi. "When parents are alive," said the Master, "serve them according to *li.* When they die, bury them and sacrifice to them according to *li.*" [II-5]

30. Tzu Yu asked about filial piety, and the Master said: "Nowadays filial piety means the support of one's parents. But even dogs and horses are cared for by men. Without the feelings of respect, what is there to distinguish men from beasts?" [II-7]

31. Meng Wu-Po asked about filial piety, and the Master said: "Let your father and mother have no anxiety except that you be sick." [II-6]

32. Tzu Hsia asked about filial piety, and the Master said:

"It is the manner that is difficult. When anything has to be done the youngsters undertake it; when there is food and wine, the elders are served—is this merely to be respected as filial piety?" [II-8]

33. Someone asked Master K'ung, saying: "Why, Sir, are you not in government?" "It is said in the *Shu*," said the Master: "'Filial Piety! Let there be filial piety. There will be friendliness toward brothers, and this in turn will be displayed in government.' This also constitutes the exercise of government. Why must one be in office to serve in the government?" [II-21]

34. The Master said: "In serving his parents, a son may gently remonstrate with them. If they refuse to listen to his argument he should remain reverent and obedient. Even if he is belabored, he should not complain." [IV-18]

35. The Master said: "When the parents are alive, a son must not travel far. If he travels, he must specify where he goes." [IV-19]

36. The Master said: "The parents' age must be remembered, both for joy and for anxiety." [IV-21]

37. Tsai Wo, asking about the three years' mourning, suggested that one year was long enough. "If," said he, "a gentleman for three years abstains from ceremonial observances, ceremonies will certainly degenerate; if for three years he abstains from the use of music, music will certainly go to ruin. [In a year] the old crops are consumed, and the new crops have come up; the fire-striking sticks have been changed—a year would be long enough." "Would you then feel at ease in eating good rice and wearing fine clothes?" said the Master. "Quite at ease," was the reply. "If you feel at ease, then do so. But a gentleman, when in mourning, does not relish good food when he eats it; nor does he enjoy music when he hears it; nor does he feel at ease when he lives in a comfortable dwelling. Therefore he abstains from those things. But now if you would feel at ease, then go and do them." When Tsai Wo went out, the Master said: "What lack of *jen* is in Yü [i.e., Tsai Wo]! Only when a child is three years old, does he leave his parents' arms; so must three years' mourning be the universal mourning period everywhere below heaven. And Yü, did he not enjoy the loving care of his parents for three years?" [XVII-21]

38. The Master said: "In the morning I hear the *Tao*, then may I let myself die in the evening." [IV-8]

39. The Master said: "Ts'ang! there is one central idea that

runs through all my teachings." "Yes," answered Tseng Tzu. After the Master left, the disciples asked: "What did the Master mean?" "Our Master's doctrine," said Tseng Tzu, "is simply this: *chung* [loyalty] and *shu* [altruism]." [IV-15]

40. The Master said: "Who can go out [of the house] except by the door: Likewise, who can get along without following the *Tao?*" [VI-15]

41. The Master said: "Tz'u, do you think I am one who knows because of extensive learning?" "Yes, is it not so?" "No," said the Master, "there is one central idea that runs through all my teachings." [XV-2]

42. The Master said: "A man can enlarge the *Tao*, but the *Tao* cannot enlarge the man." [XV-28]

43. Tzu Kung said: "What I do not want others to do to me, I would not do to others." "Oh, Ssu!" said the Master, "you are not up to that!" [V-13]

44. Tzu Kung asked: "Is there a single word that one can live by all one's life?" "Is not *shu* [altruism] such a word?" said the Master. "Do not do to others what you do not want done to yourself." [XV-23]

45. The Master said: "Virtue dwells not alone but will always have neighbors." [IV-25]

46. The Master said: "Perfect indeed is the virtue which is in accord with the doctrine of Chun-Yung. For a long time few have had the capacity for it." [VI-27]

47. The Master said: "I have never seen a man who loves virtue as much as he loves a woman's beauty." [IX-17, XV-12]

48. The Master said: "A well-bred horse is praised not for its might but for its good qualities." [XIV-35]

49. The Master said: "Yu, those who know virtue are few." [XV-3]

50. The Master said: "The good careful villagers are the simulators of virtue." [XVII-13]

Chapter II. Moral Cultivation

Confucius stressed moral cultivation as the chief concern of life. According to his ethical teachings, man, as a moral being, can gain wisdom to improve and enrich his life through his relations with his fellow men. Therefore, a man, first of all, should demand much from himself but little from others and, next, he should be alert in his dealings with people. To Confucius the model human being was a *chün-tzu*, originally the word for an aristocrat, which came to have its present connotation of a "man of virtue" or a "true gentleman." The opposite of *chün-tzu* is *hsiao-jen,* originally the word for peasant, which came to mean a low, despicable person.

◆§ ❧◆

51. The Master said: "*Chün-tzu* is not a utensil." [II-12]

52. Tzu Kung asked about *chün-tzu,* and the Master said: "He first practices what he preaches, and then preaches what he practices." [II-13]

53. The Master said: "*Chün-tzu* is broadminded but not biased. *Hsiao-jen* is biased but not broadminded." [II-14]

54. The Master said: "There is nothing for which *chün-tzu* contends. If he has to contend, shall he do so in archery? But even then, he bows before he mounts to the archery ground. Then he comes down and exacts the forfeit of drinking. In such a contention, he is still a *chün-tzu.*" [III-7]

55. The Master said: "*Chün-tzu* in his dealings with the world has neither enmities nor affections, but he sides with what is righteous." [IV-10]

56. The Master said: "While *chün-tzu* cherishes virtue, *hsiao-jen* cherishes the possessions, and while *chün-tzu* thinks of sanctions, *hsiao-jen* thinks only of favors." [IV-11]

57. The Master said: "*Chün-tzu* is informed in what is righteous; *hsiao-jen* is informed in what is profitable." [IV-16]

58. The Master speaking to Tzu Hsia said: "Be a noble-minded literati not a small-minded literati." [VI-11]

59. The Master said: "*Chün-tzu* is always calm and at ease; *hsiao-jen* is always worried and full of distress." [VII-36]

60. The Master said: "That one's words are good and sincere we may grant. But is he a *chün-tzu,* or is he merely acting like one?" [XI-20]

61. Szu-ma Niu asked about *chün-tzu,* and the Master said: "*Chün-tzu* has neither anxiety nor fear." "Neither anxiety nor fear," echoed Szu-ma Niu, "is this what is meant by being a *chün-tzu?*" "When he looks into himself and finds no cause for self-reproach," said the Master, "what is there to be anxious about? What is there to fear?" [XII-4]

62. The Master said: "*Chün-tzu* helps the people to succeed in what is good but does not help them in what is evil. *Hsiao-jen* does just the reverse of this." [XII-16]

63. The Master said: "*Chün-tzu* is conciliating but not adulating; *hsiao-jen* is adulating but not conciliating." [XIII-23]

64. The Master said: *"Chün-tzu* is easy to serve but difficult to please. For if you try to please him in a way contrary to the *Tao*, he will not be pleased; but when employing the services of others, he only expects of them according to their capacity. *Hsiao-jen* is difficult to serve but easy to please. Even though you please him in a way contrary to the *Tao*, he will still be pleased; but when he employs the services of others, he expects them to be capable of everything." [XIII-25]

65. The Master said: *"Chün-tzu* is dignified but not arrogant; *hsiao-jen* is arrogant but not dignified." [XIII-26]

66. The Master said: *"Chün-tzu* may not be *jen*-minded at all times, but *hsiao-jen* cannot be *jen*-minded at any time." [XIV-7]

67. The Master said: *"Chün-tzu* reaches upward; *hsiao-jen* reaches downward." [XIV-24]

68. The Master said: *"Chün-tzu* makes demands on himself; *hsiao-jen* makes demands on others." [XV-20]

69. The Master said: *"Chün-tzu* may not be conversant with petty details but may be intrusted with important matters. *Hsiao-jen* may not be charged with important matters but may be well versed in petty details." [IV-32]

70. Master K'ung said: "There are three things *chün-tzu* fears: he fears the will of Heaven; he fears great men; he fears the words of the sages. *Hsiao-jen* does not know the will of Heaven; he treats great men with contempt; and he scoffs at the words of the sages." [XVI-8]

71. The Master said: "The *Tao* of *chün-tzu* is threefold; being *jen*-minded, he is free from anxiety; being wise, he is free from perplexity; being brave, he is free from fear. I myself have not yet attained any of them." "But, Master," said Tzu Kung, "this is your own way." [XIV-30]

72. Tzu Lu asked about *chün-tzu,* and the Master said: "He cultivates himself with reverence." "Is that all?" asked Tzu Lu. "He cultivates himself," said the Master, "so as to bring comfort to others." "Is that all?" asked Tzu Lu. "He cultivates himself," said the Master, "so as to bring comfort to the people—even Yao and Shun fell short of this." [XIV-45]

73. The Master said: *"Chün-tzu* bases his character on righteousness, conducts himself according to propriety, expresses himself in modesty, and becomes complete in sincerity; such is *chün-tzu*." [XV-17]

74. The Master said: *"Chün-tzu* is worried about his lack of ability, but he is never worried that others do not know him." [XV-18]

75. Tzu Lu asked: "Does *chün-tzu* esteem courage?"
"*Chün-tzu* holds righteousness in the highest esteem," said the
Master. "*Chün-tzu*, having courage without righteousness,
will be turbulent. *Hsiao-jen*, having courage without righteousness, will commit robbery." [xvii-23]

76. The Master said: "*Chün-tzu* regrets that after his death
his name will no longer be mentioned." [xv-19]

77. The Master said: "*Chün-tzu* has self-respect but is not
contentious; he is sociable but not biased. [xv-21]

78. The Master said: "*Chün-tzu* does not exalt a man because of his words; nor does he spurn good words because
of the man." [xv-22]

79. The Master said: "*Chün-tzu* occupies himself with the
Tao and not with his livelihood. One may attend to farming
and yet may sometimes be short of food. One may attend to
learning and yet may be rewarded with emolument. Therefore, what *chün-tzu* worries about is the *Tao* and not poverty." [xv-31]

80. The Master said: "*Chün-tzu* holds fast to his uprightness but not fidelity." [xv-36]

81. Master K'ung said: "There are nine things which occupy the thought of *chün-tzu:* In seeing, he sees clearly; in
hearing, he hears distinctly; in his looks, he is kind; in his
manner, he is respectful; in his speech, he is sincere; in his
work, he is serious; when in doubt, he asks questions; when
in anger, he considers the consequence; and when he sees
gains, he thinks of righteousness." [xvi-10]

82. Master K'ung said: "There are three things against
which *chün-tzu* is on his guard. In his youth, when his blood
and vital powers are not fully developed and settled, he is
on his guard against lust. In his manhood, when his blood
and vital powers are vigorous and strong, he is on his guard
against strife. In his old age, when his blood and vital powers
are weak and decaying, he is on his guard against greed of
gain." [xvi-7]

83. The Master said: "It is beyond my hope to meet a
sage; could I see *chün-tzu*, that would make me content. It
is beyond my hope to meet a good man; could I see a man of
constancy, that would make me content. When a man who
does not have pretends to have, who is empty pretends to be
full, who is rigid pretends to be at ease; such a man does not
possess constancy." [vii-25]

84. The Master said: "*Chün-tzu*, if not solemn, will not
inspire awe, and his learning will not be solid. He holds with

loyalty and sincerity and has no friends who do not come up to him. If he has faults, he will not fear to amend them." [II-8]

85. Tzu Chang asked about the *Tao* of the good man, and the Master said: "Not treading in the track, a man cannot find his way into the chamber." [XI-19]

86. Tzu Chang asked: "What must an official do to merit his distinction?" "What, I wonder," said the Master, "do you mean by distinction?" "When he is in the service of the state, he is certain to make himself known; when he is in the service of the ruling family, he is certain to make himself known." "This is popularity," said the Master; "it's not distinction. Now the man of distinction is one who is by nature upright and loves righteousness. He watches men's words and observes their looks; he is modest and deferring to others. Such a man, whether in the service of the state or in that of the ruling family, will certainly achieve distinction. The man of mere popularity, on the other hand, assumes the appearance of *jen,* but his actions are contrary to it; he makes his claims with sufficient self-assurance. Such a man is sure to be popular either in the state or in the ruling family." [XII-20]

87. Tzu Kung asked: "What must an official do to merit his name?" "A man who in his private conduct," said the Master, "shows a sense of shame and as an envoy abroad does not disgrace his prince's commission; such a man may be called a true official." "I venture to ask who would rank next?" "He must be the man," said the Master, "who is praised for his filial piety by his kinsmen and for his deference to elders by his fellow villagers." "I venture to ask who would come next?" "He who keeps his words and sticks to his course," said the Master; "such a man, though little-minded, may be considered to come next." "What would you say of those who are now in government?" "Ugh!" said the Master. "Those ricebags! They are not worth taking into account." [XIII-20]

88. The Master said: "Since I cannot find the moderate men to associate with, I turn to the ambitious and the prudent. The ambitious push themselves forward, whereas the prudent refrain from assertion." [XIII-21]

89. Tzu Lu asked: "What must a scholar[1] do to merit his name?" "A man is earnest and diligent; friendly and affable; then he may be called a true scholar. Toward his friends, he

1. The Chinese term *shih* stands for a class of men, meaning both scholars and officials, as distinguished from farmers, artisans, and merchants.

is earnest and diligent; to his brothers, he is friendly and affable." [XIII-28]

90. The Master said: "A scholar who cherishes his own comfort does not merit his name." [XIV-3]

91. Tzu Lu asked about the perfect man, and the Master said: "Suppose there were a man with the wisdom of Tsang Wu-chung, the uncovetousness of Meng King-ch'o, the courage of Pien Chuang-tzu, and the talents of Jen Chiu; in addition, he is well versed in ceremonials and music: such a man may be considered a perfect man." Then the Master added: "But the perfect man of today need not be like that. In view of gain, he thinks of righteousness; in view of danger, he is ready to sacrifice his life; in addition, he never forgets his promise, however far back; such a man may also be considered a perfect man." [XIV-13]

92. Tzu Kung asked: "What would you say of a man who is poor and does not flatter; rich and not arrogant?" "That is fine," said the Master, "but it is still better to be poor and yet happy; rich and yet fond of propriety [li]." Then Tzu Kung said: "The Shih [Odes] reads:

> As you cut and then file;
> As you carve and then polish.

Does this refer to what you have just said?" "Ssu," said the Master, "with you I can talk about the Shih, for when I allude to the past, you know what is to follow." [I-15]

93. Tzu Chang was studying with a view to official emolument. The Master said: "Hear much, and set aside those which seem doubtful, and be cautious in speaking of the rest; then you will be free from error. See much, and put aside those that seem perilous, and be cautious in acting upon the rest; then you will be free from regrets. Let your speech be free from error and your actions be free from regrets: therein lies official emolument." [II-18]

94. The Master said: "How am I to regard those who, in high office, are not magnanimous, who perform ceremonies without reference, and who conduct mourning without grief?" [III-26]

95. The Master said: "A scholar who is devoted to the Tao and yet is ashamed of bad clothes and bad food is not worth talking to." [IV-9]

96. The Master said: "When you see a man of worth, think of attaining to his excellence. When you see an un-

worthy one, then look within and examine yourself." [IV-17]

97. The Master said: "The ancients were reserved in their speech, lest their actions might not come up to their words." [IV-21]

98. The Master said: "One who is strict with oneself rarely errs." [IV-23]

99. The Master said: "*Chün-tzu* wishes to be slow in speech but prompt in action." [IV-24]

100. The Master said: "Clever words, flattering looks, and fulsome respect—Tso Ch'iu Ming was ashamed of them, and I, Ch'iu, am also ashamed of them. To conceal resentment and appear friendly—Tso Ch'iu Ming was ashamed of such conduct, and I, Ch'iu, am also ashamed of such conduct." [V-24]

101. The Master said: "That is all over! I have not yet seen a man who can perceive his own faults and inwardly reproach himself." [V-26]

102. The Master said: "In a hamlet of ten families, there must be men as conscientious and sincere as myself, but none as fond of learning as I am." [V-27]

103. The Master said: "When nature exceeds culture, we have the rustic. When culture exceeds nature, we have the pedant. Only when nature and culture are balanced, do we have *chün-tzu*." [VI-16]

104. The Master said: "To know *Tao* is not as good as to love it, and to love it is not as good as to practice it." [VI-18]

105. The Master said: "Neglect in the cultivation of virtues; lack of thoroughness in study; inability to move towards righteousness; and inability to amend my faults: these are my worries." [VII-3]

106. The Master said: "Be devoted to the *Tao;* cling to virtue; rely on *jen;* and then study the polite arts." [VII-6]

107. The Master said: "While I am in a party of three, I am sure to have teachers. What is good in them I should follow, and what is not good in them I should correct." [VII-21]

108. The Master said: "In learning, I am perhaps equal to others; but I have not yet attained to living the life of *chün-tzu*." [VII-32]

109. The Master said: "Though a man has the qualities of the Duke of Chou, yet if he is arrogant and avaricious, nothing in him will merit our attention." [VIII-11]

110. The Master said: "It is not easy to find a man who after three years of study has never thought of reward." [VIII-12]

111. Standing by a stream, the Master said: "Ah, that which is passing is just like this, never ceasing day or night." [IX-16]

112. The Master said: "Let me take this illustration: If in raising a mound, I stop working before the last load is placed, the fact remains that I have stopped. On the other hand, if in leveling it to the ground, I advance my work by but one load at a time, the fact remains that I am advancing." [IX-19]

113. The Master said: "There are sprouting crops which never come into ear; there are others, which, having come into ear, never ripen into grain." [IX-21]

114. The Master said: "The Young men are to be respected. Who knows but that the future generation will surpass the present. But to those who have made no name for themselves by the ripe age of forty and fifty, no respect is due." [IX-22]

115. The Master said: "Can we refuse to follow the words of just admonition? But what matters is reformation. Can we refuse to be pleased with the words of kindly advice? But what matters is meditation. If a man is pleased with advice but will not meditate on it, or if a man follows admonition but does not reform, I do not know what to do with him." [IX-23]

116. The Master said: "Hold with loyalty and sincerity; have no friend inferior to yourself; should you have faults, do not fear to amend them." [IX-24]

117. The Master said: "The Three Armies may be robbed of their commander, but a common man can never be deprived of his will." [IX-25]

118. The Master said: "It is only when the winter comes, that we know the pine and cypress to be the last to fade." [IX-27]

119. The Master said: "There are some with whom we can join in study but who are not yet able to approach the *Tao;* there are others with whom we can approach the *Tao* but who are not yet able to take a firm stand [on *li*]; and there are others with whom we can take a firm stand but who are not yet able to follow the desires of their minds." [IX-29]

120. Tzu Chang asked how to exalt virtue and discern delusion. The Master said: "Hold with loyalty and sincerity, and follow the path of righteousness—this is the way of exalting virtue. To love a thing means wanting it to live, to hate a thing means wanting it to perish. But suppose you

want something to live and at the same time want it to perish
—this is the case of delusion." The *Shih* says: "Truly not for
wealth, only for a change." [XII-10]

121. When strolling with Master K'ung under the Rain-
Dance Altars, Fan Ch'i asked how to exalt virtue, how to
rectify cherished evils, and how to discern delusion. The
Master said: "A good question, indeed! Duty first, and reward second; is this not a way of exalting virtue? Attack the
evil in one's self, not that in others; is this not a way of
rectifying cherished evils. For a sudden fit of anger to disregard one's own life and involve one's parents; is this not
a case of delusion?" [XII-21]

122. The Master said: "The man of the south has a saying:
A man without constancy will not make a witch-doctor.'
Well said!" [The *I Ching* says:] 'A man without constancy
will bring disgrace upon himself.' "This arises simply from not
consulting oracles." [XIII-22]

123. The Master said: "A man who is boastful in words
will be indolent in action." [XIV-21]

124. The Master said: "*Chün-tzu* is ashamed to let his
words exceed his action." [XIV-28]

125. The Master said: "Hopeless is the case of those who
herd together all day long without talking about righteousness but being fond of smart and petty wits." [xv-16]

126. The Master said: "The real fault is to have faults and
not to amend them." [xv-29]

127. Master K'ung said: "There are three kinds of enjoyments which are beneficial and three kinds of enjoyments
which are detrimental. To enjoy performance of ceremonies
and music, to enjoy speaking of other's goodness, and to enjoy the company of worthy friends are beneficial. To enjoy
extravagant pleasures, to enjoy licentious idleness, and to
enjoy wild feastings are detrimental." [xvi-5]

128. Master K'ung said: "'When you see the good, act as
though you were not equal to it; when you see the evil, act
as though you would try the boiling water.' I have seen such
men and heard such words. 'Live in seclusion, and work out
your aims; practice righteousness and achieve the *Tao*.' I
have heard such words, but have not yet seen such men."
[XVI-11]

129. The Master said: "A man who is stern in appearance
but weak in mind is comparable to *hsiao-jen;* is he not like
a sneaking thief who breaks into a house by night?" [XVII-12]

130. The Master said: "To tell what has been heard on the way is to cast aside virtue." [XVII-14]

131. The Master said: "It is hard with a man who just eats and sits idle the whole day without occupying his mind on anything. Are there no chess games? To play them would be better than doing nothing at all." [XVII-22]

132. The Master said: "If a man at forty is still repelling to people, he is finished for life." [XVII-26]

133. The Master said: "Not to know Fate [Ming] cannot be a *chün-tzu;* not to know *li* is to have no means of standing; not to know the correct usage in speech is not to understand men." [XX-3]

Chapter III. The Way of Life

The teachings of Confucius, as we noted above, emphasize human relationships and teach men how to live in harmony with one another. Without involving himself in metaphysical and supernatural speculations, he set forth clear and concrete rules of conduct which can be applied in daily life. In fact, he taught a good way of life which is both practical and practicable, with a personal appeal that went directly to the heart of the listener. In this way, his teachings, so long dominant in the intellectual and moral life of the nation, could work down to the masses at the base.

❧

134. The Master said: "Grieve not that men do not know you; grieve that you do not know men." [I-16]

135. The Master said: "Observe a man's actions; scrutinize his motives; and study what makes him content. How can a man conceal himself?" [II-10]

136. The Master said: "I do not know how a man without sincerity can get on. How can a wagon without yoke bar, a carriage without cross bar, be made to go?" [II-22]

137. The Master said: "To sacrifice to a spirit not related to you is mere flattery. To shirk what is righteous shows want of courage." [II-24]

138. The Master said: "A man who acts merely for his own advantage will make himself many enemies." [IV-12]

139. The Master said: "Do not worry about not being in office; worry about qualifying yourself for office. Do not worry that no one knows you, but seek to be worthy of being known." [IV-14]

140. The Master said: "Even though a man has only the good looks of Prince Chao of Sung, without the eloquence of the Priest T'o, he will still find it difficult nowadays to get through." [vi-14]

141. The Master said: "Man is upright by birth. If he loses uprightness and yet lives, it is mere good luck." [vi-17]

142. The Master said: "Be sincere and fond of learning; hold firm to death for the perfection of the *Tao*. Do not enter a tottering state or remain in a rebellious state. When the *Tao* prevails in the world, then show yourself; when the *Tao* does not prevail in the world, then withdraw yourself. When the *Tao* prevails in the state, it is a disgrace to be poor and malicious; when the *Tao* does not prevail in the state, it is a disgrace to be rich and honored." [viii-13]

143. The Master said: "A man who is fond of courage but is dissatisfied with poverty will proceed to violence. So will any man who is not *jen*-minded, if his sufferings are very great." [viii-10]

144. The Master said: "A man who is out of office should not meddle in the government." [viii-14]

145. Tzu Chang asked what constituted "enlightenment." The Master said: "A man who is influenced neither by the soaking poison of slander nor by the assault of denunciation may be called enlightened indeed. Aye, such a man, influenced neither by the soaking poison of slander nor by the assault of denunciation, may well be called magnanimous." [xii-6]

146. Tzu Kung asked about a friend, and the Master said: "Faithfully admonish him and gently guide him. If you do not succeed, then stop. Do not submit yourself to disgrace." [xii-23]

147. The Master said of Prince Ching of Wei that he knew how to manage his household. When he began to have means, he said: "Now this is just a collection." When he had more, he said: "Now this is complete." When he became rich, he said: "Now this is excellent! Perfection!" [xiii-8]

148. The Duke of Yeh said to Master K'ung: "In my part of the country there is a man so upright that when his father appropriated a sheep his son bore witness against him." "The upright men in my part of the country are different from that," said the Master. "For a father will screen his son, and a son his father; therein lies uprightness." [xiii-18]

149. Tzu Kung asked: "What would you say of a man who is beloved by all his fellow villagers?" "That is not enough,"

said the Master. "Then what of one who is hated by all fellow villagers?" "Nor is that enough," said the Master. "It would be better if among his fellow villagers, the good loved him and the wicked hated him." [XIII-24]

150. Hsien asked about the sense of shame, and the Master said: "When the *Tao* prevails in the country, one may accept emolument. When the *Tao* does not prevail in the country, it is shameful to accept emolument." [XIV-1]

151. The Master said: "When the *Tao* prevails in the land, both speech and action may be lofty. When the *Tao* does not prevail in the land, let action be lofty but speech be modest." [XIV-4]

152. The Master said: "Can one love a man without working hard for him? Can one be loyal to a man without admonishing him?" [XIV-8]

153. The Master said: "It is difficult to be poor without complaint; it is easy to be rich without arrogance." [XIV-11]

154. Tzu Lu asked how to serve a prince. The Master said: "Do not impose on him, but rather resist him." [XIV-23]

155. The Master said: "Do not worry about lack of fame; worry about lack of ability." [XIV-32]

156. The Master said: "A man should not anticipate fraud, not expect falsehood; yet if he is conscious of this beforehand —is he not a man of worth?" [XIV-33]

157. Someone asked: "What may be said of requiting injury with kindness?" "How will you then requite kindness?" said the Master. "Requite injury with justice, and kindness with kindness." [XIV-36]

158. The Master said: "Some men of worth retire from the world; those next to them withdraw from their fatherland; the next from uncongenial looks; and the next from uncongenial words." [XIV-39] The Master said: "There are seven men who have retired." [XIV-40]

159. Tzu Chang asked how a man should conduct himself. The Master said: "Let him be faithful and true in his words; let him be sincere and reverent in his actions; and then he will conduct himself even among barbarians. But if he is not faithful and true in his words, nor sincere and reverent in his actions, even among his own villagers, how can he be expected to conduct himself? When standing, see these precepts in front of you; when in a carriage, see them on the yoke. Then may you conduct yourself well wherever you go." Tzu Chang inscribed this down on his sash. [XV-5]

160. The Master said: "Not to speak with a man who can

be spoken with is to lose a man. To speak to a man who cannot be spoken with is to waste words. He who is truly wise
never loses a man; he, too, never wastes his words." [xv-7]

161. The Master said: "A man who gives no thought to
the future will have trouble at home." [xv-11]

162. The Master said: "A man who exacts much from
himself and little from others will certainly avoid resentment."
[xv-14]

163. The Master said: "In my dealing with men, whom do
I blame excessively? Whom do I praise excessively? If I do
sometimes exceed in praise, there must be something that I
put to the test. I would have the people follow the straight
path which prevailed during the Three Dynasties." [xv-24]

164. The Master said: "Clever words confound virtue.
Lack of forbearance in small matters makes a mess of greater
schemes." [xv-26]

165. The Master said: "When the multitude detests a man,
inquiry is necessary; when the multitude likes a man, inquiry
is equally necessary." [xv-27]

166. The Master said: "In serving a prince, let attention
be given to duties, and then think of emolument." [xv-37]

167. The Master said: "In the presence of a prince, one is
subject to three errors: To speak out of one's turn—this is
called rashness; to refrain from speaking in one's turn—this
is called bashfulness; to speak without observing the prince's
countenance—this is called blindness." [xvi-6]

168. Master K'ung said: "There are three kinds of friendships which are beneficial, and three kinds of friendships
which are detrimental. To make friends with the upright,
with the trustworthy, and with the learned is beneficial. On
the other hand, to make friends with the obsequious, with
the flattering, and with the glib-tongued, is detrimental."
[xvi-4]

169. The Master said: "Those malicious fellows! How can
we ever work with them to serve the prince? When they are
not in office, they are anxious to get it. When they are in
office, they worry about losing it. Worrying about losing it,
they would not scruple to do anything to keep it." [xvii-15]

170. Tzu Kung asked: "Does chün-tzu have his hatreds?"
"Yes," said the Master, "he has his hatreds. He hates those
who divulge the evils of others; he hates those who, in low
position, malign their superiors; he hates those who have
courage without propriety; he hates those who are not resolute and forward, but rash and impetuous." Then the Master

added: "Tz'e, have you also your hatreds?" [The disciple replied] "I hate those who are impetuous and consider themselves wise; I hate those who are not modest and consider themselves courageous; I hate those who attack the secrets of others and consider themselves upright." [xvii-24]

171. The Master said: "Only women and *hsiao-jen* are difficult to deal with. If you are intimate with them, they do not respect you; but if you keep at a distance, they resent it." [xvii-25]

Chapter IV. Learning and Teaching

Confucius, as we have noted in his life, was a zealous student, a devoted scholar, and an indefatigable teacher. Above all, he was an educator *par excellence*, whose success lay chiefly in his ability to cultivate intimate, personal relationships with his disciples. The following passages offer good illustrations of his passion for learning as well as his individualized tutorship. Moreover, the wealth of educational theories in his teachings will amply reward study.

◄§ ६►

172. The Master said: "To learn and frequently practice what has been learned—is this not a pleasure? To have friends coming from far-off lands—is this not a joy? To remain unconcerned even though others do not know him—is he not a *chün-tzu?*" [i-1]

173. The Master said: "At fifteen I set my mind on learning; at thirty I could stand; at forty I had no doubts; at fifty I knew the Fate; at sixty I was already obedient [to the Fate]; and at seventy I could follow my heart's desires without transgressing the standards of right." [ii-4]

174. The Master said: "I transmit but I do not create; I have faith in, and a passion for, ancient studies. In this respect, I venture to compare myself to Lao P'eng." [vii-1]

175. The Master said: "Knowing through silent reflection, learning without satiety, and teaching others without becoming weary—these are merits which I can claim." [vii-2]

176. The Master said: "As to being a sage or even a man of *jen*, how dare I make such claims? But it may be said of me that I have strived to learn without satiety and to teach others without becoming weary." Kung Hsi Hua said: "This is what we disciples fail to learn." [vii-33]

177. The Master said: "Is it true that *chün-tzu,* widely learned in culture, properly conducted in propriety, may not be far wrong?" [vi-25]

178. The Master said: "Were I to be given a few more years, I would give fifty to the study of the *Yi;* only then might I be free from grave faults." [vii-16]

179. The Duke of Yeh asked Tzu Lu about Master K'ung, and Tzu Lu did not answer him. The Master said: "Why didn't you tell him that I am a person who forgets to eat when he is in pursuit of knowledge, forgets all worries when he is in his enjoyment of it, and is not aware that old age is coming on?" [vii-18]

180. The Master said: "There are those who act without knowing why. But I am not like that. To hear much and then to select the good and follow it; to see much and then to ponder it—this comes next to true knowledge." [vii-27]

181. The Master said: "I am not one born with possession of knowledge, but, being fond of antiquity, I assiduously pursue it." [vii-19]

182. The Master said: "Sometimes I have passed a whole day without eating and a whole night without sleep, giving myself in thought. But it was of no avail. It is better to learn." [xv-30]

183. The Master said: "Study without thought is labor lost; thought without study is perilous." [ii-15]

184. The Master said: "A youth should be filial at home and fraternal when abroad. He should be earnest and sincere, feeling an affection for all and a disposition toward *jen*. If, when all is done, he still has any energy to spare, then let him study the polite arts." [i-6]

185. The Master said: "The study of heterodox doctrines is injurious indeed." [ii-16]

186. The Master said: "*Chün-tzu* does not seek satiety in his food, or comfort in his home, but he is earnest in his work and cautious in his speech; he still seeks the company of the righteous for rectification of his conduct. Such a man may rightly be said to be fond of learning." [i-14]

187. The Master said: "Learn as though you would never be able to master it; hold it as though you would be in fear of losing it." [viii-17]

188. The Master said: "In old days, men studied only for their own improvement; nowadays men study for approbation of others." [xiv-25]

189. The Master said: "In education there is no class distinction." [xv-38]

190. The Master said: "By nature men are nearly alike, but through experience they grow wide apart." [xvii-2]

191. The Master said: "To those who are above average, it is possible to discourse on the high doctrines. To those who are below average, it is impossible to do so." [vi-19]

192. The Master said: "Those who are born wise are the highest type of men; those who become wise through learning come next; those who are dull-witted and yet strive to learn come after that. Those who are dull-witted and yet make no effort to learn are the lowest type of men." [xvi-9]

193. The Master said: "The one who never changes is either the wisest of the wise or the dullest of the dull." [xvii-3]

194. The Master said: "From him who has brought his simple present of dried meat seeking to enter my school, I have never withheld instruction." [vii-7]

195. The Master said: "I won't teach a man who is not eager to learn, nor will I explain to one incapable of forming his own ideas. Nor have I anything more to say to those who, after I have made clear one corner of the subject, cannot deduce the other three." [vii-8]

196. The Master said: "To be able to acquire new knowledge while reviewing the old qualifies one as an instructor of men." [ii-11]

197. The themes on which the Master frequently discoursed were: the *Shih* [Odes], the *Shu* [History], and performance of the Rites. Of these he frequently discoursed. [vii-17]

198. The Master took four subjects for his teaching: belles-lettres and conduct, loyalty and truth. [vii-24]

199. The Master said: "My friends, do you think that I have concealed something from you? No, I conceal nothing from you. There is nothing that I do not share with you. That is my way." [vii-23]

200. The Master said: "Am I possessed of wisdom? Far from it. But if an ignorant fellow from the lower classes should come to me with a question, I would discuss the subject from beginning to end and set all I know fully before him." [ix-7]

201. The Master said: "I wish that I could do without speaking." "If my Master did not speak," said Tzu Kung, "what could we disciples transmit?" The Master said: "Does

Heaven speak? The four seasons run their course, and all things live and grow. Yet, tell me, does Heaven speak?" [xvii-19]

202. The Master said: "If language is lucid, it suffices." [xv-40]

203. The Master said: "Arrogant and yet not upright, ignorant and yet not honest, stupid and yet not sincere; to such persons I give no recognition." [viii-3]

204. The Master said: "If a man does not come to me inquiring 'what of this' and 'what of that,' I can indeed do nothing with him." [xv-15]

205. The Master said: "Yu, shall I tell you what knowledge is? Only say that you know when you really know, and concede your ignorance of what you do not know." [ii-17]

206. Chi Lu asked about serving the ghosts and spirits, and the Master said: "While you are not able to serve men, how can you serve the ghosts and spirits?" When he ventured to ask about death, the Master said: "Not yet knowing life, how can you know death?" [xi-11]

207. Tzu Lu asked whether he should put his learning into practice. The Master said: "While your father and elder brothers are still alive, how can you do so?" When Jan Yu asked the same question, the Master said: "You should do it immediately." Kung-hsi Hua, who overheard both conversations, repeated the discrepancies of the Master's replies and said: "I am perplexed, Sir, and venture to ask for an explanation." "Ch'iu [Jan Yu] is diffident," said the Master, "so I urged him forward. Yu [Tzu Lu] is overconfident, so I held him back." [xi-21]

208. Ju Pei wished to see Master K'ung, but Master K'ung declined on the ground of being sick. When the messenger was leaving the house, the Master took up his zithern and sang to it, in order that the messenger could hear. [xvii-20]

209. Once when Yen Yuen and Tzu Lu were waiting on him, the Master said: "Why don't you tell me your wish?" "I should like to have," said Tzu Lu, "carriages and horses, and to be clad in light furs, so that I can share them with my friends. I would not mind if they should be worn out together." "I should like," said Yen Yuen, "to make no boast of my talents or display of my good deeds." Then Tzu Lu turned to the Master and said: "We should like, Sir, to hear of your wish." "It is my wish," said the Master, "to nourish

the old, to cherish the young, and to be true to friends."
[v-25]

210. Once when Tzu Lu, Tseng Hsi, Jan Yu, and Kung-
hsi Hua were sitting by him, the Master said: "Now forget
for a moment that I am older than you. As you are out of
office, you feel that you are not recognized. Let us suppose
that some one wishes to give you a government position;
what would you choose to do?" "Give me," Tzu Lu replied
hastily, "a state with a thousand chariots, hemmed in by
powerful neighbors, overrun by invading armies, with famine
and drought to boot, and I could in space of three years
teach its people courage and lead them toward right conduct." The Master smiled and asked: "What about you,
Ch'iu?" "If I had charge," replied Jan Yu, "of a territory of
sixty to seventy *li*, or one of fifty to sixty, I would in the
space of three years make the people live in abundance. As
to rites and music, I should wait for *chün-tzu*." "How about
you, Ch'ih?" "I wish to speak not of the things I can do,"
replied Kung-hsi Hua, "but of the things I wish to learn. In
ceremonials at the ancestral temple, or at the audiences of
the princes, I should like to be dressed in the straight robe
and official cap, to act as a junior assistant." "What about you,
Tien?" Tseng Hsi, while playing his zithern, pushed it aside
and rose to reply: "I fear my choice cannot compare with
those of the other three." "What harm is there in that? I just
want each of you to speak his mind." "At the end of spring,"
said Tseng Hsi, "and clad in spring clothes, with five or six
newly capped youths, and six or seven lads, I should like to
bathe in the river Yi and fan myself with breezes from the
Rain-Dance altars. Then we would return singing." At this
the Master sighed, saying: "I am with you, Tien."

After the other three had left, Tseng Hsi followed the
Master and asked: "What do you think of the words of these
three friends?" "They were merely speaking of their mind,"
said the Master. "Why did you smile at Yu?" "To rule a state,"
said the Master, "requires observance of ceremony; and his
words show want of humility, so I smiled at him."

"Didn't Ch'iu mean to rule a state?"

"Where have you ever seen 'a territory of sixty to seventy
li, or one of fifty to sixty,' that was not a state?"

"Didn't Ch'ih mean to rule a state?"

"Who but princes hold audiences in ancestral temples?
But if Ch'ih were only a minor officer in these services, who
would be the major one?" [XI-25]

Chapter V. Li *and Music*

Among the six arts which comprised the chief training of a *chün-tzu,* Confucius stressed rites and music (including poetry) in his ethical system. Music was a required study, as its performance accompanied all ceremonies, whether in religious sacrifice, court assembly, or family entertainment. *Li* governed the moral, social, and religious activities of a man. Etymologically, *li* is religious in nature, and in the course of its evolution, it came to include all forms of rituals and everything in connection with the proper conduct of the *chün-tzu.* Poetry was also studied, as it was indispensable not only for moral cultivation, but for diplomatic intercourse as well.

⋞⋟

211. The Master said: "Personal cultivation begins with poetry, is established by rites, and is perfected by music." [viii-8]

212. Chen K'ang asked of P'o Yü: "Have you learned anything different from what we all have had?" "No," replied P'o Yü, "but once when I was hurrying across the hall, where my father was standing alone, he said to me, 'Have you learned the *Odes?*' I answered, 'Not yet.' 'If you do not learn them,' he admonished, 'you will have no hold on words.' Then I retired and studied the *Odes.* On another occasion, as he was again standing by himself, I hurried across the hall to greet him. 'Have you learned the Rites?' he asked. 'Not yet,' I answered. 'Without learning the Rites,' he said, 'you will not be able to establish yourself.' So I retired and studied the Rites. Only these two things have I heard from him." Chen K'ang turned away and in delight, said: "I asked one thing and got three. I have learned about the *Odes* and the Rites; and I have learned too that *chün-tzu* is reserved toward his son." [xvi-13]

213. The Master said: "If I should summarize the three hundred *Odes* in one sentence, I would say: 'Wayward thoughts are absent.'" [ii-2]

214. The Master said: "[In the *Odes,* the first piece] *Kuan-chü* expresses joy without being licentious and grief without being injurious." [iii-20]

215. The Master said: "A man may learn the three hundred odes by heart, but if he proves himself incompetent

when given a government post, or if he cannot make a speech unaided when sent abroad on mission, then of what use to him is all his learning?" [XIII-5]

216.   The flowers of the cherry tree
            Flutter on every spray.
        It is not that I do not think of thee,
            But that thou art far away!

[Commenting on these lines], the Master said: "He did not really think of her, what does the distance mean to him?" [IX-30]

217. The Master said: "My pupils, why don't you study the *Odes?* The *Odes* are evocative of thoughts; they are material for introspection; they contribute to social intercourse, they alleviate one's frustration. From the *Odes,* one learns the immediate duty of serving one's father and the remote duty of serving one's prince. And in the *Odes* one may be better acquainted with the names of birds and beasts, plants and trees." [VII-9]

218. The Master said to P'o Yü: "Have you ever learned the odes *Chou-nan* and *Shao-nan?* A man who has not ever learned them is like one who stands with his face against the wall; is he not so?" [XIII-10]

219. Tzu Hsia asked: "What is the meaning of the following verse?

            How bewitching her artful smiles!
            How clear her beautiful eyes!
            There must be plain background
            For the application of colors!"

"The painting comes after the plain groundwork," said the Master. "Then rituals and etiquette (*li*) are secondary?" said Tzu Hsia. "It is Shang who can open new vistas to me," said the Master. "In this way, I can begin to discuss the *Odes* with him." [III-8]

220. The Master said: "A man without *jen*—what has he to do with rites? A man without *jen*—what has he to do with music?" [III-3]

221. Lin Fang asked about the basic principles of rites, and the Master said: "A great question indeed! In ceremonials at large, it is better to be sparing than extravagant; and as for mourning rites, there should be deep grief rather than minute attention to details." [III-4]

222. The Master said: "Ceremonials! Ceremonials! Do they mean no more than offerings of jade and silk? Music! Music! Does it mean no more than bells and drums?" [xvii-11]

223. The Master said: "At the Grand Sacrifice after [the pouring of] libation, I have no heart to look on." [iii-10]

224. Someone asked about the Grand Sacrifice, and the Master said: "I do not know. One who knew its meaning would find it easy to govern the world as to look on at this." And he pointed to his palm. [iii-11]

225. Sacrifice [to the dead] as if they were present; sacrifice to the spirits as if they were present. The Master said: "If I am not present at the sacrifice, it is as though there were no sacrifice at all." [iii-12]

226. The Master said: "In archery (special) emphasis is not laid on piercing the hide, for people's strength is not equal. This is the way of the ancients." [iii-16]

227. The Master said: "Extravagance begets arrogance; frugality begets niggardliness. It is better to be niggardly than arrogant." [vii-35]

228. The Master said: "Reverence without propriety li becomes labored effort; prudence without propriety becomes timidity; boldness without propriety becomes turbulence; and uprightness without propriety becomes rudeness. When the chün-tzu are kind and devoted to their own kin, the people are encouraged to jen. When the old dependents are not neglected, the people are not niggardly." [VIII-2]

229. The Master said: "So long as the ruling class is fond of propriety the people are easy to govern." [xiv-44]

230. The Master said: "Those who must first study ceremonies and music, are common people, while those later [before taking office] are chün-tzu. Should I make a choice, I would study first." [xi-1]

231. Tzu Chang asked: "Is it possible to know about things after the lapse of ten dynasties?" "We know how the Yin [Shang] modified the code of ritual when they followed upon the Hsia. We know how the Chou modified the code of ritual when they followed upon the Yin. And hence we can know the code of ritual as modified by the successors of the Chou even after one hundred dynasties." [ii-23]

232. The Master said: "I can describe the ceremonies of Hsia, but the State of Ch'ih offers no adequate evidence. I can describe the ceremonies of Yin, but the State of Sung offers no adequate evidence. This is because there is a lack

of written records. But for this lack, I should be able to corroborate my views." [III-9]

233. The Master said: "Chou had the advantage of surveying the two preceding dynasties. How elegant and complete was its culture! I follow Chou." [III-14]

234. When the chief of the Chi family was going to sacrifice on Mount Tai [which was a royal prerogative], the Master said to Jen Yu: "Cannot you save him from this?" "No, I can't" was the reply. Then the Master exclaimed: "Is that not saying that Mount Tai is not the equal of Lin Fang?" [III-6]

235. When he entered the Imperial Temple, the Master asked about everything. Someone remarked: "Who says that the son of the man from Tsou knows the Rites? When he was in the Imperial Temple, he asked about everything." The Master, hearing of this, said: "This is in accordance with the Rites." [III-15]

236. Tzu Kung proposed to do away with sacrificial sheep offering at the beginning of each month. The Master said: "Tzu! You grudge the sheep, but I love the Rites." [III-16]

237. The Master said: "One who serves the prince with all due propriety is regarded a flatterer." [III-18]

238. The Master said: "The linen cap is in conformity with ceremonies, but the modern silk cap is more economical. I follow the popular practice. The ceremonies require that one bows below the hall, but nowadays the bowing is made after ascending the hall; this is presumptuous. Though I move contrary to the popular practice, I bow below the hall." [IX-3]

239. The Master spoke of music to the Grand Music Master: "Music may be understood. While beginning [to play a piece], all parts should be prompt and united; in developing [the theme], there should be harmony, with distinct rhythm and recurrent notes, without a jarring break to the end of the piece." [III-23]

240. The Master spoke of the *Shao* [music of Emperor Shun] as being beautiful and perfect; he spoke of the *Wu* [music of Emperor Wu] as being beautiful but not perfect. [III-25]

241. When the Master was in Ch'i, he heard the *Shao* music and for three months he forgot the taste of meat, saying: "I never thought music could be so beautiful." [VII-13]

242. The Master said: "The prelude as played by the

Chief Musician and the final strains of the song *Kuan-chu* are certainly magnificent and beautiful." [vii-15]

243. The Master said: "It is only after my return to Lu from Wei that the music was revised, and then the *Yah* and *Tsong* songs were properly discriminated." [ix-14]

ˋ Chapter VI. Paternal Government

Confucius, as a great humanist, looked at all political problems in terms of human relations. He based all his judgments on the moral codes, from which he evolved his ethical-political system of a paternal government. The good behavior of the ruler was a prerequisite for successful government. As taught by Confucius, a ruler had nine basic duties:

1. To cultivate his personal conduct
2. To honor men of worth
3. To cherish affection for his kinsmen
4. To show respect to great ministers
5. To have an interest in the welfare of all officials
6. To take paternal care of the common people
7. To promote all useful crafts
8. To be hospitable to strangers
9. To be friendly to the neighboring princes

It was especially important for a ruler to cultivate his own conduct, so that he could set a perfect moral example for his officials and for his people. The moral attributes of a ruler were the same as those of a *chün-tzu*. For a ruler, as well as for a *chün-tzu*, the cardinal virtues were *jen, li, yi,* and *hsin* [good faith], as illustrated in his teachings.

◦§ ɓ◦

244. The Master said: "To rule a state of a thousand chariots, there must be reverent attention to duties and sincerity, economy in expenditure and love for the people, working them only at the proper seasons." [i-5]

245. The Master said: "One who governs by virtue is comparable to the polar star, which remains in its place while all the stars turn towards it." [ii-1]

246. The Master said: "Govern the people by laws and regulate them by penalties, and the people will try to do no wrong, but they will lose the sense of shame. Govern the people by virtue and restrain them by rules of propriety, and

the people will have a sense of shame and be reformed of themselves." [ii-3]

247. Duke Ai asked: "What should I do to secure the submission of the people?" "Promote the upright and banish the crooked," said the Master; "then the people will be submissive. Promote the crooked and banish the upright; then the people will not be submissive." [ii-19]

248. Chi Kang Tzu asked: "What should be done to make the people respectful and be encouraged to cultivate virtues?" "Approach the people with dignity," said the Master, "and they will be respectful. Show filial piety and kindness, and they will be loyal. Promote those who are worthy, and train those who are incompetent; and they will be encouraged to cultivate virtues." [ii-20]

249. Duke Ting asked how a prince should employ his ministers and how ministers should serve their prince. Master K'ung said: "A prince should employ his ministers with propriety; ministers should serve their prince with loyalty." [iii-19]

250. The Master said: "If a prince governs his state with propriety and courtesy, what difficulty will he have? But if not, of what use are rituals?" [iv-13]

251. The Master said: "Yung would be a ruler." Then Chung Kung [Yung] asked about Tzu-sang Po-tzu. "He would be, too," said the Master, "but he is lax." "Such a man might be a ruler," said Chung Kung, "if he were scrupulous in his own conduct and lax only in his dealing with the people. But a man who was lax in his own conduct as well as in government would be too lax." The Master said: "What Yung says is true." [vi-1]

252. [Alluding to the States of Ch'i and Lu], the Master said: "Ch'i, by one change, might attain to the level of Lu; and Lu, by one change, might attain to the *Tao!*" [vi-22]

253. The Master said: "A cornered vessel that has no corners. What a cornered vessel! What a cornered vessel!" [vi-23]

254. The Master said: "The people may be made to follow but not to understand." [viii-9]

255. Tzu Kung asked about government, and the Master said: "The essentials [of good government] are sufficient food, sufficient arms, and the confidence of the people." "But," asked Tzu Kung, "if you have to part with one of the three, which would you give up?" "Arms," said the Master. "But suppose," said Tzu Kung, "one of the remaining two has to

be relinquished, which would it be?" "Food," said the Master. "From time immemorial, death has been the lot of all men, but a people without confidence is lost indeed." [XII-7]

256. Duke Ching asked Master K'ung about government, and Master K'ung said: "Let the ruler be ruler; the minister, minister; the father, father, and the son, son." "Good!" said the Duke. "For truly if the ruler be not ruler, the minister not minister; if the father be not father, and the son not son, then with all the grain in my possession, should I be able to relish it?" [XII-11]

257. The Master said: "In hearing lawsuits, I am no better than other men, but my aim is to bring about the end of lawsuits." [XII-13]

258. Tzu Chang asked about government, and the Master said: "Attend to its affairs untiringly, and carry it out loyally." [XII-14]

259. Chi Kang Tzu asked Master K'ung about government, and Master K'ung said: "To govern means to rectify. If you, Sir, lead the people in rectitude, who dares not to be rectified?" [XII-17]

260. Chi Kang Tzu, being troubled by burglars, asked Master K'ung what he should do, and Master K'ung said: "If only you, Sir, are free from desire [for wealth], they will not steal even though you pay them." [XII-18]

261. Chi Kang Tzu asked Master K'ung about government, saying: "Suppose I kill the *Tao*-less for the good of the *Tao*-abiding, what do you think of it?" "What need, Sir," said Master K'ung, "is there of killing in your administration? Let you desire good, and the people will be good. The virtue of the prince [*chün-tzu*] is the wind, and that of the common people [*hsiao-jen*) the grass. The grass bends in the direction of the wind." [XII-19]

262. Tzu Lu asked about government, and the Master said: "Go before the people and be diligent in their affairs." When asked for further instruction, the Master said: "Be not weary." [XIII-1]

263. Chung Kung, chief minister of the Chi family, asked about government, and the Master said: "Employ first the services of your men, overlook minor faults, and then promote men of worth and talents." "How do I know a man of worth and talents in order to promote him?" said Chung Kung. "Promote those whom you know," said the Master.

"Those whom you do not know others will certainly not neglect." [XIII-2]

264. Tzu Lu said: "The prince of Wei is awaiting you, Sir, to join his government. What will you do first, Sir?"

The Master said: "The first thing needed is the rectification of names."

"So, indeed!" said Tzu Lu. "How pedantic it sounds! Why must there be such rectification?" "Yu! How rude you are!" said the Master. "*Chün-tzu* abstains from what he does not know. If names are not correct, then words are inappropriate; when the words are inappropriate, then things cannot be accomplished. Then rites and music will not flourish, punishments will not be properly administered, and the people have nowhere to put hand or foot. Therefore *chün-tzu* designates what can be properly stated, and only speaks of what can be properly carried into effect. *Chün-tzu*, in what he says, leaves nothing that is remiss." [XIII-3]

265. The Master said: "If a prince himself is upright, all will go well without orders. But if he himself is not upright, even though he gives orders, they will not be obeyed." [XIII-6]

266. The Master said: "In their governments, Lu and Wei are still brothers." [XIII-7]

267. When the Master went to Wei, Jan Yu acted as driver of his carriage. The Master said: "How thriving is the population here!" "Since it is so thriving," asked Jan Yu, "what more shall be done for the people?" "Enrich them!" was the Master's reply. "And when they are enriched, what more shall be done?" "Educate them!" said the Master. [XIII-9]

268. The Master said: "Were any prince to employ me, in a year something could be done; in three years, the work could be completed." [XIII-10]

269. The Master said: "'Only if good men were to govern a country for one hundred years, would it be really possible to transform the evil and do away with killings.' How true is the saying!" [XIII-11]

270. The Master said: "If a prince has rendered himself upright, he will have no difficulty in governing the people. But if he cannot rectify himself, how can he hope to rectify the people?" [XIII-13]

271. The Master said: "If a sage-king were to arise, *jen* would prevail within one generation." [XIII-12]

272. Once when Jan Yu returned from the court, the Master asked: "Why are you so late?" "There were state

affairs," said Jan Yu. "You must mean family affairs," said the Master. "If there had been state affairs, although I am not now in office, I too should have heard of them." [XIII-14]

273. Duke Ting asked: "Is there a single phrase that suffices to save a country?" The Master said: "No phrase could ever be like that. But here is one coming near to it. There is a saying among men: 'It is difficult to be a prince and not easy to be a minister.' A prince who really knows the difficulty of being a prince would have been close to saving his country by a single phrase." Then Duke Ting asked again: "Is there a single phrase that could ruin a country?" The Master said: "No phrase could ever be like that. But here is one coming near to it. There is a saying among men: 'What pleasure is there in being a prince unless no one contradicts his words.' So long as what he says is good, it is for the good that no one contradicts him. But if what he says is bad, and no one contradicts him, will it not come near to ruining his country by a single phrase?" [XIII-15]

274. The Duke of Yeh asked about government, and the Master said: "Those near are pleased, and those far off are attracted." [XII-15]

275. Tzu Hsia, being the magistrate of Chu-fu, asked about government, and the Master said: "Do not seek quick results, nor look for small gains. Seek quick results, and you will not achieve success; look for small gains, and you will not accomplish big projects." [XIII-17]

276. The Master said: "A good man instructs the people seven years, and then they be employed in war." [XIII-29]

277. The Master said: "To take an untrained multitude into battle is equivalent to throwing it away." [XIII-30]

278. The Master said: "In preparing an official document, P'i Ch'en made the rough draft; Shih-shu studied it; Tzu Yu— the minister in charge of interstate affairs—polished it; and Tzu-chan of Lung-li gave the final touch." [XIV-9]

279. The Master was speaking of the bad government of Duke Ling of Wei. Kang Tzu said: "Since he is like that, how has he not lost his throne?" "He has Chung Shu Yu to deal with envoys and guests"; said the Master, "the priest T'o to regulate ancestral worship; Wang Sun Chia to command his armies. Why then should he lose his throne?" [XIV-20]

280. The Master said: "To govern by *Wu-wei* [inaction or noninterference], Shun was the one! What did he do? He

merely made himself reverent and majestically occupied his royal throne." [xv-4]

281. Yen Yuen asked how to rule a state, and the Master said: "Follow the calendar of Hsia; ride in the carriage of Yin; wear the cap of Chou. Adopt the music of *Shao* with its pantomime; banish the songs of *Cheng;* and keep away from glib talkers. For the song of Cheng is licentious and glib talkers are dangerous." [xv-10]

282. The Master said: "Suppose a prince has sufficient wisdom to attain power, but he has no *jen* to secure it. Though he gets it, he will certainly lose it. Suppose his wisdom brings him to power, and he has *jen* to secure it; if there is no dignity in his rule, the people will not show respect. Suppose his wisdom has brought him into power; he has *jen* to secure it and rules with dignity. However, if he acts contrary to the code of rituals, he is still not a good ruler." [xv-32]

283. Master K'ung said: "When the *Tao* prevails in the world, ceremonies, music, and punitive expeditions proceed from the Emperor. When the *Tao* fails in the world, ceremonies, music, and military expeditions proceed from the feudal princes. When they proceed from a feudal prince, his power can seldom survive for ten generations. When they proceed from a state minister, his power can seldom survive for five generations. When a subordinate officer holds power in the kingdom, his power can seldom survive for three generations. When there is *Tao* in the world, the power is not in the hands of ministers. And when there is *Tao* in the world, the people do not even discuss government affairs." [xvi-2]

284. Master K'ung said: "For five generations the revenue has departed from the Ducal House [of Lu], and for four generations the government has been in the hands of ministers. That is why the descendants of the three Huan [the three powerful families] are so losing their powers!" [xvi-3]

285. Tzu Chang asked Master K'ung: "What must a man do to qualify himself for government position?" "Let him honor the five merits and banish the four demerits," said the Master, "then may he serve in the government." "What are the five merits?" asked Tzu Chang. "A *chün-tzu* is bounteous without extravagance; he works the people without causing their resentment; he has desires, but he is not covetous; he is dignified but not arrogant; he is majestic but not ferocious." "What do you mean by 'being bounteous without extravagance'?" said Tzu Chang. "Let him spend on what the people

find advantageous; is this not being bounteous without extravagance? Let him work the people during the proper seasons; who will resent? Let him long for *jen* and become *jen*-minded; how can he be covetous? Whether he deals with many people or few, with the small or with the great, he never presumes to be arrogant; is this not being dignified but not arrogant? When he is properly dressed, with dignified manners, he will inspire awe on the onlookers; is this not being majestic but not ferocious?" Then Tzu Chang asked again: "What are the four demerits?" "To put the people to death without giving instruction," said the Master; "this is cruelty. To require accomplishment without previous warning; this is tyranny. To delay orders and hasten its execution; this is oppression. And to make offers but grudge to carry them out; this is the way of the petty officials." [xx-2]

Chapter VII. Comments of Confucius

286. The Master said: "Great indeed was Yao as a sovereign! How exalted! It is only Heaven that is great, and only Yao was equal to it. So boundless was [his virtue] that the people could find no name for it. How sublime were his achievements! How glorious were his institutions!" [viii-19]

287. The Master said: "Sublime were Shun and Yu! Though they ruled the whole world, yet they remained aloof from it." [viii-18]

288. Shun had five ministers, and the world was well governed. King Wu once said: "I have ten able ministers." Master K'ung said: "Talents are difficult to find, isn't it true? The turn of the T'ang and Yu dynasties was the time famous for men of talent. [As for King Wu], there were only nine men, one being a woman. The Chou had two thirds of the world and yet still submitted to the Yin. The virtue of the Chou may, indeed, be said to have attained to its supremacy." [viii-20]

289. The Master said: "In Yu I can find no flaw. Abstemious in his own food and drink, he displayed the utmost devotion in his offerings to spirits and divinities. Content with his poor ordinary garments, he displayed the utmost elegance in his sacrificial cap and apron. He lived in a low, humble house, but he spent all his energy on the ditches and water channels. I can find no flaw in Yu." [viii-21]

290. The Master said: "T'ai P'o [ancestor of the Chou] may indeed be said to have attained to moral perfection.

Thrice he declined to kingdom, without letting the people praise him for it." [VIII-1]

291. The Master said: "P'o Yi and Shu Chi never bore old ills in mind, and hence they had few resentments." [V-22]

292. "Among those who were noted for withdrawal into private life were P'o Yi and Shu Chi, Yu Chung, Yi I, Chu Chang, Liu Hsia Hui, and Shao Lien. Neither surrendering their high purpose nor disregarding their persons, were these not P'o Yi and Shu Chi? As to Liu Hsia Hui and Shao Lien, while they surrendered their high purpose and disgraced their persons, their words were consonant with moral principles and their actions were in accord with prudence; this is all and no more. As to Yu Chung and Yi I, though in seclusion they were free in their utterances, yet they sustained their personal purity; their self-renouncement was in accord with the emergency. However, I am different from all these men. I have no course of action but depend on exigency of the occasion." [XVIII-8]

293. The Viscount of Wei withdrew from serving [Chou, the last ruler of Yin]; the Viscount of Chi became his slave; Pi Kan remonstrated with him and suffered death. Master K'ung said of these: "The Yin had three men of jen." [XVIII-1]

294. The Master said: "Duke Wen of Tsin was crafty but not upright; Duke Huan of Ch'i was upright but not crafty." [XIV-16]

295. The Master said: "Kuan Chung was a man of small capacity!" Someone asked: "Was Kuan Chung temperate?" "Kuan Chung had three lots of wives," said the Master, "and his officials performed no double duties. How can he be considered temperate?" "Then did Kuan Chung know etiquette [li]?" "Only the sovereign of a state may build a screen in front of his gate, but Kuan Chung had likewise such a screen. Only the sovereign of a state, when he had friendly meeting with other princes, may use a stand for his inverted pledge cup; but Kuan Chung had also such a stand. If Kuan Chung could be considered to know etiquette, who does not know etiquette?" [III-22]

296. Tzu Lu said: "Duke Huan [of Ch'i] had [his brother] prince Chiu put to death. Shao Hu died [for the prince], but Kuan Chung did not. May I say that he was short of jen?" The Master said: "Duke Huan nine times convened the feudal princes without resorting to chariots of war, and all this was through the ability of Kuan Chung. That was his jen! That was his jen!" [XIV-17]

297. Tzu Kung said: "Was Kuan Chung short of *jen?* When Duke Huan had prince Chiu put to death, Kuan Chung did not die; moreover, he became prime minister to Duke Huan." The Master said: "After Kuan Chung became minister to Duke Huan, he made the Duke leader of all feudal princes and achieved unity for the world. Even to the present day the people are recipients of his benefactions. But for Kuan Chung, we might now be wearing our hair loose and folding our garments to the left [like the barbarians]. We must not expect him to behave like common men and common women who showed their fidelity by committing suicide in a stream or a ditch, unknown to the world." [xiv-18]

298. The Master said: "Chang Wen-chung kept the sacred tortoise in a hall where its pillars were carved with mountains and its beams were painted with reeds. How could he be considered wise?" [v-17]

299. The Master said: "Was Chang Wen-chung a stealer of other men's ranks? He knew the worth of Liu-hsia Hui but failed to make him a colleague at court." [xv-13]

300. The Master said: "Chang Wen-chung occupied the fief of Fang and demanded that a successor be appointed to him in Lu. It is said that he brought no pressure on the prince, but I do not believe it." [xiv-15]

301. Tzu Chang asked: "Minister Tzu Wen was appointed to office three times, but he displayed no sign of elation. Three times he was removed from office, but he showed no sign of disappointment. Each time, he duly informed the new minister of the way of his administration. What would you say of him?" The Master said: "He was certainly loyal." "Was he a man of *jen?*" "I am not sure," said the Master, "but how could he be a man of *jen?*"

302. [Tzu Chang said:] "When Ts'ui Tzu murdered the prince of Ch'i, Chen Wen Tzu, though he had an estate of ten chariots, gave it up and left the country. Coming to another state, he said, 'They are here like our Minister Ts'ui Tzu,' and then he went away. Coming to the next state, he said again, 'They are here like our Minister Ts'ui Tzu,' and then he went away. What would you say of him, Sir?" The Master said: "He was certainly scrupulous." "Was he a man of *jen?*" "I am not sure," said the Master, "but how could he be a man of *jen?*" [v-18]

303. Chi Wen Tzu used to think thrice before he acted. The Master, hearing of it, said: "Twice is quite enough." [v-19]

304. The Master said: "When the *Tao* prevailed in the country, he showed his wisdom; but when the *Tao* failed in the country, he feigned ignorance. We can attain to his wisdom but not to his ignorance." [v-20]

305. The Master said: "Meng Kung Ch'o would be excellent to be the chief officer of the Chao family or Wei family, but he was unfit to be a minister of even a small state like Teng or Hsieh." [xIV-12]

306. Of Tzu Ch'an, the Master said: "He possessed four virtues of a *chün-tzu:* He was courteous in his conduct, punctilious in serving his prince, kind in dealing with the people, and righteous in working them." [v-17]

307. Someone asked about Tzu Ch'an, and the Master said: "He was a kind man." Asked about Tzu Hsi, he said: "That man! That man!" Asked about Kuan Chung, he said: "He was the sort of man who could seize the fief of P'ien with its three hundred villages, from the P'o family; yet the P'o family, though lived on coarse food to their dying days, never uttered a single word of resentment." [xIV-10]

308. The Master said: "Yin Ping Chung knows well how to maintain friendly relations with his fellow men. However long the acquaintance may be, he always remains respectful toward others." [v-18]

309. [Master K'ung said:] "Duke Ching of Ch'i possessed one thousand and four horse teams, but on the day of his death, the people could not find a single value to praise. P'o Yi and Shu Chi starved at the foot of Shou Yang, and the people praise them down to the present day. 'Truly not for wealth, merely for difference in virtue.' Is not this saying illustrated by this?" [xVI-12]

310. The Master asked Kung-ming Chia about Kung-shu Wen Tzu: "Is it true that your master speaks not, laughs not, and takes not?" "The people who told you this were exaggerating," said Kung-ming Chia: "my master speaks only when it is the time to do so, so the people do not weary of his talking; he laughs only when he is delighted, so the people do not weary of laughing; he takes only when it is righteous to do so, so the people do not weary of his taking." "Is that so?" said the Master, "but is that so with him?" [xIV-14]

311. Kung-shu Wen Tzu brought with him and presented to the Duke his household attendant Chuan as his colleague at court. The Master, hearing of it, said: "He deserved his name—*wen* [culture]." [xIV-19]

312. Master K'ung said of the Chi family, which had the eight rows of dancers [a royal prerogative] performing in their temple yard: "If they can be endured, who cannot be endured?" [III-1]

313. The Three Families used the *Yung Ode* during the removal of sacrificial vessels. The Master said: "How can the following lines be used in the hall of the Three Families?

Princes and lords come to attend,
The Emperor looks austere and profound." [III-2]

314. The Chi family was about to attack Chuan-yu [a small state within the borders of Lu]. Jan Yu and Tzu Lu came to see Master K'ung and said: "The Chi family is going to have an incident with Chuan-yu." "Ch'iu [Jan Yu]," said Master K'ung, "is it not you who must be held responsible for this incident? Chuan-yu was long ago appointed by the former kings [of Chou] to preside over the sacrifices to Mount Tung-meng; besides, it is situated within the confines of the State [*lu*], and its ruler is a vassal of our state. How can you justify such an attack?" Jan Yu said: "This is the wish of our master, not that of either of us two ministers." "Ch'iu," said Master K'ung, "there is a saying by Chou Jen: 'One who can put forth his ability steps into the ranks; one who cannot, resigns.' Of what use to a master are the ministers, who cannot help him when he is in danger and who cannot support when he totters? And, further, your pleas are wrong. For if a tiger or rhinoceros breaks out of the cage, or if a piece of sacred jade is damaged in the casket—who is to be blamed?" "But Chuan-yu is now fortified," said Jan Yu, "and situated close to P'i. If it is not taken at present, it is sure to be a menace to Ch'i's descendants." "Ch'iu," said the Master, "*chün-tzu* detests a man who declines to make manifest his wishes but frames pretexts to cover them up. I have heard that the man at the head of a state or of a family should not be concerned about insufficiency but about inequitable distribution, nor should he be concerned about poverty but about discontentment. For where there is equitable distribution, there is no poverty; where there is harmony, there is no insufficiency; where there is contentment, there is no trouble. Therefore, if the people of far-off lands fail to submit, the ruler will attract them by cultivating culture and virtue; when they have been so attracted, then he will make them feel contented. Now with you two, Yu and Ch'iu, acting as ministers

to your master, the people of far-off lands fail to submit, and
he cannot attract them; the country is divided and disrupted,
and he cannot hold it together. Now plans are being made
for taking up arms within the borders of the State. I am
afraid that the troubles of the Ch'i-sun family do not lie in
Chuan-yu, but right within the walls of their own court."
[XVI-1]

315. The Master said: "Upright indeed was the histogra-
pher Yu! When the *Tao* prevailed in the land, he was [up-
right] as an arrow; when the *Tao* failed in the land, he was
still [upright] as an arrow. A *chün-tzu* was indeed Ch'u P'o
Yu! When the *Tao* prevailed in the land, he was found in
office; when the *Tao* failed in the land, he retired to roll up
[his wisdom] in his bosom." [xv-6]

316. Tzu Kung asked: "How did K'ung Wen Tzu get that
title of *wen* [culture]?" The Master said: "He was diligent and
fond of learning; he was not ashamed to learn from his inferiors. That is why he was named *wen*." [v-14]

317. The Master said: "Who says of Wei Sheng Kao that
he is upright? Someone once begged vinegar of him, but he
begged it of a neighbor and gave it (as if it were his own)."
[v-23]

318. The Master said: "Men Tzu-fan is not a boaster. He
lagged once in the flight, but upon entering the gate, he
whipped up his horse and said: 'It is not that I dared to be
the last; my horse would not advance!' " [vi-13]

319. Yuan Zang squatted on his heels while waiting for
the Master. The Master said: "As a youth, you were not
humble; as an adult, you did nothing worth speaking of; and
now as an old man, you are not decent enough to die. You
are merely a pest!" And the Master hit him on the shins with
his staff. [xiv-46]

320. The Master said: "The barbarians of the east and
north have their princes and are not like the Chinese, who
have none." [iii-5]

321. The Master said: "In my time I have come upon the
scribe who would leave out what was doubtful, and the
owner who would lend his horse to others to ride. But such
things are no longer seen today." [xv-25]

322. The Master said: "In ancient times the people had
three failings which are probably not to be found today. In
ancient times the high-minded people disregarded small
things; in the present day they are utterly unrestrained. In
ancient times the serious-minded people were austere and

approachable; in the present day they are quarrelsome and perverse. In ancient times the simple-minded people were honest; in the present day they are deceitful." [xvii-16]

Part Two: The Personality of Confucius

For many centuries, Confucius, the great teacher of antiquity, has been grossly misrepresented. As time passed, much of his life became so distorted and obscure that a great deal of misunderstanding arose. In fact, the Master was no mystic, nor was he a saint. The following passages from the *Analects* furnish us with the most intimate knowledge of the personality and character of Confucius. Reading these passages, we can rediscover the historical Confucius, accessible and human, placid and sincere. His outlook was serious yet kind; his deportment was respectful yet natural. He appeared taciturn, but he spoke convincingly. In his relations with his fellow men, he was always accessible and inspiring, sincere and earnest. This was a way of living in which Confucius led the younger generation—and, in fact, the entire Chinese people.

❧ ☙

Chapter VIII. The Daily Life of Confucius

323. In his leisure hours the Master was easy in his manner and cheerful in his looks. [vii-4]

324. The Master was gentle yet strict, dignified yet not awesome, respectful yet at ease. [vii-37]

325. The Master was cautious in regard to fasting, war, and sickness. [vii-12]

326. The Master never spoke of prodigies, prowess, rebellions, or the supernatural. [vii-20]

327. The Master seldom spoke of profit or fate or *jen*. [ix-1]

328. When the Master sang in company, if someone sang a song that pleased him, he would have it repeated, joining in the melody himself. [vii-31]

329. The Master fished but not with a net; he shot but not at a roosting bird. [vii-26]

330. When he dined by the side of a person in mourning, he never ate to the full. He never sang on the day when he had mourned. [vii-9]

331. When he saw a man in mourning dress or in official costume, or a blind man, even though such a man was younger, the Master would stand up. When passing him, he would quicken his steps. [ix-9]

332. When he saw a man in mourning dress, even a close friend, the Master would change countenance; when he saw anyone in official costume, or a blind man, even a well-known person, the Master would assume the appropriate attitude. If [from his carriage] he saw a man in mourning dress, he would bow forward to its cross bar; in the same manner he would also bow to the bearer of the census tables. [x-16]

333. When a sumptuous banquet was laid before him, the Master's countenance would change, and he would stand up. [x-16]

334. At a sudden clap of thunder, or a violent wind, the Master would change countenance. [x-16]

335. When the Master was among his village folks, he looked simple and sincere, as if he were inept at speaking. But when in the ancestral temple or at court, he spoke cautiously. [x-1]

336. At court, when conversing with the lower ministers, the Master spoke gently and kindly. When conversing with the higher ministers, he spoke affably and precisely. When in presence of the prince, he was reverent in his movement and solemn in his demeanor. [x-2]

337. When the prince summoned him to receive a visitor, his countenance seemed to change, and he would turn to do obeisance. He would salute those among whom he took up his position, using his right hand or the left and holding the lower part of his robe in proper position both front and back. Then he would hasten forward, with elbows evenly bent outward. When the visitor withdrew, he would report to the prince, saying: "The visitor no longer looks back." [x-3]

338. When he entered the palace gate, the Master would bend his body as if it were not high enough to admit him. When he halted, he would never stand in the middle of the gateway; nor when moving about, would he ever tread upon the threshold. When passing the throne, his countenance seemed to change, and he would turn to do obeisance; then his words seemed to fail him. On ascending the audience hall, he would hold up his robe and bend his body forward, holding his breath as if he would not breathe. On coming out, as soon as he descended one step, he began to relax his countenance and appeared satisfied and relieved. On reaching the

bottom of the steps, he would quicken his pace, with elbows evenly bent outward. On resuming his position, he would appear reverent in every movement. [x-4]

339. When holding the scepter, he would bend his body as though he were not able to bear its weight. Then he would raise it as though he were making a bow; he lowered it as though he were presenting a gift. His countenance seemed to change, and he looked apprehensive; his gait seemed retarded as though he were following the line. When he presented the gifts of ceremony, he appeared calm and at ease. But at the private interview, he would be cordial and affable. [x-5]

340. When sending a message of inquiry to someone in another state, the Master would bow twice on seeing the messenger away. [x-11]

341. Chi Kang once sent the Master some medicine. He bowed and received it but said: "As I do not know its properties, I dare not taste it." [xi-11]

342. When the prince sent the Master a present of food, he would adjust his mat and be the first to taste it. If the prince's present was one of raw meat, he would have it cooked and make an oblation of it. If the present was a live animal, he would keep it alive. When he was in attendance, and at a meal with the prince, he would first taste the food while the prince made the offering. [x-13]

343. When the Master was ill and the prince came to see him, he would turn his face towards the east and put on his court robes with belts across them. [x-13]

344. When the prince summoned him, he would start off on foot without waiting for his carriage. [x-13]

345. When he entered the Imperial Temple, the Master asked about everything. [x-14]

346. When a friend died, leaving no relatives, he would say: "Let me take care of the funeral." For a friend's gift, even though it might be a carriage and horses, he would not bow unless it was meat for sacrifice. [x-15]

347. The Master would use no deep purple or bright blue in the ornaments of his clothing. Nor would he have red or orange color in his ordinary garments. In summer he wore a single gown, of either coarse or fine hemp, but he would have an outer garment over it. [In winter] he wore a black robe, lined with lamb's fur, a white one, lined with fawn's fur, and a yellow one, lined with fox fur. His ordinary furred robe was long, but the right sleeve was shortened. He would needs

have his sleeping garment one and a half times his body. When staying at home, he wore thick furs of the fox or the badger. When he left off mourning, he would wear all his insignia on his waist belt. Apart from his court robe, all his garments were cut narrow above and wide below. He would wear lamb's fur or a black cap when he went on visits of condolence to mourners. On the first day of the new moon, he had to have his court robe and present himself at court. [x-6]

348. When observing his fasts, he thought it necessary to have bright, shiny garments, made of linen. At such times he had to vary his food and move his seat to another part of his dwelling room. [x-7]

349. As to his food, the Master never tired of rice so long as it was clean and pure, nor of hashed meats when finely minced. Rice spoiled by damp and turned sour, he would not touch, nor tainted fish or bad meat. He would not eat anything of a bad color or smell, nor anything ill cooked or out of season. He would not eat anything that was not properly cut or that was not served with its proper sauce. Although there might be an abundance of meat, he would not take an amount to exceed the due proportion for the rice. Only in the matter of wine did he set himself no limit, but he never drank so much as to confuse himself. He would not touch wine and dried meat bought from the market, nor would he remove ginger from the table during the meal. He never let himself overeat. The meat from the official offerings he would not keep overnight; nor would he keep the meat of his own offerings over three days, for after three days none were to eat it. [x-8]

350. The Master would not carry on discourse when at meals; he would not say a word when in bed. [x-8]

351. Even though an offering consisted of coarse rice and vegetable broth or melons, the Master would make it with reverence. [x-8]

352. He would not sit on a mat that was not properly laid. [x-9]

353. At the banquet of his villagers the Master would leave after the elders had left. When the villages were exorcising pestilence, he would put on his court robe and stand on the eastern steps. [x-10]

354. In bed the Master did not lie like one dead, and at home he was easy in his manners. [x-16]

355. When he was about to mount his carriage, the Master

would stand [up] erect, holding on by his strap. When he was in the carriage, he would not turn his head round; nor would he talk hastily; nor would he point with his hands. [x-17]

356. The Master said: "Ah! No one knows of me." Tzu Kung asked: "Why do you say that none knows you?" "I have no complaint against Heaven," said the Master, "nor do I lay the blame on men. I study all earthly things and reflect on transcendental matters. And if I am known anywhere, is it not Heaven?" [xiv-37]

Chapter IX. Some Anecdotes of Confucius

357. The people of Ch'i presented a number of female musicians. Chi Huan Tzu [the great minister of Lu] accepted; for three days no audience was held. Master K'ung then left. [xviii-4]

358. Duke Ching of Ch'i, in regard to his reception for Master K'ung, said: "I cannot treat him as I would the chief of the Chi family. I should accord him a rank between the Chi and Meng families." Then he added: "I am old and cannot avail myself of him." Master K'ung then left. [xviii-3]

359. The Master said: "Heaven has bestowed [the] virtue in me. Huan Tui—what can he do to me?" [vii-22]

360. When he was in jeopardy in K'uang, the Master said: "Since the death of King Wen, has the cause of culture rested only with me? Should Heaven let this culture perish, posterity would never again share its heritage. As Heaven has not yet destroyed this culture, what can the men of K'uang do to me?" [ix-5]

361. When the Master was in jeopardy in K'uang, Yen Yuen lagged behind. The Master said: "I thought you were dead." "Would I dare die," replied Yen Yuen, "while you were alive?" [xi-22]

362. When the Master was very ill, Tzu Lu asked leave to pray for him. The Master said: "Is there such a thing?" "Yes," replied Tzu Lu, "it is written in the *Eulogies:* 'Pray to the spirits of Heaven above and on earth below.'" But the Master said: "Ah, long have I prayed!" [vii-34]

363. The Master called on Nan-tzu, and Tzu Lu was displeased. The Master declared solemnly: "If I have done wrong, may Heaven forsake me! May Heaven forsake me!" [vi-26]

364. Duke Ling of Wei asked Master K'ung about the

alignment of an army. Master K'ung said: "I have learned the arrangements of sacrificial vessels, but I have not studied military matters." The next day he left. [xv-1]

365. Jan Yu asked: "Is our Master working for the Duke of Wei?" "Yes," said Tzu Kung, "I'll ask him about that." He went in and asked, "What sort of men were Po Yi and Shu Chi?" The Master said, "They were ancient worthies." "Did they repine?" "They sought *jen* and attained to it," said the Master. "Why should they repine?" Tzu Kung went out and said, "Our Master is not working for him." [vii-14]

366. Chen Heng assassinated Duke Chien of Ch'i. Master K'ung, bathing himself, went to court and reported to Duke Ai: "Chen Heng has slain his prince. I beg you to punish him." The Duke said: "Inform the chiefs of the Three Families of it." Master K'ung said: "As I rank next to the great ministers, I am obliged to report. But now your Highness says: 'Inform the chiefs of the Three Families of it.'" Then he went to the three chiefs and informed them. They refused to listen to him. Master K'ung said: "As I rank next to the great ministers, I could not but report." [xiv-22]

367. Yang Ho wished to see Master K'ung, but Master K'ung would not see him. He sent Master K'ung a suckling pig. Master K'ung, choosing a time when Yang Ho was not at home, went to pay respects but met him on the way. Yang Ho said to Master K'ung: "Come here; let me speak with you." Then he asked: "Can a man be called *jen*-minded if he hides his jewel in his bosom and leaves his country to confusion?" "Certainly not," said Master K'ung. "Can a man be called wise if he longs to serve the public and yet misses the opportunity to do so?" "Certainly not." Then the other added: "The days and months are passing away; the years do not wait for us." "All right," said Master K'ung, "I shall accept public office." [xvii-1]

368. Kung Po Liao slandered Tzu Lu before Chi Sun, and Tzu-fu Ching P'o informed the Master, saying: "Our chief is certainly being led astray by Kung Po Liao, but my influence is still strong enough to have him punished and exposed." The Master said: "If the *Tao* is going to prevail, it is through Fate. If the *Tao* is going to fail, it is through Fate. What can Kung Po Liao do against Fate?" [xiv-38]

369. Kung Shan Fu Zao revolted at P'i [against the Chi family] and sent for the Master. The Master inclined to go, but Tzu Lu was displeased, saying: "Since we haven't gone to anyone else, why must we go to Kung Shan?" "Can it be

without reason that he has sent for me?" said the Master. "If there were one willing to employ me, I might create an Eastern Chou? (He meant revival of the old Chou culture.)" [XVII-5]

370. Pi Hsi sent for the Master, and the Master inclined to go. But Tzu Lu said: "I heard you once say, 'Chün-tzu will not associate with a person who is in his own person doing evil.' Now Pi Hsi revolts in Chung-mou, and you want to join him. How do you think of this?" "It is true," said the Master, "that I made such a saying. But isn't there this saying?

Being really hard,
No grounding can render it thin;
Being really white,
No dying can make it black.

Am I then a bitter gourd, good enough to be hung up to dry, but never eaten?" [XVII-7]

371. The Minister of Chen asked: "Does Duke Chao know rites?" "Yes," said Master K'ung, "he knows rites." Master K'ung having left, the minister received Wu-ma Chi and said: "I have heard that chün-tzu is impartial. May chün-tzu be partial? The prince married a Wu girl, of the same clan name with himself, and called her Wu Meng Tzu. If the prince knows rites, who does not know rites?" Wu-ma Chi reported these remarks, and the Master said: "I am fortunate; if I make a mistake, people are sure to know it." [VII-30]

372. Chu P'o-yu sent a messenger to Master K'ung. Master K'ung sat with him and asked: "What is your master doing?" "My master is trying," replied the messenger, "to diminish his faults, but he has not yet succeeded." When the messenger went out, the Master said: "A messenger, indeed! "A messenger, indeed!" [XIV-26]

373. The Master said: "If my Tao fails, I would like to board a raft on the sea. And who would follow me but Tzu Lu?" Hearing of this, Tzu Lu was delighted; whereupon the Master said: "Yu [Tzu Lu] is more venturesome than I, but he lacks judgment." [V-6]

374. The Master entertained the wish of making his home among the nine tribes of the east. Someone said: "They are barbarous. How could you live with them?" "Where chün-tzu has his home, what savagery could there exist?" said the Master. [IX-13]

375. The Master said of Kung-yeh Ch'ang: "He is a fit

person to choose as a husband; it was not his fault that he had been imprisoned." He married him to his daughter. [v-1]

376. The Master said of Nan Jung: "In a country where the *Tao* prevails, he will not be overlooked; in a country where the *Tao* fails, he will manage to avoid punishment and disgrace." He married him to the daughter of his elder brother. [v-2]

377. Nan Jung, in reciting the *Odes,* often repeated the verse about the sceptre of white jade.[1] Master K'ung married him to his elder brother's daughter. [xi-5]

378. Tzu Hua having been sent on a mission to Ch'i, Jan Tzu, on behalf of Tzu Hua's mother, requested an allowance of grain. The Master said: "Give her six measures." Jan Tzu asked for more, and the Master said: "Give her sixteen measures." But Jan Tzu gave her eighty measures. "Tzu Hua," said the Master, "on his mission to Ch'i, has fat horses and fine furs. I have heard that *chün-tzu* helps the poor to meet urgent needs, not the rich to be richer." [vi-3]

379. When Yuen Szu was appointed a district magistrate, he was given an allowance of nine hundred measures of grain. He, however, declined to accept the grain. "Do not decline it," said the Master. "May the grain not be of use to the villages and hamlets around you?" [vi-3]

380. When Tzu Yu was magistrate of Wu-cheng, the Master asked, "Have you found any good man there?" "Yes," replied Tzu Yu, "there is a man, by the name of T'an-t'ai Mieh-ming, who never walks on bypaths; nor has he ever come to my house except on public business." [vi-12]

381. The Master, having come to Wu-cheng, heard singing accompanied by stringed instruments. He said with a smile: "Why does one use an ox-cleaver to kill a fowl?" "Sir," replied Tzu Yu, "I once heard you say: 'When *chün-tzu* learns the *Tao,* he loves men. When *hsiao-jen* learns the *Tao,* he is easily led.'" "My disciples," said the Master, "what Yen says is quite true. What I said just now was only in jest." [xvii-4]

382. P'o Niu was very ill, and the Master went to see him. Holding his hand through the window, the Master said: "It's all over with him! This is Fate! Alas, that such a man should have such a sickness! That such a man should have such a sickness!" [vi-8]

---

1. The verse reads as follows:
   Blemishes on the sceptre can be removed;
   Blemishes in one's speech cannot be removed.

383. When Yen Yuen died, [his father] Yen Lu requested the Master to use his carriage as a hearse. The Master said: "Whether he has talents or not, a son is a son to his own father. When [my son] Li died, he had only a coffin without hearse. As I rank next to the great ministers, I cannot go on foot." [xi-7]

384. On the death of Yen Yuen, the Master said: "Alas! Heaven has forsaken me! Heaven has forsaken me!" [xi-8]

385. On the death of Yen Yuen, the Master wailed unrestrainedly. His disciples said: "Sir, your grief is excessive!" "Is it indeed excessive?" said the Master. "If not for this man, for whom then should I mourn?" [xi-9]

386. On the death of Yen Yuen, his disciples wished to give him a sumptuous funeral, but the Master said: "It is better not." Nevertheless, they gave him a sumptuous funeral. "Hui looked upon me as his father," said the Master, "but I have failed to treat him as my son. It is, however, not my fault; it is yours, my pupils." [xi-10]

387. The people of Hu Village were hard to deal with, and a young boy presented himself for an interview. The disciples were in two minds about showing him in. But the Master said: "I admit his approach to me without sanctioning what he will do when he retires. Why make so much ado? If a man purifies himself to see me, I accept this purification. I am not concerned with his past." [vii-28]

388. A young boy from the village of Ch'ueh used to come with messages. Someone asked about him, saying: "Is he improving himself?" The Master said: "I see him sitting in the grown-up's places and walking shoulder to shoulder with elders. He is not seeking to improve himself, but he wants to grow up quickly." [xiv-47]

389. The Master said: "Alas, how much I have fallen! For long I have not dreamed as of yore that I saw the Duke of Chou." [vii-5]

390. The Master said: "The phoenix does not come; nor does the River send forth charts. It is all over with me!" [ix-8]

391. The Master said: "If riches could be sought, I would do so even though I should become a carriage driver to get them. Since riches cannot thus be sought, I will continue to follow my cherished way." [vii-11]

392. The Master said: "Living on coarse food and plain water, with bent arm for a pillow—herein lies true happiness.

Ill-gotten riches and honors are to me like floating clouds." [vII-15]

393. Tzu Kung asked: "I have here a beautiful piece of jade. Should I hide it away in a casket, or should I seek for a good price to sell it?" "Sell it! Sell it!" said the Master. "I too am waiting to be sold, at a right price." [IX-12]

394. Once when the stable was burned down, on his return from the court, the Master said: "Has any person been injured?" He did not inquire as to the horses. [X-12]

395.   Let a man move at the first sign,
And he will rise up and settle down.

Upon this, [the Master] said:

The hen-pheasant of the hill-bridge
Comes just in season, just in season.
When Tzu Lu made a motion to the bird,
It sniffed thrice before it flew away. [X-18]

Chapter X. Comments on Confucius

396. Tzu Ch'in asked Tzu Kung [about the Master], saying: "When our Master comes to a country, he is sure to find out its administration. Does he demand this information or do the people tell him of their own accord?" Tzu Kung said: "Our Master is gentle, upright, courteous, temperate, and compliant, and thus he gets the information. That is his way of inquiry—a different matter from the way in which inquiries are generally made." [1-10]

397. Tzu Kung said: "We can comprehend our Master's views on culture and arts, but we cannot comprehend his discourses about man's nature and the *Tao* of Heaven." [v-12]

398. Yen Hui, [in admiration of the Master's wisdom], once said with a long sigh: "The more I gaze up towards it, the higher it soars; the deeper I drill down into it, the harder it becomes. One moment it appears before me; the next it is behind. Step by step the Master gently and skillfully lures me on. He has broadened me by culture and restrained me by ceremonies. And now, even though I want to stop, I cannot. Having exhausted all my abilities, I seem to see something stand out in front of me, sharp and clear, but while I want to follow it, the way is closed." [IX-10]

399. A man from Ta-hsiang said: "What a great man is Master K'ung! His learning is vast, yet in nothing does he make himself a name!" The Master, hearing this, said to his disciples: "What shall I take up? Shall I take up charioteer-

ing? Or shall I take up archery? Let me take up chariot-eering." [ix-2]

400. The great minister [of Wu] asked Tzu Kung, saying: "Your Master is surely a Sage. What varied acquirements he has!" "Of a truth," said Tzu Kung, "Heaven has endowed him with sageness, and he has also many acquirements." The Master, hearing of this, said: "Does the great minister know me? When I was young, my condition was low; that is why I have many acquirements in lowly pursuits. Must *chün-tzu* have many acquirements? No, he is in no need of such ac-quirements at all."

Lao said: "The Master used to say: 'I have not been of-ficially employed, so that I have acquired many arts.'" [ix-6]

401. Nan-kung Kuo questioned Master K'ung, saying: "Yi was well versed in archery, and Ao could shape the boat, yet neither of them died a natural death; whereas Yü and Chi, both engaged personally in farming, came into possession of the world." At the time the Master made no reply. When Nan-kung Kuo had left, the Master said: "A *chün-tzu* is in-deed this man! A lover of virtue is indeed this man!" [xiv-6]

402. The Border Officer of Yi district requested to be presented to the Master, saying: "Whenever a *chün-tzu* comes here, I never fail to meet him." The followers pre-sented him to the Master, and, on leaving, he said: "My friends, why are you disheartened by his failure? The world has long been without the *Tao;* but now Heaven is going to use the Master as a wooden bell [to arouse the populace]." [iii-24]

403. Tzu Lu happened to pass the night in Shi-men. The gatekeeper asked: "Where are you from?" "From Master K'ung's," was the reply. "Is he not the one," said the man, "who knows that what he does is in vain yet keeps on trying to do so?" [xiv-41]

404. The Master was playing on a stone chime one day in Wei, when a man with a straw basket passed by his house and said: "His heart is full who thus strikes the sounding stone!" A little later, he added: "Oh, for shame! Why this contemptible tinkling note! If one doesn't gain recognition, why not quit at once?—that's all. 'In deep water, cross it with your clothes on; in shallow water, wade in it with your clothes lifted.'"[1] Master K'ung hearing of this, said: "Where there is a will, there is a way." [xiv-42]

1. This is a verse from the *Odes*—meaning that one should act in accord-ance with circumstances.

405. Chieh Yü, a madman of Ch'u, as he passed by Master K'ung, sang:

> O Phoenix! O Phoenix!
> How your virtue is in decay!
> As the past is over,
> The future is still in sight.
> Hopeless! Alas!
> Court attended is dangerous in these days.

Master K'ung alighted wishing to talk with him, but the madman hurried along and avoided him, so that the Master failed to get a word with him. [xviii-5]

406. Ch'ang Chü and Chieh Nih were working together in the fields. Master K'ung, happening to pass by them, sent Tzu Lu to ask them where the river could be forded. Ch'ang Chü said: "Who is that man who holds the reins?" "K'ung Chiu," said Tzu Lu. "K'ung Chiu of Lu?" and Tzu Lu assented. "Then he should know where the ford is," said the man. So Tzu Lu turned to Chieh Nih, and the latter said: "Who are you?" "Tzu Lu," was the reply. "A disciple of K'ung Chiu of Lu?" "Yes." "All the world is a swelling torrent," said Chieh Nih, "and who is there to change it? As for you, instead of following a man who flees from one man to another, would it not be better to follow those who withdraw from the world altogether?" With that he went on hoeing. Tzu Lu went back and reported to the Master. The Master said, with a sigh: "It is impossible to herd with birds and beasts. If I do not associate with our fellow men, with whom should I live? If the *Tao* prevails in the world, there is no need for me to change it." [xviii-6]

407. Once when Tzu Lu was following the Master on a journey, he happened to lag behind. He met an old man carrying a weeding basket on his staff and asked: "Have you, Sir, seen my Master?" "You," said the old man, "do not toil with your four limbs; nor can you distinguish the five grains. Who may your Master be?" With these words, he planted his staff in the ground and proceeded to weed. Tzu Lu joined his hands in salutation and stood waiting. Then the old man ended up by taking Tzu Lu home for the night; he killed a fowl, boiled millet to feed him, and also introduced his two sons. Next morning Tzu Lu went his way and reported his adventure. "He is a recluse," said the Master, and sent Tzu Lu back to find the man. But when Tzu Lu went there, the

old man was gone. Whereupon Tzu Lu said: "To refuse to serve in the government is contrary to righteousness. Since the regulations between old and young cannot be set aside, how can the duties between the sovereign and ministers be neglected? In his desire to maintain his own personal purity, he subverts the great relationships of mankind. *Chün-tzu* tries to go into office, because he holds it righteous to do so; the fact that the *Tao* fails to prevail, he knows already." [xvɪɪɪ-7]

408. Wei-sun Mou said to Master K'ung: "Ch'iu, how is it that you keep perching from one place to another? Is it to show your eloquency?" "I dare not show my eloquency," said Master K'ung, "but I detest obstinacy." [xɪv-34]

409. Kung-sun Chao of Wei asked Tzu Kung: "From whom did Chung-ni [Master K'ung] get all his learning?" "The *Tao* of kings Wen and Wu [founders of Chou] has not been lost to this world," said Tzu Kung, "but is still to be found among men. The men of worth have recorded the major teachings of the *Tao*, while those of less worth recorded its minor teachings. They, however, all share in varying degrees the *Tao* of Wen and Wu. From whom indeed did our Master not learn? But what need had he of a regular teacher?" [xɪx-22]

410. Shu-sun Wu-shu said to the officials at court: "Tzu Kung is superior to Chung-ni." Tzu-fu Ching-p'o told this to Tzu Kung, and Tzu Kung said: "Let me take as an example the palace walls. My walls reach only to the shoulder, and the people outside may see the attractive chambers and rooms within. But the walls of our Master rise fathoms high, and if one is not let in by the door, one cannot have a good look inside at the beauty of the ancestral temple or the grandeur of the hundred officers. But few indeed are those who have found the gate. What Shu-sun said is therefore to be expected, is it not?" [xɪx-24]

411. [On another occasion] Shu-sun Wu-shu spoke derogatorily of Chung-ni, and Tzu Kung said: "You mustn't do that. You cannot hurt Chung-ni. The goodness of other men is like hillocks or mounds which one may step over. But [the goodness of] Chung-ni is like the sun and moon, which one cannot step over. Although a man may deny himself to the sun and moon, what damage can he cause to either of them? It only shows that he did not know his own measure." [xɪx-24]

412. Chen Tzu-chin said to Tzu Kung: "You must be too modest. How can Chung-ni be superior to you?" "*Chün-tzu,*

for a single assertion, may be deemed wise or otherwise," said Tzu Kung. "One must be careful of one's assertions. Just as Heaven cannot be reached by ladders, so our Master cannot be attained. Were our Master ever in control of a state or of a family, it would have been as is said in the following remarks:

He raised the people, and so they remain;
He guides the people, and so they follow;
He makes the people content, and so they come;
He labors the people, and so they act in accord.
When he lives, he is honored;
When he dies, he is mourned.

How can one be a peer to our Master?" [xix-25]

Part Three: The Disciples of Confucius

As a young man, Confucius started to teach in his native state of Lu. In his last days, when he retired into private life, he had attracted young men of promise from all parts of China, but mostly from Lu, Wei, Ch'en, Ch'i, Ts'ai, and a few from the border states of Ch'in, Ch'u, and Wu. It may be an exaggeration that no fewer than three thousand students received his instruction, but, according to the more reliable source, the names of seventy-seven students can be ascertained. As Confucius himself said, among the students who accompanied him to wander about and who enjoyed his personal teachings, there were four classes of ancient worthies: (1) those who were noted in virtues were Yen Yuen, Min-tzu Chien, Jan P'o-niu, and Jan Yung; (2) those who were gifted in the art of speech were Tsai Nge and Tzu Kung; (3) those who were distinguished in the government were Tzu Lu and Jan Yu; and (4) those who were eminent in literature were Tzu Yu and Tzu Hsia [Analects xi-2]. In the opinion of posterity, however, the most important of Confucian scholars was Tseng Tzu [Tseng Ts'an], noted for his filial piety and knowledge of ancient ceremonies. He has been credited with the authorship of the Classic of Filial Piety. In the Analects there are more dialogues between Confucius and him than between the Master and others. It has been believed that the anonymous editor of the *Analects* was a follower of Tseng Tzu [Master Tseng], who, alone of the Master's disciples, was called by the title of Master Tzu, while the others, with the exception of Master Yu [Yu Tzu], were only mentioned by name.

Generally speaking, the disciples of Confucius may be classified into two categories: those senior students who came to Confucius before he went on his travels and those junior students who gathered around him in his last days in Lu. Whereas most of the senior students were interested in the arts of government and of speech, as they aspired to high government positions, the group of junior scholars distinguished themselves in the fields of literature and philosophy; it was largely through these junior scholars that Confucius exerted a great influence on the development of Chinese culture.

❧ ☙

Chapter XI. The Sayings of the Disciples

413. Yu said: "A man who is filial and fraternal seldom shows a disposition to offend his superiors. A man who is not fond of offending his superiors will never be fond of stirring up a revolt. *Chün-tzu* devotes himself to the fundamental, for once the fundamental is well established, the *Tao* naturally evolves. Is it not filial piety and fraternal love that constitute the very foundation of *jen?*" [1-2]

414. Yu Tzu said: "In the usages of ceremonies, harmony is to be stressed. In the regulations of ancient kings, this was the admirable feature, the one which should prevail in all occasions. If things go amiss and one who knows the significance of harmony does not regulate them by ceremonies, they likewise will go amiss." [1-12]

415. Yu Tzu said: "When sincerity is in accord with righteousness, we take a person at his words. When reverence is in accord with ritual, we may avoid shame and disgrace. When confidence is placed on a person who merits our confidence, we may rely on his guidance." [1-13]

416. Duke Ai [of Lu] asked Yu Tzu: "The harvest fails and my revenue is insufficient; what am I to do?" "Why not apply the tithing statute?" replied Yu Tzu. "With two-tenths," said the Duke, "I find my revenue insufficient; what would be the good of applying the tithing statute?" "So long as the people have plenty," said Yu Tzu, "who will leave their

prince alone in want? So long as the people are in want, who will leave their prince alone to enjoy plenty?" [XII-9]

417. Tseng Tzu said: "Every day I examine myself on three points: Have I been self-interested in what I have done for others? Have I been unfaithful in my association with friends? And have I failed to embody in life the Master's teachings?" [I-4]

418. Tseng Tzu said: "When proper solicitude is given on the death of parents and periodical offerings [to them] are made, the morals of the people will be renewed and cherished." [I-9]

419. Tseng Tzu was very ill; he sent for his disciples and said: "Uncover my feet, uncover my hands. The *Shih* says:

> In fear and trembling,
> With caution and care,
> As if standing by a deep abyss,
> As if treading on thin ice.

My pupils, from now on, I know I shall be free from injury to my person!" [VIII-3]

420. When Tseng Tzu was very ill, Meng Ching Tzu came to see him. Tseng Tzu said: "When a bird is about to die, its cry is mournful; when a man is about to die, his words are good and true. *Chün-tzu*, in following the *Tao*, values three things: In his deportment, he is free from arrogance or violence; in his countenance, he inspires sincerity; in his words, he avoids vulgarity. As for details of sacrifices, these can be left to the care of those in charge." [VIII-4]

421. Tseng Tzu said: "Capable yet consulting those less capable, possessed of much yet consulting those possessed of little, having yet seeming not to have, full yet seeming empty, offended against yet never entering into contest; once I had a friend who conducted himself in this manner." [VIII-5]

422. Tseng Tzu said: "A man is entrusted with the care of an orphan and given authority over a state of a hundred *li;* no emergency, however great, can shake him. Can such a man be a true *chün-tzu?* He is indeed a true *chün-tzu.*" [VIII-6]

423. Tseng Tzu said: "The scholar should be broad-shouldered and strong-minded, for his responsibility is heavy and his course [*Tao*] is long. *Jen* is his personal responsibility—is it not heavy? Only with death does his course cease—is it not long?" [VIII-7]

424. Tseng Tzu said: "*Chün-tzu* gathers friends by culture and furthers *jen* with friendship." [xii-24]

425. Tseng Tzu said: "*Chün-tzu* keeps his mind on his own duties." [xiv-27]

426. Tseng Tzu said: "Chang is so self-imposing. Being with him, it is hard to achieve *jen*." [xix-16]

427. Tseng Tzu said: "I once heard the Master say: 'One may never show one's true self, and yet one is certain to do so on the occasion of the death of one's parents.'" [xix-17]

428. Tseng Tzu said: "I once heard the Master say: 'In regard to the filial piety of Meng Chuang Tzu, it is possible for others to equal him. However, he made no changes either in the ministers of his father or in his father's policies—this would indeed be hard to equal.'" [xix-18]

429. When the chief of the Meng Family appointed Yang Fu as the Chief of Criminal Administration, the latter came for advice to Tseng Tzu. Tseng Tzu said: "It is long since those above have failed in their duties that the people have gone astray. When you find out the truth of the crime, you will feel grief and pity but take no joy." [XIX-19]

430. Tzu Hsia said: "If a man instead of loving beauty loves true worth; if he serves his parents to the utmost; if he devotes his life to the service of his sovereign; if in dealing with his friends he is sincere in his words; although others assert that he has not studied, I will assert that he is a learned man." [1-7]

431. Szu-ma Niu, being worried, said: "All else have brothers; I alone have none." Tzu Hsia said: "I have heard this: 'Life and death are allotted by Fate; riches and honor depend upon Heaven. Let *chün-tzu* be reverent and make no fault; let him be respectful to others and observant of ritual; then all within the four seas will be his brothers.' Why should *chün-tzu* be worried that he has no brothers?" [xii-5]

432. Tzu Hsia said: "Even the minor studies [of knowledge] contain something of truth, but if pursued too far, they will prove inapplicable. Therefore, *chün-tzu* refuses to cultivate them." [xix-4]

433. Tzu Hsia said: "If a man is daily aware of what he lacks and every month remembers what he has learned, he is indeed fond of learning." [xix-5]

434. Tzu Hsia said: "Study widely and hold fast to purpose, inquire earnestly and continue to think—therein lies *jen*." [xix-6]

435. Tzu Hsia said: "Just as the artisans stay in workshop

to accomplish their work, so *chün-tzu* remains in studies to attain the *Tao*." [xix-7]

436. Tzu Hsia said: "*Hsiao-jen* always glosses over his faults." [xix-8]

437. Tzu Hsia said: "*Chün-tzu* presents three different aspects: On first look, he appears stern and forbidding; on closer acquaintance, he becomes gentle and mild; and when he is heard to speak, he becomes firm and decisive." [xix-9]

438. Tzu Hsia said: "A prince, having won the confidence of the people, may then impose labor on them; without their confidence, they feel that they are being exploited. Similarly, a man, having won the confidence of others, may remonstrate with them; without their confidence, they feel that they are being slandered." [xix-10]

439. Tzu Hsia said: "A man may not transgress the bounds of major morals but may make errors in minor morals." [xix-11]

440. Tzu Hsia said: "An official, having discharged his duties, should devote himself to learning. A scholar, having completed his learning, should devote himself to public office." [xix-13]

441. Tzu Yu said: "The disciples and followers of Tzu Hsia learn well as to the matters of sprinkling and sweeping, answering questions and receiving visitors, but these are mere trifles. They are all at a loss in the fundamental and important studies. What a pity!" Tzu Hsia, hearing of this, said: "Alas! Yen Yu is mistaken. In learning the *Tao* of *chün-tzu*, there are certain things which should be transmitted first and others withheld until later. This is comparable to the growth of plants and trees developing through different stages. How can there be any deceit in learning the *Tao* of *chün-tzu*? It is only the sage who embraces in himself the whole process of learning." [xix-12]

442. Tzu Yu said: "Let mourning stop when one's grief is fully expressed." [xix-14]

443. Tzu Yu said: "My friend Chang can be hardly equalled in his accomplishment, but he is not yet considered a *jen*-minded man." [xix-15]

444. Chi Tzu-ch'eng said: "*Chün-tzu* can be a *chün-tzu* in virtue of his innate substance; what need has he of refined ornament?" "Ah! Sir," said Tzu Kung, "I regret to hear your words about *chün-tzu*. For a team of four horses can never overtake the tongue! Refined ornament is much the same as innate substance, and innate substance as refined ornament.

Likewise, a tiger's or leopard's skin resembles that of a dog or sheep when the hair has been removed." [XII-8]

445. Tzu Kung said: "Chou [the tyrant] was blamed for more wickedness than he did. Therefore *chün-tzu* shuns 'dwelling in the low ground,' where all the evils of the world flow in upon him." [XIX-20]

446. Tzu Kung said: "The faults of *chün-tzu* may be compared to the eclipses of the sun and moon. When he has faults, everyone sees them; but once he corrects them, everyone turns up toward him." [XIX-21]

447. When Tzu Lu heard [any teaching from the Master] and was still unable to practice it, he was only afraid lest he might hear some fresh teaching. [V-13]

448. The Chi family sent a messenger to ask Min Tzu Chien to be governor of P'i. Min Tzu Chien, declining the offer, said: "Kindly make some excuse for me. But if anyone comes with a second invitation, I shall have to retire to the banks of the river Wen." [VI-7]

449. Tzu Chang said: "The scholar, in the face of danger, is ready to offer his life; when he sees the opportunity of gain, he thinks of righteousness; when he performs sacrifice, he shows reverence; in mourning he feels grief. Such a man deserves our approbation." [XIX-1]

450. Tzu Chang said: "If a man fails to have a firm hold of virtue and has no firm faith in the *Tao*, what account can be made of him if he lives? What account can be made of him if he dies?" [XIX-2]

451. The disciples of Tzu Hsia asked Tzu Chang about choice of friends. Tzu Chang said: "What does Tzu Hsia tell you?" They replied: "Tzu Hsia says:

Make friends with those whom you approve;
Keep at a distance those whom you disapprove."

Tzu Chang said: "This is different from what I have heard:

Chün-tzu shows respect to the worthy and yet maintains a proper concern for all;
He praises the good and yet has pity on the incompetent.

If I am virtuous and worthy, for whom should I not maintain a proper concern? If I am not virtuous and worthy, people will keep me at a distance. So why should I keep others at a distance?" [XIX-3]

Chapter XII. Confucius' Comments on His Disciples

452. When the Master was in Chen, he said: "Let's go home! Let's go home! The little children of my school are getting impetuous and ambitious. They are well accomplished and cultured, but they still do not know how to shape themselves." [v-21]

453. The Master said: "None of those that accompanied me to Chen and Tsai was then in government service."

Noted for moral character were Yen Yuen, Min-tzu Chine, Jan P'o-niu, and Ch'ung Kung; for the art of speech were Tsai Nge and Tzu Kung; for administrative ability were Jan Yu and Tzu Lu; and for literature and learning were Tzu Yu and Tzu Hsia. [XI-2]

454. While they were waiting on the Master, Min Tzu looked upright and firm; Tzu Lu, frank and bold; Jan Yu and Tzu Kung, genial and affable. The Master was pleased.

[The Master said:] "A man like Yu [Tzu Lu] will not die a natural death." [XI-12]

455. [The Master said:] "Ch'ai [Tzu Kao] is dull; Shen [Tseng Tzu] is slow-witted; Sh'ih [Tzu Kung] is specious; Yu is lacking in polish." [XI-17]

456. Tzu Kung asked: "Who is better, Sh'ih [Tzu Chang] or Shang [Tzu Hsia]?" The Master said: "Sh'ih is overdoing things, and Shang is falling short." "In that case," said Tzu Kung, "is Sh'ih better?" The Master said: "To overdo things is as bad as to fall short." [XI-15]

457. The Master said: "Hui [Yen Yuen] comes very near to [jen]. He is often empty. Szu [Tzu Kung] does not bow to Fate and hoards up his wealth. In his calculations he often hits the mark." [XI-18]

458. The Master asked Tzu Kung: "Who is better, you or Hui?" "How can I be compared with Hui? Hui hears one point and knows the whole ten; I hear one point and know only two." The Master said: "Not equal to him; you and I are indeed not equal to him." [v-8]

459. The Master said to Yen Yuen: " 'When wanted, go and serve; when released, retire and hide.' Only you and I have attained to this." Tzu Lu said: "Supposing you were in charge of the Three Armies, whom would you take to work with?" "The man who 'will rouse the tiger or rush the river' —thereby recklessly dying with no regret; that sort of man I should not take. I should certainly take someone who is

keenly conscious of responsibility and fond of success through strategy." [vii-10]

460. Meng Wu P'o asked: "Is Tzu Lu jen-minded?" "I do not know," said the Master. On his repeating the question, the Master said: "In a country of a thousand chariots, Yu might be appointed to the administration of its revenues, but whether he is jen-minded, I do not know." "What do you say then of Ch'iu?" "As for Ch'iu," said the Master, "in a city of a thousand families, or a ruling family with a hundred chariots, he might be appointed as its minister, but whether he is jen-minded, I do not know." "Take Ch'ih [Tzu Hua] then; what of him?" "Ch'ih," said the Master, "dressed in official robes and standing in a court might be appointed to converse with the guests, but whether or not he is jen-minded I do not know." [v-7]

461. Chi Kang-tzu asked: "Is Tzu Lu suited for official employment?" "Yu," said the Master, "is a man of decision; what difficulty would he find therein?" "Is Tzu Kung suited for official employment?" "Szu," said the Master, "is a man of penetration; what difficulty would he find therein?" "Then is Jan Ch'iu suited for official employment?" "Ch'iu," said the Master, "is a man of much proficiency; what difficulty would he find therein?" [vi-6]

462. Chi Tzu-zan asked: "Can Tzu Lu and Jan Ch'iu be called great ministers?" The Master said: "I thought you would ask about something else, and you only ask about Yu and Ch'iu. What is called a great minister is one who will serve his prince according to the Tao, and when he finds he cannot do so, he will resign. But Yu and Ch'iu can only be regarded as ordinary ministers." Then Chi Tzu-zan said: "Will they merely act as they are told?" "So far as to slay their father or their prince," said the Master, "they will refuse." [xi-23]

463. The Master said: "I talked to Hui a whole day, and he did not differ from me as if he were stupid. When he retired, I inquired into his conduct and found him able to elaborate my teachings. Hui is not stupid at all!" [ii-9]

464. Duke Ai asked which of the disciples loved learning, and Master K'ung said: "There was Yen Hui who loved learning. He never vented his anger upon others nor would he repeat the same fault. Unfortunately, he was short-lived and died. At present there are none, and I have not yet heard of anyone who loves learning." [vi-2]

465. The Master said: "As to Hui, for three months his

mind did not deviate from *jen*. The others may attain to this for a day or for a month, but there they end." [vɪ-5]

466. The Master said: "A worthy man indeed was Hui! With a bamboo bowl of rice and a gourd basin of water, he lived in a mean lane. Others could not endure such distress, and yet Hui was invariable with his cheerfulness. How worthy a man indeed was Hui!" [vɪ-9]

467. The Master said: "Never listless when spoken to— such is Hui!" [ɪx-19]

468. The Master said of Yen Yuen: "Alas! I saw him advance but never saw him stop in his progress." [ɪx-20]

469. The Master said: "Hui gave me no assistance, but he was delighted in what I said." [xɪ-3]

470. Someone said: "Jan Yung is *jen*-minded, but he is a poor talker." The Master said: "Of what use is it to be a good talker? One who wins people by fluency of words procures only hatred. Whether or not he is *jen*-minded, I do not know. But why must he be a good talker?" [v-4]

471. The Master said of Jan Yung: "If the calf of a brindled cow is red in color and horned, although men may not wish to take it [for sacrifice], would [the spirits of] the hills and streams reject it?" [vɪ-4]

472. When the men of Lu were rebuilding the Long Treasury, Min Tzu-chien said: "Would the old building not be adequate? Why must it be rebuilt?" The Master said: "That man seldom speaks, but when he does, he is certain to hit the mark." [xɪ-13]

473. Tzu Kung asked: "Sir, what do you say of me?" "You are a utensil," said the Master. "What kind of utensil?" asked the disciple. "An ornate temple vessel of jade," said the Master. [v-3]

474. The Master said: "Filial indeed is Min Tzu-chien! None can say anything of him different from the words of his parents or brothers." [xɪ-4]

475. Tzu Kung was fond of criticizing others. The Master said: "Is Szu really a worthy man himself? I myself have no time to spare for this." [xɪv-31]

476. Of Tzu Chien, the Master said: "*Chün-tzu* is indeed such a man! If there were no *chün-tzu* in Lu, how could this man have become as he is?" [v-2]

477. The Master wanted Chi-tiao Kai to take office, but the latter replied: "I have not yet had confidence for that." And the Master was delighted. [v-5]

478. The Master said: "Dressed in a shabby gown quilted

with hemp, yet standing unabashed with those clad in furs
of fox and badger—who could do it but Yu?"

> Who harms none, covets nothing,
> Does only what is good!

Tzu Lu [Yu] kept on humming over the lines. But the
Master said: "How should the *Tao* contained in them be
worth treasuring to that extent?" [IX-26]

479. The Master said: "What business has the lute of Yu
to twang at my door!" The disciples began not to respect Tzu
Lu. The Master said: "[Yu] has climbed to the hall, though
he has not yet passed into the inner chamber." [XI-14]

480. Tzu Lu put Tzu Kao in charge of Pi district. The
Master said: "You are only doing harm to a man's son." Tzu
Lu said: "When a man has the people and a country to
administer, should his learning consist only in reading books?"
The Master said: "It is for remarks of that kind that I dislike
glib people." [XI-24]

481. The Master said: "Who could settle litigation upon
hearing one side but Yu? Tzu Lu never slept over a promise."
[XII-12]

482. Jan Ch'iu once said: "It is not that I fail to delight
in your *Tao*, but that my ability cannot follow it." The Master
said: "One whose ability gives out collapses in the middle
of the *Tao*, but you set a limit to yourself." [VI-12]

483. The chief of the Chi family was richer than the Duke of
Chou, and yet Ch'iu still collected duties to add to his wealth.
The Master said: "He is no disciple of mine. Boys, you may
beat the drum and assail him." [XI-16]

484. Duke Ai asked Tsai Nge about an altar [to be erected
for the worship of Earth]. Tsai Nge replied: "The Hsias
planted pines there; the Ying, cedars; the Chous, chestnut
trees, meaning thereby to inspire the people with fear and
trembling."[1] The Master, hearing of it, said: "For things that
are done, no explanations need be made; for things that are
already in progress, no remonstrations; for things that are
past, no blame." [III-21]

485. Tsai Yü used to sleep during the daytime. The Master
said: "Rotten wood cannot be carved, nor can a wall of dried
dung be trowelled. This Yü—what's the use of my denouncing
him any more?" [V-9]

486. The Master said: "In my early dealings with men, I

---

1. In Chinese the words "chestnut" and "trembling" have the same sound.

used to listen to their words and take their deeds on trust.
Now I am obliged to give ear to what they say and then keep
a watchful eye on what they do. It was my experience with
Tsai Yü that brought about this change." [v-9]

487. The Master said: "I have never yet seen a man of
strong character." Someone replied: "Shen Ch'eng." "Shen
Ch'eng is covetous," said the Master; "how can he be considered as a man of strong character?" [v-10]

488. Fan Chi asked to be instructed in agriculture. The
Master said: "I am not so good as an old farmer." When
asked about gardening, the Master said: "I am not so good
as an old gardener." When Fan Chi left, the Master said:
"What a little-minded man [hsiao-jen] is Fan Chi! When those
above love propriety [li], the people will be bound to be
respectful; when those above love righteousness, the people
will be bound to be obedient; when those above love good
faith, the people will be bound to be honest. When all these
things prevail, then people from all quarters will flock to them
with their little ones. What need have those above to practice
farming?" [xiii-4]

Part Four: Miscellaneous Records

489. Tzu Chang said: "The *Shu* [Book of History] says:
"Kai Tsung, while observing the imperial mourning, did not
speak for three years. What does this mean?" The Master
said: "Why Kai Tsung in particular? In fact, all the men of
old did this. When a prince died, the ministers attended to
their several duties and acted on the instruction of the Prime
Minister for three years." [xiv-43]

490. The wife of a prince is addressed by her husband as
"Madam"; the queen calls herself "Little Maiden." The people address her as "Queen." In addressing other states, she
calls herself "Humble Small Princess." The other states address her as "Queen." [xvi-14]

491. Liu Hsia Hui, the minister of justice, was thrice dismissed. Someone said to him: "Is it not time for you to leave
the country?" He said: "If I serve men in an upright way,
where should I go and not be thrice dismissed? Were I to
serve men in a crooked way, why need I leave the land of my
parents?" [xviii-2]

492. The Chief Musician, Chih, went to Ch'i. Ken, the music
master at the second repast, went to Ch'u; Liao the

music master at the third repast went to Ts'ai. Ch'ueh the music master at the fourth repast went to Ch'in. Feng Shu, the drummer, went to the bank of the river, and Wu, the master of the hand drum, withdrew to the River Han. Yang, the junior music-master, and Hsiang, the master of stone chimes, withdrew to the seacoast. [xviii-9]

493. The Duke of Chou said to the Duke of Lu [his son]: "A good prince [*chün-tzu*] does not neglect his kinsmen; nor does he make his ministers complain for not being employed. He does not discard his old ministers without grave cause; nor does he expect one man to be capable of everything." [xviii-10]

494. During the Chou dynasty, there were eight famous officers [being four pairs of twins]: the eldest pair, Ta and Kwo; the next, Tu and Hwu; the third, Yah and Hsia; the youngest, Sui and Kwa. [xviii-11]

495. Yao said: "Oh, you Shun [Yao's successor]:

> Upon you rests the Heavenly succession;
> Hold fast to the center.
> The Four Seas may run dry,
> But Heaven's blessing lasts forever."

Shun also used the same words to admonish Yü [founder of the Hsai dynasty].

[T'ang, the founder of the Shang-Yin dynasty] said: "I, Li, Thy humble servant, venture to offer this sacrifice and to announce this prayer before Thee:

> Oh, most august sovereign God!
> Those who are guilty, I dare not pardon;
> But Thy minister's sins, I will not screen,
> As they are evident to Thee.
> Should I commit offenses,
> Pray never let the people suffer.
> Should the people commit offenses,
> Pray let the blame be imputed to me."

When the Chous were bestowed with blessings, it was the good who were enriched.

> They [The Shangs] have Chou kinsmen,
> Yet they are not equal to *jen*-minded men.
> When the people commit offenses,
> Let me alone bear the blame.

He [King Wu of the Chou dynasty] attended to the weights and measures, codified the laws and rules, and restored the discarded officers. Then good government prevailed in the world. He also restored the subjugated states, revived the broken families, and nominated the retired virtuous men. Then the hearts of the people throughout the world turned to him. He stressed the people's food, funeral rituals, and sacrifices. By his magnanimity, he won the multitude; by his sincerity, he had the people's confidence; by his diligence, he had achievements; by his justice, all the people were gratified. [xx-1]

CONTENTS

Mencius (Meng K'o) is the Latinized form of the Chinese name Meng Tzu or Master Meng. He lived in the fourth century B.C., his approximate dates being 372-289 B.C. He was born in the small state of Tsou (the modern district of Tsou Hsien, Shantung). Having lost his father when he was only three years old, he was brought up under the devoted care and instruction of Mother Meng, whose name is proverbial even to this day. The favorite story about Mother Meng is that she moved three times in order to provide her son with a favorable environment. They first lived near a cemetery until the mother discovered that her son took to playing at burying and mourning the dead. They moved at once, near a market place, where the boy was soon mimicking the merchants, which also displeased the mother. So they moved again, this time to the vicinity of a school, where the sensitive boy began to pattern his actions after those of pupils and teachers. This story, and many like it, have served to inspire countless mothers ever since.

When Mencius grew up, he studied with a disciple of Confucius' grandson, Tzu Ssu, and he was thus initiated into the great school of Confucius. Early in his life, Mencius came to regard Confucius as his greatest inspiration. He once said: "What I desire to do is to study to be like Confucius." (The Meng Tzu, IIA, 2). With his eloquence, moral courage, and deep conviction, he had widely popularized the teachings of Confucius, at the same time attacking with great zeal the heterodox teachings of other schools. However, he was different from Confucius in temperament. While Confucius was an introvert and a true chün-tzu, cautious and deliberate in speech, Mencius was an extrovert and a great oracle of age, widely noted for his wit. When asked a difficult question or when under a verbal attack, Confucius often became helpless and called on Heaven to witness. Mencius, however, would lash out at his opponents and drive them into defensive positions.

Most of his working life was in the second half of the

fourth century B.C., when the old China was beginning to disappear and great changes were in progress. This period, known in history as that of the Warring States, was one of social disturbance, political instability, and intellectual anarchy. Mencius' attempts at political reform, therefore, met with no greater success than had those of his model. The *Shih Chi* (Historical Records), written by Ssu-ma Ch'ien (ca. 100 B.C.), says in its biography of Mencius:

> . . . When he had achieved full comprehension of his learning, he traveled to serve King Hsüan of Ch'i, but the latter was unable to find a post for him. Thence he went to the state of Liang; but King Hui of Liang did not listen to his advice, for he felt that Mencius was pedantic and his words had no basis in fact. At this time the state of Ch'in was adopting the policies of Lord Shang to enrich its state and strengthen its armies: the states of Ch'u and Wei were employing the strategist Wu Ch'i to attack and conquer their weaker neighbors; and Kings Wei and Hsüan of Ch'i were employing such strategists as Sun Wu and T'ien Chi, with the result that the feudal lords faced the east so as to pay homage to Ch'i. The world was then engaged in forming the vertical [which ran from north to south] and horizontal [which ran from west to east] alliances, and fighting was held as something worthy. It was under such circumstances that Mencius was transmitting the virtues of Yao, Shun, and the Three Dynasties, but those whom he visited were not willing to listen to him. So he withdrew home and together with his disciple, Wan Chang, and others, wrote prefaces to the *Shih* [Odes] and the *Shu* [History], transmitted the teachings of Confucius, and composed the *Meng Tzu* in seven books. (Ch. 74, p. 1)

Like Confucius, Mencius was an educator *par excellence*. Among his disciples he was greatly loved. As to himself, Mencius said that there were three things in which he delighted, but to be sovereign of the world was not one of them. Obtaining the young men of the finest talent in the world and educating them was his great delight. In 289 B.C., at the age of eighty-four, Mencius died in his native state. For his contributions to Confucianism, as well as for his defense of the great tradition, Mencius has been generally recognized as the greatest philosopher after Confucius, "the Second Sage."

✎ᶳ The Works of Mencius, or Meng Tzu

The Works of Mencius consists of a series of discourses
Mencius had with the feudal lords, ministers, friends, and
disciples, and now ranks as one of the famous "Four Books,"
the other three being the *Analects, The Great Learning,* and
The Doctrine of the Mean. Compared with the ancient classics, Mencius' work excels particularly because of its interesting content and its beautiful and lucid style. Although the
authenticity of Mencius' personal authorship has at times
been questioned, the opinion—as stated by Ssu-ma Ch'ien—
that Mencius, along with such disciples as Wan Chang, composed the book *Meng Tzu* in seven books has subsequently
met with general acceptance. It is believed that at one time
the complete work consisted of eleven books, but only seven
books have come down to us.

The current copy, edited by Chu Hsi, the pre-eminent
philosopher of the Sung period, is divided into fourteen chapters. However, we have rearranged the entire text into four
parts. The numbers of chapters and sections within the
brackets as noted at the end of each paragraph correspond to
those given in the original text.

Part One: The Doctrine of Human Nature

As we have noted, amid the mass of thought that Confucius developed, the doctrine of *jen* stands out as the central
thesis of the system. *Jen,* as the prime virtue of life, prompts
a man to positive efforts for others. Mencius, as an apostle of
the Confucian school, naturally gave *jen* the first place in his
life ideal but claimed that for the cultivation of virtues *jen*
should be coupled with *yi,* or righteousness. According to
Mencius, *jen* is the sound principle of warranting internal
sentiment, while *yi* is the proper way of guiding external
conduct. In his effort to develop these ethical ideas, Mencius
made the discovery of the innate goodness of human nature,
his chief contribution to Chinese thought.

Much controversy had arisen among the followers of Confucius as to the moral quality of human nature. Hsun Tzu of
the third century B.C. contended that the nature of man is
evil. Tzu Ssu, the grandson of Confucius, advanced the opinion that human nature, as conferred by Heaven, is essentially

good, but Mencius was the first to enunciate distinctly the doctrine that the nature of man inclines him to goodness and kindness as surely as the nature of water compels it to flow downward. There were in Mencius' time three different theories on this subject. One theory, advanced by Kao Tzu, with whom Mencius had many arguments, held that human nature was neither good nor bad. Another maintained that human nature could be either good or bad, depending upon circumstances. The third theory stated that the nature of some men was good while that of others was bad. These scholars seem to have been more interested in the educability of nature than in its original constitution. The following passages in the *Works of Mencius,* referring to this controversy are worth considering because they imply that education is growth, a theory much stressed by modern writers.

ᘿᏱᏱᕔ

Chapter I. The Goodness of Human Nature

1. Kung-tu Tzu said: "Kau Tzu says that human nature is neither good nor bad. Some say that human nature can be turned either to be good or bad. Thus when [the sage kings] Wen and Wu were in power, the people were fond of goodness; when [the wicked kings] Yu and Li were in power, the people were fond of violence. Still others say that some natures are good and some are bad. Thus while [the sage] Yao was sovereign, there was [a bad man like] Hsiang; [a bad father like] Kusou had [a good son] Shun [the sage king]; even with [the wicked] Chou for their sovereign and the son of their elder brother besides, there were [men of virtue like] Ch'i, the Viscount of Wei, and the Prince Pi-kan. Now, you say that human nature is good. Are the others all wrong?"

Master Meng said: "It is by virtue of its innate quality that human nature can be considered good. This is why I say it is good. If it becomes evil, it is not the fault of its innate quality. The sense of compassion is common to all men; the sense of shame is common to all men; the sense of respect is common to all men; the sense of right and wrong is common to all men. The sense of compassion constitutes humanity [*jen*]; the sense of shame constitutes righteousness [*yi*]; the sense of respect constitutes propriety [*li*]; the sense of right and wrong constitutes wisdom [*chih*]. Humanity, righteousness, propriety, and wisdom are not taught; they are inherent

in our nature. Sometimes we fail to think of them." As the
saying goes, "Seek [them] and you will find [them]; neglect
[them] and you will lose [them]." [Men have these virtues in
varying degrees]—some twice as much as others, some five
times as much, and some to an incalculable amount; this is
because those others have failed to develop fully their innate
capacities. It is said in the *Shih* [Odes]:

> Heaven creates the teeming multitudes;
> All things are governed by their proper principles.
> Abide by the normal nature of man,
> And all will love these beautiful virtues.

Commenting on this poem Master K'ung said: 'The writer of
this poem knows the *Tao!* Therefore, everything must have a
proper principle. As the people abide by their normal nature,
they will come to love these beautiful virtues.' " [VIA-6]

2. Kao Tzu said: "The nature of man is like the willow
tree, whereas righteousness is like a wooden bowl or a wicker
basket. Turning man's nature into humanity and righteousness
is like turning a willow tree into bowls and baskets."

Master Meng said: "Sir, can you follow the nature of the
willow tree, when you make the bowls and baskets? Or must
you violate its nature to make the bowls and baskets? If you
must violate the nature of the willow tree to turn it into
bowls and baskets, would you violate the nature of man to
turn it into *jen* and righteousness? It must be due to your
words that everyone in the world thinks of *jen* and righteousness as a curse!" [VIA-1]

3. Kao Tzu said: "The nature of man is like a swift current of water. If a breech is made to the east, it flows to the
east; if a breech is made in the west, it flows to the west. And
just as water is neither disposed to east nor west, so the nature
of man is neither disposed to good nor to evil."

Master Meng said: "It is true that water tends to flow
neither to the east nor the west, but will it tend equally to
flow upward and downward? Human nature tends toward
goodness just as water tends to flow downward. There is no
man who does not show tendency to be good; there is no
water but flows downward. Now, by splashing water, you
may cause it to fly over your head, and, by damming water,
you may make it go up the hills. But is this the nature of
water? It is, of course, external force that causes it to do so.
Likewise, if a man does other than good, his nature is being
forced in a similar way." [VIA-2]

4. Kao Tzu said: "What is born in us is called nature." Master Meng said: "What is born in us is called nature—is it not in the same sense that white is called white?" The reply was: "Yes." Master Meng continued: "Is the whiteness of a white feather the same as the whiteness of white snow? And is the whiteness of white snow the same as the whiteness of white jade?" Kau Tzu replied: "Yes." "Very well," said Master Meng. "Is the nature of a dog the same as the nature of an ox? And is the nature of an ox the same as the nature of a man?" [VIA-3]

5. Master Meng said: "The trees on the Bull Mountain were once beautiful. But being on the outskirts of a great state, they were hewn down with axes and hatchets, could they retain their beauty? Even so, moistened by rain and dew, with the force of growth operating day and night, the stumps began to send forth fresh sprouts. But soon cattle and sheep came to browse on them, and in the end the mountain became denuded as it is now. And seeing it thus, people think that it was never wooded. But is this the nature of the mountain?

"So it is with human nature. How can it be said that man is devoid of *jen* and righteousness? The reason is that he has lost his good heart in the same way that the trees have been felled by axes and hatchets. Assailed day after day, can the heart retain its goodness? Even so, nourished by the calm air of dawn, with the force of life operating day and night, man develops in his heart desires and aversions that are proper to man. But soon these good feelings are fettered and destroyed by the inroads of the day's work. Thus, fettered again and again, they wither, and the nourishing influence of night is no longer able to keep them alive. So in the end man reverts to a state not much different from that of birds and beasts, and seeing him thus, people think that man never had good feelings. But is this the nature of man? Therefore, [we conclude]:

If rightly tended, anything thrives;
If left untended, anything pines away.

Master K'ung said: 'Hold fast, and you shall keep it; let go, and you will lose it. It comes and goes without keeping time; no one knows where it lodges.' Was it not the human heart of which he spoke?" [VIA-8]

6. Master Meng said: "In good years young people tend

to be indolent; in bad years they tend to be violent. It is not that they vary because of their innate qualities conferred by Heaven; it is because their hearts are ensnared and drowned by circumstances. Now take barley as an instance. Let the seed be sown and covered up; the ground being the same, and the time of sowing likewise the same, they all germinate and grow rapidly. When the time comes, they all are found to be ripe. If there is any difference in the crops, it is due to differences in the fertility of the sites, or to unequal nourishment afforded by rain and dew, or to the variations in the ways in which they are cultivated. Therefore, all things which are the same in kind are alike by nature. In regard to men, why should we doubt that it is so? The sage and we are the same in kind.

"In reference to this, Lung Tzu once said: 'Even if a man makes sandals without knowing the size of all feet, he will not make them like baskets.' Sandals are all alike because all men's feet are alike.

"So with the mouth and flavors—all men have common tastes and relishes. Yih Ya [an ancient gourmand] knew what our mouths relish. Suppose that the nature of his mouth was not the same as that of other men, as is the case with dogs or horses, which are not the same in kind with us, why should all men be fond of following Yih Ya in their relishes? In the matter of tastes the whole world follows Yih Ya; that is, all men's mouths are alike.

"And so also it is with the ear and hearing; in the matter of music, the whole world follows the music master K'wang; that is, all men's ears are alike.

"And so also it is with the eye and seeing; no men in the world but recognize that Tzu Tu was beautiful. Anyone who would not have recognized the beauty of Tzu Tu must have had no eyes.

"Therefore I say: in the matter of flavors, men's mouths have the same taste; in the matter of music, their ears enjoy the same sounds; in the matter of beauty, their eyes recognize the same beauty. Shall their minds be an exception, sharing nothing in common? What is it, then, that the minds of men have in common? It is, I say, reason and righteousness. It is the Sage who apprehends first what is common to our minds. Therefore reason and righteousness please our minds, just as meats please our mouths." [VIA-7]

7. Master Meng said: "The mouth desires [delicious] food, the eye desires [beautiful] objects, the ear desires [fine]

music, the nose desires [sweet] odors, and the four limbs desire ease and rest; all these desires are human nature, but their enjoyment depends upon Fate. For this reason, *chün-tzu* does not say that these innate desires are human nature.

"*Jen* in relating to father and son, *Yi* in relation to sovereign and minister, *li* in relation to guest and host, *Chih* in relation to men of worth, and the sage in relation to the *Tao* of Heaven; all these relationships are submissive to Fate, but their observance depends upon human nature. Hence *chün-tzu* does not say that these relationships are submissive to Fate." [VIIB-24]

8. Kung-tu Tzu asked: "All are equally men, but some are great men and some are small men. How is this?" Master Meng said: "Those who follow the great part of themselves are great men, and those who follow the small part of themselves are small men."

[Kung-tu Tzu] continued: "All are equally men, but some follow the great part of themselves, and some follow the small part of themselves. How is this?" And [Master Meng] answered: "Ears and eyes do not think but are obscured by [external] things. When they come into contact with [external] things, they are thus distracted away. The mind, on the other hand, governs the faculty of thinking. By thinking, it obtains [what is good]; by not thinking, it fails to do this. Therefore, taking what Heaven confers upon us, let us first establish the great part of ourselves [i.e., the mind] and the small part [i.e., ears and eyes] will not be able to snatch it away. It is simply this which constitutes the great man." [VIA-15]

9. Master Meng said: "That which makes man different from the birds and beasts is but slight. The mass of people cast it away, whereas *chün-tzu* preserves it. Shun clearly understood [the nature of] all things, and carefully studied [the principles of] human relationships. He conducted himself with *jen* and *yi*; he did not need to pursue them." [IVB-19]

10. Master Meng said: "The hungry find any food good, and the thirsty find any drink good. They cannot judge food and drink properly, because their judgment has been impaired by hunger and thirst. Is it only 'the mouth and belly' which are injured by hunger and thirst? Man's mind is also injured [by hunger and thirst]. If a man can preserve his mind from the ravages of hunger and thirst, he need not worry about not being as good as other men." [VIIA-27]

Chapter II. The Manifestation of Innate Goodness

11. Master Meng said: "All men have a heart for com-miseration. The ancient kings had this commiserating heart and hence a commiserating government. When they conducted a commiserating government from a commiserating heart, they were able to rule the whole world as if they were turning it on the palm. This is why I say all men have a heart for commiseration. Take a man who suddenly sees a child about to fall into a well. Invariably he will feel a sense of alarm and distress. This is not so he will win the gratitude of the child's parents, nor so he may seek the praise of his neighbors and friends, nor because of fear of blame if he does not save the child.

"From this case we see that one who lacks a sense of com-passion is not a man; that one who lacks a sense of shame and dislike is not a man; that one who lacks a sense of mod-esty and yielding is not a man; and that one who lacks a sense of right and wrong is not a man. The sense of compassion is the beginning of *jen;* the sense of shame and dislike is the beginning of *yi;* the sense of modesty and yielding is the beginning of *li;* and the sense of right and wrong is the begin-ning of wisdom [*chih*]. Man has these four beginnings just as he has four limbs.

"When, having these four beginnings, he says of himself that he is incapable [of exercising them], he is injuring him-self. And when he says of his sovereign that he is incapable, he is injuring his sovereign. Since all men have these four beginnings in themselves, let us know how to expand and de-velop them. The result will be like fire that has begun to burn or a spring that has begun to find vent. Let one expand and develop [these four beginnings], and one will suffice to pro-tect all within the four seas. Let one fail to do so, and one will not suffice to serve one's parents." [IIA-6]

12. Master Meng said: "*Jen* is man's heart; *yi* is man's path. Alas for those who abandon the path and follow it not! Alas for those who lose the heart and seek it not! When men lose their fowls and dogs, they know to seek them. But they lose their hearts and do not know how to seek them. The way to learning is nothing else but the search for the lost heart." [VIA-11]

13. Kao Tzu said: "The desire for food and sex is [part of]

human nature. *Jen* comes from within and not from without; *yi* comes from without and not from within."

Master Meng asked: "What do you mean by saying that *jen* comes from within and *yi* comes from without?"

Kao Tzu replied: "Here is a man who is old, and I regard him as old. This regard for age is not a part within myself. It is just as there is a man who is white, and I regard him as white, because his whiteness is outside of myself. For this reason, I say *yi* comes from without."

Master Meng said: "It may be true that there is no difference between regarding the white horse as white and the white man as white. But is there really no difference between one's regard for age in an old horse and one's regard in an old man? Moreover, is it old age itself or our regard for old age which constitutes what is called *yi?*"

Kao Tzu said: "My younger brother I love; the brother of a man of Ch'in I do not love. Here the feeling is determined by myself; therefore, I say that [*jen*] comes from within. An old man of Ch'u I regard as old, just as an old man among my own people I regard as old. Here the feeling is determined by the age; therefore, I say that *yi* comes from without."

But Master Meng retorted: "We enjoy the pork roasted by a man of Ch'in as much as the pork roasted by our own men. Here the feeling is aroused by the thing itself. Then will you likewise say that our enjoyment of the roast comes from without?" [VIA-4]

14. Meng Chi Tzu asked Kung-tu Tzu: "On what ground is it said that *yi* comes from within?" Kung-tu Tzu said: "We act out of the sense of respect, and, therefore, I say that it comes from within."

[The other asked]: "Suppose that here is a villager who is older than your elder brother by one year; to whom would you show the greater respect?"

"To my elder brother," was the reply.

"If serving wine, whom would you serve first?"

"The villager."

[Meng Chi Tzu argued]: "Now you show greater respect to the one, and now you have regard for age to the other; this is certainly determined by what is without and does not proceed from within."

Kung-tu Tzu could not answer him, and he told Master Meng about it.

Master Meng said: "[Ask him,] 'To whom will you show

the greater respect—your uncle or your younger brother?' He will answer, 'To my uncle.' Then ask him, 'If your younger brother be impersonating a dead ancestor [at a sacrifice], to whom will you show the greater respect?' He will answer, 'To my younger brother.' Then you may ask, 'Well, what is the respect due, as you said, to your uncle?' He will answer: 'Because of the position which my younger occupies,' and you may likewise say, 'So my respect to the villager is because of his position. Ordinarily one should show the greater respect to one's elder brother, but on special occasions, one should show the greater respect to the villager.' "

Chi Tzu, hearing of this, said: "A man respects his uncle in one way, and his younger brother in another way; this is certainly determined by what is without, and does not proceed from within."

Kung-tu Tzu said: "In winter we like to drink hot broth, and in summer we like to drink cold water. Because of this fact, could you say that the desire for food and drink comes from without?" [VIA-5]

15. Master Meng said: "When all in the world speaks about the nature of things, their reasonings are already known. The reasonings, however, must be in their natural state. What I dislike about those wise men is the way they frame their reasonings. If they would only act as Yü did when he drained the waters [after the flood], there would be nothing to dislike in their wisdom. When Yü drained away the waters, he merely followed their nature. If those wise men would also follow the nature of things [in their studies], their wisdom would be great. Thus, though the sky is high and the stars are far away, if we have followed their nature, we may easily calculate the solstices of a thousand years." [IVB-26]

16. Master Meng said: "All men feel they cannot endure [seeing] some things; extend that feeling to what they can endure [to see], and this is jen. All men feel they cannot endure doing some things; extend that feeling to what they can endure to do, and this is righteousness [yi].

"If a man can fully develop the feeling not to injure others, his humanity will not be exhausted. If a man can fully develop the feeling not to commit anything malicious, his righteousness will not be exhausted. If a man can fully develop the feeling not to be addressed disgracefully, he will be righteous wherever he goes.

"If a man speaks what he ought not to speak, he seeks

favor by speech. If he does not speak what he ought to speak, he seeks favor by silence. In both cases he is malicious and shameless." [VIIB-31]

17. Master Meng said: "A man who has exercised his mind to the utmost, knows his nature. Knowing his nature, he knows Heaven. Therefore, to preserve one's mind and nourish one's nature is the way to serve Heaven. A man worries about neither untimely death nor long life but cultivates his personal character and waits for its natural development; this is to stand in accord with Fate." [VIIA-1]

18. Master Meng said: "All things are determined by Fate, and one should accept what is conferred [by Fate]. Therefore, one who knows Fate will not stand beneath a precipitous wall. Death sustained as a result of fulfilling one's duties may be ascribed to Fate. Death sustained as a penalty cannot be ascribed to Fate." [VIIA-2]

19. Master Meng said: "The great man is he who has not lost his child's heart." [IVB-12]

20. Master Meng said: "Stature and complexion belong to our Heavenly nature. Only the sage can conform to the design of his stature." [VIIA-38]

21. Master Meng said: "Is the arrow-maker less *jen*-hearted than the armor-maker? The arrow-maker's sole fear is that his arrow will not hurt men, while the armor-maker's sole fear is that his armor will not protect men from being hurt. So it is with the priest and the coffin-maker. One should use caution in the choice of a profession. Master K'ung once said: 'It is best to live in the company of *jen*. If a man chooses not to live where *jen* prevails, how can he be considered wise?' Now, *jen* is an honored endowment by Heaven and a peaceful abode among men. Since no one can prevent us from doing so, it is not wise that we should fail to abide by *jen*.

"Whoever is devoid of *jen* and wisdom, lacks a sense of *yi* and *li*; such a man will be the servant of others. To be the servant of others and yet ashamed of servitude is like a bow-maker being ashamed of making bows, or an arrow-maker being ashamed of making arrows. If one be ashamed of one's self, the best course for one is to abide by *jen*.

"The man who abides by *jen* is like the archer. The archer first adjusts himself and then shoots. If he misses, he bears no grudge against those who surpass him. He simply turns inward to examine his own self." [IIA-7]

22. Master Meng said: "*Jen* subdues inhumanity just as water subdues fire. However, man nowadays abides by *jen*

in a manner comparable to using a cupful of water to extinguish the flames in a wagonload of fuel. When his efforts were in vain, he would claim that water cannot subdue fire. This view, moreover, greatly encourages those who are not *jen*-minded, and in the end there will be total loss of *jen*." [VIA-18]

23. Master Meng said: "Here is a man whose fourth finger is bent and cannot be stretched out. It does not cause him any pain or inconvenience in his work. And yet if there is anyone who can make it straight, he will not think the journey from Ch'in [in the north] to Ch'u [in the south] too far [to go to him], because his finger is not like that of other men.

"When a man's finger is not like that of other people, he feels dissatisfied. But when his mind is not like that of other people, he does not feel dissatisfaction. This is called ignorance of the relative importance of things." [VIA-12]

24. Master Meng said: "In regard to the trees *t'ung* and *tzu*, which may be grasped either with both hands or with one, anyone who wishes to cultivate them knows how to nourish them. But in regard to his own person, man does not know how to nourish it. Does this mean that the love for his own person is less than that for the trees *t'ung* and *tzu?* This shows indeed want of thought!" [VIA-13]

25. Master Meng said: "There is no part of his own person which a man does not love; because he loves all, he must nourish all. There is not an inch of skin which he does not love, and so there is not an inch of skin which he does not nourish. As to whether [his way of nourishing] be good or not, who can tell but the man himself? Some parts of the body are superior, and some inferior; some parts of the body are great, and some small. One must not injure the great for the small; nor must one injure the superior for the inferior. He who nourishes that part of himself which is small becomes a small man, and he who nourishes that of himself which is great becomes a great man.

"Here is a gardener, who neglects [the valuable trees] *wu* and *chia,* and cultivates the worthless wild date trees; he is indeed a poor gardener. Likewise, here is a man who nourishes one of his fingers and neglects his shoulder and back, without knowing [their relative importance]; he is indeed like a hurried wolf.

"A man who only eats and drinks is condemned by others, because he nourishes what is small to the neglect of what is great. If a man, fond of eating and drinking, neglects nothing else, his mouth and belly will mean more to him than an inch of skin." [VIA-14]

26. Master Meng said: "The *chün-tzu* differs from other men in the attitude of his heart. The *chün-tzu* in his heart upholds *jen* and *li. Jen* is the love due to men. *Li* is the respect due to men. He who loves men will certainly be loved by men. He who respects men will certainly be respected by men.

"Here is a man who treats me improperly and unreasonably. As a *chün-tzu* I turn inward to examine myself: 'I must have been devoid of *jen;* I must have been devoid of *li;* otherwise, how should this have happened to me?'

"I examine myself and I abide by *jen;* I examine myself, and I abide by *li.* If the man still treats me improperly and unreasonably, then as a *chün-tzu* I turn inward to examine myself: 'I must have been devoid of loyalty.' I examine myself, and I abide by *chung.* But if the man still treats me improperly and unreasonably, then as a *chün-tzu,* I would say: 'This is a man utterly wanting in reason! When he conducts himself in this way, what is there to distinguish him from the birds and beasts? Why should I bother myself with birds and beasts?'

"Therefore, the *chün-tzu* has a life-long anxiety but not one morning's trouble. What is worrying him is this: 'Shun was a man, and so am I. But Shun became a model to the world, and [his conduct] was transmitted to later ages, while I am no better than a villager. Indeed, this is a matter for [one's] anxiety.' In what way may he relieve his anxiety? The only way is to be like Shun.

"There is no trouble for the *chün-tzu* to be worried about. He does nothing contrary to *jen;* he does nothing contrary to *li.* Should there be one morning's trouble, the *chün-tzu* is never worried about it." [IVB-28]

27. Master Meng said: "All things are complete within us. There is no greater delight than to find sincerity when one turns inward to examine oneself. If one endeavors one's utmost to abide by *shü* [altruism], one is close to *jen.*" [VIIA-4]

28. Master Meng said: "To nourish the heart, there is no better way than to make the desires few. When a man's desires are few, it is seldom that he loses his heart. On the other hand, when a man's desires are many, it is seldom that he keeps his heart." [VIIB-35]

29. Tsao Chiao asked: "Is it true that all men may be Yao and Shun [sage-kings of antiquity]?" Master Meng said: "It

is true." Tsao Chiao said: "I have heard that King Wen was ten feet tall and T'ang nine feet tall. Now I am nine feet, four inches, in height, and all I have done is but to eat grains. What am I to do to be like Yao and Shun?"

Master Meng said: "What has one's height to do with the matter? All lies in one's own efforts. Here is a man whose strength is not enough to carry a duckling; he is considered a man of no strength. But now he says that he is capable of lifting a weight of three thousand catties; he is considered a man of strength. Therefore, a man who can lift the weight which Wu Huo [an ancient noted for strength] lifted is merely another Wu Huo. Why should men be anxious about lacking ability? They just will not do the thing.

"To walk slowly and keep behind the elders is to conform to the duty of a younger; to walk hurriedly and keep ahead of the elders is to act contrary to the proper conduct of a younger. Now is this impossible for a man to walk slowly? No, he just does not do it. The *Tao* of Yao and Shun is simply filial piety and fraternal love. If you wear Yao's clothes, speak Yao's words, and do Yao's deeds, then you too will be a Yao—that is all! On the other hand, if you wear Chieh [the tyrant]'s clothes, speak Chieh's words, and do Chieh's deeds, then you too will be a Chieh—that is all!"

Tsao Chiao said: "I am going to have an interview with the prince of Tsou. If he can provide me with lodging here, I should like to remain and receive your instruction."

Master Meng answered: "The *Tao* is like a great road, and it is not difficult to recognize. The trouble with most men is that they do not seek it. You just go home and search for it; then you will find many teachers." [vɪʙ-2]

30. Ch'u Tzu said: "Master, the king sent men secretly to watch to see if you are really different from other men." Master Meng said: "How should I be different from other men? Even Yao and Shun were just the same as other men." [ɪvʙ-32]

31. Master Meng said: " 'Only when one seeks something one finds it, and only if one neglects something will one lose it'; this is true only if seeking leads to obtaining and that which is sought is within the man himself.

" 'Although one seeks according to *Tao,* [yet] one's obtaining still depends on Fate'; this applies when seeking is of no use to obtaining and that which is sought is not within the man himself." [vɪɪA-3]

Part Two: The Political and Economic Measures

Like Confucius, Mencius was concerned with achieving good government, or, as he called it, "[humane] *jen*-government." True to the Confucian tradition, Mencius maintained that good government depends not upon brute force but on the good example of the ruler. Mencius exalted government of the *wang* [king] who "upholds *jen* through virtuous conduct" and deprecated that of the *pa* [feudal leader] who "employs force under a cloak of *jen*." Reacting to the chaotic world, he deduced his theory of government from his general doctrine that human nature is good, and growing out of his concept of "*jen*-government" was his recognition of the importance of the role of the people in the government. He emphasized that the people are not only the root but also the final judge of government.

Mencius also granted the "Mandate of Heaven" doctrine found in the *Shu* [History] that the people have the right to depose a wicked king. It is worth mentioning that Mencius's theory of government antedates John Locke's theories about the consent of the governed and right of revolution by about two thousand years.

More specifically, the way of good government, as taught by Mencius, consisted, first, in enriching the people generally and improving their over-all welfare by means of reforms such as land tenure, reduction of taxes, and what might be called "old-age pensions" and, secondly, in educating the people in personal cultivation, in social order, and in national loyalty. These ideal policies will be noted in the following passages.

◈

Chapter III. Jen-Government

32. Master Meng went to see King Hui of Liang. The King said: "Sir, since you have not considered a thousand *li* too far to come here, may I ask what advice you will give to profit my kingdom?" Master Meng replied: "Why must you speak of profit? What I have to offer are *jen* [humanity] and *yi* [righteousness], and nothing else. If the sovereign says, 'What will profit my kingdom?' the chief ministers will say, 'What will profit our ministers?' and the inferior officials and the common people will say, 'What will profit our-

selves?' Then high and low will fight one another for profit, and the kingdom will be in danger. In the kingdom of ten thousand chariots, the murderer of its sovereign shall be the chief of the family of a thousand chariots. In the kingdom of a thousand chariots, the murderer of its sovereign shall be the chief of the family of a hundred chariots. To have a thousand [chariots] in [a kingdom of] ten thousand, or to have a hundred [chariots] in [a kingdom of] a thousand, is by no means a small allotment, but if [righteousness] be placed last and profit be placed first, [these] chiefs will not be satisfied unless they deprive others of their possessions. There never has been a man upholding *jen* who deserted his parents; nor has there been a man upholding *yi* who neglected his sovereign. Let Your Majesty speak of humanity and righteousness and of nothing else. Why must you speak of profit?" [IA-1]

33. King Hui of Liang said: "I should like very much to receive your instruction." Master Meng replied: "Is killing a man with a club any different from killing him with a sword?" The King said: "No, there is no difference."

"Is killing him with a sword any different from killing him by misrule?" "No, there is no difference," was the reply. Then Master Meng said: "In your kitchen there is fat meat; in your stables there are fat horses; but the people look hungry, and starved bodies lie along the countryside. This incites beasts to devour men. Men hate even beasts that devour one another. If a prince, being the parent of his [people] cannot govern without inciting beasts to devour men, wherein is he the parent of his people?

"Chung-ni [Master K'ung] said: 'May the man who first made wooden images to bury with the dead have been without posterity!' This is because that man used the images of men. So what will be said of a prince who causes his people to die of hunger?" [IA-4]

34. King Hui of Liang said: "Sir, as you know, there was not in the world a stronger state than Tsin.[1] But in my time we were defeated by Ch'i on the east, and then my eldest son was killed; on the west we lost seven hundred *li* of territory to Ch'in; and on the south we suffered disgrace at the hands of Ch'u. I am ashamed of myself for all this, and wish on the account of the dead to wipe out this [humiliation]. What course should I pursue?"

Master Meng replied: "With a territory of one hundred *li*

1. In the period of Warring States, Tsin was divided into three states—Wei (also known as Liang), Chao, and Han.

one can still assume 'kingly sway' [*wang*]. If Your Majesty
will indeed practice '*jen* government,' abating severe punishment, lightening taxes and levies, causing the farms to be
attended with care and industry, and enabling the strong-
bodied in their leisure days to cultivate their filial piety,
fraternal love, loyalty, and sincerity, so that at home they
will serve their fathers and elder brothers and abroad their
elders and superiors—[under conditions such as these] your
people can be employed with wooden staffs to oppose the
strong nail and sharp weapons of the troops of Ch'in and
Ch'u. For those rulers [of Ch'in and Ch'u] encroach upon
their people's time, so that they cannot attend to the farming
to support their parents. As a consequence, their parents
suffer from cold and hunger; brothers, wives, and children
are separated and scattered abroad. Those rulers drive their
people into distress and suffering. If Your Majesty go to
punish them, who will resist you? Here is the saying: 'The
jen-hearted man has no enemies.' I beg your Majesty not to
doubt my words." [IA-5]

35. Master Meng said: "It was by *jen* that the Three Dynasties won the world, and by want of *jen* that they lost it.
It is by the same reason that states decay and flourish, preserve and perish. If the emperor is devoid of *jen*, he cannot
safeguard the world. If a feudal prince is devoid of *jen*, he
cannot safeguard his kingdom. If a minister is devoid of *jen*,
he cannot safeguard his ancestral temple. If a scholar or
common man is devoid of *jen*, he cannot safeguard his four
limbs. Now people hate death and yet delight in want of *jen*
—this is as if one hates to be drunk and yet obliges oneself
to drink wine." [IVA-3]

36. Master Meng said: "If the sovereign is *jen*-hearted, all
will be *jen*-hearted. If the sovereign is righteous, all will be
righteous." [IVB-5]

37. Master Meng said: "If one subdues men by one's
goodness, one will not be able to subdue them. If one nourishes men by one's goodness, one will be able to subdue the
whole world. Never has one become a king without winning
the heart of the world." [IVB-16]

38. Master Meng said: "There are cases where a man devoid of *jen* has won a state, but there is not a single case
where a man devoid of *jen* has ever won the world." [VIIB-13]

39. Master Meng said: "One who employs force under a
cloak of *jen* is the *pa* [feudal lord]. To be a *pa* one must have
a large state. On the other hand, one who upholds *jen* with

virtuous conduct is the *wang* [true king]. To be a *wang* one need not have a large state. T'ang [founder of the Shang dynasty] had only a territory of seventy *li*, and King Wen [founder of the Chou dynasty] only a hundred. When men are subdued by force, they do not submit in heart; they submit because they cannot resist. When men are won by virtue, they are pleased in their hearts and their submission is sincere, just as the seventy disciples were submissive to Master K'ung. This is what is meant in the *Shih* [Ode]:

> From the west, from the east,
> From the south, from the north,
> None thought of not submitting." [IIA-3]

40. Master Meng said: "Under the rule of the *pa*, the people look cheerful; under the rule of the *wang*, the people show deep contentment. When he puts them to death, they show no resentment. When he benefits them, they never think of his merit. From day to day they make progress toward goodness, without knowing who makes them progress. Wherever the Chun-Tzu [i.e., prince] conducts himself, he transforms [the people]; whatever he preserves [in his heart], is divine. His influence, exerting far and wide, can be comparable to that of Heaven and Earth. How can it be said that he benefits the people but slightly?" [VIIA-13]

41. Sung K'eng was on his way to Ch'u when Master Meng met him at Shih-chiu. Master Meng asked: "Sir, where are you going?" Sung K'eng replied: "I have heard that there will be war between Ch'in and Ch'u. I am going to see the king of Ch'u and persuade him to stop it. If he is not pleased with me, I shall go to see the king of Ch'in and persuade him to stop it. Of the two kings, I shall certainly succeed with one."

Master Meng said: "I do not venture to ask about the details of your plan, but I should like to hear its general scope. How are you going to persuade them?" Sung K'eng replied: "I will tell them that they will not be profited by fighting." Master Meng said: "Sir, your purpose is grand, but your reasoning is not good. If you persuade the kings of Ch'in and Ch'u with profit, and if those kings are pleased with the consideration of profit to recall their armies, then all the officers and soldiers will delight in the cessation of war and take pleasure in the pursuit of profit. Ministers will serve their sovereign for the consideration of profit; sons will serve their fathers for the consideration of profit; and younger brothers will serve their elder brothers for the consideration of profit; in the end, sovereign and minister, father and son, younger brother and elder will all abandon *jen* and *yi* and only think of profit in their dealings with one another. Under conditions such as these, there has never been a state without ruin.

"On the other hand, if you persuade the kings of Ch'in and Ch'u with *jen* and *yi*, and if those kings are pleased with them and recall their armies, then all the officers and soldiers will delight in the cessation of war and take pleasure in *jen* and *yi*. Ministers will serve their sovereign for them; sons will serve their fathers for them; and younger brothers will serve their elder brothers for them. In the end, sovereign and minister, father and son, younger brother and elder will all abandon the thought of profit and cherish *jen* and *yi* in their dealings with one another. Under conditions such as these, there has never been a state which did not rise to be a true king [*wang*]. Why must you speak of profit?" [vɪʙ-4]

42. Master Meng said: "Let the people be employed to secure their ease and comfort, and they will not complain, even though they be labored. Let those [criminals] be put to death to preserve lives [of other people], and they will not resent him who puts them to death, even though they die." [vɪɪᴀ-12]

43. Master Meng said: "When the *Tao* prevails in the world, the less virtuous submit to the more virtuous, and the less worthy to the more worthy. When the *Tao* fails to prevail in the world, the small submit to the great and the weak to the strong. Both these cases are ordained by Heaven. Those who act in accord with Heaven survive, and those who act contrary to Heaven perish.

"Duke Ching of Ch'i once said: 'Not to be able to command others, and yet to refuse to receive commands of others is to cut one's self off from others.' So in tears he gave his daughter to be married to the prince of Wu.

"Now the small states follow the large states, and yet are ashamed to receive their commands. This is like a pupil's being ashamed to receive the instructions of his teacher. If a prince is ashamed to receive commands, the best way is to follow King Wen. Let one follow King Wen, and in five years, if his state is large, or in seven years, if his state is small, he will be sure to rule the whole world. It is said in the *Shih* [Odes]:

The descendants of Shang
Are in number more than one hundred thousand;
But Heaven has passed its mandate,
So they are submissive to Chou.
They are submissive to Chou,
Because Heaven's mandate is irrevocable;
Yin's [i.e., Shang] officers, being admirable
    and alert,
Pour libations and assist at Chou's capital.

Master K'ung said: 'The *jen*-hearted man cannot be resisted by the multitude.' Thus if the sovereign of a state is fond of *jen,* he has no enemies in the world. Now the sovereigns of states wish to have no enemies in the world, but they refuse to uphold humanity. This is like a man grasping a heated substance and not first wetting the hand. It is said in the *Shih* [Odes]:

Who can grasp a heated substance,
Without first wetting the hands?" [IVA-7]

44. Master Meng went to see King Hsiang of Liang. On coming out [after the interview], he said to somebody: "When I looked at him from a distance, he did not appear to me like a sovereign, and when I drew near to him, I saw nothing in him to command awe and respect. Suddenly he asked me, 'How may the world be at peace?' I replied, 'When there is unity, there will be peace.' 'But who can unify the world?' I replied, 'He who does not delight in killing men can unify it.' 'Who will follow him?' I replied, 'All the people of the world will follow him. Does Your Majesty know the way of growing grain? During the seventh and eighth moons when there is drought, the plants wither. Then dense clouds collect in the heavens, and torrents of rain begin to pour down, so that the withering plants erect themselves. Such is the case; who can repress the revival of the plants? Now among the 'shepherds of men' [i.e., rulers] throughout the world, there is none who does not delight in killing men. If there were one who did not delight in killing men, all the people in the world would look up to him with outstretched necks. Such being the case, the people would flock to him as water flows downward. Who will be able to repress such a rush of the multitude?" [IA-6]

Chapter IV. The Policies of Jen-Government

1. POLITICAL ECONOMY

45. King Hui of Liang said: "I have exerted my heart to the utmost for the welfare of my kingdom. [For instance,] when there was famine in Ho-ney, I removed its inhabitants to Ho-t'ung and transferred grain to Ho-ney. When there was famine in Ho-t'ung, I took the same relief. On examining the government of the neighboring states, I find no sovereign who employs his heart as I do. But the people of the neighboring states do not decrease, nor do my people increase. Why is this so?" Master Meng replied: "Your Majesty is fond of war, and let me take an illustration from war. Suppose that after the drums have beaten, and swords have been crossed, our soldiers throw off their armor, trail their weapons behind them, and flee, some a hundred paces and others fifty paces; what would you say, if the men who ran only fifty paces laughed at those who ran a hundred paces?"

The king said: "They should not do so; they also flee, though not a hundred paces."

Master Meng said: "Since Your Majesty knows this, you must not expect to have more people than your neighboring states.

"If the seasons for farming are not interfered with, there will be more grains than can be consumed. If close-meshed nets are not allowed in the pools and lakes, there will be more fish and turtles than can be consumed. If the axes and hatchets are brought to the forest only at the proper time, there will be more timber than can be used. When the people have more grain, fish, and turtles than they can eat, and more timber than they can use, they will be able to feed the living and bury the dead without any undue worry. To ensure this for his people marks the beginning of the 'kingly sway' [wang tao].

"Let the homesteads of five mu be planted with mulberry, and all persons over fifty may have silk to wear. Let proper seasons be not neglected in the breeding of poultry, pigs, dogs, and swine, and all persons over seventy may have meat to eat. Let a farm of a hundred mu not be of its labor at the time proper for its farming, and a family of several mouths will stave off the pangs of hunger. Let attention be paid to teaching in schools, with special regard to filial piety and fraternal reverence, and gray-haired men will not be seen on the roads bearing heavy loads. No ruler under whom the aged have silk to wear and meat to eat, and the common people suffer neither from hunger nor cold, has ever failed to be a [true] king [of the whole world].

"Now dogs and swine eat the food of men, and you know not how to stop the waste. On the roads people are starving to death, and you know not how to relieve them out of your stores. When people die, you say: 'It is not my fault; it is due to the bad year.' This is a plea no better than if you stabbed a man to death and then said: 'It was not I; it was the knife.' Do not lay the blame on the year, O King, and you will find the people of the whole world flocking to you." [IA-3]

46. King Hsüan of Ch'i said: ". . . I am stupid, and I cannot advance to this. I should like you, my Master, to advise and enlighten me with your instruction. Though I am not intelligent, I will try to do my best."

Master Meng said: "Only the true scholar is capable of maintaining, without certain means of livelihood, a steadfast heart. As for the people, they cannot maintain a steadfast heart when they have no certain means of livelihood. Without a steadfast heart, they are apt to abandon themselves to all manner of depravity. If the sovereign does nothing until they are involved in crime and then metes out punishment, this serves only to entrap the people. How can a *jen*-hearted ruler permit such a thing as entrapping the people under his government?

"Therefore, when an enlightened ruler regulates the livelihood of the people, [he] makes sure that they will have enough to serve their parents, on the one hand, and to support their wives and children, on the other. In good years they all may have abundant food, and in bad years they will not die of starvation. Thus he urges them on toward goodness, and the people will follow him readily. But now the livelihood of the people is so regulated that they do not have enough to serve their parents, on the one hand, or to support their wives and children, on the other. Even in good years they must toil all the year round, and in bad years they cannot escape death. Under such cicumstances, they are only anxiously trying to save themselves from death; what leisure have they to cultivate *li* and *yi*? If Your Majesty wishes to practice *jen* government, why not reverse your present policy and turn to what is fundamental? . . ." [IA-7, para. 19-23]

47. Duke Wen of T'eng asked about the way of governing

a kingdom. Master Meng replied: "The farming of the people must not be neglected. It is said in the *Shih* [Odes]:

> In the morning go and gather the grass,
> And at night make ropes;
> Make haste to repair the roofs,
> And you shall have time to sow the grain.

The way of [governing] the people is thus:

"[First] if they have a certain means of livelihood, they will maintain a steadfast heart. If they have no certain means of livelihood, they cannot maintain a steadfast heart. Without a steadfast heart, they are apt to abandon themselves to all manner of depravity. If the sovereign does nothing till they are involved in crime and then metes out punishment, this serves only to entrap the people. How can a *jen*-hearted ruler permit such a thing as entrapping the people under his government?

"Therefore, the good sovereign upholds reverence and temperance and shows respectful politeness to his subordinates. He takes from the people only in accordance with regulated limits.

"Yang Hu once said: 'One who seeks to be rich is seldom *jen*-hearted; one who wishes to be *jen*-hearted is seldom rich.'

"Under the Hsia tribute was paid on the fifty-*mu* allotment; under the Yin, mutual aid was rendered on the seventy-*mu* allotment; under the Chou, share was assessed on the hundred-*mu* allotment. In fact, in every case, the actual amount was one-tenth [of the produce]. The share system [of Chou] means mutual division, while the aid system [of Yin] means mutual dependence.

"Lung Tzu once said: 'In the matter of land regulation, there is no better system than that of mutual aid; nor is there a system worse than that of tribute. By the tribute system, the regular amount was fixed by taking the average for several years. As a result, in good years the grain is abundant and the people can afford to pay more, without being oppressed, but only the fixed amount can be taken. Whereas in bad years, the produce is not enough to repay the manuring, but the fixed amount must be taken. The sovereign, as a parent to the people, causes them to toil hard all the year round, and yet they are not able to feed their parents. Then they proceed to borrow to make up the deficiency, with the result that the old people and children are found dying in the ditches and canals; wherein is he a parent to his people?'

"The system of hereditary pension [in connection with the produce of the public lands] has been in use in T'eng. It is said in the *Shih* [Odes]:

> May the rain fall on our public field,
> And then upon our private fields.

Only under the system of mutual aid, is there a public field, and from this passage it may be said that even in the Chou dynasty, the mutual-aid system still existed.

"[Next,] establish *hsiang, hsü, hsüeh,* and *hsiao* for the instruction of the people. The *hsiang* is to nourish, the *hsiao* is to teach, and the *hsü* is for archery. The Hsia dynasty used the name *hsiao,* the Yin dynasty the name *hsü,* and the Chou dynasty the name *hsiang.* The name *hsüeh* has been common to all the three dynasties. All these institutions serve to illustrate the human relationships. When these human relationships are illustrated by those of the ruling class, kindly feeling will prevail among the common people. Should a real king arise, he will certainly come to take you as a model, and thus you will be a true king's teacher. It is said in the *Shih:*

> Although Chou is an old state,
> Its mandate is new.

This is said in reference to King Wen. If you practice these things with vigor you will make new your kingdom."

[The Duke afterwards] sent Pi Chan to ask about the well-field land system.[1] Master Meng said: "Now your prince wishes to practice *jen* government, so he appoints you to carry it out. You will certainly do your best. The first thing toward *jen* government must be land division and demarcation. If land division and demarcation are not defined clearly, then the well-field farms are not equally distributed [among the farmers] or grain for emoluments is not equitably appor-

---

1. This is known as the ***ching***-*tien* system, a form of cooperative agriculture, inherited from earlier times, which prevailed during the early part of the Chou dynasty. ***Ching*** means "well," and *tien* means "field." If the ***ching*** is put within a square, it will form a field divided into nine equal squares. The central lot is the public field, being cultivated jointly by the eight households.

ching   *tien*   *ching* within square

tioned [among the ministers]. For this reason, oppressive rulers and corrupt ministers are sure to neglect land division and demarcation. When lands are clearly divided and demarcated, the distribution of land and regulation of emolument can be easily determined.

"Although T'eng is a small state, yet there must be those who are *chün-tzu*, those who are countrymen. Without the former, there would be none to rule the countrymen; without the latter, there would be none to feed the *chün-tzu*.

"In the outlying districts let the land tax be fixed at one part in nine to be paid on the system of mutual aid, while in metropolitan areas let it be one-tenth [of produce] to be paid by the people for themselves. All officers, from the chief ministers down, are each allotted an extra sacrificial land, consisting of fifty *mu*. All extra-quota males are each given twenty-five *mu* of land. Whether in burying its dead or in removing its residence, a family shall not go beyond the district. Within the district, those whose farms belong to the same well-field unit have friendly relations to one another, help one another in keeping watch and ward, and uphold one another in sickness. Thus the people will be brought to live in affection and harmony.

"Each square *li* of land should be divided into nine plots, the whole containing nine hundred *mu*. The central plot will be the public field, and the eight households, each owning a hundred-*mu* farm, will collaborate in cultivating the public field. Not until the public field has been properly attended, may each household attend to [its] private plot. This is how the country men should be required to learn.

"The above are the main features of the system. As to its modifications and adaptation, it is up to you and your prince." [IIIA-3]

48. Tai Ying-chih said: "I am not able at present to adopt a tithe taxation, or to abolish altogether the levy of tolls and duties at the passes and in the markets. However, I will lighten both the tax and duties, and wait until next year to abolish them. What do you think of such a measure?"

Master Meng said: "Here is a man who everyday appropriates stray fowls from his neighbor. Someone says to him, 'This is not the way of a *chün-tzu*,' and he replies, 'I will reduce my appropriations, and will take only one fowl a month, and wait till next year to stop this practice altogether.'

"If you know that this is contrary to righteousness, then stop it at once; why wait till next year?" [IIIB-8]

49. Master Meng said: "Let the fields be well cultivated and tax and duties be reduced; then the people will be made rich.

"Let food be consumed in proper seasons, and things be used with propriety; then their wealth will be more than can be consumed.

"The people cannot live without water and fire. If you knock at a man's door in the evening to ask for water and fire, no one will refuse you, because water and fire are in abundance. The Sage who governs the world will make food supplies as abundant as water and fire. When food supplies are as abundant as water and fire, how can the people be other than *jen*-hearted?" [VIIA-23]

50. Master Meng said: "When Jan Ch'iu was chief minister to the Chi Family, he was not only unable to change the character of his chief, but also doubled the old grain tax. Master K'ung said: 'He is no disciple of mine. Boys, you may beat the drum and assail him.'

"From this case, [we may say that] when a sovereign failed to practice *jen* government, whoever enriched him would be rejected by Master K'ung. How quickly would those who make their sovereign strong in warfare be rejected? When they fight for territory, slaughtered men fill the fields; when they fight for a city, slaughtered men fill the city. This is what is called 'inciting the land to devour men'—a crime for which death is not enough to atone. "Therefore, those who are skillful in warfare deserve the severest punishment; next would come those who unite the feudal lords into alliances, and next should come those who open up uncultivated lands and force the people to till on them." [IV-14]

51. Master Meng said: "P'o-yi, avoiding Chow [the tyrant], lived on the coast of the North Sea. When he heard of the rise of King Wen, he was delighted and said: 'Why should I not go to him? I have heard that the chief of the west serves the old well.' T'ai-kung, avoiding Chow, lived on the coast of the East Sea. When he heard of the rise of King Wen, he was delighted and said: 'Why should I not go to him? I have heard that the chief of the west serves the old well.'

"These two old men were the greatest old men of the world. When they went to King Wen, all the fathers of the world would go to him. When all the fathers of the world went to him, to whom else could the sons go?

"If any of the princes practices the government of King

Wen, within seven years he will certainly govern the whole world." [IVA-13]

52. Master Meng said: "P'o-yi, avoiding Chow, lived on the coast of the North Sea. When he heard of the rise of King Wen, he was delighted and said: 'Why should I not go to him? I have heard that the chief of the west serves the old well.' T'ai-kung, avoiding Chow, lived on the coast of the East Sea. When he heard of the rise of King Wen, he was delighted and said: 'Why should I not go to him? I have heard that the chief of the west serves the old well.'

"When there is a sovereign in the world who serves the old well, all *jen*-hearted men will go to him.

"Let homesteads of five *mu* be planted with mulberry, along their walls, and let the women feed silkworms; thus the old may be able to wear silk. Let each family have five hens and two sows, and let the proper seasons be observed in their breeding; thus the old may be able to eat meat. Let a farm of a hundred *mu* be cultivated by the husbandmen, and thus a family of eight mouths may never go hungry.

"When we say that the chief of the west served the old well, we mean that he regulated the fields and homesteads, taught the people to plant mulberry and to raise animals, and instructed the wives and children, so as to make them nourish the old. Once beyond fifty, man cannot keep his body warm without silks; over seventy, man cannot satisfy his appetite without meat. Man lacking in warmth or meat supplies is said to suffer from cold and hunger. Among the people of King Wen, no old man suffered from cold and hunger. This is what we mean by the expression: 'King Wen serves the old well.' " [VIIA-22]

53. Master Meng said: "There are levies on cloth and silk, on grain, and on manual labor. The sovereign should employ but one of these at a time and defer the other two. If he employs two of them at a time, the people will die of hunger. If he employs all the three at the same time, then fathers and sons will be separated." [VIIB-27]

54. Master Meng said: "If the sovereign honors men of worth and employs those who are capable and fills offices with men of distinction and mark, then all scholars in the world will be pleased and wish to serve in his court.

"If in the market place he either levies a tax on houses without taxing the goods or enforces the proper regulations without levying a tax, then all the merchants in the world will be pleased and wish to store their stocks in his market place.

"If at the frontier passes there is inspection but no taxation, then all the travelers in the world will be pleased and wish to travel on his roads.

"If he institutes the mutual-aid system without taxing the farmers on their produce, all the farmers in the world will be pleased and wish to till his fields.

"If he exacts no exorbitant taxes on persons or estates, all the people in the world will be pleased and wish to be his people.

"If a sovereign can truly carry out these five things, then the people of neighboring states will look up to him as to a parent. Since the birth of mankind, never has anyone succeeded in leading children to attack their parents. Thus such a sovereign will have no enemies in the world. One who has no enemies in the world is the minister of Heaven. Never has there been a sovereign with such achievement who did not attain a kingly sway [over the other states]." [IIA-5]

2. THREE TREASURES OF A SOVEREIGN

55. Master Meng said: "The treasures of a sovereign are three—territory, people, and good administration. If he treasures pearls and jades instead, calamity is sure to befall him." [VIIB-28]

56. Master Meng said: "Opportunities of time are not as important as advantages of situation, and advantages of situation are not so important as united efforts of the people. Now the people surround and attack a city with an inner wall of three *li* and an outer wall of seven *li*. They must have chosen the opportunity of time, but they are not able to take the city. This is because opportunities of time are not so important as advantages of situation.

"Now the people defend a city where the walls are high, the moats are deep, the weapons and shields strong and sharp, and the food supplies abundant. Yet they give up and abandon the city. This is because advantages of situation are not so important as the united efforts of the people.

"Therefore it is said, 'The containment of a people does not depend upon the limits of dikes and borders; nor does the security of a country depend upon the strategic defense of mountains and rivers; nor does the conquest of the world depend upon the sharpness and strength of weapons and

shields.' He who abides by the *Tao* has many supporters. On
the other hand, he who acts contrary to the *Tao* has few
supporters. He who has few supporters is even abandoned by
his own relations. But he who has many supporters is followed by the whole world. Then one who has the support
of the whole world may attack those who are abandoned by
their own relations. Therefore, the true sovereign will prefer
not to fight; but when he must fight, he is sure to win."
[IIB-1]

57. Master Meng said: "If confidence is not placed on men
of *jen* and worth, a state will become empty and void. If the
rules of *li* [propriety] and *yi* [righteousness] are not observed, distinctions between the high and the low will become confused. If the administration is not well conducted,
wealth will not be sufficient for the expenditure." [VIIB-12]

58. Master Meng said: "It is not appropriate to criticize
the officers, or to blame the administration. It is only the
great man who can rectify what is wrong in the sovereign's
heart. Let the sovereign be *jen*-hearted, and all men under
him will be *jen*-hearted. Let the sovereign be righteous, and
all men under him will be righteous. Let the sovereign be
rectified, and all men under him will be rectified. Once the
sovereign himself is rectified, the state will be settled."
[IVA-20]

59. Master Meng said: "Even if one has the vision of Li
Lou and the skill of Kung-shu Tzu, without the compass and
rule one cannot make squares and circles. Even if one has
the acute ear of the music master K'uang, without the six
tuning tubes one cannot determine the five notes. It is likewise with the *Tao* of Yao and Shun. Without a humane government one cannot secure peace and order in the world.
Now there are sovereigns who have *jen*-hearts and a reputation for *jen*, but the people [under them] receive no benefits
from them, nor will they leave any example to future ages,
because they fail to follow the *Tao* of the early kings. Therefore, it is said, 'Goodness alone cannot constitute good government; nor can laws alone enforce themselves.' It is said in the
Shih:

> Transgress not, forget not;
> But follow the ancient ways.

Never has there been anyone who followed the laws of the
early kings and who fell into errors.

"When the Sage has used his vision, he employs the compass, the rule, the level, and the line to make various objects square, round, level, and straight—more tools than need be used. When the Sage has used his hearing, he employs the six tuning tubes to rectify the five notes—more music than may be necessary. When the Sage has used his mind to the utmost, he practices compassionate government, so that the world will be benefited through his *jen*. Therefore, it is said, 'To build high, one must begin from the top of a hill; to dig deep, one must begin from the bottom of a river.' If in administration a sovereign does not proceed by following the *Tao* of early kings, can he be considered wise? For this reason, only he who abides by *jen* is fit to occupy high position. When one who lacks *jen* occupies a high position, his evils will spread among the people.

"[For when the *Tao* of early kings is neglected,] the sovereign will have no way to guide his administration, and his ministers will have no laws to discharge their duties. When the officers in the court do not believe in the *Tao* [of early kings], the workers in general will not abide by regulations. As a consequence, the men of the ruling class violate righteousness, and the common people violate prohibitions. In such a condition, it would be good luck if a state survives. Therefore, it is said, 'It is not weak city walls or a scarcity of war weapons, that constitute the calamity of a state; it is not fallow farms and fields, or dispersed goods and wealth, that constitute the harm of a state.' When those of the ruling class do not observe propriety and the common people do not receive instructions, the evil men will rise and overrun the country, and the state will perish in no time.

"It is said in the *Shih:*

> Heaven now causes commotion;
> Don't be so much at chattering!

'Chattering'—that is, 'garrulous.' When a man serves his sovereign without *yi* and conducts himself without regard to *li* [propriety], and when in his words, he disapproves the *Tao* of early kings, he is said to be garrulous. Therefore, we may say: 'To urge one's sovereign to do what is difficult is to show him respect; to present what is good and repress what is evil is to show him reverence; but to say "My sovereign is incapable" is to do him harm.' " [IVA-1]

60. Master Meng said: "The compass and rule produce perfect circles and squares. The Sage represents the apogee

of the human relationships. As a sovereign, one should follow
the *Tao* of the sovereign. As a minister, one should follow
the *Tao* of the minister. Both need only to take Yao and Shun
as their models. If a minister does not serve his sovereign as
Shun served Yao, he does not respect his sovereign. If a sovereign does not treat his people as Yao treated his, he does
harm to the people. Master K'ung once said: 'There are but
two ways—*jen* and want of *jen*.' When a sovereign oppresses
his people, in the extreme case, he will himself be slain and
his state will perish; even in the less extreme case, he will endanger his own life and his state will be weakened. Moreover,
he will be styled 'Yu' [*the dark*] or 'Li' [*the cruel*]. Even
though he may have filial sons and affectionate grandsons, this
hideous designation will stand unchanged for a hundred generations. This is what is meant in the *Shih:*

> The example of Yin was not remote;
> It was in the time of Hsia lord!" [IVA-2]

61. Kung-sun Ch'o asked: "Master, if you were given the
power of government in Ch'i, could you promise yourself to
do anew what Kuan Chung and Yin Tzu had accomplished?"
Master Meng said: "You are indeed a man of Ch'i. All you
know about is Kuan Chung and Yin Tzu. Someone once
asked Tseng Hsi, 'Sir, who is more worthy—you or [and]
Tzu Lu?' [Upon hearing this,] Tseng Hsi became embarrassed
and said, 'Even my grandfather had a feeling of awe for
him.' 'Then,' asked the other again, 'who is more worthy—
you [or] Kuan Chung?' Tseng Hsi was greatly displeased and
said, 'How dare you compare me with Kuan Chung? He had
the complete confidence of his sovereign and was in power
for such a long period, but he achieved very little for his
country. How can you compare me to him?'"

Then Master Meng concluded: "Tseng Hsi would not think
Kuan Chung worthy of emulation. Do you think that I desire to be like him?"

Kung-sun Ch'ou asked: "Kuan Chung enabled his sovereign to become the leader of the feudal lords, while Yin Tzu
made his sovereign famous throughout the world. Why do
you think that they were still unworthy of emulation?"
Master Meng said: "Enabling Ch'i to attain a kingly sway
would be as easy as turning over the hand."

"If that is so," said the other, "your disciple is very much
perplexed. Notwithstanding his great virtues and long ad-

ministration, lasting about one hundred years, King Wen at
the time of his death was still not able to win the whole world.
It was not till King Wu and the Duke of Chou continued his
work that the rule prevailed. Now you say that it is easy to
attain a kingly sway [over the other states]; is King Wen
then not worthy of emulation?"

Master Meng said: "How can King Wen be compared?
From the time of T'ang [founder of Yin (Shang) dynasty]
to Wu-ting, there had been six or seven worthy and sage
kings. The whole world had long been turned toward Yin.
After such a long regime it is difficult to induce changes. For
Wu-ting to have all feudal princes coming to his court and to
win the world, it was as easy as turning over the hand. Chow
[the last ruler of Yin] did not come long after Wu-ting, so
some of the old families, old customs, old traditions, and the
good administration of the last regime were still preserved.
Moreover, there were the Viscount of Wei, Wei Chung,
Prince Pi-kan, the Viscount of Chi, and Chiao-ko, all of them
men of worth, who mutually assisted Chow in his government. Therefore, it took a long time for him to lose the world.
In his time, every foot of land in the world was under his
rule, and every man was his subject. On the other hand, King
Wen made his beginning with a territory of only one hundred
square li; this is why there were difficulties [for him to attain
a kingly sway].

"The people of Ch'i have a saying: 'Even though man has
wisdom and intelligence, yet it is best to wait for the favorable opportunity; even though man has all the farm implements, yet it is best to wait for the farming season.' Now's
the time to attain a kingly sway! Even in their flourishing
periods, none of the Hsia, Yin, and Chou dynasties possessed
a territory of more than one thousand li, but now Ch'i embraces so much territory. Ch'i possesses so many people that
the barking dogs and crowing cocks can be heard throughout
the length and breadth of its land. There is no need to extend
its territory; nor is there need to increase its population. If
its sovereign adopts a jen-government, no one will be able
to prevent him from attaining a kingly sway over the other
states.

"Moreover, there has never been a time so devoid of a true
sovereign as at present; there has never been a time when
people suffered more from tyrannical rule. We all know that
the hungry are easily fed and the thirsty easily slaked. Master
K'ung once said: 'The spread of virtue is more rapid than the

transmission of imperial orders by stages and couriers.' So now, if *jen*-government were practiced in a country of ten thousand chariots, its people would be as pleased as men relieved from hanging by their heels. It is only in times like these that, with only half the labor of the ancients, one can achieve twice as much." [IIA-1]

62. Master Meng said to King Hsüan of Ch'i: "If Your Majesty's minister, while going on a journey to Ch'u, had entrusted his wife and children to a friend, and upon his return discovered that his wife and children had been cold and starved, what should he do to his friend?" The king said: "Cast him off!" Master Meng proceeded. "If your chief judge could not regulate the offices under him, what should be done?" "Dismiss him," was the reply. Master Meng again said: "If within the four borders of your kingdom there is no good government, what should be done?" The king looked uneasy and changed the subject. [IB-6]

63. King Hsüan of Ch'i asked: "May I hear from you the transactions of Huan of Ch'i and Wen of Tsin?" Master Meng replied: "The disciples of Chung-ni did not speak about the affairs of Huan and Wen, and therefore no records have been transmitted to posterity. Hence your servant has never heard them. If you will have me speak, I would like to talk about kingly sway."

The king said: "What virtue must I have to attain a kingly sway?" Master Meng said: "If you love and protect the people, no power will be able to prevent you from attaining it." The king said again: "Is such a ruler as I competent to love and protect the people?" "Yes," was the reply. "How do you know that I am competent?" "I heard the following story from Hu Ho: 'The king was sitting in the hall when someone leading an ox passed by its front. The king saw him and asked, 'Where is the ox going?' The man replied, 'We are going to consecrate a bell.' The king said, 'Let it go. I cannot bear its trembling and frightened looks, as if it were an innocent person on the way to death.' The man said, 'Then shall we cancel the consecration of the bell?' The king said, 'How can it be cancelled? Change it for a sheep.' I do not know whether this story is true." The king said, "It is true," and Master Meng said: "Such a heart warrants that you are capable of attaining the kingly sway. The mass of the people might suppose that Your Majesty grudged the animal, but I know surely, that Your Majesty could not bear the sight."

The king said: "Yes, there were people who thought as you

said. Though Ch'i is a small state, how should I grudge an ox? I simply could not endure its trembling and frightened looks, as if it were an innocent person on the way to death. That is why I changed it for a sheep."

Master Meng said: "Let not Your Majesty be surprised that the people should think you were grudging the animal. When you exchanged a large animal for a small one, how could they know the reason? If you pitied the innocent being led to death, what was there to choose between an ox and a sheep?" The king said with a smile: "What was really the reason in my heart for doing so? It certainly was not because I grudged its expense and changed it for a sheep. The people might have good reason to say that I grudged it."

Master Meng said: "There is no harm in what they said. Your conduct was in accord with the ways of *jen*. You saw the ox, and had not seen the sheep. The *chün-tzu*, in regard to birds and beasts, having seen them alive, cannot bear to see them die; having heard their dying cries, cannot bear to eat their flesh. Therefore, he stays away from the kitchen."

The king was pleased and said: "It is said in the *Shih:*

> Thoughts in the hearts of others,
> I am able to conjecture.

My Master, this can be applied to you. I did the thing, but when I turned inside and examined it, I could not say why I did it in my heart. Now you have spoken to my heart, and I feel deeply moved. How is it that this heart makes me competent to attain the kingly sway?"

Master Meng said: "Suppose someone said to you, 'I am strong enough to lift a load of three thousand *catties*, but I am not strong enough to pick up one feather. My sight is sharp enough to see the tip of a hair, but I cannot see a wagonload of faggots.' Would Your Majesty believe him?" "No," was the answer, and Master Meng continued: "Now, your kindness is sufficient to reach birds and beasts, but no benefits are extended to the people. Why is this so? A man fails to pick up one feather, because he does not use his strength; he fails to see a wagonload of faggots, because he does not employ his vision. A sovereign fails to love and protect his people, because he does not extend his kindness. Therefore, Your Majesty does not attain a kingly sway, because you do not do it, and not because you are not able to do it."

The king said: "What is the difference between 'not doing' and 'not able to do'?" Master Meng replied: "Suppose a man were asked to lift up the T'ai Mountain and leap over the North Sea, and he said: 'I am not able to do it'; that is a case of 'not being able.' Suppose he were asked to break off a branch for the elder, and he said: 'I am not able to do it'; that is a case of 'not doing' and not that of 'not being able.' Your Majesty's not attaining the kingly sway is not comparable to lifting up the T'ai Mountain and leaping over the North Sea; your not being able to attain the kingly sway is comparable to breaking off a branch.

"Treat as befits old age the elders in your own family, so as to extend this treatment to the elders of others; treat as befits youth the young in your own family, so as to extend this treatment to the young of others. If you follow this, the world can be made to revolve in your palm. It is said in the *Shih:*

> His example first affected his wife,
> And then reached to his brothers.
> Thereby he governed his home and the state.

These words show how one's heart must be extended to embrace all others. Thus if one extends one's kindliness to others, it will suffice to protect all within the four seas. If one does not extend this kindliness, it will not be sufficient to protect one's own wife and children. The way in which the ancients greatly surpassed other men was none other than this: Simply to extend widely what they did, so as to affect others. Now your kindliness is sufficient to reach to birds and beasts, but no benefits are extended to the people. Why is this so? By weighing, one knows what is heavy and what is light; by measuring, one knows what is long and what is short. This is true of things, and especially of the heart. I beg Your Majesty to measure it. You raise your armaments, endanger your soldiers and officers, and excite the resentment of other sovereigns. Do you find pleasure in these things?"

The king replied: "No, how should I find pleasure in these things? But I would do these things to seek what I greatly desire." Master Meng said: "May I hear from you what you greatly desire?" The king only smiled and did not speak. Then Master Meng continued: "Is it because you do not have enough rich and sweet food for your mouth? Or is it because you do not have enough fine and warm clothing for your body? Or is it because you do not have enough beautiful things to delight your eyes? Or is it because you do not have enough music and songs to please your ears? Is it because you do not have enough attendants and courtiers to wait on you? Your Majesty's ministers are quite able to provide all these things. How can Your Majesty still entertain such a desire for these things?" "No," the king said, "I do not desire these things." Master Meng added: "Then I know what Your Majesty greatly desires. You wish to extend your territory, to have Ch'in and Ch'u wait at your court, to rule the Middle Kingdom, and to submit all the barbarian tribes. To do what you are doing to [gain] what you desire is like climbing a tree to look for fish."

The king said: "Is it as bad as that?" "It is even worse," said Master Meng. "When a man climbs a tree to seek for fish, though he fails to catch fish, he suffers no subsequent calamity. But to do what you are doing to seek for what you desire, and to do it with all your heart, you will certainly meet with calamities." The king asked: "Would you mind telling about them?" Master Meng said: "Suppose that the people of Tsou were fighting with the people of Ch'u; who does Your Majesty think would win?" "The people of Ch'u would win." "Yes," said Master Meng, "the small cannot resist against the large; nor can the few contend with the many; nor can the weak fight with the strong. In the world there are now nine states, each possessing a territory of one thousand *li*. Ch'i is but one of them. When one state attempts to subdue the other eight, how would that be different from Tsou fighting with Ch'u? Let us turn to what is fundamental.

"Now if Your Majesty practices humanity in your government, you will make all the officers in the world wish to serve in your court, all the farmers in the world wish to work in your fields, all the merchants and traders wish to store their stocks in your market place, all the travelers wish to travel on your roads, and all those in the world who feel aggrieved by their sovereigns wish to come to you with their complaints. Under these conditions, who would be able to resist you?" [1A-7, para. 1-18]

64. Master Meng said: "A sovereign, abiding by *jen*, attains glory; devoid of *jen*, he brings disgrace upon himself. Now the sovereign who hates disgrace and yet acts contrary to *jen* is like one who hates damp and yet dwells on the low ground. If he hates disgrace, the best way for him is to esteem virtue and honor scholars. Let men of worth occupy posi-

tions of honor, and let men of ability hold posts of trust;
then the country will be at peace and free from troubles. The
sovereign will take advantage of such a moment to enlighten
his administration. Then even the large states will stand in
awe of him. It is said in the *Shih:*

> Before it grows cloudy and begins to rain,
> I gather the bark from mulberry trees,
> And twine it into the window and door;
> Now all ye people below,
> What blame dare ye lay on me?

Master K'ung once said: 'Did not he who wrote the ode
know the *Tao?*' If the sovereign governs his state well, who
will dare to blame him?

"But now the country is at peace and free from troubles,
and the sovereign takes advantage of the time to abandon
himself to pleasure and indolence. This is the way to seek
calamities for himself. In fact calamity and good fortune are
man's own seeking. It is said in the *Shih:*

> Forever abide by Heaven's mandate;
> May ye receive good fortunes!

On the other hand, it is said in the *Shu* [History]:

> When Heaven sends down calamities,
> Man may escape from them,
> If a man occasions calamities himself,
> He will no longer be able to live. [Ch. *Tai-Chia*]

Both passages illustrate what I said above." [IIA-4]

65. Master Meng, having an interview with King Hsüan
of Ch'i, said to him: "When you are going to build a large
mansion, you will surely ask the chief of workmen to look
for large timber. When he finds the large timber, you will be
pleased, thinking that he has done his work well. But should
the workmen cut the timber so as to make it too small, you
will be angry, thinking that they have failed in their work.
When a man is young, he occupies himself with learning;
when he reaches manhood, he wants to practice his learning.
Suppose that Your Majesty says to him, 'For the present put
aside your learning, and follow me.' What would you say of
such a request? Now suppose that you have a piece of un-

polished jade; although it may be worth thousands of taels, yet you will certainly have a jade specialist cut and polish it. But when you would come to the government of the state, you would say, 'Put aside your learning, and follow me.' How is it that you act differently from your conduct in employing a jade specialist to cut and polish the jade?" [IB-9]

66. Master Meng said: "Administration of government is not difficult; just do not offend the ruling families. One who wins the approbation of the ruling families will win the approbation of the whole state; one who wins the approbation of the whole state will win the approbation of the world. Thus one's virtue and teachings will spread far and wide until they cover all within the four seas." [IVA-6]

67. Master Meng said: "People have this common saying, 'The world, the state, and the family.' The root of the world lies in the state; the root of the state lies in the family; and the root of the family lies in the person of an individual." [IVA-5]

68. When Duke Wen of T'eng was crown prince, he, on his way to Ch'u, went by way of Sung to see Master Meng. Master Meng told him about the goodness of human nature and frequently made laudatory references to Yao and Shun. On his return from Ch'u, the crown prince again visited Master Meng. Master Meng said: "Does Your Honor still doubt my words? There is only one *Tao*. Once Cheng-chien said to Duke Ching of Ch'i: 'They are men, and I am also a man. Why should I stand in awe of them?' Yen Yuen once said: 'What a man was Shun! What a man am I! If I exert myself I can be like him.' And Kung-ming Yi once said: '[The Duke of Chou said:] "King Wen is my teacher." How should the Duke of Chou deceive me?' Now, T'eng, taking its length with its breadth, has a territory of fifty *li*, and yet it is still large enough to make a good kingdom. It is said in the *Shu* [History]:

If the medicine does not make the patient dizzy,
His disease will not be cured." [IIIA-1]

69. Pai Kwei said: "I want to levy a tax of only one twentieth. What do you think of it?" Master Meng said: "Yours is the way of *Pai* [northern barbarian tribe]. In a country of ten thousand families, is it possible to have only one potter?" Pai Kwei said: "No, there would not be enough wares to use." Master Meng said: "In the country of *Pai* five possible

grains are not grown; only the millet is produced. There are
no fortified cities, no palaces, no temples, and no sacrificial
ceremonies; there are no princes exchanging presents and
offering entertainment. There are no officers with their various subordinates. Therefore, a tax of one-twentieth is sufficient. But now we are living in the Middle Kingdom. How
can we dispense with human relationships and have no
sovereign? If with but few potters a state cannot subsist, how
much the less without the sovereign? If you exact less revenue
than Yao or Shun, you will be like a great *Pai* or a small *Pai*
[barbarian]. If you exact more, you will be like a great *Chiu*
or a small *Chiu* [tyrant]." [VIB-10]

3. THE MANDATE OF HEAVEN

70. Wang Chang asked: "Is it true that Yao gave the world
to Shun?" Master Meng said: "No. The Emperor cannot give
the world to another." "But," said Wang Chang, "Shun had
the world. Who gave it to him?" Master Meng said: "Heaven
gave it to him." The other asked: "Heaven gave it to him!
Did Heaven confer its mandate with specific instructions?"
Master Meng said: "No. Heaven does not speak, but merely
makes its will known through man's conduct and his deeds."
"How does it make its will known through man's conduct
and his deeds?" Master Meng said: "The Emperor can present a man to Heaven, but he cannot make Heaven give that
man the world. A feudal lord can present a man to the Emperor, but he cannot cause the Emperor to make that man
a feudal lord. A minister can present a man to a feudal
lord, but he cannot cause the feudal lord to make that man
a minister. Of old, Yao presented Shun to Heaven, and
Heaven accepted him. Then Yao showed Shun to the people,
and the people accepted him. Therefore, I say, 'Heaven does
not speak. It merely makes its will known through man's
conduct and his deeds.'"

Wang Chang said: "I beg to ask how he was presented to
Heaven, and Heaven accepted him; and how he was shown
to the people, and the people accepted him." Master Meng
said: "He was made to preside over the sacrifices, and all
the spirits were well pleased with them: thus Heaven accepted him. He was made to preside over the affairs of the
state. These affairs were well administered, and the people
were satisfied: thus the people accepted him. Heaven gave
him the world, and the people gave it to him. Therefore, I

say, 'The Emperor cannot give the world to another.' Shun assisted Yao for twenty-eight years. This was more than man could have done. It was Heaven. After the death of Yao, when the three years' mourning was over, Shun withdrew from the son of Yao to the south of Nan Ho. The feudal lords, however, visiting the court, went not to the son of Yao, but to Shun. Litigants went not to the son of Yao, but to Shun. Singers sang not to the son of Yao, but to Shun. Therefore, I say, 'It was Heaven.' It was after this that he went to the Middle Kingdom and occupied the Imperial Throne. If he had already occupied Yao's palace and had applied pressure on Yao's son, it would have been usurpation, and not the gift of Heaven. This is what is meant in the *Great Declarations:*

> Heaven sees as the people see;
> Heaven hears as the people hear." [VA-5]

71. King Hsüan of Ch'i asked: "Is it true that T'ang [founder of the Yin] banished Chieh [last king of the Hsia], and that King Wu [founder of the Chou] smote Chow [last king of the Yin]?" Master Meng replied: "It is so recorded." The king said: "Then may a minister put his sovereign to death?" Master Meng said: "He who acts in defiance of *jen* is a rascal; he who outrages *yi* is a knave. The man who acts as a rascal and knave is properly called a mere ruffian. I have heard about the killing of a ruffian named Chow; I have not heard of putting a sovereign to death." [IB-8]

72. Master Meng said: "Chieh and Chow lost their world, because they lost the people. They lost the people, because they lost the people's hearts. There is a way to win the world: Win the people, and the world is thereby won. There is a way to win the people: Win their hearts, and the people are thereby won. There is a way to win their hearts: Give them what they like; collect from them according to their means; do not impose excessive levies. The people turn to a *jen*-hearted sovereign as water flows downward, and as wild beasts flee to the wilderness. Accordingly, just as the otter drives the fish into the deep waters, and the hawk drives the little birds into the thickets, so Chieh and Chow drove the people to T'ang and Wu. If among the present sovereigns of the world there were one who loved *jen*, all the other princes would drive the people to him. Even though he wished not to attain the kingly sway, he could not avoid it.

But the present sovereigns who would like to attain the kingly sway are like the patient who seeks some medical herb of three years old to cure his seven years' sickness. If no accumulations are made beforehand, he will not have to the end of his life. Likewise, if the sovereigns do not devote themselves to *jen,* all their lives will be in sorrow and disgrace, and finally they will end in ruin and death. This is what is meant in the *Shih:*

> How can they do anything good?
> They will all go down into ruin." [IVA-9]

73. Master Meng said: "The people rank highest in a state, the spirits of the Land and Grain come next, and the sovereign is of the least account. Therefore, to win the people is the way to become emperor; to win the emperor is the way to become a feudal lord; to win the feudal lord is the way to become a minister. When a feudal lord offends the spirits of the Land and Grain, he will be deposed and another appointed in his place. When the sacrificial victims have been fully grown, the vessels filled with millet and clean, and offerings made at their proper seasons, and yet there has been drought or flood, then the altars for the spirits of the Land and Grain are demolished and rebuilt." [VIIB-14]

74. Master Meng said to King Hsüan of Ch'i: "If the sovereign should treat his ministers as his hands and feet, they in turn would rely on him as their bellies and hearts. But when the sovereign looks on his ministers as his dogs and horses, then they may regard him as merely one of their fellows; if the sovereign treats them as if they were grass and dirt, then they may regard him as a brigand and an enemy." The king said: "According to the rules of propriety, a minister wears mourning for his former sovereign. How should a sovereign behave so that his ministers will thus wear mourning?" Master Meng said: "When the admonitions of a minister have been followed and his advice accepted, with the result that benefits have been extended to the people, if for some reason he leaves, the sovereign sends him an escort to conduct him out of the country and, in addition, gives advance notice to the country to which he is proceeding. Only after he has been absent three years without having returned does the sovereign take back his fields and residence. These are called the three acts of propriety. When a sovereign acts thus, his former minister will wear mourning for him.

"Nowadays, however, the objections of a minister are not considered, nor is his advice followed, so no benefits are extended to the people. When for some reason he leaves, the sovereign sends an evil report to the country to which he is proceeding. On the very day of his departure, he takes back his fields and residence. This is what is called a brigand and an enemy. What mourning can be worn for a brigand and an enemy?" [IVB-3]

75. Master Meng having an interview with King Hsüan of Ch'i, said to him: "When we speak of an ancient kingdom, we do not mean that there are lofty trees in it. We mean that there are ministers who have served their sovereigns for generations. Your Majesty does not even have ministers in whom you can place confidence. Those whom you called into office yesterday are gone today without your knowing it." The king said: "How shall I know that a man has no talent so as not to employ him?" Master Meng said: "The sovereign of a state puts a man of worth into office, as a matter of necessity, so as not to let the mean overstep the noble or strangers overstep those who are closely attached. For this reason, may he not be cautious in doing so?

"When all those near you say, 'This is a man of worth, do not believe it. When all ministers say, 'This is a man of worth,' do not believe it. But if all the people of the state say, 'This is a man of worth,' then investigate this case, and if you find him worthy, employ him. When all those near you say, 'This man is incompetent,' do not listen to them. When all ministers say, 'This man is incompetent,' do not listen to them. But if all the people of the state say, 'This man is incompetent,' then investigate the case, and if you find him incompetent, send him away. When all those about you say, 'This man deserves death,' do not listen to them. When all ministers say, 'This man deserves death,' do not listen to them. But if all the people of the state say, 'This man deserves death,' then investigate the case, and if you find that the man deserves death, put him to death. Accordingly, there is a saying: 'The people of the state have put a man to death.' If you follow this policy, you will act as a parent to the people." [IB-7]

76. King Hsüan of Ch'i asked: "Is it true that the park of King Wen contained seventy square *li?*" Master Meng said: "It is so recorded." The king said: "Was it really so large as that?" Master Meng said: "The people still considered it too small." The king said: "My park contains only forty

square *li*, but the people consider it too large. Why is it so?"
Master Meng said: "The park of King Wen contained seventy
square *li*, but the grass-cutters and fuel-gatherers went there;
the hunters of pheasants and hares went there. Thus he
shared his park with the people, and wasn't it reasonable
that they considered it small? When I first reached your
borders, I inquired about the important prohibitions in your
realm, and only then did I venture to enter. I heard that
close to the border there was a park of forty square *li* and
that whoever killed a hare there would be punished as if he
had killed a man. Thus those forty square *li* constitute a
pitfall within your realm. Is it not reasonable that your people
consider it large?" [1B-2]

77. King Hsüan of Ch'i asked: "Is there any proper way
of maintaining intercourse with neighboring states?" Master
Meng replied: "Yes, there is. Only a sovereign abiding by
jen can serve a small state with a large state, as was the case
of T'ang serving Ko and King Wen serving Kun-yi. Only a
sovereign being possessed of wisdom can serve a large state
with a small state, as was the case of King T'ai serving Hsün-yu
and Kou-chien serving Wu. He who with a large state serves
a small one conforms to Heaven. He who with a small state
serves a large one stands in awe of Heaven. He who conforms
to Heaven preserves the world, while he who stands in awe
of Heaven preserves his own state. It is said in the *Shih:*

> As he fears Heaven's might,
> He preserves its mandate!"

The king said: "Great indeed are your words! But I have
a weakness; I am fond of bravery." Master Meng replied: "I
beg Your Majesty not to be petty in your bravery. Here is
a man who brandishes his sword and with fierce looks, said,
'How dare he withstand me?'—this is the bravery of a common man, a fit [to] match for a single foe. I beg Your Majesty
to enlarge it. It is said in the *Shih:*

> The king blazed with anger,
> So he marshalled his troops
> And marched to stop invaders,
> To enhance the blessings of Chou,
> To respond to the whole world.

This was the bravery of King Wen. King Wen, in one burst
of his anger, pacified the people of the world. It is said in the
Shu [History]:

Heaven has sent among the people below
Some to be their sovereigns,
Some to be their teachers.
Only those who assist Heaven's Being
Receive His blessings.
Throughout the four corners of the world
Whoever are offenders,
Whoever are innocent,
I alone am to deal with them.
How dare one offend Heaven's will?

There was one man who pursued a violent course in the world, and King Wu was ashamed of him. This was the bravery of King Wu. He, too, through one display of anger, pacified the people of the world. Now if Your Majesty also, with one burst of anger, pacifies the people of the world, the people are afraid lest Your Majesty might renounce bravery."
[IB-3]

78. King Hsüan of Ch'i had an interview with Master Meng in the Snow Palace and said to him: "Do men of worth also find pleasure in these things?" Master Meng replied: "Yes, they do. People, however, will condemn their superiors if they cannot enjoy themselves. It is wrong for the people to condemn their superiors when they cannot enjoy themselves, but it is also wrong for the sovereigns not to share enjoyment with the people. When the sovereign rejoices in the joy of his people, they also rejoice in his joy. When he grieves at the sorrow of his people, they also grieve at his sorrow. Let him share enjoyments with the world; let him share sorrows with the world; such a sovereign has never failed to attain imperial sway.

"Formerly the Duke Ching of Ch'i asked Yen Tzu: 'I would like to make a trip of inspection to Mounts Chuan-fu and Chao-wu, and then to turn southward along the seacoast till I reach Lang-yeh. How should I conduct myself so as to make my trip worthy to be compared with the trips made by early kings?' Yen Tzu replied: 'This is a good question! When the emperor visited the feudal lords, it was called a tour of inspection; that is, he inspected the states under their rule. When the feudal lords attended the court of the emperor, it was called a report of duties; that is, they reported the administration of their governments. In no case has a trip been made without a purpose. In the spring, they inspected the farming, so as to supply deficiency; in the autumn, they inspected the harvest, so as to supply insufficiency. It is said in a proverb of the Hsia dynasty:

> If our king does not make his trip,
> How are we to have any rest?
> If our king does not take his tour,
> How are we to have any help?

Just one trip or one tour was regarded as an example to the feudal lords. Today, however, things are different. Armies march [in attendance on the sovereign's trip] and consume stores of provisions. The hungry are deprived of food; the toilers are given no rest. With eyes askance and muttering curses, the people turn to hatred. But imperial orders are violated; the people are oppressed; food and drink are wasted like water. The sovereigns yield themselves to wickedness, or they give themselves to indulgence; they are wild and they are utterly lost. These things are sorrows for the feudal lords. To lose oneself in the down-current is what I call yielding to wickedness; to fling oneself into the up-current is what I call giving oneself to indulgence. To hunt without satiety is what I call being wild; to indulge in wine without satiety is what I call being lost. The kings of old found no pleasures in wickedness and indulgence, and their conduct was free from being wild and lost. It is up to Your Honor to make the choice in the course of action.'

  "Duke Ching was pleased and issued a proclamation to the whole country. Then he moved and took up his abode in the borders. He opened his granaries to supply the wants of the people. He sent for the grand music master and said to him: 'Compose for me music about a prince and his minister pleased with each other.' These were the pieces that we know as *chih-shao* and *chüeh-shao*, in which the poem says:

> What fault is it,
> To restrain the sovereign?

To restrain is in fact to love the sovereign." [1B-4]

  79. King Hsüan of Ch'i asked: "The people all wish to demolish the Brilliant Hall. Shall I do so or not?" Master Meng replied: "The Brilliant Hall is the abode of a real king. If Your Majesty wishes to carry out the rule of such a king, then do not demolish it." The king said: "May I hear from you about the kingly rule?" Master Meng said: "Form-

erly, when King Wen governed in Ch'i, farmers cultivated one-ninth of land [for the government in lieu of tax]; officials received hereditary pensions; at passes and in the markets, persons were inspected but goods were not taxed; in the ponds and at the weirs, fishing was not prohibited; the wives and children of the guilty were not punished along with them. There were those who were old and wifeless, or widowers, those who were old and husbandless, or widows, those who were old and childless, or solitaries, and those who were young and fatherless, or orphans. These are the four classes of destitute people of the world; they have no relations to whom they can turn for help. While King Wen was governing and upholding *jen*, he attended first to these four classes of people. It is said in the *Shih:*

> It is well with the rich,
> But alas! for those helpless and destitute!"

The king said: "Good indeed are your words!" Master Meng said: "If Your Majesty thinks them good, why do you not practice them?" The king said: "I have a weakness; I am fond of wealth." Master Meng said: "Formerly, Kung Liu was fond of wealth, as it is said in the *Shih:*

> He collected; he stored;
> Then he tied up dried provisions,
> Into bags and into sacks.
> He gathered people together and glorified the state;
> When bows and arrows were displayed,
> With shields, spears, and axes,
> He began the march.

It was only when those at home had collected and stored and those in traveling had tied up dried provisions that he commenced his marches. If Your Majesty is fond of wealth, let it be shared with the people. How could it prevent you from attaining the kingly rule?"

The king said: "I have another weakness; I am fond of women." Master Meng said: "Formerly King T'ai was fond of women, and he loved his wife. It is said in the *Shih:*

> Ku-kúng Tan-fu [King T'ai]
> Set out with his horse at dawn,
> Westward along the river bank,

Till he reached the foot of Ch'i.
Along with the lady of Chiang,
Together they came and made their new home.

In those days there were no discontented spinsters at home,
nor were there any unmarried men abroad. If Your Majesty
is fond of women, let this fondness be shared with the people. Who could prevent you from attaining the kingly rule?"
[1B-5]

80. Master Meng saw King Hui of Liang. The king stood
by a pond and, looking at the large geese and deer, said: "Do
men of worth find pleasure in these things?" Master Meng replied: "Only men of worth can find pleasure in these things.
Others may have these things, but they do not find pleasure.
It is said in the *Shih:*

He designed and commenced the Divine Tower:
He planned it, and built it.
The people came to work at it,
And soon it was completed.
Though he intended not to hurry,
They came to him like children to a parent.

When the king was in the Divine Park,
The does calmly reposed.
The does looked so sleek and fat;
The white birds appeared so shining and pure.
When the king was at the Divine Pond,
How full it was of leaping fish!

"King Wen employed the people to make his tower and his
pond, but they rejoiced to do the work. They called the
tower 'Divine Tower' and the pond 'Divine Pond.' They rejoiced that there were deer, fish, and turtles. The ancients
shared the pleasure with the people, and therefore all enjoyed it the more. It is said in the *Shu* [History]:

Oh Sun [i.e., tyrant Chieh], why hasn't thou set?
May thou and I perish together!

When the people wanted to perish together with him, though
he had towers, ponds, birds, and animals, how could he have
pleasure alone?" [1A-2]

81. Chuang Pao, in an interview with Master Meng, said:

"When I had an audience with the king, His Majesty said that he was fond of music. I was then not prepared for a reply. What do you think of his love for music?" Master Meng said: "If His Majesty is really fond of music, Ch'i is about to be a state with good government."

One day Master Meng, having an interview with the king, said: "Your Majesty, I have heard, once told Chuang Pao that you are fond of music; was it so?" The king blushed and said: "I cannot love the classical music of early kings; I only enjoy the popular modern music." Master Meng said: "If Your Majesty is really fond of music, Ch'i is about to be a state of good government. The modern music is just like the ancient music." The king said: "May I hear from you about this?" Master Meng said: "Which is more enjoyable—to enjoy music yourself alone, or to enjoy it with others?" "To enjoy it with others," was the answer. Then Master Meng asked again: "Which is more enjoyable—to enjoy music with a few, or to enjoy it with many?" "To enjoy it with many," said the king. Master Meng said: "Let me tell Your Majesty about music. Suppose that Your Majesty were to give a concert here. When the people hear the sound of your bells and drums, and the notes of your fifes and pipes, they all raise their aching heads and knit their brows, saying to one another, 'How fond of having music played is our king! But why does he make us suffer such great distress? Fathers and sons cannot see one another; brothers, wives, and children are all separated and scattered.' Now suppose that Your Majesty were to hold a hunt here. When the people hear the noise of your carriages and horses, and see the beauty of your plumes and streamers, they all raise their aching heads and knit their brows, saying to one another, 'How our king is so fond of his hunting! But why does he make us suffer such great distress? Fathers and sons cannot see one another; brothers, wives, and children are separated and scattered.' There is no other reason but that you do not share pleasure with the people.

"On the other hand, suppose that Your Majesty were to have a concert held here. When the people hear the sound of your bells and drums, the notes of your fifes and pipes, they all beam with joy and say to one another, 'Our king must be free from sickness; otherwise, how could he enjoy this music?' And suppose that Your Majesty were to hold a hunt here. When the people hear the noise of your carriages and horses, and see the beauty of your plumes and streamers, they all beam with joy and say to one another: 'Our king must be free from sickness; otherwise, how could he enjoy this hunting?' There is no other reason but that you share pleasure with the people. If you will now share your pleasures with the people, you can attain the kingly rule." [IB-1]

82. Master Meng said: "Nowadays, all those who serve the sovereign say, 'We can extend the territory and enrich the treasury for our sovereign.' Such persons who are today called 'good ministers' were called 'foes of the people' in ancient time. If a sovereign does not follow the *Tao,* or does not abide by *jen,* to enrich him is to enrich a Chieh. Or they all say, 'We can for our sovereign form alliances with other states and win our battles.' Such persons who are today called 'good ministers' were called 'foes of the people' in ancient time. If a sovereign does not follow the *Tao,* or does not abide by *jen,* to make him strong in war is to strengthen a Chieh. If a sovereign pursues his present ways and does not change his present practices, even though he were given the world, he could not retain it for a single day." [VIB-9]

83. Master Meng said: "There are those who serve the sovereign; they serve him for the sake of winning his favor. There are those who serve as ministers to secure the state, and they find their pleasure in its security. There are those who are the people of Heaven, and only when they can carry out its will, do they serve the sovereign. There are those who are great men, and when they improve themselves, others are improved." [VIIA-19]

84. Master Meng said: "In ancient times frontier passes were established to guard against violence. Nowadays they are established to exercise violence." [VIIB-8]

85. Master Meng said: "Humane words do not touch men so deeply as humane deeds. Good government does not win the people as well as good instruction. The people may fear good government, but they love good instruction. Good government wins the people's wealth; good instruction wins the people's hearts." [VIIA-14]

86. Master Meng said: "There are men who say, 'I am an expert in marshalling troops; I am an expert in conducting a battle.' They are indeed great criminals. If the sovereign of a state loves *jen,* he will have no enemy in the world. When T'ang was battling in the south, the northern barbarians complained; when he was battling in the east, the western barbarians complained. They all complained, 'Why does he put us last?' When King Wu started his punitive expedition against

Yin, he had only three hundred chariots and three thousand warriors. The king said: 'Fear not! Let me bring peace to you. I am not making war against the people.' On hearing this, the people bowed their heads and prostrated themselves to the ground. 'To battle' is to rectify. Everyone wishing himself to be rectified; what need is there for war?" [viib-4]

4. POLITICAL INSTITUTIONS

87. Pei-kung Yi asked: "What was the arrangement of rank and emoluments prescribed by the House of Chou?" Master Meng said: "Its particulars cannot be learned, for the feudal lords, disliking them as detrimental to their interests, have all done away with their records. However, I still learned their general features.

"The Emperor constituted the highest rank; Dukes followed, then Marquises and Earls; Viscounts and Barons shared rank equally. Thus, there was a total of five ranks. Again, the Feudal Prince constituted the highest rank; the Chief Minister followed, then the minister and the officer of the first class; then the officer of the middle class and the officer of the lowest class. There was a total of six ranks. To the Emperor there was alloted a territory of one thousand square *li;* the Duke and the Marquis each had one hundred square *li;* the Earl had seventy *li;* the Viscount and Baron each had fifty *li.* Thus there was a total of four grades. Where the territory did not amount to fifty *li,* its ruler had no direct access to the Emperor, and his domain, being attached to the feudal princes, was called a 'subordinate state.' The chief minister of the Emperor received a territory equal to that of the marquis; the minister received as much as the Earl; and the officer of the first class as much as the Viscount or the baron. In a large state, where the territory was seventy square *li,* the prince had an income ten times that of his chief minister, the chief minister four times that of the minister, the minister twice that of the officer of the first class, the officer of the first class twice that of the officer of the middle class, the officer of the middle class twice that of the officer of the lowest class, and the officer of the lowest class received the same pay as the common people employed in the government —such a pay was equal to what they would have made by tilling the fields. In a state of next order, where the territory was seventy square *li,* the prince had an income ten times that of his chief minister, the chief minister three times that of the minister, the minister twice that of the officer of the first class, the officer of the first class twice that of the officer of the middle class, the officer of the middle class twice that of the officer of the lowest class, and the officer of the lowest received the same pay as the common people employed in the government—such a pay was equal to what they would have made by tilling the fields.

"In a small state, where the territory was fifty square *li,* the prince had an income ten times that of his chief minister, the chief minister twice that of the minister, the minister twice that of the officer of the first class, the officer of the first class twice that of the officer of the middle class, the officer of the middle class twice that of the lowest class, and the officer of the lowest class received the same pay as the common people employed in the government—such a pay was equal to what they would have made by tilling the fields. As to those who tilled the fields, each farmer received one hundred *mu* of land. If, when those *mu* of land were fertilized, its produce supported a family of ten persons, it was the first grade; if its produce supported a family of eight persons, it was the second grade; if its produce supported a family of seven persons, it was the third grade; if its produce supported a family of six persons, it was the fourth grade; if its produce only supported a family of five persons, it was the lowest grade. The pay of the common people employed in the government was regulated according to the various grades as described above." [vb-2]

88. King Hsüan of Ch'i asked about the chief ministers of state. Master Meng said: "What kind of chief minister is Your Majesty asking about?" The king said: "Are there different kinds of chief ministers?" "There are differences," said Master Meng. "There are the chief ministers who are related to the royal family and there are those who are of different family." The king said: "I beg to ask about those who are related to the royal family." Master Meng said: "If the sovereign has serious faults, they correct him. If after repeated criticisms he fails to listen to them, they proceed to dethrone him." The king, on hearing this, changed countenance. Master Meng said: "Let Your Majesty not be offended. You asked me, and I dare not speak but the truth." When the king resumed his composure, he asked about the chief ministers who are of different family. Master Meng said: "When the sovereign has serious faults, they [remonstrate with] correct him.

If after repeated criticism he fails to listen to them, they resign and leave the country." [vb-8]

89. Master Meng said: "The Five Feudal Leaders [*Pa*] committed crimes against the Three Kings [*Wang*]. The feudal lords of today commit crimes against the Five Leaders. The ministers of today commit crimes against the present feudal lords. When the emperor visited the feudal lords, he was said to be on a tour of inspection. When the feudal lords attended the court of the emperor, they were said to be rendering reports on their administration. In the spring the farming was examined, so as to supply any deficiency of seeds; in the autumn the reaping was examined, so as to assist insufficiency of crop. If, on entering a state, the emperor found that new lands were being reclaimed and old fields well cultivated, old people well nourished, and the worthy honored, and men of distinguished talents placed in office, the lord of the state was rewarded with an addition to his territory. On the other hand, if, on entering a state, the emperor found that lands were deserted and uncultivated, old people neglected, and the worthy not honored and offices filled by 'money-grubbers,' the lord of the state was censured. If the feudal lord failed to attend the court of the emperor, he was punished by demotion to a lower rank; [for] the second time, he was deprived of a portion of his territory; [for] the third time, he was removed by the imperial forces. Thus the emperor commanded punitive expeditions but did not wage wars, whereas the feudal lords waged wars but did not command punitive expeditions. The Five Feudal Leaders dragged the feudal lords to wage wars against one another. Therefore I say that they committed crimes against the Three Kings. Of the Five Feudal Leaders, Duke Huan of Ch'i was the most powerful. He called a conference of feudal lords to meet at K'uei-Ch'iu. Then they bound a sacrificial victim, and placed a written oath therein but did not slay it to drink its blood. This oath stipulated as follows:

First, the unfilial shall be put to death; an appointed heir shall not be changed; a concubine shall not be exalted to the rank of wife.

Second, the worthy shall be honored; the talented shall be educated; the virtuous shall be given distinction.

Third, the aged shall be respected; the young shall be loved. The guest and travelers shall not be neglected.

Fourth, offices shall not be hereditary; officers shall not

hold double offices; officers selected shall be fit for their positions. Ministers shall not be put to death without approval [by the emperor].

Fifth, no embankment shall be detrimental to the neighboring states; no restrictions shall be imposed on the sale of grain; no enfeoffment shall be granted without being first reported [to the Emperor]. All who have jointly taken this oath shall hereafter maintain amicable relations.

All the feudal lords of today violate these five stipulations. Therefore, I say that they commit crimes against the Five Feudal Leaders. If a minister carries out the wickedness of his lord, his crime is slight. If a minister incites his lord to wickedness, his crime is great. The ministers of today all incite their lords to wickedness. Therefore I say that they commit crimes against the present feudal lords." [VIB-7]

Part Three: The Way of Life

While basing his life ideal on the teachings of Confucius, Mencius was able to elaborate his own philosophy of life with some new ideas. As we have already seen in his statement of man's good nature, Mencius regarded man as having certain instinctive feelings—such as those of love and compassion, shame and dislike, modesty and yielding, and right and wrong—that lead to his positive efforts for the good of others. Mencius saw it as man's duty to cultivate these basic feelings, in order to achieve *jen* and *yi*. Through this cultivation, man's natural goodness would be developed and extended, so that it would be a blessing for all. Mencius called this "extending one's good heart to include others," and he viewed it as the ultimate development of *jen* and *yi*.

When man's natural goodness is thus developed and extended, he comes to feel that there is no distinction between himself and others; that is, man becomes identified with the universe as a whole. Mencius said, "All things are complete within us." Note here that Mencius went much further than Confucius in the way of individual cultivation. According to Mencius, it would not be enough to develop our moral quality; we have a responsibility to develop our spiritual quality, or, as Mencius called it, "the vital spirit" (*hao jan chih ch'i*)—the "spirit" (*ch'i*), which if properly cultivated and carefully preserved, "fills up all between Heaven and

Earth." As to how to develop this "spirit," Mencius said, "It is in accord with the *tao* and *yi*." In other words, the way of developing this spirit consists, first, in understanding the *tao* that leads to the elaboration of our mind, and, second, in accumulating *yi*—that is, what we ought to do in the universe.

❧ § ❧

Chapter V. Personal Cultivation

90. Kung-sun Ch'ou asked: "Master, if you were appointed chief minister of Ch'i and were able to practice your *tao*, it would not be surprising that you should make the sovereign become the feudal leader. In such a position, would your heart be disturbed?" Master Meng said: "No. At forty, nothing can disturb my heart." Kung-sun Ch'ou said: "In that case, you are far superior to Meng Pen." Master Meng said: "That isn't difficult. Kao Tzu could hold his heart undisturbed at an earlier age than I." Kung-sun Ch'ou asked: "Is there a way to maintain the heart undisturbed?" Master Meng said: "Yes. Pei-kung Yu had this way of cultivating his courage: He did not shrink from injury at his body, nor did he turn his eyes aside at any thrusts at them. He considered that the slightest insult inflicted on him was the same as if he were thrashed in the market place. He would not tolerate insults of a commoner in loose garments; nor would he tolerate insults of a sovereign with ten thousand chariots. He would attack a sovereign with ten thousand chariots just as he would attack a fellow in loose garments. He was not afraid of the feudal lords, and when a curse was hurled at him, he would return it.

"Meng Shih-she had his way of cultivating his courage: He said, 'Being defeated, I would fight as if I were victorious. I first study the enemy and then advance; I first make sure of victory and then fight; this is to stand in awe of the enemy's armies. How can I make sure of victory? All I can do is have no fears.' Meng-Shih-she was like Tseng Tzu, and Pei-kung Yu was like Tzu Hsia. I do not know which of the two was more courageous. However, it seems to me that Meng Shih-she possessed all the essentials. Formerly, Tseng Tzu said to Tzu Hsiang, 'Are you fond of courage? I heard from Master K'ung about great courage: "If, on self-examination, I find that I am not upright, I will not go forward even at the hints of a commoner in loose garments. On the other hand, if, on self-examination, I find that I am upright, I will go forward even against thousands and tens of thousands of people." Yet what Meng Shih-she maintained, being his spirit [ch'i], was inferior to what Tseng Tzu maintained, being all the essentials:'" Kung-sun Ch'ou asked: "Master, would you mind telling me how you maintain an undisturbed heart, and how Kao Tzu does the same?" Master Meng said: "Kao Tzu once said: 'Do not seek in the heart for what cannot be found in the words; do not seek in the spirit [ch'i] for what cannot be found in the heart.' The statement, 'Do not seek in the spirit for what cannot be found in the heart,' may be granted. But not to seek in the heart for what cannot be found in the words, cannot be granted. For the will guides the spirit, while the spirit pervades the body. The will is of the highest importance; the spirit is subordinate to it. Therefore I say: 'Hold fast to the will and the spirit will not deviate from it.'"

Kung-sun Ch'ou asked again: "Since you say, 'The will is of the highest importance, and the spirit is subordinate to it,' why do you also say, 'Hold fast to the will and never disturb the spirit?'" Master Meng said: "When the will is concentrated, it moves the spirit. When the spirit is concentrated, it moves the will. For instance, in the case of stumbling or running, this is the spirit [in operation], and yet in turn it moves the heart."

"Master, may I ask wherein you excel?" Master Meng said: "I know the right and wrong in speech, and cultivate my *hao jan chih ch'i* [vital spirit]."

"May I ask what is meant by *hao jan chih ch'i?*" "It is difficult to say," said Master Meng. "It is the *ch'i* [spirit], supremely great, supremely strong. When properly cultivated without sustaining injury, then it pervades all between Heaven and earth. Such is the *ch'i:* It is in accord with *yi* and *Tao.* Without this *ch'i,* man will be weakened. It is produced by the accumulation of *yi* and not to be obtained by incidental acts of *yi.* If one's heart feels no satisfaction in one's conduct, this *ch'i* will be weakened. Therefore I say Kao Tzu has never understood *yi,* for he thought it something external. There must be its constant practice without stopping. The heart must not forget it, nor shall effort be made to hasten its growth. Let us be like the man of Sung. There was a man of Sung who worried that his grain did not grow fast enough. So he pulled and stretched it. Then he felt quite exhausted and hurried home. He said to his people, 'I am tired today, for I have been helping the grain to grow fast.'

His son ran out to look at it, and found all the grain withered. There are few people in the world who do not try to help the grain grow. There are those who, thinking it of no benefit, leave it alone—they do not weaken their grain. Those who try to help it grow pull out their grain. What they do is not only of no benefit to it, but also injures it."

Kung-sun Ch'ou asked again: "What do you mean when you say, 'I know the right and wrong in speech?'" Master Meng said: "When words are one-sided, the mind conceals the truth; when words are obscene, the mind is perverse; when words are depraved, the mind deviates from *yi;* when words are evasive, the mind is at its wit's end. When these four types of words arise in the heart, they will injure the government. When they are displayed in the government, they will injure the conduct of affairs. Should a sage arise, he would certainly follow my words." Kung-sun Ch'ou further asked: "Tsai Wo, and Tzu Kung were well versed in speech, while Jan Nu, Ming Tzu, and Yen Yuen distinguished themselves in moral conduct. Master K'ung excelled in both qualities, and yet he said of himself, 'In speech, I am not competent.' Then, Master, have you been a sage?" Master Meng said: "Oh! How can you say this? Formerly Tzu asked Master K'ung, 'Master, are you a sage?' Master K'ung said, 'As to being a sage, I cannot make such a claim. It may be said of me that I have strived to learn without satiety, and to teach others without becoming weary.' And Tzu Kung said, 'To learn without satiety is wisdom; to teach others without being weary is *jen.* Being *jen*-hearted and wise, Master, you are a sage.' Since Master K'ung would not have made such a claim as being a sage, how can you say this?"

Kung-sun Ch'ou asked: "Formerly, Tzu Hsia, Tzu Yu, and Tzu Chang had attained some of sageness, while Jan Nu, Ming Tzu, and Yen Yuen had attained a small portion of sageness. May I ask with which of these people you compare yourself?" Master Meng said: "Let us drop this subject for the moment."

Then Kung-sun Ch'ou asked: "What do you say of Pei-yi and Yi-Yin?" Master Meng said: "Their ways differ from each other. Not to serve a sovereign whom he did not esteem or to rule over a people of whom he did not approve, to take office only when good order prevailed and to retire when disorder prevailed, to take office only when good order prevailed and to retire when disorder prevailed; this was the way of Pei-yi. Whoever was the sovereign was to be served;

whoever were the people were to be ruled. When good order prevailed, to take office; when disorder prevailed, also to take office; this was the way of Yi-Yin. To serve in government when it was proper, to keep retired when it was proper, to stay in it long when it was proper, to withdraw quickly when it was proper; this was the way of Master K'ung. These were all sages of antiquity, and I have not been able to do what they did. Now what I wish to do is to learn to be like Master K'ung."

Kung-sun Ch'ou said: "Comparing Pei-yi and Yi-Yin with Master K'ung, are they to be placed in the same rank?" Master Meng said: "No. Since the birth of mankind till now, there was no peer to Master K'ung." "Then, was there anything in common among them?" "Yes," said Master Meng. "If any one of the three had been given a state of one hundred *li*, he would bring all the feudal lords to his court and thus win the world. And none of them would commit a single unrighteous act or put to death a single innocent person in order to win the world. This is in common among them."

"May I ask in what they differed from one another?" Master Meng said: "Tsai Wo, Tzu Kung, and Yu Jo had wisdom sufficient to know the sage. They would not have exaggerated so as to flatter their favorite. Tsai Wo said, 'In my opinion, our Master is far superior to Yao and Shun.' Tzu Kung said: 'By viewing the ceremonies, he knows the government; by hearing the music, he knows virtue. Even after the lapse of one hundred generations, even though kings of one hundred dynasties might have been changed, not one of them could refute the doctrines of Master K'ung. Since the birth of mankind, there has been no peer to Master K'ung.' Yu Jo said: 'Is it only among men that it is so? There is the unicorn among four-footed animals; the phoenix among the flying birds; the Tai Mountain among mounds and hillocks, and rivers and seas among rain pools. They are the same in kind. So the sage among the people is the same in kind, but he stands out from his fellow men and rises above the level. Since the birth of mankind till now, there has been none so superior and perfect as Master K'ung.' " [IIA-2]

91. Master Meng said: "Shun rose from among the farms; Fu Yueh was called to office when he was a mason; Chiao Ko was called to office when he was a fish-and-salt dealer; Kuan Yi-wu was called to office from the hands of his jailers; Sun-shu Ao from the seashore; Pai-li Hsi from the market place. Thus, when Heaven is about to place a great responsibil-

ity upon a certain man, his heart is made to suffer bitterly, and his sinews and bones are given to severe toil. Then his body is exposed to hunger, and his person is subjected to poverty. Finally obstruction and frustration break in on all undertakings. By all these, Heaven stimulates his heart, disciplines his patience, and augments his ability. When a man is often in error, he is able to reform himself. When he is distressed in heart and perplexed in thought, then he rises to action. When things are evidenced in his looks and set forth in his words, he comes to understand them. If within its domain there are no model families and upright ministers, and if beyond its borders there are no hostile states and foreign aggressions, a state will generally perish. From these experiences, we know how we survive in sorrow and distress, how we perish in ease and comfort." [VIB-15]

92. Master Meng said: "Men who are possessed of virtue, wisdom, and talent are often found to have been in difficulties and misfortune. Thus ministers isolated from the sovereign and sons born of concubines often keep their hearts in a sense of peril and use deep precaution against calamity. On this account they excel in their intelligence." [VIIA-18]

93. Master Meng, on his way from Fan to Ch'i, saw the son of the King of Ch'i at a distance, and said with a sigh: "One's position affects one's manners as much as nutrition affects the body. Great is the influence of position! Isn't this true of all the sons of men? The residence, carriages, horses, and clothes of the king's son are not much different from those of other men. That he looks so is due to his position. How much more would the effect be if he looked upon the world as his abode? When the lord of Lu went to Sung, he called out at the Tieh-tse Gate, and the keeper said: 'This is not our lord, but how is it that his voice is so like that of our lord?' This was for no other reason than that their positions are similar." [VIIA-36]

94. Wan Chang asked: "When Master K'ung was in Chen, he said, 'Let us go home! The little children of my school are getting impetuous and ambitious; they are making progress!' He did not forget his early disciples. When Master K'ung was in Chen, why did he think of the ambitious scholars of Lu?" Master Meng said: "Since Master K'ung could not find men pursuing the doctrine of the mean to teach, he had to turn to those who were ambitious and cautious. The ambitious would make progress, while the cautious would not do anything. Did Master K'ung not wish to find men pursuing the doctrine of the mean? He was not sure of finding such men;

he therefore thought of the next best." "May I ask what type of men could be called 'ambitious'?" "Men," said Master Meng, "like Ch'in Chang, Tseng Hsi, and Mu P'i were those whom Master K'ung called 'ambitious.'" "Why were they called 'ambitious'?" Master Meng said: "They were self-important and fond of big words. They were in the habit of saying, 'The ancients! The ancients!' But their actions, when examined, did not come up to their words. When he found that he could not get the ambitious, he had to turn to those who were priggish and egoistic. Those were the cautious—a type inferior to the ambitious. Master K'ung once said, 'Of those who pass my door without entering my house, the only ones whom I do not resent are the "good careful villagers." The "good careful villagers" are the simulators of virtue.'"

"What type of men were the 'good careful villagers'?" Master Meng said: "They were those who were wont to say, 'Why are they so self-important and fond of big words? Their words have no regard for their actions, and their actions have no regard for their words.' And then they say, 'The ancients! The ancients!' Why do they appear so sluggish and so cold? They believe that men are born in this age and so should be of this age; all they need is to be good men. They—priggish and hypocritical—are but the flatterers of the age. Such are the 'good careful villagers'."

Wan Chang said: "When a man is considered good and careful in his own village, then he is so wherever he goes. How was it that Master K'ung regarded such a type as simulators of virtue?" Master Meng said: "As regards these good and careful people, if you blame them, they seem to be blameless; if you criticize them, they seem to be faultless. They follow the current customs of the world, and they agree with the bad practice of the age. They look as if they were faithful and sincere; they act as though they were honest and pure. Everybody is pleased with them, and they assert themselves. However, we cannot make them follow the *tao* of Yao and Shun. On this account they are called 'the simulators of virtue.' Master K'ung once said, "I hate what seems right but what in reality is wrong. I hate the darnel lest it be confused with the corn. I hate the glib-tongued lest he be confused with the righteous. I hate the clever talker lest he be confused with the sincere. I hate the music of Cheng lest it be confused with true music. I hate purple lest it be confused with vermillion. I hate the good careful villagers, lest they be confused with the virtuous.' The *chün-tzu* needs only to return to

the normal standard, and when this normal standard is rectified, the people will be roused to virtue. When they are so
roused, there will be no perversities and evils." [viib-37]

95. Master Meng said: "Words that are simple but profound in meaning are good words. Principles that are condensed but comprehensive in application are good principles.
The words of the *chün-tzu* concern common affairs, but the
Tao is contained therein. What the *chün-tzu* holds is to cultivate his own person, so as to pacify the world. The weakness
of men is this: they neglect their own fields and go to weed
the fields of others; what they demand of others is great, while
what they require of themselves is little." [viib-32]

96. Master Meng said: "Yao and Shun were what they
were by nature; T'ang, founder of the Shang dynasty, and
Wu, founder of the Chou dynasty, were what they were
through personal cultivation. When all the movements, in the
countenance and conduct of a man, are in accord with *li*, he
attains the perfection of supreme virtue. In mourning for the
dead, grief is expressed not because of the living; pursuing
the righteous course without deviation is not with a view to
emolument; speaking the truth is not just to appear upright.
The *chün-tzu* always follows what is right and leaves its out-
come to Fate." [viib-33]

97. Master Meng said: "It is of no use to talk to a man
who does harm to himself, just as it is of no value to cooperate
with a man who throws himself away. He who speaks contrary to *li* and *yi* does harm to himself. He who believes that
he is not able to dwell in *jen* and to pursue *yi* throws himself
away. *Jen* is man's secure abode, and *yi* his true road. Alas for
those who desert the secure abode and dwell not therein!
Alas for those who abandon the true path and follow it not!"
[iva-10]

98. Master Meng said: "If Hsi Shih [a famous beauty] had
been covered with a filthy headdress, all people would have
held their noses when passing her. On the other hand, even
a wicked man, if he purifies his thoughts, fasts and bathes,
may sacrifice to *Shang Ti* [Supreme God]." [ivb-25]

99. Master Meng said: "It is not surprising that the king
is not wise. Consider the case of a plant; however hardy it
may be, it can never grow if it is exposed to ten days' of cold
after only one day of warmth. My visits to the king are few,
and as soon as I leave, he is overrun by those who act upon
him like the cold plants. Though I may succeed in bringing up
a sprout here and there, what good can it do? Now chess

playing is but a minor art; if a man does not devote his heart to it and concentrate his will on it, he cannot succeed in learning it. Chess player Ch'iu is the best player in the country. Suppose that he is teaching two men. One of them devotes his heart to the subject and concentrates his will on it and does nothing but listen to chess player Ch'iu. The other, while listening to Ch'iu, occupies his whole heart on an approaching swan and speculates how to arrange his bow and arrow to shoot it. Although he is learning along with the first man, he does not equal him in learning capacity. Is this because his intelligence is inferior? No, I say, this is not so." [VIA-9]

100. Master Meng said to Kao Tzu: "There are footpaths along the hills; if they are persistently used, they become roads. When they are not used for a time, wild weeds will choke them up. Now wild weeds are choking your heart." [VIIB-21]

101. Hao-sheng Pu-hai asked: "What type of man is Yüeh-cheng Tzu?" Master Meng said: "He is a good man, a sincere man." "What do you mean by 'a good man'? What do you mean by 'a sincere man'?" Master Meng said: "One who is liked by all is called a good man. One who possesses goodness in himself is called a sincere man. One who develops his goodness is called 'a beautiful man.' One who develops and enlightens his goodness is called 'a great man.' One who, out of his greatness, exercises a transforming influence, is called 'a sage.' And one whose sageness is beyond our knowledge is called 'a saint.' Yüeh-cheng Tzu qualifies for the first two categories but falls short of the last four." [VIIB-25]

102. Hsü Tzu said: "Chung-ni [i.e., Master K'ung] often exclaimed in praise of water, 'O water! O water!' What did he find in water?" Master Meng said: "There is a spring of water that gushes out day and night without rest. It fills in the crevices and goes on into the four seas. Such is water that comes from a spring. It was this which he found in water. Suppose that the water does not come from a spring. In the seventh and eighth moons the rain gathers and fills up the ditches and channels, but its drying up may be expected in an instant. So chün-tzu would be ashamed if his reputation were in excess of his merits." [IVB-18]

103. Master Meng said: "When Master K'ung ascended the T'ung Mountain, Lu appeared small to him; when he ascended the T'ai Mountain, the world appeared small to him. So a man who has seen the sea finds it difficult to sat-

isfy himself with rivers; a man who has associated with sages finds it difficult to satisfy himself with words. There is an art for one to look at water; it is the rushing waves that are to be observed. The sun and the moon are possessed of brilliancy, and their light shines through each and every crevice. Just as flowing water must fill up the hollows before it proceeds to cover its entire course, so *chün-tzu,* who sets his mind on the *Tao,* must advance to it step by step before he reaches the state of perfection." [VIIA-24]

104. Master Meng said to Wan Chang: "Only when a scholar has distinguished himself in a village for his goodness shall he make friends of all the good scholars of that village. Only when a scholar has distinguished himself in a state for his goodness shall he make friends of all the good scholars of that state. Only when he has distinguished himself in the world for his goodness shall he make friends of all the good scholars of the world. When a scholar is not content with the friendship of the good scholars of the world, he may proceed upward to consider the men of antiquity. He recites their poems and reads their books. But can he be ignorant of what they were? On this account, he considers the ages in which they lived. This is the way to make friends of the men of antiquity." [VB-8]

105. Master Meng said: "A man who aims at great achievement may be compared to one digging a well. Digging a well to a depth of nine fathoms and stopping without reaching water is to throw away the well." [VIIA-29]

106. Master Meng said: "Though the wise man embraces all knowledge, he pays special attention to what is most important. Though the *jen*-hearted man extends his love to all, he attaches his earnest affection to those who are worthy. Yao and Shun did not apply their wisdom to everything but attended only to what was most important; nor did they extend their *jen* to every man but earnestly attached their affection to the worthy. For instance, a man who is not able to keep three years' mourning will be very particular about that of three months or five months. Or a man who eats and drinks without manners will make inquiries about how to avoid cutting the meat with his teeth. This is what I would call ignorance of the relative importance of things." [VIIA-46]

107. Master Meng said: "If a man stops short of where he should not, he will surely stop short in anything. If a man is grudging to those whom he should treat liberally, he will

surely be grudging to all. If a man advances with haste, he will retreat with speed." [vIIA-44]

108. Master Meng said: "Words which are false are disastrous, and words which are most disastrous are those that throw men of worth into the shade." [IVB-17]

109. Master Meng said: "When those in inferior positions fail to win the confidence of their superiors, they cannot succeed in governing the people. There is a way to win the confidence of superiors; if one is not trusted by one's friends, one cannot win the confidence of one's superiors. There is a way of obtaining the trust of one's friends; if one does not please one's parents by serving them, one cannot be trusted by one's friends. There is a way to please one's parents; if one is not sincere to oneself, one cannot please one's parents. There is a way to be sincere to oneself: if one does not understand what is good, one cannot be sincere to oneself. Therefore, sincerity is the *Tao* of Heaven, and to be sincere is the *Tao* of man. Never has there been a man who was truly sincere and yet could not influence others; conversely, never has there been a man who was not sincere and yet could influence others." [IVA-12]

110. Master Meng said: "Of the services of men, which is the greatest? The service to parents is the greatest. Of the duties of men, which is the greatest? The duty of self-preservation is the greatest. I have heard of being able to serve one's parents by preserving oneself. I have never heard of being able to serve one's parents by not preserving oneself. There are many services, but service to one's parents is the root of all services.

"There are many duties, but the duty of self-preservation is the root of all duties. Tseng Tzu always served [his father] Tseng Hsi with wine and meat. When the table was cleaned, he would ask to whom the residue should be given. If his father asked whether there was anything left, he would answer, 'Yes.' After the death of Tseng Hsi, Tseng Yüan always served [his father] Tseng Tzu with wine and meat. When the table was cleaned, he did not ask to whom the residue should be given. And if his father asked whether there was anything left, he would answer, 'No,' for he intended to serve it again. This is what we call 'to feed the mouth and body'; but Tseng Tzu may be said to have nourished the will of his father. It is proper to serve one's parents as Tseng Tzu did." [IVA-19]

111. Master Meng said: "There are three things which are unfilial, and the greatest of them is to have no posterity.

Shun married without informing his parents because of fear of having no posterity. Therefore, *chün-tzu* takes that to be the same as if he had informed his parents." [IVA-26]

112. Master Meng said: "The substance of *jen* is to serve one's parents; the substance of *yi* is to obey one's older brother. The essence of wisdom is to know these two things and not to depart from them; the essence of *li* is to perform these two things according to ritual orders; the essence of music is to rejoice in these two things. When joy is found in them, [filial piety and fraternal affection] arise; if so, how can they be repressed? When they cannot be repressed, unconsciously one's feet will dance and one's hands will flutter." [IVA-27]

113. Master Meng said: "To have supported one's parents during their lifetime may not be considered the fulfillment of one's great duty toward them. It is only in observing mourning rites after their death that we have what is considered as the great duty toward the parents." [IVB-13]

114. Master Meng went from Ch'i to Lu to bury his mother. On his return to Ch'i, he stopped over in Ying, and Ch'ung Yü said to him: "The other day you were kind enough to ignore my incompetence and to ask me to supervise the making of the coffin. Owing to the urgency of the matter, I dared not bother you with questions. Now, however, I should like to ask about the matter. The wood used for the coffin, it seemed to me, was just too good." Master Meng said: "In ancient times, there was no standard for the coffin or its outer shell. At the time of early Chou, the coffin was seven inches thick, and its outer shell the same. This applied to all, from the emperor to the common people. This was not solely to make its appearance beautiful, but also to satisfy the feeling of men's hearts. Men would not be happy if their coffins could not be made in this way; nor would they be happy if they could not have money to make such coffins. When these coffins were available and there was money, all the ancients used them. Why should I alone not do so? Moreover, if the earth be prevented from touching the bodies of the dead, won't the feelings of men's hearts be satisfied? I have heard that the *chün-tzu* will not for the world be grudging to serve his parents." [IIB-7]

115. Kung-tu Tzu said: "Throughout the country Kuang Chang is known to everybody for being unfilial. But, Master, you keep company with him and even treat him with respect. I venture to ask why you do so." Master Meng said: "There

are five things which are generally considered unfilial. The first is laziness in the use of one's limbs while neglecting the support of one's parents. The second is gambling, chess-playing, and fondness for wine, resulting in neglect of the support of one's parents. The third is fondness for goods and wealth, and special favor shown to one's wife and children, while neglecting the support of one's parents. The fourth is sensual gratifications of one's ears and eyes, bringing disgrace on one's parents. Has Kuang Chang committed himself to any one of these things? Now in the case of Kuang Chang, there arose disagreement between father and son, when they admonished each other to do good. To admonish each other to do good is the way of friends; but such admonition between father and son is detrimental to the affection between them. Didn't Kuang Chang wish to enjoy the relationships of husband and wife, of child and mother? But because he had offended his father, he could not approach them: he divorced his wife and drove out his son, thereby depriving himself of their care and support all his life. He felt in his heart that if he did not act in this way, he would have been guilty of the greatest of crimes. Such is the case of Kuang Chang and nothing more!" [IVB-30]

116. When Duke Ting of T'eng died, the crown prince said to Jan-yu: "Formerly, Master Meng and I met in Sung, and in my heart I have never forgotten what he had said to me. Now I am unfortunate having this great duty to my father. I should like to send you to ask Master Meng how I am to proceed." Jan-yu went to Tsou and inquired of Master Meng. Master Meng said: "This is indeed good! In the funeral service of his parents, a man feels constrained to exert his utmost. Tseng Tzu said, 'While parents are alive, serve them according to li; when they die, bury them according to li; and make the offerings to them according to li. Thus may a man be considered a filial son.' I have never learned the rituals observed by the feudal lords. However, the three-year period of mourning, the garments of coarse cloth, and the eating of porridge are prescribed for all, from the emperor down to the mass of the people. This practice was common among the Three Dynasties." Jan-yu returned and reported his mission. It was then decided that the three years' mourning should be observed. But the elders and officers did not wish to accept this decision, and they said: "None of the former lords of our ancestral state of Lu observed this ceremony, and none of our own former lords observed it. It is not proper for you to act contrary to their practice. Moreover, the Records say, 'In

funeral services and sacrifices follow the example of your ancestors.'" The crown prince said: "I act in accordance with instruction." Then he said to Jan-yu: "In my early days, I did not occupy myself with studies, but I was fond of horsemanship and sword exercise. Now the elders and officers are not satisfied with my decision, so I am afraid I may not be able to perform this great duty well. On my behalf, go and ask Master Meng about it." So Jan-yu went to Tsou and saw Master Meng. Master Meng said: "In a case such as this, he may not ask of others. Master K'ung said: 'When the sovereign dies, the administration is left in the hands of the chief minister. The heir eats porridge, and his face is of deep black. He remains in his place and weeps. Then all the officers and those in office will join in the lamentation, taking the heir as their example. What the superior is fond of doing, his inferiors usually do with zest. The *chün-tzu* [prince] is the wind; the *hsiao-jen* [common people] the grass, and the grass bends in the direction of the wind.' Therefore, all depends on the prince." Jan-yu returned and reported his mission. The crown prince said: "It is true that all depends on myself alone." So for five months he remained in the shed, without giving orders or instructions. The officers and his relatives all said he had knowledge of *li*. On the day of internment, people from all quarters of the world came to witness the ceremony. Those who came to offer condolences were greatly pleased by his solemn expression and deep mourning. [IIIA-2]

117. Kung-sun Ch'ou said: "*Chün-tzu* does not teach his own son—why is that?" Master Meng said: "In the nature of their relationship it will not do. In teaching there must be insistence on good conduct. If conduct is not good, anger follows, and when anger follows, the mutual affections are wounded. [And the son will say,] 'My father teaches me good conduct, but his own conduct does not proceed from what is good.' Then there is an estrangement between father and son. In ancient times fathers taught one another's sons. Between father and son, there should be no reproaches. Such reproaches lead to estrangement, and there is nothing more disastrous than estrangement [between father and son]." [IVA-18]

118. King Hsüan of Ch'i wanted to shorten the period of mourning. Kung-sun Ch'ou said: "Isn't one year's mourning better than no mourning at all?" Master Meng said: "This is like someone twisting the arm of his older brother, and you merely tell him to do it gently. You should, instead, teach him

filial piety and fraternal duty." It happened that the mother of one of the king's sons died, and his tutor requested that he observe a few months of mourning. Kung-sun Ch'ou said: "What do you say of this case?" Master Meng said: "In this case, the son wanted to observe the full period of mourning, but he could not do so. So the addition of even a single day would be better than no mourning at all. I was speaking of those who, under no prohibition, neglected to do things themselves." [VIIA-39]

119. "From this time on, I know the serious consequences of killing a man's near relations. If a man kills another's father, others will kill his father; if he kills another's older brother, others will kill his older brother. Although he does not himself kill his father and older brother, their deaths must be attributed to him." [VIIB-7]

120. Master Meng said: "The common fault of men is that they like to be teachers of others." [IVA-23]

121. Master Meng said: "Those who know the golden mean cultivate those who do not, and those who have talent cultivate those who have not. For this reason men rejoice in having fathers and elders who are men of worth. If those who know the golden mean spurn those who do not, and those who have talents spurn those who have not, then the difference between the worthy and the unworthy is indeed slight." [IVB-7]

122. Master Meng said: "The chün-tzu earnestly devotes himself to the study of the Tao, in order to attain a firm hold of it. Only when he attains a firm hold of the Tao will he abide by it securely. When he abides by the Tao, he will use it inexhaustibly, and only then will he be possessed of the Tao so as to sustain him in whatever he does. It is on this account that the chün-tzu wishes to attain a firm hold of the Tao." [IVB-14]

123. Master Meng said: "One must ponder one's learning extensively and then expound on it in detail, so that one may synthesize what is essential." [IVB-15]

124. Master Meng said: "There are five ways in which chün-tzu can transmit his teachings: There are some whom he transforms like seasonal rain; some whom he urges to cultivate their virtue; some whom he helps to develop their talents; some whom he helps to solve difficult problems; and some whom he enables to learn by themselves. These are the five ways in which the chün-tzu can transmit teachings." [VIIA-40]

125. Master Meng said: "There are many ways of teaching. I teach a man by refusing to teach him; this is one way of teaching." [VIB-16]

126. Master Meng said: "There are three things in which the *chün-tzu* delights, and to be the sovereign of the world is not one of them. That his parents are both living and that his brothers live in harmony is one delight. That he looks up to Heaven with a clear conscience and looks out upon men without shame is his second delight. That he obtains the young men of finest talent in the world and educates them is his third delight. There are three things in which the noble man delights, but to be the sovereign of the world is not one of them." [VIIA-20]

127. Master Meng said: "The influence of *chün-tzu* usually lasts for five generations, as does that of a common man. I could not be a disciple of Master K'ung himself, so I have endeavored to learn his teachings through others." [IVB-22]

128. Kung-tu Tzu said: "When Ten Keng [brother of the prince of Teng] was among the disciples of your school, it seemed proper to treat him with politeness. But you did not answer him. Why was that?" Master Meng said: "I do not answer a man who makes inquiries on the presumption of his nobility, nor a man who makes inquiries on the presumption of his talents, nor a man who makes inquiries on the presumption of his seniority, nor a man who makes inquiries on the presumption of services performed to me, nor a man who makes inquiries on the presumption of old acquaintance. Two of these five presumptions might be attributable to Teng Keng." [VIIA-43]

129. Kung-sun Ch'ou said: "Your *Tao* is indeed lofty and admirable! It may well be compared to ascending the heavens, for it seems unreachable. Why don't you make it within the reach of those who daily exert themselves?" Master Meng said: "A great craftsman does not alter or abolish the rules of workmanship, in order to suit the unskilled workmen; nor did Yi [the great archer] reduce the bend of the bows in order to suit the unskilled archer. The *chün-tzu* draws [the bow], but he does not discharge [the arrow], so as to present a clear position (to the onlookers). He stands firm in the middle of *Tao*, and waits for the competent to follow him." [VIIA-41]

130. Master Meng said: "A carpenter or a carriage-maker may teach men how to use the compass and square but cannot make them skillful in the use of them." [VIIB-5]

131. Master Meng said: "Just as Yi [the archer], in teach-

ing men archery, made it a rule to draw a full bow, so the scholar must conform to the same rule. Just as a master-workman, in teaching men, uses the compass and square as his standard, so the scholar must follow the same standard." [VIA-20]

132. Master Meng said: "A populous and wide territory may be what *chün-tzu* desires, but such a desire is not his true delight. Standing in the center of the world and bringing peace to all the people within the four seas may be what *chün-tzu* delights in, but such a delight does not express his very nature. *Chün-tzu* abides by his nature, which cannot be increased by his achievements in governing the world nor diminished by his retirement in enjoying private life; on this account it is apportioned to him by Heaven. *Jen, yi, li*, and wisdom, which come naturally to *chün-tzu*, are rooted in his heart. They manifest themselves in his countenance, his manners, and his movements, and hence they are evident to all men." [VIIA-21]

133. Master Meng said: "The great man will not observe the ceremonies which are contrary to the rules of *li;* nor will he perform the act of *yi*, which is not really righteous." [IVB-6]

134. Master Meng said: "A man must refrain from doing what he ought not to do; then he will be able to achieve what he ought to do." [IVB-8]

135. Master Meng said: "I like fish and I also like bear's paws. If I cannot have them both together, I will leave fish and take the bear's paws. [So] I like life, and I also like *yi*. If I cannot have them both together, I will leave life and keep *yi*. I like life indeed, but if there is something which I like more than life, I will not seek to keep it improperly. I dislike death indeed, but if there is something which I dislike more than death, I will not seek to evade death. If there is nothing which a man likes more than life, why shall he not be justified to use every means to preserve it? If there is nothing which he dislikes more than death, why shall he not be justified to do everything to evade it? There are many ways to preserve life, and yet men do not use them; there are many ways to evade death, and yet men do not do them. Therefore, there is something which men like more than life, and something which men dislike more than death. Such a state of heart is not peculiar to men of worth but is common to all men. It is only that men of worth are not able to lose it. Here is a basket of rice and a platter of soup; if one gets

them, one lives; if not, one dies. But if they are offered with an insulting voice, even a vagabond will not accept them; or if they are offered with a kick, even a beggar will not stoop to accept them. However, a man will accept an emolument of ten thousand measures of grain without regard for *li* [propriety] and *yi* [righteousness]. What good can this offer do him? Is it that he may live in a beautiful mansion, that he may secure the services of wives and concubines, or that he may help his poor and needy acquaintances? Formerly a man spurned a bounty even should it save him from death, and now he accepts the emolument for the sake of a beautiful mansion; formerly he spurned the bounty even if it would have saved him from death, and now he accepts the emolument for the services of wives and concubines; formerly he spurned the bounty even if it would have saved him from death, and now he accepts the emolument for the gratitude of his poor and needy acquaintances. Was it then impossible to decline the emolument? This is what I call 'the loss of a man's innate heart.'" [VIA-10]

136. Master Meng said: "Do not do what you ought not to do; do not desire what you ought not to desire. That is all." [VIIA-17]

137. Master Meng said: "The common people wait for a sage ruler like King Wen in order to rouse themselves in action. But men of superior character, without a King Wen, arouse themselves to action." [VIIA-10]

138. Master Meng said: "A man who gets up early in the morning and devotes himself to the practice of goodness is a follower of Shun. A man who gets up early in the morning and devotes himself to the pursuit of profit is a follower of robber Shih. If we want to distinguish Shun from Shih, we need only to know the difference between profit and goodness." [VIIA-25]

139. Master Meng said: "A man may not be without a sense of shame. If he is ashamed of having no sense of shame, then he will not commit what is shameful." [VIIA-6]

140. Master Meng said: "The sense of shame is very important to a man. Those who resort to trickeries and deceitful schemes are making no use of the sense of shame. When a man is not ashamed of being inferior to others, what will he have in common with men?" [VIIA-7]

141. Master Meng said: "To act without understanding the reason, and to behave habitually without looking into the conduct, thus all life long without knowing the proper

way of what has been done—this is the way of multitudes."
[VIIA-5]

142. Prince Tien [of Ch'i] asked: "What is the occupation
of the scholar?" Master Meng said: "He is in the pursuit of
high ideals." "What do you mean by 'the pursuit of high
ideals'?" Master Meng said: "He pursues only *jen* and *yi*. To
kill a single innocent person is contrary to *jen;* to take what
is not one's own is contrary to *yi*. Where should one's dwelling be? *jen;* what should one's path be? *yi*. When one lives
in *jen* and follows *yi,* one occupies oneself with what the
great man should be occupied." [VIIA-33]

143. Master Meng said: "Just as a man who has sufficient
wealth will not suffer death in a bad year, so a man who is
possessed of complete virtue will hold his own in a corrupt
age." [VIIB-10]

144. Master Meng said: "There is that which is conferred
by Heaven. There is that which is conferred by man. *Jen, yi,*
loyalty, and sincerity, with unlimited delight in goodness,
are conferred by Heaven. Duchies, ministries, and grand officers are those which are conferred by man. In ancient times
men cultivated the heavenly qualities, and the man-made
ranks of nobility followed. Nowadays men cultivate the
heavenly qualities for the purpose of gaining the man-made
ranks of nobility, and when they acquire the ranks, they
discard the qualities; in this way they utterly delude themselves. In the end they must lose the ranks of nobility as
well." [VIA-16]

145. Master Meng said: "The desire for honors is common
among the hearts of men. And all men possess something
honorable within themselves, but they simply do not think of it.
The honor which men grant is not true honor. Those whom
Chao Meng honors he in turn can disgrace. It is said in the
Shih:

> He has filled us with wine;
> He has satiated us with virtues.

That is to say that a man who is satiated with *jen* and *yi*
does not desire exquisite food. When a man enjoys good
fame and far-reaching praise, he does not crave elegant embroidered garments." [VIA-17]

146. Master Meng said: "*Jen* is inherent in the nature of
man. When a man abides by *jen,* he follows the *Tao*." [VIIB-
16]

147. Master Meng said: "The five kinds of grains are the

best of all seeds. If, however, they are not ripe, they are not equal to cockles. So the value of *jen* depends entirely on its being brought to perfection." [VIA-19]

148. A man of *jen* asked Wu-lu Lien: "Which is more important, *li* or food?" "*Li* is more important," was the answer. "Which is more important, *li* or the rules of marriage?" "*Li* is more important," was again the answer. Then the man asked again: "If acting according to *li*, one would starve to death, whereas acting contrary to *li*, one might get food, would it still be necessary to follow *li*? If following *li* to fetch the bride, one would not get a wife, whereas disregarding *li*, he would get a wife, must one still follow *li* to fetch the bride?" Wu-lu Lien was unable to answer these questions, and the next day he went to Tsou and told Master Meng about it. Master Meng said: "Why is it difficult to answer these questions? Suppose that in comparing two things, you neglect their extremities but place their tops on a level; then a piece of wood an inch square may be made taller than a high tower. Gold is heavier than feathers; does it refer to a comparison between a single clasp of gold and a wagon-load of feathers? When you take an extreme case of food and compare it with the least important aspect of *li*, how should the food not be more important? When you take an extreme case of sex and compare it with the least important aspect of *li*, why should the sex not be more important?

"You should go and answer him thus: 'If by twisting the arm of your older brother and robbing him you can get food for yourself, while by not so doing you cannot get food, will you so twist his arm? If by jumping over the wall of your eastern neighbor and carrying away his maiden daughter, you can get a wife, while by not so doing you cannot get a wife, will you so carry her away?'" [VIB-1]

Chapter VI. The Temperament of Mencius

149. Duke P'ing of Lu was about to leave his palace when his favorite Tsang T'sang asked him: "On other days when Your Majesty left the palace, the officers were sure to be informed of where you were going. But now the carriage is ready, and yet the officers do not know where Your Majesty is going. I venture to ask." The Duke said: "I am going to see Master Meng." "Why?" said the other. "You demean yourself by calling first on a common man. Is it that he is a

man of worth? The observance of *li* and *yi* proceeds from men of worth. But Master Meng let his observance of a later funeral service [for his mother] exceed that of an earlier one [for his father]. I beg Your Majesty not to go to see him." The Duke said: "I shall not."

Yüeh-cheng Tzu came to see the Duke and said: "Why was it that Your Majesty did not go to see Meng K'o?" The Duke said: "Someone told me that Master Meng let his observance of a later funeral service exceed that of an earlier one. It is on this account that I have not gone to see him." "Why?" said Yüeh-cheng Tzu. "By what you call 'exceeding,' do you mean that on the earlier occasion he used rites for the scholar, and on the later occasion he used rites for the officer? Or do you mean that he first used three tripods and later five tripods?" The Duke said: "No. I refer to the difference in the splendor of the coffins and burial-clothes." Yüeh-cheng Tzu said: "That cannot be called 'exceeding.' That was the difference between poverty and wealth." Then Yüeh-cheng Tzu saw Master Meng and said: "I told His Majesty about you, and he was about to call on you. But his favorite Tsang T'sang stopped him, and therefore he did not come to see you." But Master Meng said: "What prevails may be advanced by others; what fails may also be retarded by others. But what will prevail or fail is beyond the control of men. My failure to meet the Duke of Lu must be due to Heaven. How could the son of Tsang prevent me from meeting the Duke?" [IB-16]

150. When Master Meng was going to court, the king sent a messenger with this word: "I wish to come and see you, but on account of a cold, I may not expose myself to the wind. Tomorrow morning I shall hold my court. May I request the pleasure of your company at that time?" Master Meng replied: "Unfortunately, I am also ill and shall not be able to attend His Majesty." The next day, however, he went out to pay a visit of condolence at the home of Tung-kuo. Kung-sun Ch'ou said: "Yesterday, you declined an invitation to the court on the ground of illness, but today you are making a visit of condolence. May this not be regarded as improper?" Master Meng said: "Yesterday I was ill; today I am better. Why should I not pay this visit of condolence?" In the meantime, the king sent a messenger with a physician to look after his health. Meng Chung Tzu said to them: "Yesterday, when His Majesty sent for him, he was ill and could not go to the court. Today he is a little better and is

on his way to the court. I do not know whether he has
arrived or not." At the same time, Meng Chung Tzu dis-
patched several men to waylay Master Meng and say to him:
"Before you return home, you must pay His Majesty a visit."
Master Meng felt himself obliged to go to Cheng Ch'ou's
and there spend the night. Chung Tzu said to him: "At home
there is the relation of father and son; in government there
is the relation of sovereign and minister. These are two great
relationships of men. Between father and son the ruling principle is kindness; between sovereign and minister, the ruling
principle is respect. I have seen His Majesty's respect to you,
but I have not seen how you show respect to His Majesty."
"Oh!" said Master Meng, "what words are these? Among the
people of Ch'i there is no one who speaks to His Majesty
about *jen* and *yi*. Is it that *jen* and *yi* are not magnificent?
They must say in their hearts: 'The king is not fit to know
about *jen* and *yi*.' There is no greater disrespect than that!
I dare not speak to His Majesty of anything but the *Tao* of
Yao and Shun. Therefore, there is no one in Ch'i who shows
as much respect to His Majesty as I do." Ching Tzu said:
"No, that was not what I meant. It is said in the *li* [Rites],
'When a man is sent for by his father, he must go to him
immediately. When a man is sent for by his sovereign, he
must hasten without waiting for his carriage.' You were going to the court, but you changed your mind when you heard
the king's order. It seems to me that your conduct was not in
accord with the rules of etiquette." Master Meng said: "Is that
what you mean by my conduct? Tseng Tzu once said, 'The
wealth of Tsin and Ch'u cannot be matched. They have
their wealth, but I have my *jen;* they have their ranks of
nobility, but I have my· *yi*. Why should I be dissatisfied?'
Are the words of Tseng Tzu not right? There is some truth
in his words. In the world there are three things which command universal respect and honor; these are nobility, age,
and virtue. At court nobility is the most important; in the
village age is the most important; in exercising influence over
the people, these two cannot match virtue. How can one in
possession of only one of these spurn another who possesses
the other two? Therefore, a sovereign who is making great
achievements must have ministers whom he does not summon. When he wishes to consult with them, he goes to them.
The sovereign who does not honor the virtuous and rejoice
in the right principles is not worthy of help in making great
achievements. Accordingly, T'ang first learned of Yi-yin and

then had him as his minister, so as to become Emperor without difficulty. And, again, Duke Huan of Ch'i first learned of Kuan Chung and then had him as his minister, so as to become the leader of the feudal lords without difficulty. Now throughout the world all the states are equal in territory and in power, and none is superior to others. This is due to no other reason than the sovereigns being fond of having as ministers those whom they teach rather than those by whom they might be taught. T'ang would not venture to summon Yi-yin; nor would Duke Huan venture to summon Kuan Chung. If Kuan Chung could not be summoned, how much the less is a man, who would not liken himself to Kuan Chung, to be summoned?" [IIB-2]

151. When Master Meng was the state councillor of Ch'i, he went on a mission of condolence to T'eng. The king also sent Wang Huan, the governor of Ko, as assistant commissioner. They were together night and day, but on the whole trip to T'eng and back, never once did Master Meng speak to Wang Huan about their mission. Kung-sun Ch'ou said: "The position of state councillor of Ch'i is not a low one; the trip from Ch'i to T'eng is not a short one. Why did you never once speak to Wang Huan about your mission?" Master Meng said: "He seems to have performed his mission. What need was there for me to speak about it?" [IIB-6]

152. When Kung Hang Tzu lost his son, Wang Huan went to offer his condolence. When he entered the house, some advanced forward and spoke with him, and others moved up to his seat and spoke with him. But Master Meng did not speak to him. Kuang Huan was displeased and said: "All the gentlemen came to speak to me. Master Meng was the only man who did not speak to me, thereby belittling me." Master Meng, hearing of this remark, said: "According to the rules of etiquette, at court one does not leave one's seat to speak to others, nor does one pass from one's rank to greet others. I merely want to observe the rules of etiquette, but Wang Huan thinks that I was belittling him. Is not this strange?" [IVB-27]

153. Ch'i was suffering from famine, and Chen Ch'in said: "The people of the state all think that you will again request that the granary of T'ang be opened for them. But you will not do so a second time, will you?" Master Meng said: "To do it would be to act like Feng Fu. There was in Tsin a man by the name of Feng Fu, famous for his skill in seizing tigers. Later he became a good scholar. One day when he

was out in the wild country, he came upon a crowd in pursuit of a tiger. The tiger had been cornered, but no one dared to attack it. When they saw Feng Fu from afar, they rushed to meet him. Feng Fu rolled up his sleeves and descended from his carriage. The people were delighted with him, but the scholars laughed at him." [viiB-23]

154. Master Meng resigned his office and was about to return to his native state. The king called on him and said: "Formerly, I wished to meet you, but I had no chance. Since you came and joined the court, I have been very happy. But now again you leave me and return home. May I look forward to meeting you again?" Master Meng replied: "This is what I wish, though I dare not request such an honor." Another day, the king said to Shih Tzu, "I wish to give Master Meng a house right in the center of the kingdom, and to support his disciples with ten thousand bushels of grain, so that all the ministers and the people will respect them and follow their guidance. You had better tell him this for me!" Shih Tzu had this message conveyed to Master Meng through Chen Tzu, and Master Meng, on hearing it, said: "Well, how should Shih Tzu know that this proposal is unacceptable? If I wanted to be rich, would I have resigned an office paying 100,000 bushels of grain, to accept another paying only 10,000? Is this to show that I want to be rich?"

"Chi Sun once said, 'Strange indeed is Tzu Shu-ni! When he failed to obtain office for himself, he should have retired. However, he again schemed to secure high offices for his disciples. Who would not desire riches and honors? But this man, in seeking riches and honors, tried to monopolize the high mound.' In the good old days, the market traders exchanged what they had for what they had not, and the officer was there merely to keep order among them. It happened that there was a wretch who sought to occupy a high mound. Then he watched to net all the market's profits. The people all thought his practice malicious, and therefore they proceeded to levy a tax on his goods. Taxation on traders began with this wretch." [iiB-10]

155. Master Meng said to Ch'ih-wa: "You declined the governorship of Ling-Ch'iu and requested to be appointed censor. The reason for such a change seems to be that you may be able to remonstrate with the king. Now several months have elapsed, and is it still not the time for you to speak to the king?" Thereafter, Ch'ih-wa remonstrated with the king and, his advice not being accepted, resigned and

left the country. The people of Ch'i said: "The advice given
to Ch'ih-wa was indeed good, but we do not know as to what
he [i.e., Master Meng] is doing for himself." Kung-tu Tzu
reported these words to Master Meng, and Master Meng said:
"I have heard that a man who holds an office, when he is
prevented from performing his duties, ought to resign, and
that a man who is charged to remonstrate with the king, when
his advice is not accepted, ought to resign. But I hold no
office; nor am I charged to remonstrate with the king. Why
should I not be free to stay or leave, without any restraint?"
[IIB-5]

156. Master Meng, on his way out of Ch'i, passed his first
night in Chou. There was a man who persuaded him to stay
for the king. Master Meng even refused to speak with the
man; instead, he leaned upon his stool and slept. The man
was displeased and said: "I passed the night in respect so
as to speak to you, but you, Master, slept and did not listen.
I dare not see you again." Master Meng said: "Sit down, and
I will be frank to speak to you. Formerly, Duke Mu of Lu,
in order to induce Tzu-szu to stay, had kept a person by the
side of Tzu-szu. Hsieh-liu and Shen-hsiang, in order to feel
secure in their persons, had had a friend by the side of Duke
Mu. You have been trying to look out for me, but you do
not treat me as Tzu-szu was treated. Is it you, Sir, who have
failed me? Or is it I who have failed you?"[IIB-11]

157. When Master Meng left Ch'i, Yin Shih said to others:
"If Master Meng did not know that the king could not be
made a sage-king like T'ang and Wu, he is indeed not
judicious. If he knew that the king could not be made such,
and yet come to his court, he was looking for honors. He
came from a thousand *li* to see the king, and took his leave
because of disagreement with him. But he lingered at Chou
for three nights; why was he so tardy to leave that place?
I am displeased on account of this." Kao Tzu informed
Master Meng of these remarks. Master Meng said: "How
could Yin Shih understand me? I came a thousand *li* to see
the king, because it was what I desired. I took my leave
because of a disagreement; was that what I desired to do?
I had to leave. I lingered at Chou for three nights, and yet in
my heart I still considered my departure hasty. I was hoping
that the king might change. If the king had changed, he
would certainly have sent another message of recall. But it
did not come when I left Chou. Then I made up my mind to
leave for my homeland. However, I have not entirely given

up the king. The king, after all, can be made to do what is good. If he were to employ me, it would be not only for the welfare of the people of Ch'i, but also for the good of the whole world. I am still hoping that the king changes his mind! Why should I be like a narrow-minded man? He remonstrates with his sovereign, and when his advice is not accepted, he gets angry and shows his anger in his face. Then he takes his leave and travels all day long before he stops for the night." Yin Shih, on hearing of this, said: "I am indeed a low-minded man." [IIB-12]

158. When Master Meng left Ch'i, Ch'ung Yü asked on the way: "Master, you look quite unhappy. The other day I heard you say, 'The *chün-tzu* does not complain against Heaven, nor does he grudge against men.'" Master Meng said: "That was one time, and this is another. As a rule, a true sovereign is sure to arise in the course of five hundred years, and during that period there should be men of virtue and worth. Since the rise of the Chou dynasty, more than seven hundred years have elapsed. According to the number of years, the time is overdue; but considering the cyclical changes of the age, it is time for the rise of the kingly rule. But Heaven does not wish that the world should enjoy tranquility and good order. If Heaven wished this, who is there today, besides myself, to bring it about? Why shouldn't I be unhappy?" [IIB-13]

159. When Master Meng left Ch'i, he dwelt in Hsiu. There Kung-sun Ch'ou asked: "Was it the way of the ancients to hold office without accepting emolument?" Master Meng said: "No; when I first met the king at Ch'ung, I made up my mind to leave the country. After that did I not change my mind, and therefore I declined to accept the emolument? As the king was occupied with military campaigns, it would have been improper for me to ask to leave. But to tarry so long in Ch'i was not my intention." [IIB-14]

160. Ch'en Chen asked: "When you were in Ch'i, the king sent a present of 2,400 taels of fine silver and you refused to accept it. But in Sung you accepted the present of 1,680 taels and in Hsieh you again accepted the present of 1,200 taels. If it was right to decline the present on one occasion, then it was wrong to accept the present on other occasions. Or if it was right to accept the present on the latter occasions, then it was wrong to decline the present on the former occasion. You must have been wrong on one of the occasions." Master Meng said: "I was right on all the occasions. When

I was in Sung, I was about to take a long journey. A traveler must be accorded money for traveling expenses, and the king's message was, 'A present for traveling expenses.' Why should I decline it? When I was in Hsieh, I was apprehensive for my safety. The king's message was, 'Having heard of your apprehension, here is a present to help you procure arms.' Why should I decline it? But when I was in Ch'i, there was no occasion for a present. To send a man a present on no occasion is to bribe him. How should *chün-tzu* be won over with a bribe?" [IIB-3]

161. When Master Meng was living in Tsou, Chi Jen, as a guardian of Jen, sent him a present of silks. It was accepted without acknowledgment. When Master Meng was dwelling in P'ing-lu, Ch'u Tzu, as chief minister of Ch'i, sent him a present of some silks. Likewise, it was accepted without acknowledgment. Later when traveling from Tsou to Jen, Master Meng called on Chi Jen; but when he went from P'ing-lu to Ch'i, he did not call on Ch'u Tzu. Wu-lu Tzu was delighted and said: "This is my opportunity to ask for instruction." Then he asked: "When you went to Jen, you called on Ch'i Jen, but when you went to Ch'i, you did not call on Ch'u Tzu. Was it because Ch'u Tzu was only a minister?" Master Meng said: "No, it is said in the *Shu*, 'In offering a gift one should show due etiquette and respect. If etiquette and respect are not in accord with the gift, it may be said that no gift is offered. The will of offering is absent.' This is because the gift offered does not constitute a proper offering." Wu-lu Tzu was thereby pleased, and when someone asked him, he said: "Chi Tzu could not go to Tsou [to see Master Meng], but Ch'u Tzu could have gone to P'ing-lu." [VIB-5]

162. Chén Tai said: "In refusing to serve any of the feudal lords, you seem to me to be scrupulously biased. If now you were to serve them, you would make one of them attain kingly rule, or at least the position of feudal leader. It is said in the records, 'Bend one cubit and you may make eight cubits straight.' It seems to me worthwhile for you to try it." Master Meng said: "Formerly, Duke Ching of Ch'i was hunting and summoned the officer in charge of the forests by a flag [which was contrary to propriety]. The officer would not come, and the Duke wanted to put him to death. [As regards this incident, Master K'ung] said, 'The strong-willed man never deviates from his course, even at the threat of being thrown into a ditch or a stream. The brave man never submits to his enemies even at the threat of being killed.' What was it in

the officer that Master K'ung thus praised? He praised him because he did not go to the duke for his inappropriate summons. If a man goes to a sovereign without waiting to be
summoned, what will the people think of him? Moreover, this
saying, 'Bend one cubit and you may make eight cubits
straight,' refers to the gain that may be obtained. If we act
in view of gain, will we do it when gain can be obtained by
bending eight cubits to make one cubit straight?

"And again, Chao Chien-tzu once sent Wang Liang to act as
charioteer for his favorite Hsi. In the course of a whole day,
not a bird was caught. The favorite Hsi, on his return to Chao
Chien-tzu, said, 'Wang Liang is the poorest charioteer in the
world.' On being informed of this remark, Wang Liang said,
'Let me drive again.' Only after repeated requests was this
accorded to him, and in one morning ten birds were caught.
Then the favorite Hsi on return said, 'Wang Liang is the best
charioteer in the world.' Chien-tzu said, 'I will make him your
charioteer.' When this was reported to Wang Liang, he said,
'When I followed the proper rules to drive for him, not a
single bird was caught in the whole day. But when I engaged
in deceptive trapping, in one morning ten birds were caught.
It is said in the *Shih*:

When one follows the proper rule for driving, One is sure
to shoot one's subjects.

I am not used to driving for a mean man, and I beg leave to
decline.' Thus a charioteer even was ashamed to accommo-
date himself to a poor archer, even though by so doing they
could thereby catch a pile of game. So how can I deviate
from the *Tao* to follow those sovereigns? And your reasoning
is wrong! Never has there been a man who bends himself
and yet is able to make others straight." [IIIB-1]

163. Kung-sun Ch'ou asked: "What is there in *yi* that
prevents you from going to see the feudal lords?" Master
Meng said: "In ancient times a man who was not in the service of a state would not go to see the sovereign. Tuan-kan Mu
leaped over his wall to avoid the Duke of Wei, and Hsieh-
liu shut his door and would not admit the Duke of Lu. They
both went too far. If the sovereign is sincere, it is proper to
see him. Yang Hu wished to meet Master K'ung, but he did
not want to overstep the bounds of *li*. According to the rules
of etiquette, when a minister sends a present to a scholar
during his absence, the scholar will call on the minister to

pay his respects. Yang Hu watched that Master K'ung was out and then sent him a present of roasted pig. Master K'ung likewise watched that Yang Hu was out and then called on him to pay his respects. At that time, if Yang Hu had called on Master K'ung first, how could he have failed to meet him? Tseng Tzu said, 'One who shrugs shoulders and feigns flattering smiles is more exhausted than a field laborer toiling in summer.' Tzu Lu also said, 'There are those who talk with people with whom they have nothing in common; so they blush with shame. I do not understand why they do so.' From these remarks, it is possible to know the character and temperament of *chün-tzu*." [LIIB-7]

164. Wang Chang said: "I venture to ask what there is in *yi* that prevents you from going to see the feudal lords." Master Meng said: "Those in the metropolitan areas are called city subjects, and those in the countryside are called farming subjects. In both cases they are common men. It is quite in accord with *li* that common men who do not offer presents to the sovereign and become his subjects, should not venture to call on the sovereign." Wang Chang said: "When a common man is summoned to perform service, he goes and performs it. But when the sovereign wishes to see a scholar and summons him, why should the scholar not go to the interview?" Master Meng said: "It is a man's duty to go and perform service, but it is not his duty to go and see the sovereign. For what reason does the sovereign wish to see the scholar?" Wang Chang said: "Because of his extensive knowledge or because of his worth and talents." Master Meng said: "If a man possesses extensive knowledge, he is a teacher. Even the emperor does not summon a teacher, so how much the less may the sovereign of a state do so? If he is a man of worth and talents, I have never heard that a sovereign summons a man of worth and talents when he wishes to see him. Duke Mu of Lu had frequent interviews with Tzu Szu, and once he said, 'In ancient times, a sovereign of a state of a thousand chariots wished to make friends with a scholar; how do you think of it?' Tzu Szu was displeased and said, 'The ancients said to serve him! Did they say to befriend him?' Tzu Szu was thus displeased because he reasoned, 'As regards position, you are my sovereign, and I am your subject. How can I presume to be a friend of the sovereign? As regards virtue, you ought to serve me as a teacher. How may you treat me merely as a friend?' When the sovereign of a state of a thousand chariots failed in his effort to

seek for a man of worth, how much less could the sovereign summon him? Duke Ching of Ch'i was hunting and summoned the officer in charge of the forest with a flag. The officer would not come, and the Duke wanted to put him to death. [As regards this incident, Master K'ung] said, 'The strong-willed man never deviated from his course, even at the threat of being thrown into a ditch or a stream. The brave man never submitted to his enemies, even at the threat of being killed.' What was it in the officer that Master K'ung thus praised? He praised him because he did not go to the Duke for his inappropriate summons." Then Wang Chang asked: "May I ask how the officer should be summoned?" Master Meng said: "He should be summoned with a fur cap. A common man should be summoned with a plain banner, a scholar with an embroidered flag, and a minister with a feathered flag. When the sovereign used the flag appropriate to the ministers to summon the officer in charge of the forest, the officer did not presume to go, even at the cost of his life. If the sovereign were to use what is appropriate to scholars to summon common men, how should they presume to go? How much less should a man of worth go when he is summoned in an improper way. When a sovereign wishes to see a man of worth and yet does not approach him in the proper way, it is as if he wished a man to enter the house and shut the door in his face. *Yi* is the way, and *li* is the door. Only *chün-tzu* can follow the way of *yi* and pass the door of *li*. It is said in the *Shih:*

> The great road is as even as a whetstone,
>   And as straight as an arrow;
> While noble men tread on it,
>   Mean men look at it."

Wang Chang said: "It is said of Master K'ung, 'When the sovereign summoned him, he went without waiting for his carriage.' Was Master K'ung wrong?" "But," said Master Meng, "Master Kung was then in office and had duties, and he was summoned on the business of his office." [VB-7]

165. P'eng Keng asked: "Is it not an extravagance to go from one state to another and live upon the feudal lords, with an escort of tens of carriages and hundreds of men?" Master Meng said: "If it is contrary to the *Tao*, even a basketful of rice may not be accepted from a man. If it is in accord with the *Tao*, it is not excessive for Shun to accept the whole

world from Yao. Do you think it was excessive?" P'eng Keng said: "No. But I consider it improper for a scholar rendering no service to accept support." Master Meng said: "If you do not have interchange of the products of labor and exchange of services, so that one's surplus may supply another's deficiency, then farmers will have surplus of grain, and women will have surplus of cloth. If you have such an exchange, then carpenters and cartwrights may all get food from you. Now here is a man who, at home, is filial, and abroad fraternal; he abides by the *Tao* of early kings for the benefits of the later scholars. Nevertheless, you would not support him. How is it that you esteem the carpenter and cartwright, and spun him who upholds *jen* and *yi*?" P'eng Keng said: "The carpenter and cartwright carry on their trades for the purpose of earning a living. Does the *chün-tzu* practice the *Tao* for the purpose of earning a living?" Master Meng said: "What have you to do with his purpose? If he is of service to you, he deserves to be remunerated and should be remunerated. But do you remunerate him for his purpose or for his service?" "For his purpose," was the reply. But Master Meng added: "Suppose that there is a man who breaks your tiles and blemishes your walls. Even if his purpose is to earn a living, will you remunerate him?" "No," said P'eng Keng. Master Meng concluded: "Then, after all, it is not the purpose which is remunerated, but the service rendered." [IIIB-4]

166. Wan Chang asked: "I venture to ask what the feeling of the heart should be when friends exchange gifts." Master Meng said: "There must be the feeling of respect." Wan Chang said: "Why is it considered disrespectful to decline a gift?" Master Meng said: "When the elder gives you a gift, before you accept it, you consider whether he gives it in accordance with *yi* or not; this is deemed disrespectful. For this reason one must not decline a present." Then Wan Chang asked again: "A man may not expressly decline a present, but if he believes that it has been taken contrary to *yi* from the people, may he not make some excuse for declining it?" Master Meng said: "When a man has good reason to give a present and the offer is made in accordance with *li*, even Master K'ung would have accepted it." Wan Chang asked: "Suppose that a man robs people outside the city gates. He has good reason to give a present and the offer is made in accordance with *li*. Would it be proper to accept the present so acquired by robbery?" "No," said Master Meng, "it would not be proper. It is said in the *Shu*:

Those who kill people and rob them of their goods are reckless and fearless of death. Let them be detested by all.

These persons are to be put to death, without being given instructions. This was the general rule under the Three Dynasties, and it cannot be questioned. To the present day this rule is still strictly enforced. How can such a present be accepted?" Wan Chang said: "At present the feudal lords take from their people just as a robber plunders his victims. If they offer their presents with appropriate *li*, then the *chün-tzu* accepts them. I venture to ask how you explain it." Master Meng said: "Do you think that if there should arise a real king, he would put all feudal lords to death? Or would he admonish them first, and then, on their not reforming themselves, put them to death? If you claim that whoever takes what does not properly belong to him is a robber, you apply resemblance and insist on *yi* to the utmost. When Master K'ung was in office in Lu, the people used to contest the game from the hunt, and he also joined with them in the contest. If this contest for the captured game was considered proper, how much more may the presents of the sovereigns be accepted!" "Then," Wan Chang argued, "may we suppose that Master K'ung held office not for the purpose of practicing the *Tao?*" Master Meng said: "Yes, he desired to practice the *Tao.*" Then Wan Chang asked, "If he desired to practice the *Tao*, why should he join in the contest for the captured game?" Master Meng said: "Master K'ung first recorded how to rectify the vessels of sacrifice, without regard to food gathered from every quarter." Then Wan Chang asked again: "Why did he not go away?" "He wished to have a trial," said Master Meng, "in order to show that the *Tao* might be practiced. If he failed in his trial, then he would go away. Therefore, he had never remained in a state longer than three years. Master K'ung was in office when he saw that the *Tao* might be practiced; or when he was received with *li*; or when men of worth were honored. In his relation with Chi Huan Tzu, he saw the possibility of practicing the *Tao*; in his relation with Duke Ling of Wei, he had been received with *li*; and in his relation with Duke Hsiao of Wei, he was convinced that men of worth would be honored." [VB-5]

167. Wan Chang said: "Why is it that a scholar may not accept the support from the sovereign of another state?" Master Meng said: "It would be presumptuous for him to do so. When a sovereign loses his state, he is in accord with *li*

to accept the support from the sovereign of another state. But it is contrary to *li* for a scholar to accept the support from any of the feudal lords." Wan Chang said: "If the sovereign sends him a present of grain, may he accept it?" Master Meng said: "He may accept it." "On what ground does he accept it?" "The sovereign ought to provide relief for the people." Then Wan Chang asked again: "Why is it that the scholar will thus accept the sovereign's relief but will not accept his emolument?" "It would be presumptuous for him to do so." "I venture to ask why it is presumptuous to do so." "Even gatekeepers and night watchmen," said Master Meng, "have their regular duties, for which they are supported by the sovereign. But it is disrespectful for one who has no regular duties to accept emolument from the sovereign." Wan Chang said: "If the sovereign sends a gift, it is accepted. But may this gift be constantly repeated?" Master Meng said: "Duke Mu frequently inquired after Tzu Szu's health and sent him presents of cooked meat. Tzu Szu was thereby displeased. Finally he let the messenger stand outside the door, bowed his head to the ground with his face to the north, made obeisance twice, and then declined the present, saying, 'Now I know that the sovereign feeds me as a dog or a horse.' Since then there have been no messengers with gifts. If a sovereign is pleased with a man of worth and yet can neither employ nor support him, can he be said to be pleased with the man of worth?" Wan Chang asked again: "I venture to ask how the sovereign should proceed properly if he wishes to support a *chün-tzu*." Master Meng said: "When a present is offered for the first time in the sovereign's name, the recipient will make obeisance twice with his head bowed to the ground to accept it. Thereafter the stewards will continue to send grain and the chefs to send meat without using the name of the sovereign. Tzu Szu thought that it was not proper to support a *chün-tzu* when the meat from the cauldrons gave him much trouble of constantly making obeisance. For instance, Yao honored Shun thus: he sent his nine sons to serve him, and gave him his two daughters in marriage, with all his officers, cattle and stores of provisions for his use on the farm, and then exalted him to the highest position. Therefore this is the way for the kings to honor men of worth." [VB-6]

168. Chou Hsiao asked: "In ancient times, did *chün-tzu* wish to serve in the government?" Master Meng said: "Yes, they did. It is said in the records, 'When Master K'ung was out of office for three months, he would be anxious and un-

happy; so on leaving for a state, he always had with him gifts for its sovereign.' Kung-ming Yi once said, 'In ancient times, one was condoled upon being out of office for a duration of three months.' " Chou Hsiao said: "One is condoled upon being out of office for three months; is this not rather too urgent?" Master Meng said: "The loss of an office to a scholar is like the loss of a kingdom to a sovereign. It is said in the *Li*: 'The sovereign plows with the assistance of the people, so as to supply millet for sacrifice. The queen tends silkworms and unwinds the cocoons, so as to make garments for sacrifice. If the sacrificial animals are not full grown, the sacrificial millet was not pure, and if the sacrificial garments are not complete, the sovereign dare not offer sacrifices. If a scholar, out of office, has no sacrificial land, he does not offer sacrifices.' When the sacrificial animals, vessels, and garments are not complete, one dares not sacrifice and therefore there is no entertainment. Is this not sufficient reason for condolence?" Chou Hsiao asked again: "On leaving for a state, why need he take gifts?" Master Meng said: "A scholar's being in office is comparable to the farmer's plowing. Does a farmer part with his plow when he leaves his country?" Chou Hsiao pursued: "There are many official posts in the Kingdom of Tsin, but I have never heard of anyone being thus anxious to be in office. Since a *chün-tzu* is urgent about being in office, why does his taking it become so difficult?" Master Meng said: "When a son is born, what is desired is to get him a wife; when a daughter is born, what is desired is to get her a husband. The heart of parents is common to all men and women. If the young people, without waiting for the order of their parents and arrangements of the mediators, bore holes to catch sight of each other, or jump over walls to be with each other, then their parents and all the people will have contempt for them. The ancients were indeed anxious to be in office, but they disliked ignoring the *Tao*. For one to be in office without following the *Tao* is similar to the young people who bore holes." [IIIB-3]

169. Ch'en Tzu asked: "In ancient times, under what conditions did the noble man accept office?" Master Meng said: "There were three conditions under which he would accept office and three conditions under which he would leave. If he were received with respect and accorded *li*, and he were convinced that his advice would be adopted, then he would accept office. Although still accorded *li* and courtesy, he would leave if his advice were not adopted. Next, although

his advice could not be adopted, if he were received with respect and accorded *li*, he would accept office. If he were not
accorded *li* and courtesy, he would leave. And lastly, he had
nothing to eat, day and night, and was so famished that he
could not depart from his abode; on hearing of this the sovereign said, 'I cannot practice his teachings, nor can I follow
his advice, but I am ashamed to let him suffer hunger in my
country,' then relief offered might be accepted, but only for
the purpose of averting death." [VIB-14]

170. Master Meng said: "To hold office is not on account
of poverty, but sometimes one seeks office for that reason. To
take a wife is not for the sake of her service, although at times
one marries for that reason. If a man takes office because of
poverty, he will certainly decline an honorable position and
occupy a humble one; he will certainly refuse high emolument
and accept low pay. For what position will such a man be fit?
For such a petty office as that of gatekeeper or a night watch-
man. Master K'ung was once a keeper of stores, and he then
said, 'I merely attend to keeping a correct account.' When he
was in charge of the public fields, he then said, 'I merely attend to making the cattle and sheep fat and strong.' When a
man occupies a low position, it is wrong for him to speak of
high matters. When he occupies a high position at court, and
yet the *Tao* fails to prevail, he should be ashamed of himself." [VB-5]

171. Shun-yü K'un said: "A man who stresses a good name
and meritorious service always works for the benefit of others.
On the other hand, a man who cares not for a good name and
meritorious service is always content to live for himself. You,
Master, were ranked among the three chief ministers, and yet
before you established a good name and meritorious service,
either among the ruling class or among the people, you have
left your place. Is this the way of *jen*?" Master Meng said:
"There was Po-yi, who, in a low position, would not, as a
man of worth, serve a corrupt sovereign. There was Yi-yin,
who sought five times to serve T'ang [founder of Shang] and
five times to serve Chieh [last ruler of Hsia]. There was Liu
Hsia Huei, who did not disdain to serve a vile sovereign, nor
did he decline a petty office. These three men were different
in the pursuit of the *Tao*, but their aim was one and the
same." "What was their one and the same aim?" Master Meng
continued: "*Jen!* And so it suffices that *chün-tzu* abides by
jen. Why should they pursue the same *Tao*?" Shun-yü K'un
said: "During the reign of Duke Mu of Lu, the government

was in the hands of Kung-yi Tzu, while Liu Tzu and Tzu Szu were ministers. And yet the territory of Lu diminished exceedingly. How was it that men of worth were of no advantage to a state?" Master Meng said: "The sovereign of Yü could not keep Pai-li Hsi, and thereby lost his state, while Duke Mu of Ch'in made use of Pai-li Hsi's service, and thereby became the leader of the feudal lords. By not employing men of worth, the sovereign was in danger of losing his state. How can it result merely in the diminution of territory?" Shun-yü K'un said: "Formerly, when Wang Pao dwelt on the banks of the Ch'i, the people of Wei all became good singers. When Mien Chü dwelt in Kao-t'ang, the people in western Ch'i all became good singers. The wives of Hua Chou and Ch'i Liang mourned the death of their husbands so properly that they changed the customs of the country. What is within the will manifests itself without. I have never seen the man who was devoted to his work and yet failed to achieve results. Therefore there are now no men of worth. If there were, I should know them." Master Meng said: "When Master K'ung was Minister of Crime in Lu, his advice was not adopted. He stayed on till the time of the state sacrifice, and when no sacrificial meat was sent to the Minister of Crime, he hastened to leave. Those who did not know him thought it was on account of the sacrificial meat. Those who knew him thought that his departure was due to the neglect of *li*. In fact, Master K'ung preferred to leave for this singular incident rather than for no apparent reason. The conduct of a *chün-tzu* cannot be understood by the people." [vIB-6]

172. Shun-yü K'un said: "Is it a rule of etiquette that men and women should not touch hands when passing things to one another?" Master Meng said: "It is." Shun-yü K'un pursued: "Suppose a man's sister-in-law were drowning, should he rescue her with his hands?" Master Meng said: "Certainly he should. Not to rescue one's sister-in-law from drowning would be beastly inhumanity. It is a general rule for men and women not to touch hands; whereas to rescue a drowning sister-in-law with one's hands is merely expediency." Shun-yü K'un said: "The whole world is drowning. How is it that you, Master, will not rescue it with your hands?" Master Meng said: "A drowning world is to be rescued by the *Tao;* a drowning sister-in-law with the hand. Do you expect me to rescue the world with my hand?" [IVA-17]

173. Yü and Chi, in an age of a peaceful world, were so earnest in their work that they three times passed their homes

without entering. Master K'ung considered them men of worth. Yen Tzu, in an age of great confusion, lived in a low alleyway with only a bamboo bowl and a gourd cup of water. No ordinary man could have endured such misery, but mirth never failed Yen Tzu. Master K'ung also considered him a man of worth. Master Meng said: "Yü, Chi, and Yen Hui abide by the same *Tao*. Yü thought that if anyone in the world were drowned, it would be his fault. Chi thought that if anyone in the world suffered hunger, it would be his fault. It was for this reason that they were so earnest in their work. If these three men of worth exchanged places, each would do what the other did. If people were fighting in the same house, you would separate them. It would be proper for you to part them even with hair dishevelled and cap untied. But suppose people were fighting in the village or neighborhood, it would be an error for you to part them with hair dishevelled and cap untied. In such a case it would be allowable for you to shut your door." [IVB-29]

174. When Tseng Tzu dwelt in Wu-ch'eng, the Yüeh came to attack the city. Someone said: "The enemy is coming. Why not leave the city?" Then Tseng Tzu said to the caretaker: "Do not let anyone lodge in my house or damage the trees and shrubs." When the enemy left, he sent word: "Repair the house, for I am about to return." When the enemy went away, Tseng Tzu came back. His followers said: "Our Master has been treated with loyalty and respect, but on the coming of the enemy, he set an example to the people by being the first to run away, and then he returned when the enemy had left. Was his conduct improper?" But Shen Yu-hsing said: "There is something which you do not know. Formerly, there was in this place a revolt of the grass-cutters, and then our Master was here with seventy of his followers, but none of them became involved in the matter." When Tzu Szu dwelt in Wei, the Ch'i came to attack the country. Someone said: "The enemy is coming. Why not leave the country?" Tzu Szu said: "If I leave, whom will the sovereign have to defend the country?" Master Meng said: "Tseng Tzu and Tzu Szu abide by the same *Tao*. Tseng Tzu was a teacher, and his position was like that of a father and an elder brother. On the other hand, Tzu Szu was a state minister, and his position was that of a subordinate. Should Tseng Tzu and Tzu Szu have exchanged places, each would have done what the other did." [IVB-31]

175. Wan Chang asked: "I venture to ask about friend-

ship." Master Meng said: "Friendship should be maintained without any presumption on the ground of seniority, or superiority, or relationship. In other words, friendship is something based on virtue, and there should be no presumption whatever. Meng Hsien-tzu, chief of a family of one hundred chariots, had five friends—namely, Yüeh-Cheng Ch'iu, Mu Chung, and three others whose names I have forgotten. Hsien-tzu maintained friendship with these five men without presumption on account of his family. If he presumed upon his family, they would not care to be his friends. And this is true not only in the case of the chief of a family of one hundred chariots, but also with the sovereign of a small state. Duke Hui of Pi once said, 'I treat Tzu Szu as my teacher and Yen Pan as my friend. As to Wang Shun and Ch'ang Hsi, they are my subordinates.' And this is true not only in the case of the sovereign of a small state, but also with the sovereign of a large state. This might be illustrated in the relationship of Duke P'ing of Tsin with Hai T'ang: when Hai T'ang asked him to come in, he came; when he asked him to sit, he sat; when he asked him to eat, he ate. Even though there were plain food and vegetable soup, the Duke always ate his full, never daring not to do so. But their relationship was confined to this and went no further. He never called Hai T'ang to share his royal position, or to govern his royal office, or to partake of his royal emoluments. He showed him the respect which a scholar would show to a man of worth, not that granted by a sovereign on a man of worth. When Shun went to see Emperor Yao, he was lodged in the second palace. The emperor often went there to dine with Shun. Thus he acted as host and guest alternately. Here was the case where the emperor maintained friendship with a common man. When an inferior shows respect to his superiors, he is said to esteem men of nobility. When a superior shows respect to his inferiors, he is said to honor men of worth. In either case, the *yi* is the same." [vb-3]

176. Master Meng said: "When somebody told Tzu Lu of his fault, he rejoined. When Yü heard good words, he bowed. Great Shun was still better. He regarded the goodness of other men as his own, and thereby he would yield his own and follow that of others, so as to delight learning goodness from others. From the time when he was a farmer, a potter, and a fisherman to the time when he became emperor, he was always learning from others. To learn goodness from others is to encourage them to be good. Accordingly, for *chün-tzu,*

nothing is more important than encouraging men to be good."
[IIA-8]

177. Master Meng said: "When you love people, and they
fail to return the love, you turn to yourself and examine your
jen. When you try to govern people, and they refuse to be
governed, you turn to yourself and examine your wisdom.
When you treat people with *li*, and they do not return it, you
turn to yourself and examine your reverence. When our conduct does not yield what we desire, we turn inward and
examine ourselves. If a man's person is upright, the whole
world will turn to him. It is said in the *Shih:*

> Forever abide by Heaven's mandate,
> And you will be blessed with good fortune." [IVA-4]

178. Master Meng said: "One who is respectful does not
disdain others. One who is temperate does not plunder others.
A sovereign who disdains and plunders men is only afraid lest
they should be disobedient. How can he ever be regarded as
respectful and temperate? How can respect and temperance
be expressed in pleasant words and facial expressions?" [IVA-
16]

179. Master Meng said: "No part of a man's body is more
vital than the pupil of the eye. The pupil cannot conceal a
man's wickedness. If within his breast he is upright, the pupil
is bright. If within his breast he is not upright, the pupil is
dull. Listen to his words and look into his pupils; how can a
man conceal his true self?" [IVA-15]

180. Master Meng said: "A man may receive unexpected
praises and reproaches when he tries to be perfect." [IVA-21]

181. Master Meng said: "A man who is apt to be impru-
dent in his words is not accountable for his actions." [IVA-22]

182. Yüeh-cheng Tzu went to Ch'i in company with Wang
Huan. He came to see Master Meng, who said to him: "So
you have come to see me!" Yüeh-cheng Tzu said: "Master,
why do you speak such words?" Master Meng asked: "How
long have you been here?" "I arrived here the day before
yesterday." "The day before yesterday! Is it not proper that
I speak thus?" Yüeh-cheng Tzu explained: "I was not yet
settled." "Have you heard that a man must be settled before
he calls on an elder?" Yüeh-cheng Tzu conceded: "I am
wrong." [IVA-24]

183. Master Meng said to Yüeh-cheng Tzu: "Your coming
here in company with Wang Huan was merely for the food

and drink. I have never thought that you, having learned the *Tao* of the ancients, would have been occupied solely in the food and drink." [IVA-25]

184. Master Meng said: "What troubles will beset a man who speaks ill of others!" [IVB-9]

185. Master Meng said: "Chung-ni [i.e., Master K'ung] would never go to extremes." [IVB-10]

186. Master Meng said: "In the case of a great man, his words may not be sincere and his actions may not be resolute; he simply speaks and acts in accord with *yi*." [IVB-11]

187. Master Meng said: "If a man takes a thing when he should not take it, to take it is contrary to prudence. If a man gives a thing when he should not give it, to give it is contrary to kindness. If a man dares death when he should not do so, to dare it is contrary to bravery." [IVB-23]

188. There was a man of Ch'i who lived with his wife and concubine. Every morning he went out all alone and returned at night, well filled with wine and meat. When his wife asked with whom he had been dining and drinking, he would say that they were all men of wealth and honor. So the wife said to the concubine: "Every day our husband goes out and returns, well filled with wine and meat. When I ask him with whom he dined and drank, he says that they are all men of wealth and honor. But since no men of distinction ever come here, I will spy out where he goes." Accordingly, she got up early in the morning and secretly followed wherever her husband went. As he walked through the whole city, not a soul stopped to talk with him. At last he came to a graveyard in the eastern suburb and begged for scraps of meat that were left over from the sacrifices. Not being satisfied, he looked about and went to others; this was the way in which he got himself satiated. Then the wife hurried back and said to the concubine: "A husband is to be admired and relied upon for a lifetime. Now we have such a man as our husband." In utter shame of their husband, the two women stood together in the middle of the courtyard, weeping and wailing. Meanwhile, the man, unaware of what had happened, came strutting home with his usual jaunty air in the presence of his wife and concubine. Master Meng commented: "In the eyes of a *chün-tzu*, as to the way by which men seek riches and honors, success and gain, there are few wives and concubines who would not weep together for shame." [IVB-33].

189. Master Meng said: "Ancient kings of worth were fond of a man's goodness and oblivious to their own power.

How could ancient men of worth be otherwise? They delighted in their own *Tao* and were indifferent to the power of the sovereigns. Therefore, if a sovereign did not show them respect and treat them with *li*, they would not let him come frequently to visit them. If he were unable to visit them frequently, how much less could he employ them as his ministers?" [VIIA-8]

190. Master Meng said to Sung Kuo-chien: "Are you fond, Sir, of traveling to different states? Let me tell you the proper way of doing it. If a sovereign knows you, calm yourself and be content. If no one knows you, be the same." Sung Kuo-chien asked: "What should one do in order to calm oneself and be content?" Master Meng said: "Honor virtue and delight in *yi*, and you will calm yourself and be content. Therefore, a scholar, when in poverty, does not neglect *yi*, when in prosperity, he does not deviate from the *Tao*. If he does not neglect *yi* in poverty, he is able to hold himself. If he does not deviate from the *Tao* in prosperity, the people do not lose their faith in him. When the ancients achieved their purposes, the people received benefits. When they did not achieve their purposes, they cultivated their own persons and became known in the world. Likewise, when they were out of office, they would attend to their own persons. When they were in power, they would better the whole world." [VIIA-9]

191. Kung-sun Ch'ou said: "It is said in the *Shih*, 'Let us not eat without cause!' How is it that *chün-tzu* eat but do not labor?" Master Meng said: "When a *chün-tzu* stays in a state, if its sovereign employs his counsel, he enjoys security, wealth, honor, and glory. If its young men follow his instructions, they observe filial piety, fraternal duty, loyalty and sincerity. As to the saying, 'Let us not eat without cause,' who abides by it more than *chün-tzu?*" [VIIA-32]

192. Master Meng said: "To feed a man without love is to treat him like a pig. To love him without respect, is to treat him like a pet animal. Respect and reverence form the substance of gifts. A *chün-tzu* will not be retained by such artificial means as gifts not accompanied with respect and reverence." [VIIA-37]

193. Master Meng said: "When the *Tao* prevails in the world, the *Tao* must exist along with one's person. When the *Tao* fails to prevail in the world, one's person must retire along with the *Tao*. But I have never heard that the *Tao* can be sacrificed on account of men." [VIIA-42]

194. Master Meng said: "In regard to animals, the *chün-

tzu is kind but not loving. In regard to the people in general, he is loving but not devoted. Only when he is devoted to his parents, is he loving to the people in general. Only when he is loving to the people in general, is he kind to animals." [VIIA-45]

195. Master Meng said: "If a man himself does not practice the *Tao*, he cannot make his wife and children practice it. If a man does not govern the people according to the *Tao*, he cannot command the obedience of his wife and children." [VIIB-9]

196. Master Meng said: "A man who cares for his good name may be willing to decline a state of one thousand chariots, but if he is not that sort of man, he will not part with even a dish of rice or a platter of soup without manifesting displeasure on his countenance." [VIIB-11]

197. Master Meng said: "Only when a man of worth has himself been enlightened, does he try to enlighten others. Nowadays, however, one tries to enlighten others while oneself is in darkness." [VIIB-20]

198. Hé Chi said: "There is much gossip about me." Master Meng said: "There is no harm in it. Scholars often suffer from gossip. It is said in the *Shih:*

> My sad heart is in distress;
> I am resented by petty men.

This may be said of Master K'ung. And, again:

> Though I cannot stop their resentment,
> Yet my good name is not harmed.

This may be said of King Wen." [VIIB-19]

199. When Master Meng went to T'eng, he was lodged in the upper palace. A pair of sandals had been left by the window, and when the attendant came to look for them, they were missing. Someone asked: "Could your followers have hidden them?" Master Meng said: "Do you think that my men came here to steal sandals?" The man said: "Maybe not." Master Meng said: "When I offer instructions to my pupils, I do not inquire into their past, nor do I turn them away. If they come with the heart to learn, I receive them with no more ado." [VIIB-30]

200. Master Meng said: "When a man gives counsel to great personages, he should ignore their importance and take

no heed of their pomp and grandeur. They live in large and richly decorated mansions; but these, if I were in power, I would not have. They dine with plenty of dishes and are waited on by hundreds of attendant girls, but these, if I were in power, I would not have. They indulge themselves in wine and hunting, with thousands of chariots following after them; but these, if I were in power, I would not have. What they enjoy having is not what pleases me; what I care for are the regulations of the ancients. For this reason, why should I stand in awe of those great personages?" [VIIB-34]

Part Four: The Comments of Mencius

As we have seen, the period of the Warring States was not only an age of intense political confusion, but one of feverish intellectual activity in which various schools of thought vied for supremacy. This aspect of the age is most significant for our study of the following passages, since it provided the stimulus for Mencius' brilliant lifelong defense of Confucius' doctrines, as well as for his approval of the tradition of the sages.

ᵥᵉᶠ ᶠᵉᵥ

Chapter VII. On Teachings of the Other Schools

201. Kung-tu Tzu said: "Master, people all say that you are fond of arguing. May I venture to ask why?" Master Meng said: "Indeed, why should I love arguing? But how can I help it? The world has been in existence for a long time. In one period there has been good order, and in another period there has been confusion. In the time of Yau, the waters overflowed their channels and inundated the central domain. Snakes and dragons took their abode everywhere, and the people had no place to settle themselves. In the low regions they made nests, and in the high regions they lived in caves. It is said in the *Shu*, 'The overflowing waters warned us.' The overflowing waters were the Flood. Yü was asked to control the Flood. He cleared the channels and conducted the waters to the sea. He drove out snakes and dragons and forced them into the marshes. The waters [i.e., the Kiang, the Huai, the Ho, and the Han] were confined within their channels. When these menaces were removed and when the birds and beasts which were harmful to men were out of sight, the

people returned to live again on the plains. After the death of Yao and Shun, the *Tao* of the sages fell into decay, and cruel sovereigns arose one after another. Dwellings were pulled down to make ponds and lakes, with the result that the people had no places to stay and rest. Farms were appropriated to be turned into gardens and parks, with the result that the people could not get clothes and food. Then there arose vicious teachings and oppressive deeds; gardens and parks, ponds and lakes increased in number; birds and beasts swarmed in the marshes and thickets. By the time of Chow [last ruler of the Yin dynasty], the world was again in great confusion. Then the Duke of Chou assisted King Wu in annihilating Chow and smiting the state of Yin. After three years, the ruler of Yen was put to death, and Fei Lien was driven to a corner by the sea and killed. The states which had been subdued amounted to fifty. Tigers, leopards, rhinoceroses, and elephants were driven away to remote regions, and the whole world was greatly pleased. It is said in the *Shu:*

> How great and splendid were the plans of King Wen!
> How great and eminent were the achievements of King Wu!
> In all these they afford illustrious examples to the people of later generations;
> They are so righteous and perfect!

And again the world fell into decay, and the *Tao* declined. There arose again vicious teachings and oppressive deeds; there were ministers who murdered their sovereigns, and sons who murdered their fathers. Master K'ung wrote the *Ch'un Ch'iu* [Spring and Autumn Annals] to express his anxiety about the turn of events. The *Ch'un Ch'iu* recorded all major events of the world. On this account Master K'ung said, 'It is the *Ch'un Ch'iu* by which I shall be known to posterity, and it is the *Ch'un Ch'iu* by which I shall be condemned to the posterity.' Again, there are no sage kings, and the feudal lords give rein to their lusts. Unemployed scholars indulge in open criticism. The words of Yang Chu and Mo Ti fill the whole world. In their discourses, the people have adopted the views either of Yang or of Mo. Yang's principle of 'each one for himself' excludes the claims of the sovereign. Mo's principle of 'all-embracing love' leaves out the claims of the father. Abolition of fatherhood and princehood is the reduction of mankind to the level of wild beasts.

Kung-ming Yi said, 'In their kitchens, there is fat meat; in their stables, there are fat horses; but the people look hungry and starved bodies lie along the countryside. This is letting beasts devour men.' If the doctrines of Yang and Mo are not checked, and the doctrine of Master K'ung is not promoted, perverse teachings will delude the people and block the way to *jen* and *yi*. If these are blocked, beasts will be led to devour men, and men will devour one another. I am alarmed by the spread of these perverse teachings and therefore defend the doctrines of the ancient sages and oppose those of Yang and Mo. I banish depraved doctrines, so that such heretics shall not show themselves. When these heresies arise in men's hearts, they are injurious to the personal conduct. When they arise in men's conduct, they are pernicious to the government. When sages rise again, they will not change my words. In ancient times, Yü controlled floods and the world was returned to order. The Duke of Chou absorbed the Yi and the Ti [barbarian tribes] and drove away all ferocious animals, and the people enjoyed repose. Master K'ung completed the *Ch'un Ch'iu*, and rebellious ministers and villainous sons were struck with fear. It is said in the *Shih:*

> He smote the Yi and the Ti;
> He punished Hsin and Shu;
> No one dared to resist us.

Those who acknowledged neither father nor sovereign would have been smitten by the Duke of Chou. I also wish to rectify the hearts of men and put an end to heresies; to oppose evil conduct and put away depraved doctrines, so as to continue the work of the three sages. Do I do so because I am fond of arguing? No, it is simply that I cannot do otherwise. Any one who lifts his voice against Yang and Mo is worthy to be a disciple of the sages." [IIIB-9]

202. Master Meng said: "The principle of Yang Tzu was 'each one for himself,' and he would not pluck out a single hair from his body to benefit the world. Mo Ti's principle is 'all-embracing love,' and he was bent on saving the world even though he had to rub his body smooth from head to foot. Tzu Mo held the mean between these two extremes; by holding the mean, one is nearer to the true way. But by holding the mean without adapting oneself to the exigency of circumstances, one is merely like the extremists. The reason why I detest the extremists is that they pervert the true way

by exalting one point and ignoring a hundred others." [VIIA-26]

203. Master Meng said: "Those who are fleeing from Mo turn out to be the adherents of Yang, and those who are fleeing from Yang turn out to be the adherents of Ju [Confucianists]. When they turn to us, they should be received. But we now challenge the adherents of Yang and Mo, as if we were pursuing a stray pig which has entered the pen, and yet we proceed to tie its leg." [VIIB-26]

204. The Mohist, Yi Tzu, sought, through Hsü Pi, to be presented to Master Meng. Master Meng said: "I indeed wish to see him, but now I am still ill. When I am well, I shall go and see him. Please ask Yi Tzu not to come." Later Yi Tzu again sought to be presented to Master Meng. Master Meng said: "Now I am able to see him. But if I do not speak with him frankly, our doctrines will not be made clear. Let me first be frank with him. I understand that Yi Tzu is an adherent of Mo, and the Mohists advocate simple observance in the matter of funeral rites. Since Yi Tzu would convert the world in conformity with Mohist teachings, he must regard them as if they were the best. Notwithstanding his views, Yi Tzu buried his parents in a sumptuous manner, and so he served his parents in the way which he depised." Hsü Tzu informed Yi Tzu of these remarks. Yi Tzu said: "According to the Confucian doctrine, the ancients treated the people 'as if they were nursing an infant.' What does this mean? To me it seems that love is without difference of degree, but its manifestation must begin with one's own parents." Hsü Tzu reported this reply to Master Meng, and Master Meng said: "Now does Yi Tzu really believe that a brother's son is no dearer to him than a neighbor's child? What is meant in that statement is simply this: Suppose an infant crawling about falls into a well, it is no crime for the infant. Moreover, all creatures under Heaven have only one root [parenthood], but Yi Tzu makes them to have two roots. In the most ancient times there were some who did not bury their parents. When their parents died, they took them up and threw them into some open ditch. Afterwards, when they passed them by, there would be foxes and wild cats devouring them, and flies and gnats biting at them. Perspiration started out on their foreheads, and they turned aside, unable to bear the sight. They perspired not because of the reproaches of other people. The emotions of their faces affected their faces. Then they hurried back and returned with baskets and spades, so

as to cover the bodies. If it is indeed right to cover the bodies, the filial son and *jen*-hearted man must also have the proper way to bury their parents." Hsü Tzu again informed Yi Tzu of these remarks. Yi Tzu, after a pause and with a sigh, said, "Master Meng has instructed me." [IIIA-5]

205. There was a man, Hsü Hsing by name, who practiced the teachings of Shene Nung.[1] He came from Ch'u to T'eng. He called on Duke Wen and said: "We are the people of a remote country. We have heard that Your Majesty is practicing *jen*-government and wish to receive a site for a house so as to become your people." Duke Wen gave him a dwelling place. His disciples, amounting to scores, all dressed in haircloth, wove mats and plaited sandals for a living.

It happened that Ch'en Hsiang, a disciple of Chen Liang, together with his younger brother Hsin, with their plough handles and shares on their backs, came from Sung to T'eng, saying: "We have heard that Your Majesty is practicing the government of a Sage, showing that Your Majesty is a Sage. We wish to become the people of a Sage." When Ch'en Hsiang saw Hsü Hsing, he was greatly pleased with him and abandoned entirely his studies, so as to become a disciple of Hsü Hsing. He came to visit Master Meng and reiterated Hsü Hsing's words as follows: "The prince of T'eng is indeed a worthy prince, but he has not yet heard the true *Tao*. The worthy ruler labors in the fields with his people and eats [the fruit of his labor]. He prepares his own meals, morning and evening, while carrying on the work of the government. But the lord of T'eng has barns and granaries, storehouses and treasuries; he is actually oppressing the people to nourish himself. How can he be a really worthy prince?" Master Meng said: "Hsü Tzu, I presume, sows the grain and eats his own produce."

"Yes."

"Does he also weave the cloth he wears?"

"No. Hsü Tzu wears clothes of haircloth."

"Has Hsü Tzu a cap?"

"Yes, he wears one."

"What kind of cap?"

"A plain one."

"Did he weave it himself?"

1. Shen Nung, a legendary emperor, was supposed to have been the first to have taught the Chinese how to farm—hence his name, "Divine Husband-man." Hsü Hsing, a leader of the Agricultural School, who claimed his inspiration came from Shen Nung, practiced farming in the country, and while in the city wove sandals for a living.

"No. He bartered grain for it."

"Why didn't he weave it himself?"

"That would have interfered with his farming."

"Does Hsü Tzu use pots and pans for cooking, and iron shares for ploughing?"

"Yes."

"Did he make those articles himself?"

"No. He bartered grain for them."

"Well," said Master Meng, "if he did no harm to the potter and smith when he bartered his grain for their articles, why should the husbandman be harmed when the potter and smith bartered their articles for his grain? Moreover, why does not Hsü Tzu take up the crafts of the potter and smith, supplying himself with the articles made on his own premises? Why does he not carry on all this multifarious dealing with a hundred craftsmen? Why does he not spare himself so much trouble?" Ch'en Hsiang said: "Why, the work of farming cannot be carried on along with a number of other trades." Then Master Meng pursued: "Is it then the government of a state which alone can be carried on along with the work of farming? There is certain work which is assigned to those of the ruling class, just as there is certain work which is imposed on the common people. Moreover, the needs of one man must be supplied with the products of the various artisans. But if he himself must make all the articles for his own use, everybody in the world would be thrown into confusion. Therefore it is said, 'Some toil with their minds, and some toil with their bodies.' Those who toil with their minds govern others, while those who toil with their bodies are governed by others. Those who are governed by others produce food; those who govern others receive food. This is a principle universally recognized. In the time of Yao the world had not yet been reduced to order because of overwhelming floods. Grass and trees were luxuriant, and birds and beasts flourished. Various kinds of grain could not grow; the birds and beasts encroached upon men. The paths marked by the feet of beasts and prints of birds criss-crossed throughout the Imperial Domain. More than anyone else, Yao worried about this state of affairs, so that he raised Shun to office and adopted measures of relief. Shun put Yi in charge of the fire to burn down the jungles on the mountains and in the marshes, so that all the birds and beasts fled away and hid themselves. Yü was appointed to separate the courses of the nine rivers. He cleared the course of the Chi and T'a and

conducted them into the sea. He opened up the blocked Ju
and Han and regulated the course of the Huai and Ssu, so
that they all flowed into the Yangtze River. Only then did it
become possible for the people of the Imperial Domain to
produce food. During that time, Yü was away from home for
eight years, and, though he thrice passed his home, he did
not once enter. Even though he had wished to cultivate the
land, could he have done so?

"Then the minister of agriculture taught the people sowing
and reaping—how to plant and cultivate the five kinds of
grain. When the grain was harvested the people were nourished. But there is a *Tao* for all men: If the people with
plenty to eat and plenty to wear merely live in comfort without education, then they are nearly like the birds and beasts.
The Sage [Shun] worried about this and appointed Hsieh
minister of education to teach the people the human relationships: between father and son there was affection; between
sovereign and minister, *yi;* between husband and wife, distinction of functions; between old and young, a proper order
of precedence; and between friends, sincerity. So Yao said
to Hsieh, 'Urge the people to be industrious, rectify them
with *yi*, and then give them education. Thus the people will
enable themselves to be possessed of their own goodness. And
again, rouse them up and confer on them all aids and benefits.'
When the sage was thus concerned about the people, had
he the leisure to cultivate the land?

"Yao was concerned that he could not obtain a man like
Shun. Shun was concerned that he could not obtain men like
Yü and Kao Yao. But one whose concern was the improper
cultivation of his hundred-*mu* land was a mere husbandman.
To distribute to others of one's wealth is called kindness. To
teach others goodness is called faithfulness. To find the best
man to govern the world is called *jen*. Hence to give the
world to another man would be easy; to find the best man
to govern the world would be difficult. Master K'ung once
said, 'Great indeed was Yao as a sovereign! It is only Heaven
that is great, and only Yao was equal to it. So boundless was
his virtue that the people could find no name for it. A true
sovereign indeed was Shun! So grand was Shun that he
possessed the world and yet remained aloof from it.' In their
governing the world, did Yao and Shun have nothing with
which to occupy their minds? Only they did not employ their
minds on the cultivation of lands.

"I have heard of converting the Yi people [eastern bar-

barians] by the Hsia people [Chinese], but I have never heard
of the converting of the Hsia people by the Yi people. Ch'en
Liang was a native of Ch'u, and, being pleased with the *Tao*
of Duke Chou and Master K'ung, came northwards to the
Imperial Domain to study their teachings. Among the northern scholars, there was perhaps none who excelled him. He
was what you call a leading scholar of distinguished abilities.
You and your younger brother studied under him for some
tens of years, and when your teacher died, you turned your
back on him. Formerly, when Master K'ung died, after three
years [of mourning] his disciples packed up and were ready
to leave for home. When they went to take leave of Tzu
Kung, they looked toward one another and wailed till they
lost their voices. After they all left, Tzu Kung built a shed
by the side of the grave and stayed there for another three
years before he returned home. At a later time, Tzu Hsia,
Tzu Chang, and Tzu You, thinking that Yu Jo resembled the
sage, wished to serve him with the same respect that they had
served Master K'ung. They tried to persuade Tseng Tzu to
join them, but he said, 'This cannot be done. What has been
washed in the Yangtze and the Han, and bleached in the
summer sun, is so pure and shining that nothing can surpass
it.' Now here is the shrill-tongued man from the barbarian
south, whose teachings are in accord with those of the ancient
kings. You turn away from your master and study under him.
You are indeed different from Tseng Tzu. I have heard that
birds leave dark valleys to live in lofty trees, but I have never
heard that they descend from lofty trees to enter into dark
valleys. It is said in the *Shih:*

> He smote the Yung and the Ti [barbarians of the west and
>   north],
> And he punished Ching and Shu [barbarian states].
>   (*On the Prince of Lu*)

Thus the Duke of Chou would be sure to smite these barbarians, and yet you study under them. It is indeed no good
for you to make such a change."

Ch'en Hsiang said: "If Hsü's teachings were followed,
there would not be two prices in the market, nor would there
be any deceit in the country. Even if a child were sent to the
market, no one would impose on him. All cloth of the same
length would be the same in price; it would not differ with
prices for hemp and silk of the same weight; with the same

amount of five kinds of grain; and with the same size sandal."
But Master Meng answered: "To be unequal in quality is
the very nature of things. Their worth may vary as much as
from two to ten thousand times. If you arbitrarily reduced
them all to one standard, the world will be thrown into confusion. For instance, suppose large sandals and small sandals
were of the same price, who would make them? If the teachings of Hsü Tzu were followed, people would lead one another into deception. How can such a country be well governed?" [IIIA-4]

206. K'uang Chang said: "Is not Ch'en Chung Tzu a
scholar of true simplicity and honesty? While living in Wu-
ling, he went three days without food till he could neither
hear nor see. By the side of a well, there grew a plum tree,
the fruit of which had been more than half eaten by worms.
He crawled to it and ate some of the fruit. After swallowing
three mouthfuls he recovered his sight and hearing." Master
Meng said: "Among the scholars of Ch'i, I must regard Chung
Tzu the most prominent. However, how can Chung Tzu be
considered a man of true simplicity and honesty? To carry
out the teachings of Chung Tzu, one must be an earthworm,
which feeds on the dry mold above and drinks from the
muddy spring below. Was the house where Chung Tzu dwells
built by a good man like Po-yi or by a robber like Chih? Was
the millet which he eats planted by a good man like Po-yi
or by a robber like Chih? These facts cannot be ascertained."
"But," said K'uang Chang, "what does it matter? He himself
wove sandals of hemp, while his wife twisted hempen threads.
He barters them [for the necessaries]." Master Meng said:
"Chung Tzu comes of an ancient and noble family of Ch'i.
His elder brother Tai received from the region of Ko a
revenue of ten thousand measures, but he himself considers
his brother's emolument to be unrighteous, and so does not
eat of it; he likewise considers his brother's house to be unrighteous, and so does not dwell in it. Avoiding his brother
and leaving his mother, he lives in Wu-ling. One day, when
he went to his brother's house, someone presented his brother
with a live goose. Knitting his brow, he complained, 'For
what is this cackle-cackle here?' But soon afterwards, his
mother killed the goose and served it to him. At this very
moment his brother returned from abroad, and said: 'Don't
you know that this is the flesh of the cackle-cackle?' Thereupon he went out and vomited it. Thus he will not eat the
food of his mother, but he takes the food from his wife. He

will not dwell in his brother's house, but he lives in Wu-ling. How can his conduct be consistent with his teachings? To be like Chung Tzu, a man must be an earthworm, and then he can carry out his teachings." [IIIB-10]

207. Master Meng said: "Ch'en Chung Tzu would not accept the whole state of Ch'i, if it were offered to him contrary to *yi;* all people believe in him. But this is only the *yi* which declines a dish of rice or a platter of soup. A man can have no greater fault than to sever his relation with his family and to neglect his service to the sovereign. How can such a man be credited with the great moral responsibility because he has shown some small virtue?" [VIIA-34]

Chapter VIII. On Traditions of the Sages

208. Master Meng said: "Shun was born in Chu-feng, moved to Fu-hsia, and died in Ming-t'iao; he came of the eastern barbarian tribes. King Wen was born in Chou, by Mount Ch'i, and died in Pi-ying; he came of the western barbarian tribes. These two men were separated by a distance of more than one thousand *li* and lived in ages more than one thousand years apart. But their rise and success in the Imperial Domain complement each other like the two halves of a split tally. The teachings taught by the sages—both the earlier and the later—are found to be the same." [IVB-1]

209. Wan Chang asked: "Shun once went to the field, and wept and cried aloud to Heaven. Why did he weep and cry aloud?" Master Meng said: "He resented [lack of parents' love] and longed for it." Wan Chang said: "When his parents love him, a son rejoices and forgets them not. When his parents dislike him, he works hard and resents them not. Did Shun resent his parents?" Master Meng answered: "Once Chang Hsi asked Kung-ming Kao, 'As to Shun's going to the fields, I have had your instruction, but I still do not know about his weeping and crying aloud to Heaven and to his parents.' Kung-ming Kao said, 'You do not understand this matter.' For Kung-ming Kao supposed that the heart of a filial son could not be so free of resentment. Shun wondered, 'I exert myself to the utmost to cultivate the fields, so as to discharge my duties as a son. What fault can there be in me that my parents do not love me?' Emperor Yao ordered his nine sons, two daughters, all his officers, cattle and sheep, storehouses and granaries, all to be placed in the service of Shun in the fields. Most of the scholars of the world flocked

to him. Then Emperor Yao was about to ask Shun to govern the world along with him, and later to hand it over to him entirely. However, Shun felt like a poor man without a home, because his parents did not show affection for him. The compliment of the scholars of the world is what men desire, but this was not sufficient to relieve him of sorrow. The enjoyment of beauty is what men desire, and Shun had the emperor's two daughters for wives, but this was not sufficient to relieve him of sorrow. Riches are what men desire, and Shun was rich in possessions of the world, but this was not sufficient to relieve him of sorrow. Honors are what men desire, and Shun had the honor of being emperor, but this was not sufficient to relieve him of sorrow. Popular compliment, enjoyment of beauty, riches and honors were not sufficient to relieve him of sorrow; it was only the affection of his parents that could relieve him of sorrow. When a man is young, his affection is toward father and mother. When he becomes conscious of the attraction of physical love, his affection is toward the young beauties. When he has a wife and children, his affection is toward them. When he takes office, his affection is toward his sovereign; if he fails to win the favor of his sovereign, he is deeply worried in his heart. But the man of great filiality centers his affection on his parents during the whole of life. In the case of the great Shun I see the case of a man whose affection at the age of fifty was toward his parents." [VA-1]

210. Wan Chang asked: "It is said in the *Shih:*

In marrying a wife, how should a man proceed?
He must first inform his parents.

In accordance with this verse, no man would have followed the rule as Shun. How was it that Shun did not inform his parents before he married?" Master Meng said: "If he had informed his parents, he would not have been able to marry. The union of male and female is the greatest of human relations. Suppose that Shun had informed his parents, he would have relinquished this greatest of relationships, thereby incurring resentment against his parents. On this account, he did not inform them." Wan Chang said: "I have heard the reason why Shun married without informing his parents; but how was it that the Emperor Yao did not inform Shun's parents when he married his daughters to him?" Master Meng said: "The emperor also knew that if he informed them, he could not marry his daughters to Shun."

Then Wang Chang said: "Shun's parents sent him to repair a granary; the ladder to the granary was removed, and his father, Ku-sou, set fire to it. At another time they sent him to dig a well; without knowing that he had got out, they proceeded to seal it up. Hsiang [Shun's half-brother] said, 'The credit for scheming to cover up the city-lord [Shun] is all mine. Let my parents have his cattle and sheep; let them have his storehouses and granaries. His shield and spear shall be mine; his lute and bow shall be mine. My two sisters-in-law will be my chambermaids.' Then Hsiang went to Shun's palace and there was Shun on his couch playing on his lute. 'I am worried about you,' said Hsiang, but he blushed with shame. Shun said, 'There are all my officers and people. Would you assist me in my rule over them?' I do not know whether Shun was aware of Hsiang's intention to kill him." Master Meng said: "How could he be ignorant of that? But he was sad when Hsiang was sad, and he was happy only when Hsiang was happy."

"In that case, did Shun pretend to be happy?" asked Wan Chang.

"No," said Master Meng. "Formerly someone presented Tzu-Ch'an of Cheng a live fish. He ordered his officer to keep it in the pond, but the officer cooked it and then reported, 'When I set the fish free in the pond, it could hardly move about. A little while later, it became somewhat at ease, and then it swam swiftly away.' Tzu-Ch'an said, 'It has found its proper place! It has found its proper place!' The officer then went out and said, 'Who says that Tzu-Ch'an is a wise man? I had cooked the fish, and yet he still says, "It has found its proper place! It has found its proper place!"' Therefore a noble man may be deceived by what seems to be reasonable, but he cannot be entrapped by what is contrary to the true *Tao*. Hsiang came in the attitude of one who loved one's elder brother, and thereby Shun sincerely believed him, and was happy. Why should he pretend to be happy?" [VA-2]

211. Wan Chang asked: "Hsiang had always plotted to kill Shun. When Shun was made emperor, how was it that he only banished him?" Master Meng said: "He conferred lordship on him, but some might say that it was equal to banishment." Wan Chang said: "Shun exiled the superintendent of public works to You-Chou and banished Huan-Tou to Chung-Shan. He killed the prince of San-Miao at San-Wei and imprisoned K'un in Yü-Shan. These four offenders were thus punished with the approval of the world, for he had punished

those who were destitute of *jen*. But Hsiang was the most destitute of *jen*, and Shun conferred lordship on him in Yu-Pi. Of what crimes were the people of Yu-Pi guilty? Does a *jen*-hearted man act in this way? In the case of other men, he punished them; in the case of his younger brother, he conferred lordship on him." Master Meng said: "As regards his younger brother, a *jen*-hearted man does not cherish anger nor harbor hatred but feels affection and love toward him. Because he feels affection toward his brother, he wishes him to be honorable; because he loves his brother, he wishes him to be rich. To confer lordship on Hsiang was to enrich and ennoble him. Suppose that Shun, himself being emperor, had allowed his younger brother to be a common man; could he have been said to feel affection and love for his brother?"

"May I venture to ask why some people said that it was a banishment?" asked Wan Chang. Master Meng said: "Hsiang could not do anything in his state. The emperor appointed an officer to rule over the state and to levy taxes and tributes. On this account it was considered a banishment. How could Shun let the people be oppressed? Nevertheless, Shun wished to see his brother often, and so Hsiang constantly presented himself at court, as said [in the Old Records]: 'He did not wait for the tribute time, to receive the lord of Yu-Pi on state affairs.' " [VA-3]

212. Hsien-ch'iu Meng asked: "There is the saying: 'A scholar of perfect virtue may not be treated as a minister by his sovereign, nor may he be treated as a son by his father.' When Shun, as emperor, stood with his face to the south, Yao, along with all the feudal lords, attended his court with his face to the north. Ku-sou [his father] also did the same. When Shun saw Ku-sou, he became uneasy." Master K'ung said: "At this time, the world was in jeopardy! It was indeed perilous!" "I do not know whether this is true or not." Master Meng said: "No. This is not the saying of a *chün-tzu*, but that of a country folk in the east of Ch'i. When Yao was getting old, Shun was asked to act as a regent. It is said in the *Shu:* 'After twenty-eight years Yao died and the people mourned his death as the loss of their own parent. During the three years of mourning and throughout the whole world, all kinds of music were hushed.' [Canon of Yao] Master K'ung said, 'A Heaven has not two suns, so the people should not have two kings!' If Shun had been emperor, when he led all the feudal lords to observe the three years' mourning for Yao, there would be two emperors at one time."

Hsien-ch'iu Meng said: "As to Shun's not treating Yao as a minister, I have heard your instruction. It is said in the *Shih:*

> Under the whole heaven,
>   All is the sovereign's land;
> Within the borders of seas,
>   All are the sovereign's subjects.

So once Shun became emperor, I venture to ask how it was that Ku-sou would not be one of his subjects." Master Meng said: "This is not what is meant by the ode. It refers to someone who worked hard in the service of the sovereign and yet was unable to nourish his own parents, as its author said, 'Since this is all the sovereign's business, how is it that I alone am supposed to have ability and am made to work hard?' Therefore, in interpreting the *Shih*, one may not insist on one word so as to distort a phrase, nor may one insist on a phrase so as to distort the general purport of a poem. One must read the inherent thought so as to fathom its general purport. If we just take one sentence out of its context, then when it is said in the *Shih*, 'Of the people of Chou, not a single person is alive,' we would believe that not a single individual among the people of Chou was left. As to the duty of a filial son, there is nothing greater than honoring his parents. As to honoring one's parents, there is nothing greater than nourishing them with the whole world. To be the father of the emperor is the highest honor; to nourish him with the whole world is the highest nourishment. This is exactly what is said in the *Shih:*

> He is ever cherishing filial thoughts;
> His filial thoughts become a norm to all.

It is said in the *Shu* [Histories]: 'Shun always served Ku-sou with respect; he was so attentive and full of awe that Ku-sou believed him and conformed to virtue.' This is a case where a father was transformed by his son." [VA-4]

213. Master Meng said: "When Shun was living in the deep mountain, he dwelt amid the trees and rocks and consorted with the deer and swine. The differences between Shun and the mountainous barbarians was slight. But when he heard any good word or saw any good action, he would follow it like a river bursting its banks and flowing out in an irresistible flood." [VIIA-16]

214. T'ao Ying asked: "When Shun was emperor and Kao-yao was the minister of justice, if Ku-sou had murdered a man, what would have been done?" Master Meng said: "Kao-yao would simply have arrested him."

"But would not Shun have forbidden it?"

"How could Shun have forbidden it? Kao-yao had been invested with authority."

"In that case what would Shun have done?"

"Shun would have abandoned the imperial throne just as he would have thrown away a worn-out sandal. He would privately have carried his father on his back and retired into concealment somewhere along the seacoast. There he would have spent the rest of his life, cheerful and happy to forget the whole world." [VIIA-35]

215. Master Meng said: "Yao and Shun possessed [jen and yi] by nature; T'ang and Wu cultivated them; the five feudal leaders feigned them. When they feigned for long and for long did not relinquish them, how could they know that they did not possess them?" [VIIA-31]

216. Master Meng said: "When Shun ate parched grains and wild herbs, he was as much at ease as if he had done so all his life. When he became emperor, and had embroidered robes to wear, the lute to play, and Yao's two daughters to wait on him, he remained the same as if he made nothing of those things." [VIIB-6]

217. Wan Chang asked: "People say that in the time of Yü there was a decline in virtue, for he passed on the Imperial Throne not to the man of worth but to his son. Is this true?" Master Meng said: "No; it is not so. When Heaven gave the imperial throne to the man of worth, it was given to the man of worth. When Heaven gave it to a son, it was given to a son. Formerly Shun presented Yü to Heaven. Seventeen years elapsed, and Shun died. When the three years' mourning was over, Yü withdrew from Shun's son to Yang-Ch'eng. The people of the world, however, followed him, just as they had followed Shun and not Yao's son after the death of Yao. Yü present Yi [Yü's minister] to Heaven. Seven years elapsed, and Yü died. When the three years' mourning was over, Yi withdrew from Yü's son to the north of Mount Chi. However, those paying homage and those engaged in litigations went not to Yi but to Ch'i [Yü's son], saying, 'He is the son of our sovereign.' Those who sang the emperor's praises did not sing to Yi, but to Ch'i, saying, 'He is the son of our sovereign.' Chu [Yao's son], prince of Tan, was not virtuous, nor was

Shun's son virtuous. Shun assisted Yao and Yü assisted Shun over a period of many years, conferring benefits on the people. Moreover, Ch'i was worthy and capable of respectfully carrying on the way of Yü. But Yi had not assisted Yü for a long period, nor did he long to confer benefits on the people. Hence the assistance given by Shun, Yü, and Yi varied in time; that their sons were worthy or virtuous was due to Heaven, and not something which man could have brought about. That which is done without man's effort is due to Heaven. That which happens out of man's wish is due to Fate.

"When a common man obtains the world, his virtue must be equal to that of Shun and Yü, and at the same time he must have the emperor presenting him [to Heaven]. This is why Master K'ung did not obtain the world. When a sovereign who inherits the world is to be displaced by Heaven, he must be like a Chieh or a Chou. This is why Yi, Yi Yin, and the Duke of Chou did not obtain the world. Yi Yin assisted T'ang to become sovereign over the world. After the death of T'ang, his heir T'ai-ting died before assuming the succession; Wai-ping reigned two years, and Chung-jen reigned four. When T'ai-chia [T'ai-ting's son] became emperor, he nullified T'ang's institutions and statutes. Thereupon Yi Yin banished him to Tung for three years. There T'ai-chia regretted his wrongdoing and condemned and reformed himself. In Tung he began to abide by *jen* and follow *yi;* during these three years he listened to the instruction of Yi Yin. Then he returned with Yi Yin to Po [the capital]. The Duke of Chou's not obtaining the world was like the case of Yi under the Hsia and that of Yi Yin under the Yin. Master K'ung said, 'T'ang [yao] and Yu [shun] passed the throne to the man of worth. Hsia, Yin, and Chou passed on the throne to their sons. In all the cases, the principle of *yi* is the same.' " [VA-6]

218. Master Meng said: "Suppose that the whole world came in great delight under one's rule. Only Shun was capable of regarding the whole world thus coming under his rule as a bundle of grass. He believed that as long as he failed to win the love of his parents, he could not consider himself a man, and that as long as he failed to live in accord with his parents, he could not consider himself a son. Therefore, Shun did his utmost to serve his parents until Ku-sou became pleased with him. When Ku-sou became pleased, the whole world was transformed. When Ku-sou became pleased, all fathers and sons in the world were pacified. This is called great filial piety." [IVA-28]

219. Master Meng said: "Between Yao and Shun to T'ang there passed more than five hundred years. Yü and Kao-yao knew [these sages] as they saw them in person, while T'ang knew them as he heard of them. Between T'ang and King Wen there passed more than five hundred years. Yi-Yin and Lai-Chu knew [T'ang] as they saw him in person, while King Wen knew him as he heard of him. Between King Wen and Master K'ung there were more than five hundred years. T'ai-kung Wang and San-i Sheng knew [King Wen] as they saw him in person, while Master K'ung knew him as he heard of him. Between Master K'ung and the present, more than one hundred years have passed. Thus we are not yet far from the time of the sage and we are very near to his residence. Yet there is no one who knew the sage [in person] nor is there anyone who knows of him." [VIIB-38]

220. Master Meng said: "Yü hated sweet wine, but he loved good words. T'ang held fast to the mean and employed men of worth without regard to class distinctions. King Wen treated the people as though they were wounded, and he looked toward the *Tao* as though it were out of sight. King Wu did not spurn those at hand, nor did he forget those at a distance. The Duke of Chou wanted to unite in himself the sage-kings of the three dynasties, and to practice the four things [as mentioned above]. If there were anything not in accord with their teachings, he would think of it day and night. When he was fortunate enough to overcome the difficulty, he would sit waiting for the morning [in order to carry it out]." [IVB-20]

221. Kao Tzu said: "The music of Yü was superior to that of King Wen." Master Meng said: "Why do you think so?" Kao Tzu said: "Because the bosses of Yü's bells were worn out." Master Meng said: "Is that a sufficient proof? Are the ruts at a city-gate made by a single chariot drawn by two horses?" [VIIB-22]

222. Master Meng said: "Po-yi would not serve a sovereign whom he did not esteem, nor would he make friends with a man of whom he did not approve. He would not attend the court of a bad ruler, nor would he speak with a bad man. To attend the court of a bad ruler, or to speak with a bad man, would have been to him the same as to sit with his court robes and court cap amid dirt and ashes. He had such an aversion to evils that if he happened to stand with a villager whose cap was not properly adjusted, he would turn away in disdain as if he had been defiled. Accordingly, when the

feudal lords invited him to join their service, he would not accept the invitation. He would not accept it, thinking that it was improper for him to go to them.

"On the other hand, Liu-hsia Hui did not feel shame to serve a wicked sovereign, nor did he think it low to accept a humble office. When he was in office, he would not conceal his worth and ability, but he acted in accord with his principles. When he was neglected and left out of office, he would not complain; nor would he grieve when he was straitened by poverty. Accordingly, he said, 'Let you go your way and I will go mine. Although you stand by my side with bare shoulders or even naked, how can you defile me?' So he was quite at ease in the company of such men, without losing himself. When pressed to remain in office, he would stay. He would remain in office if pressed to do so, thinking that it was improper to go away.

"Po-yi was narrow-minded, and Liu-hsia Hui lacked self-respect. The *chün-tzu* will follow neither." [IIA-9]

223. Master Meng said: "Po-yi would not look at a bad sight; nor would he listen to a bad sound. He would not serve a sovereign whom he did not esteem, nor would he command a people of whom he did not approve. In a time of good government he would take office, and on occurrence of confusion he would retire. He could not bear to attend a corrupt court, nor to live among an unruly people. He considered his being in company with a villager as if he were to sit amid dirt and ashes with his court robes and court cap. In the time of Chow, he dwelt on the shores of the North Sea, awaiting the purification of the world. Therefore, when the people came under the influence of Po-yi, the corrupt became honest and the timid became self-reliant.

"Yi-yin said, 'Whom may I not serve? What people may I not command?' In a time of good government he would take office, and when disorder prevailed he would also take office. He said, 'Heaven gave birth to the people and appointed the first seers to teach those who came after, and those who were first in apprehension to teach those who were later in apprehension. I am one of the Heaven-created people who are first in apprehension, and I shall teach the people the *Tao*.' He thought that, among all the people of the world, if there were any men or women who did not enjoy the benefits of Yao and Shun, it would be as though he himself had pushed them into a ditch. He himself assumed the burden of the world.

"Liu-hsia Hui did not feel shame to serve a wicked sover-

eign, nor did he refuse a humble office. When he was in
office, he would not conceal his worth and ability, but he
acted in accord with his principles. When he was neglected
and left out of office, he would not complain; nor would he
grieve when he was straitened by poverty. When he was in
company with the villagers, he was quite at ease and could
not bear to leave them. He said, 'You go your way, and I
will go my way. Although you stand by my side with bare
shoulders or even naked, how can you defile me?' Therefore,
when the people came under the influence of Liu-hsia Hui,
the mean became generous, and the narrow-minded became
liberal.

"When Master K'ung was leaving Ch'i, he went off in great
haste. When he left Lu, he said, 'I will set out slowly!' This
was the proper way of leaving the mother country. When
it was proper to hasten away, he hastened; when it was
proper to stay long, he stayed long; when it was proper to
retire, he retired; when it was proper to accept office, he
accepted it: such was Master K'ung."

Then Master Meng concluded: "Among the sages, Po-yi
was the pure one; Yi-yin was the responsible one; Liu-hsia
Hui was the accommodating one; and Master K'ung was the
timely one. In Master K'ung was assimilated all that was best
in the ancient sages. Such an assimilation may be comparable
to a complete symphony. In a complete symphony the metal
instruments make their sounds first, and then the stone instruments follow. The metal sound signals its commencement,
while the stone notes proclaim its completion. What is commenced is the work of wisdom. What is completed is the work
of sageness. Wisdom may be compared to skill and sagacity to
strength. In a game of archery from a distance of a hundred
paces, you reach the distance because of your strength, but
you hit the mark not because of your strength [but your
skill]." [VB-1]

224. Wan Chang asked: "People say that Yi Yin sought to
be introduced to T'ang by his culinary art. Is this true?"
Master Meng said: "No; this is not true. Yi Yin was engaged
in farming in the country of Yu-hsin and delighted in the
teachings of Yao and Shun. In any matter contrary to *yi*, or
contrary to these teachings, even though he had been offered
the whole world, he would not have paid attention to it; even
though he had been offered a thousand teams of horses, he
would not have looked at them. In any matter contrary to *yi*
or contrary to these teachings, he would neither have given

nor taken a trifle, not even a single straw. T'ang sent messengers with presents of silk to invite him to join his service.
With indifference and complacence, he said: 'What can I do
with those presents of silk from T'ang? Is it not best for me to
dwell on my farm so as to delight in the teachings of Yao and
Shun?' T'ang thrice sent messengers to invite him, and finally
he changed his mind, saying, 'Rather than dwell on my farm
to delight in the teachings of Yao and Shun, hadn't I better
make this sovereign a sovereign like Yao or Shun and this people like the people of Yao or Shun? Hadn't I better see the
realization of these teachings in my own person? Heaven gave
birth to the people and appointed the first seers to teach those
who came after, and those who are first in apprehension to
teach those who were later in apprehension. I am one of the
Heaven-created people who are first in apprehension, and I
shall teach the people the *Tao*. If I do not teach them, who
will?' He thought that among all the people of the world,
if there were any man or woman who did not enjoy the benefits of Yao and Shun, it would be as though he himself pushed
them into a ditch. He himself assumed the burden of the
world, so that he went to T'ang and persuaded him to attack
Hsia and save the people. I have never heard of a man who,
being dishonest himself, could make others upright; how
much less could a man, having disgraced himself, rectify the
whole world? The actions of the sages have been different.
Some have kept at a distance, some have stayed near; others
have lived in retirement, and others have remained in office.
One thing, however, which they have in common, is that they
keep their persons pure. I have heard that Yi Yin sought to
be introduced to T'ang by the teachings of Yao and Shun. I
have never heard that he did so by his culinary art. It is said
in the *Shu:*

> Heaven's punishment of Chieh commenced in his palace Mu;
> My punishment [of T'ai-chia] commenced in Po." [*Instruc-
> tion of Yi Yin,* VA-7]

225. Master Meng said: "A sage is the teacher of one hundred generations. This is true of Po-Yi and Liu-hsia Hui.
Therefore, when the people came under the influence of Po-
Yi, the corrupt became honest and the timid became self-
reliant. When the people came under the influence of Liu-
hsia Hui, the mean became generous, and the narrow-minded
became liberal. They distinguished themselves hundreds of

generations ago, and they are inspirations to all succeeding generations. Could they have exercised such great influence if they had not been sages. How much more did they affect those who had personal contact with the sages?" [VIIB-15]

226. Kung-sun Ch'ou said: "Yi-Yin said, 'I cannot tolerate a man who acts contrary to *yi*.' Thereupon he banished T'ai-chia to T'ung, and the people were much pleased. When T'ai-chia became virtuous, he restored him to his throne, and the people were again much pleased. When a man of worth serving a minister finds that his sovereign is not virtuous, may he indeed banish the sovereign?" Master Meng said: "He may do so if he has the moral purpose of Yi-Yin. If he has not the same moral purpose, it would be an act of usurpation." [VIIA-31]

227. Master Meng said: "Liu-hsia Hui would not change his firm purpose of life, even if he were offered the three highest offices of state." [VIIA-28]

228. Wen Chang asked: "Some say that when Master K'ung was in Wei, he had as his host Yong Chu [a physician], and when he was in Ch'i, he had as his host the attendant Chi Huan. Is this true?" Master Meng said: "No; this is not true. This was the invention of curious men. When he was in Wei, he lived with Yen Ch'ou-yu. The wives of Mi Tzu and Tzu Lu were sisters, and Mi Tzu said to Tzu Lu, 'If Master K'ung has me as his host, he may be appointed a grand minister of Wei.' When Tzu Lu informed Master K'ung of this, he said, 'That depends on Fate.' Master K'ung went to office according to *li*, and he retired from it according to *yi*. Whether he obtained his office or not, he would say, 'That depends on Fate.' If he had had as his hosts Yong Chu and the attendant Chi Hua'n, he would have acted contrary to *yi* and Fate. Master K'ung was displeased in Lu and Wei and met with Huan of Sung, a high military officer, who attempted to intercept and kill him so that he had to pass through in disguise. At that time, though he was in distress, he had as his host Chen Tzu, minister of Sung, and he was in the service of Duke Chou of Chen. I have heard that ministers at home may be estimated by those whom they entertain, while ministers abroad may be estimated by those who entertain them. If Master K'ung had had Yong Chu and the attendant Chi Hua'n as his hosts, how could he have been Master K'ung?" [VA-8]

229. Master Meng said: "When Master K'ung was leaving Lu, he said, 'I will set out slowly'; this was the proper way of leaving the mother country. When he was leaving Ch'i, he

went off in great haste; this was the proper way of leaving a foreign country." [VIIB-17]

230. Master Meng said: "The *chün-tzu* [i.e., Master K'ung] was in distress between Ch'en and Ts'ai, because he had not communicated with the sovereigns or their ministers." [VIIB-18]

231. Tseng Hai was fond of sheep dates, and [after his death his son] Tseng Tzu could not bear to eat them. Therefore, Kung-sun Ch'ou asked: "Whis is better, minced meat or sheep dates?" Master Meng said: "Minced meat, of course." Kung-sun Ch'ou said: "Well, then, why did Tseng Tzu eat minced meat, but not sheep dates?" Master Meng answered: "The desire for minced meat is common to all, while that for sheep dates is peculiar. We avoid the name, but not the surname. The surname is common, and the name is particular." [VIIB-36]

Chapter IX. Miscellaneous Comments

232. Ching Ch'un said: "Are not Kung-sun Yen and Chang Yi truly great men? When they are angry, all the feudal lords tremble with fear; when they remain quiet, the world is at peace." Master Meng said: "How can they be great men? Have you not learned the rules of etiquette? At the capping of a young man, his father admonishes him. At the marriage of a young woman, her mother admonishes her. The mother escorts the bride to the door and cautions her, 'You are going to your home. You must be respectful; you must be prudent. Do not disobey your husband.' To regard obedience as the proper way of conduct is the rule for women. Let one abide by *jen*, stand on *li*, and follow the path of *yi*. When one is in power, let one lead the people to practice one's principles. When one is out of office, let one practice one's principles by oneself. Riches and honors cannot make one dissipated; nor can poverty and distress make one deviate from one's cherished principles; nor can power and force make one weaken one's will. These are the characteristics of the great man." [IIIB-2]

233. Wan Chang asked: "Some say that Po-li Hsi sold himself to a cattleman of Ch'in for five sheep skins, and fed his oxen, so as to find an introduction to Duke Mu of Ch'in. Is this true?" Master Meng said: "No; this is not true. This was the invention of curious men. Po-li Hsi was a man of Yü. The people of Tsin offered jades of Ch'ui-chi and horses of Ch'ü

breed for a passage through Yü to attack Kuo. Kung-chih Ch'i
remonstrated against accepting the offer, but Po-li Hsi did not.
Knowing that the Duke of Yü was not to be remonstrated
with, he left for Ch'i, being already seventy years old. If by
then he did not know that he would degrade himself to seek
an introduction to Duke Mu of Ch'in by feeding oxen, could
he be called wise? But by not remonstrating where remon-
strance would be of no avail, could he be called unwise? He
knew that the Duke of Mu would lose his kingdom, and he
left ahead of him; he could not be called unwise. When he
was called to office in Ch'in, he knew that some achievements
would be possible with Duke Mu, and so he became minister
to him; could he be called unwise? When he was chief minister of Ch'in, he made his sovereign distinguished throughout
the world, and worthy of being admired by the future generations. If he had not been a man of worth and ability, could
he have done this? Even a villager who had a regard for himself would not sell himself in order to help his sovereign. Shall
we say that a man of worth would do such a thing?" [VA-9]

234. When Tzu-ch'an was chief minister of Cheng, he used
his own carriages to carry the people across the Chen and
the Wei. Master Meng said: "He was kind, but he did not
know about government. Suppose that in the eleventh month
of the year the footbridges are built, and the carriage bridges
in the twelfth month; the people will not have the trouble of
wading streams. When the *chün-tzu* is just and fair in his
rule, he may cause people to be removed out of his path. How
can he carry everybody across the rivers in his own carriage?
Therefore, if he tries to please everybody, he will not have
sufficient time to do so." [IVB-2]

235. P'eng Meng learned archery with Yi. When he had
acquired all that Yi could teach him, he thought that Yi was
the only man in the world superior to himself in archery, and
so he slew him. Master Meng said: "Yi himself was also to
blame. Kung-ming Yi said, 'It would seem that he could not
be blamed.' His blame was indeed slight, but how could he
be considered blameless? Cheng sent Tzu-cho Yu-tzu to attack
Wei, and Wei then sent Yü-kung Chih'ssu to pursue him. Tzu-
cho Yu-tzu said, 'Today I am sick, and I cannot hold my bow.
I am a dead man!' Then he asked his driver, 'Who is it that is
pursuing me?' The driver said, 'It is Yü-kung Chih-ssu.' Then
he said, 'I shall live.' The driver said, 'Yü-kung Chih-ssu is the
best archer of Wei, and you say that you will live. What do
you mean?' He said, 'Yü-kung Chih-ssu learned archery from

Yin-kung Chih-tai, and Yin-kung Chih-tai learned archery from me. Yin-kung Chih-tai is an upright man, and his friends must be also upright.' When Yü-kung Chih-ssu came near, he said, 'Master, do you not hold your bow?' 'Today I am sick,' said the other, 'and I cannot hold my bow.' Thereupon Yü-kung Chih-ssu said: 'I learned archery from Yin-kung Chih-tai, and Yin-kung Chih-tai learned it from you. I cannot bear to injure you with that which you taught others. However, today I am on a mission for the sovereign, which I dare not neglect.' Then he took his arrows, knocked off their metal points, discharged them, and turned back." [IVB-24]

236. Master Meng said: "King Hui of Liang is indeed devoid of *jen!* Those who are *jen*-hearted extend what they love to what they do not love. Those who are devoid of *jen* extend what they do not love to what they love." Kung-sun Ch'ou asked: "What do you mean?" Master Meng said: "King Hui of Liang, for the sake of territory, oppressed the people by sending them to war. Suffering a great defeat, he wanted to revenge himself, but was afraid that he could not win. Therefore, he forced his beloved sons and brothers to sacrifice themselves to the war. This is what I call 'extending what one does not love to what one loves.'" [VIIB-1]

237. When P'en-ch'eng Kua was appointed an official in Ch'i, Master Meng said: "P'en-ch'eng Kua is sure to die!" Later P'en-ch'eng Kua was killed, and the disciples asked: "How did you know, Master, that he would be killed?" Master Meng said: "He was a man of little ability, and he had not learned the great principles of the *chün-tzu.* Thus he would only bring death upon himself." [VIIB-29]

238. There was an armed clash between Tsou and Lu, and King Mu of Tsou asked: "Thirty-three of my officers were killed and none of my people would die to defend them. If I put them to death, I cannot kill them all. If I do not put them to death, I allow the people to look on at the death of their superiors without attempting to save them. What should I do?" Master Meng replied: "In years of famine and calamities, the old and weak of your people who were found dying in the ditches and channels and the able-bodied who were scattered abroad to all quarters amounted to several thousands. Yet your granaries are stored with grain, and your treasuries are full. None of your officers told you of the people's distress. Thus the officers have been negligent in their duties to the sovereign and cruel to the people. Tseng Tzu said: 'Beware! Beware! What you do unto others will be done unto you.' Now the peo-

ple have done what has been done unto them. You must not blame them. If you practice a *jen*-government, your people will love their superiors and will die for them." [IB-12]

239. Duke Wen of T'eng asked: "T'eng is a small state, bordering between Ch'i and Ch'u. Shall I serve Ch'i? Or shall I serve Ch'u?" Master Meng replied: "Such counseling is beyond my abilities. If I must counsel you, I would like to suggest one thing. Deepen your moats, raise your walls, and then defend them along with the people. Be ready to die and the people will not leave you. This is a proper course." [IB-13]

240. Duke Wen of T'eng asked: "The people of Ch'i are going to erect fortifications in Hsieh. I am greatly alarmed. What should I do?" Master Meng replied: "Formerly, when King Tai dwelt in Pin, the Ti people invaded his territory. He therefore abandoned it and moved to live at the foot of Mount Ch'i. He took that situation, not as a matter of choice, but by necessity. If you do good, there will be one among your descendants who will attain the kingly rule. A sovereign lays the foundation and then bequeaths his achievements to his successors to be continued by them. But the final accomplishment depends upon Heaven. What else can you do? Be strong in doing good—that is all!" [IB-14]

241. Duke Wen of T'eng asked: "T'eng is a small state. Though I do my utmost to serve the strong neighboring states, I cannot escape their incursions. What should I do?" Master Meng said: "Formerly, when King Tai dwelt in Pin, the Ti people invaded his territory. He first offered them skins and silks, and he could not escape their incursions; then he offered them horses and dogs, and he still could not escape their incursions; and again he offered them pearls and jades, and he still could not escape their incursions. Then he assembled the elders and announced to them, saying, 'What the Ti people want is my territory. I have heard that a ruler does not harm the people with what he nourishes them. My friends, why should you be worried about having no sovereign? I am leaving this place.' Thereupon he left Pin, crossed the Mount Liang, and settled at the foot of Mount Ch'i. But the people of Pin said, 'He is a man of *jen*. We cannot lose him.' Those who followed him were like crowds flocking to the market. However, there are those who would say, 'A kingdom is kept for generations, and it cannot be disposed of in one's own person. Let one be ready to die for it.' I ask you to make your election between these two courses of action." [IB-15]

242. The people of Ch'i attacked Yen and conquered it.

King Hsüan of Ch'i asked: "Some advise me not to take it, and others advise me to take it. When a state of ten thousand chariots attacks another state of the same strength and completes its conquest within fifty days, this is an achievement beyond the power of man. If I do not take it, Heaven will send down curses on me. What do you say to my taking it?" Master Meng replied: "If the people of Yen will be pleased by your taking it, then take it. Among the ancients, the one who acted on this principle was King Wu. If the people of Yen will not be pleased by your taking it, then do not take it. Among the ancients, the one who acted on this principle was King Wen. When your state of one thousand chariots attacked another state of the same strength, the people brought baskets of rice and bowls of congee to welcome your armies; could there be any other reason than that they hoped to be rescued from their plight of water and fire? If you make the water deeper and the fire more fierce, they will turn to another to rescue them." [1B-10]

243. The people of Ch'i attacked Yen and took it, with the result that the feudal lords decided to rescue Yen. King Hsüen of Ch'i said: "The feudal lords are now conspiring to attack me. How should I deal with them?" Master Meng replied: "I have heard that with a territory of seventy li one could practice good government over the world. That was T'ang. I have never heard that with a territory of one thousand li a sovereign stood in fear of other states. It is said in the *Shu:* 'T'ang began his campaigns first against Ko, and the whole world had confidence in him. When he was battling in the east, the tribes in the west complained; when he was battling in the south, the tribes in the north complained. They all complained, "Why does he make us last?" The people looked for his coming in the same way that those suffering from draught look for clouds and rainbows. The merchants and traders did not stop coming, nor did the farmers and peasants stop working while he killed their sovereigns and consoled the people. His coming was like the falling of opportune rain, and the people were greatly delighted. It is said again in the *Shu:* 'We are waiting for the sovereign. When he comes, we shall be relieved.'

"Now the ruler of Yen was oppressing the people, and you sent armies to punish him. The people thought that you were delivering them out of the water and fire, and so they brought baskets of rice and bowls of congee to welcome your armies. If you kill their elders, imprison their youths, pull down their ancestral temples, and remove their precious vessels, how can such action be deemed proper? The world is indeed jealous of the power of Ch'i. Now you double the size of your territory, but you do not practice *jen*-government. This is why the world is rising in arms against you. Let you immediately issue orders to set free the old folks and children, to stop the removal of the precious vessels, to consult with the people of Yen, to appoint for them a new ruler, and to withdraw your armies; only then will you be able to evade their combined attack." [IB-11]

244. Shen T'ung on his own account asked: "May Yen be attacked?" Master Meng said: "Yes. Tzu-k'uai [King of Yen] has no right to give Yen to another man, nor does Tzu-chih [minister of Yen] have the right to accept Yen from Tzu-k'uai. Suppose that there is an officer with whom you are pleased, and suppose that, without informing the king, you privately give up your rank and emoluments in his favor. And suppose that this officer, without the king's orders, privately accepts them from you. Would this be permissible? And yet how would this differ from what has happened in Yen?"

When Ch'i attacked Yen, someone asked: "Is it true that you advised Ch'i to attack Yen?" Master Meng said: "No. Shen T'ung asked me whether Yen might be attacked, and I answered, 'Yes.' Thereupon he thought it right to attack Yen. If he had asked, 'Who may attack Yen?' I would have answered, 'One who acts in accord with the mandate of Heaven may attack Yen.' Suppose that there is a murderer, and that one asks me, 'May he be put to death?' The answer would be 'Yes.' If one asks me, 'Who may put the murderer to death?' I will answer, 'The minister of justice may put him to death.' But now when Yen is attacked by a state which is no better than Yen, how should I advise this state?" [IIB-8]

245. When the people of Yen revolted, the king of Ch'i said: "I feel ashamed for not following the advice of Master Meng." Ch'en Chia [the king's minister] said: "Let not Your Majesty be grieved. In your opinion, who is the more *jen*-hearted and wise, yourself or the Duke of Chou?" The king said: "Oh! what sort of comparison is this!" "Well," said Ch'en Chia, "the Duke of Chou made Kuan-shu [his elder brother] supervise the territory left in the hands of the Yin people, but Kuan-shu later led them in revolt against Chou. If the Duke of Chou appointed Kuan-shu, knowing what would happen, he was devoid of *jen*. If he appointed Kuan-shu, not knowing what would happen, he was devoid of wisdom. So if the Duke of Chou was devoid of *jen* and wisdom, how much the less

can Your Majesty be expected not to be so? I beg to see Master Meng and explain this matter."

On seeing Master Meng, Ch'en Chia asked: "What kind of man was the Duke of Chou?" Master Meng said: "He was an ancient sage."

"Is it true that he made Kuan-shu supervise the territory left in the hands of the Yin people, but Kuan-shu later led them in revolt?"

"Yes."

"Did the Duke of Chou appoint Kuan-shu, knowing what would happen?"

"He did not know."

"Then even a sage made errors, didn't he?"

"Well," said Master Meng, "the Duke of Chou was the younger brother, and Kuan-shu was his elder brother. Wasn't the error of the Duke of Chou something quite excusable? Moreover, when the *chün-tzu* of old days made errors, they corrected them. But nowadays when the *chün-tzu* make errors, they abide by them. In old days, the errors of the *chün-tzu* were like eclipses of the sun and moon, so that all the people could see their errors. But when they corrected their errors, the people all looked up to them in admiration. Nowadays, the *chün-tzu* not only abide by their errors, but also try to justify them." [IIB-9]

246. Lu wanted to make Shen Tzu commander of the army. Master Meng said: "To make use of an untaught people [in war] is to bring calamity upon them. To bring calamity upon the people was not tolerated in the time of Yao and Shun. Moreover, even though by a single battle you were to subdue Ch'i and occupy Nan-yang, such a thing ought not to be done." In a burst of displeasure, Shen Tzu said: "This is what I cannot understand." "Let me explain it to you," said Master Meng. "The emperor has a domain of one thousand *li*; without a thousand *li*, it would be insufficient for him to treat the feudal lords. The feudal lord has a domain of one hundred *li*; without one hundred *li*, it would be insufficient for him to observe the code of rituals relative to ancestral temples. When the Duke of Chou was invested with Lu, its territory was one hundred *li*. There was plenty of land, but he was given not more than one hundred *li*. When T'ai-kung was invested with Ch'i, its territory was one hundred *li*. There was plenty of land, but he was given not more than one hundred *li*. Now the territory of Lu is five times one hundred *li*. If there should arise a real king, do you think he would reduce or enlarge the

domain of Lu? One who is *jen*-hearted will not take from one
to add to another; how much the less will he kill people in
order to occupy the land? When a *chün-tzu* serves his sovereign, he will lead the sovereign to follow the *Tao* and direct
him to *jen*." [VIB-8]

247. Wan Chang asked: "Sung is a small state, and its
sovereign intends to practice *jen*-government. Ch'i and Ch'u
are disgusted and attack him. What will you do about it?"
Master Meng said: "When T'ang dwelt in Po, he had Ko as
his neighbor. The chief of Ko was dissolute and neglected
sacrifices. When T'ang sent messengers to ask why he did not
make offerings, he said, 'I have no sacrificial animals.' Thereupon T'ang sent him cattle and sheep, but he ate them and
still failed to make offerings. Again T'ang sent messengers to
ask why he did not make offerings, and he said, 'I have no
sacrificial grain.' Thereupon T'ang sent the people of Po to
farm for him, while the old and weak carried food for them.
The chief of Ko then led his people to attack those who thus
brought wine, food, millet, and rice and plundered them.
Those who refused to part with their provisions were killed.
A boy who brought millet and meat for the farmers was thus
killed and robbed. With reference to this, it is said in the *Shu*,
'The chief of Ko was hostile to food-carriers.' Because he had
killed this boy, T'ang proceeded to punish him. Throughout
the world people said, 'It is not because he desires the riches
of the world, but that he takes revenge for the common man
and woman [upon the murderer].' T'ang commenced his punitive campaigns with Ko, and, in his eleven different campaigns, he had not an enemy in the world. When he was
battling in the east, the Yi tribes in the west complained; when
he was battling in the south, the Ti tribes in the north complained. They all complained, 'Why does he make us last?'
The people looked for his coming in the same way that those
suffering from drought look for rain. The merchants and
traders did not stop coming, nor did the farmers and peasants
stop working, while he killed their sovereigns and consoled
the people. His coming was like the falling of opportune rain,
and the people were greatly delighted. It is said again in the
Shu, 'We are waiting for our sovereign. When he comes, we
shall be relieved.' [And of King Wu of Chou it says,] 'There
were some who would not submit to Chou. King Wu proceeded with his punitive campaign in the east and brought
peace to the people. They welcomed him with baskets of

black and yellow silks, and presented themselves to serve the king of Chou so as to enjoy repose with him. Thus they became the subjects of the great Chou Empire.' The *chün-tzu* of Yin filled their baskets with black and yellow silk to welcome the *chün-tzu* of Chou, while the common men of Yin brought baskets of rice and bowls of congee to welcome the common men of Chou. King Wu delivered the people from the plight of water and fire, by cutting off their oppressors. It is said in the *Shu:* 'Let our power be extended so as to invade the land of Yin. Let us seize the oppressor so as to put an end to his evils. So shall our accomplishments be more glorious than those of T'ang. [*T'ai Shin*]' The sovereign of Sung does not, as you say, practice *jen*-government. Should he practice *jen*-government, the people within the four seas would lift up their heads and look up to him, wishing him for their sovereign. Then, great as Ch'i and Ch'u are, would there be need to fear them?" [IIIB-5]

248. Master Meng said to Tai Pu-sheng: "Do you wish your king to be virtuous? Let me tell you: Suppose here in Ch'i was an envoy from Ch'u who wanted his son to learn the speech of Ch'i. Whom should he employ to teach his son, a man of Ch'i or a man of Ch'u?" Tai Pu-sheng said: "Of course, he should employ a man of Ch'i to teach his son." Master Meng said: "With one man of Ch'i teaching him [Ch'i's language] and all the Ch'u men continually shouting at him [in his own dialect], the boy would never be able to learn the language even if he were thrashed every day. On the other hand, if the boy lived alone in Chuang-Yüeh [the interior of Ch'i] for several years, he would not be able to speak the language of Ch'u even if he were thrashed every day. You have told me that Hsieh-Chü-chou is a man of virtue and he has been placed in attendance on the king. Suppose all those attending the king, old and young, high and low, were Hsieh Chü-chou; with whom would the king do evil? On the other hand, suppose all those in attendance on the king, old and young, high and low, were not Hsieh Chü-chou; with whom would the king do good? If there were only one Hsieh Chü-chou, what could he have done for the king of Sung?" [IIIB-6]

249. The sovereign of Lu wanted to put Yüeh-cheng Tzu in charge of the government. Master Meng said: "When I heard of this, I was so happy that I could not sleep." Kung-sun Ch'ou asked: "Is Yüeh-cheng Tzu resolute?"

"No."

"Is he wise and sagacious?"

"No."

"Is he a man of wide learning?"

"No."

"Then why were you so happy that you could not sleep?"

"He is a man who loves what is good."

"Is the love of what is good sufficient?"

"If a man loves what is good, he is qualified to rule over the world; how much more so to rule over Lu! If a man loves what is good, all within four seas will not mind traveling a thousand *li* in order to come and tell him what is good. On the other hand, if a man does not love what is good, people will say, 'He is self-conceited and seems to be already aware of it.' This attitude of self-conceit will keep men away at a distance of a thousand *li*. When good men are kept away at a distance of a thousand *li*, calumniators and flatterers will come. When a man lives among calumniators and flatterers, how is it possible for him to govern his country well?" [VIB-13]

250. When Master Meng was in P'ing-lu, he said to its magistrate: "Suppose that one of your armed guards falls out of the ranks three times in one day; would you dismiss him or not?" "I would not wait for three times," was the answer. Master Meng said: "Then you yourself have likewise fallen out of the ranks a good many times. In the years of bad harvest and calamities, of your people, thousands of the old and weak have been found dying in the ditches and canals, and thousands of the young and able-bodied have been scattered abroad to all quarters." The magistrate said: "This is a state of things in which it is beyond my power to act." Master Meng said: "Here is a man who is entrusted with the care of the cattle and sheep. It is his duty to search for pasturage and fodder for them. If he fails to find pasturage and fodder, will he return the cattle and sheep to the owner, or will he stand by and see them die?" Then the magistrate said: "This is my fault." Another day, when Master Meng saw the king, he said: "Of the magistrates of Your Majesty, I am acquainted with five, but the only one of them who knows his fault is K'ung Chü-hsin." Then he related to the king the conversation with the magistrate. The king said: "This is my fault." [IIB-4]

251. Pai Kuei said: "My way of regulating floods is superior to that of Yü." Master Meng said: "You are wrong. Yü's regulation of floods was in accord with the natural way. He therefore caused the four seas to be the ditches of floods, while you

make the neighboring states their ditches. Water, when regulated contrary to its nature, will overflow, and overflowing causes a great flood. This is what a *jen*-hearted man detests. You are wrong." [VIB-11]

252. Master Meng said: "It would be better to be without written records than to believe everything that has been written. In the chapter on Wu-cheng [of the *Shu*] I only accept two or three passages. The *jen*-hearted man has no enemy in the world. And when the most *jen*-hearted fought against the one who was the least *jen*-hearted, how could so much blood have flowed till it floated pestles [as described in the chapter]?" [VIIB-3]

253. Master Meng said: "During the *Ch'un Ch'iu* [Spring-Autumn] period, there were no righteous wars. There are instances where one war was more equitable than another. A punitive campaign might be waged by a superior authority against his subordinates. Among hostile states there should be no punitive campaigns against one another." [VIIB-2]

254. Kung-sun Ch'ou said: "Kao Tzu says, 'The *Hsiao Pien* is the ode of a low fellow.'" Master Meng said: "What made you say so?" "Resentment," was the reply. "Bigoted indeed is old Kao's explanation of the ode. Suppose that here is a man, and a native of Yüeh bends his bow to shoot him. You will dissuade him merely with talks and smiles, for no other reason than that he is not related to you. But if your own brother bends his bow to shoot that man, you will dissuade him in tears, for no other reason than that he is related to you. The resentment expressed in the *Hsiao Pien* is that of affection between relatives, and that affection shows *jen*. Bigoted indeed is old Kao's explanation of the ode." Then Kung-sun Ch'ou said: "Why is there no resentment expressed in the *K'ai-fung* ode?" Master Meng said: "The parent's fault, as mentioned in *K'ai-fung* ode, is small, while the one mentioned in the *Hsiao-pien* ode is great. When the parent's fault is great, the estrangement will be aggravated by not expressing resentment. When the parent's fault is small, the ill-feeling will be irritated by expressing resentment. To aggravate the estrangement will be unfilial, and to irritate the ill-feeling will also be unfilial. Master K'ung said, 'Shun was indeed most filial. Even at the age of fifty, he was still longing for his parents!'" [VIB-3]

255. Master Meng said: "When the kingly rule no longer prevailed, the *Shih* came to an end. When the *Shih* came to an end, the *Ch'un Ch'iu* (Spring-Autumn Annals) was made.

The *Cheng* of Tsin, the *Tao Wu* of Ch'u, and the *Ch'un Ch'iu* of Lu were annals of the same character. The events dealt with were those of [Dukes] Huan of Ch'i and Wen of Tsin, and the narrative was historical. Master K'ung said, 'I particularly respected its righteous principles.' " [IVB-21]

⋖§ THREE: HSÜN TZU §⋗

CONTENTS

CONTENTS

⇜§ THREE: HSÜN TZU §⇝

⇜§ INTRODUCTION

Hsün Tzu, whose personal name was K'uang (he was also known as Ch'ing), was a native of the Chao State, on the edge of Shansi. Although the dates of his birth and death are not precisely known, it is established that his working life fell into the third century B.C. Thus, he was a witness to the bloody climax of the period of the Warring States and was strongly influenced by what he saw.

Not much is known of his life. The *Shih Chi* or *Historical Records* says of him (ch. 74):

> ... When he was fifty, he first came to spread his teachings abroad in Ch'i. ... T'ien P'ien and the other scholars associated with him were all dead during the time of King Hsiang of Ch'i [283-265 B.C.], and Hsün Ch'ing was the most eminent learned scholar. ... He acted three times in the capacity of a libation officer at the great temple sacrifices. Among the people of Ch'i were some who provoked scandals against him, and he thereupon went to Ch'u, where Prince Ch'un-sun made him magistrate of Lan-ling. When Prince Ch'un-sun died [in 238 B.C.], Hsün Ch'ing lost his Lan-ling position.

In Lan-ling, Hsün Tzu surrounded himself with a group of young men, some of whom rose to eminence as scholars and politicians. Among his disciples, the two most famous were Li Ssu, prime minister of the First Emperor of the Ch'in dynasty, and Han Fei, a distinguished legalist, both of whom stood for firm and authoritative government and for using laws as the framework of the social order. The results of their views are seen in the strong measures which consolidated the conquests of all-powerful Ch'in into an administrative and cultural whole. There were Confucian scholars who insisted that Hsün Tzu, although classified with Confucianists, had paved the way for the legalist triumph which culminated in the burning of books in 213, including the classics so dear to him. Hsün Tzu died about 238 B.C.

His manner of life was much like that of Confucius. Mourn-

ing over the degeneracy of his time, he became a social and
political reformer. At first he sought to effect his objectives by
taking part in politics and setting an example of good government, as well as by giving instruction to young men. In politics
he could not claim to have had a successful career. He had
not been able to uproot the social and political decay of his
time. But Hsün Tzu was an optimist, insisting that man would
make himself master of his social destiny. The teaching and
personality of Confucius constituted the supreme intellectual
impulse of his life and inspiration of his entire thought. Of
Confucius he said:

> Confucius was human-hearted and wise; he was not blind.
> Hence he had multitudinous learning and was worthy to be
> ranked with the early kings (*Hsün Tzu*, ch. 21).

In developing his philosophy, Hsün Tzu, however, differed
fundamentally from Mencius. On the nature of man, he rejected the doctrine so strongly advocated by Mencius, that
human nature is innately good; he contended, probably as an
outgrowth of the political and social decay, that human nature
is evil. On the conception of heaven, Hsün Tzu leaned far in
the direction of the Taoists' impersonal, naturalistic *Tao*. To
him, heaven was not a moral principle or a spiritual entity, as
conceived by Mencius, but the unvarying law of natural
phenomenon:

> The stars make their rounds; the sun and moon alternately
> shine; the four seasons succeed one another; the *yin* and
> *yang* go through their mutations; wind and rain are widely
> distributed. All things acquire their harmony and have their
> lives (*ibid.*, ch. 17).

Such are the operations of the great laws, which, as Hsün Tzu
held, "a sage does not seek to know" (*ibid.*).[1]

Considering the progression from Confucius' humanism, we
see that on the one hand, Mencius elaborated on the idealistic
aspect of Confucian doctrine by exalting the supreme virtues
of *jen* and *yi* as the controlling element in human relations in
general and in government in particular. His teachings are
based on the assumption that human nature is good and

---

1. Mencius said: "A man who has exercised his mind to the utmost, knows
his nature. Knowing his nature, he knows Heaven." (*Meng Tzu*, II-17). Thus
according to Mencius, a sage must "know Heaven."

heaven will throw its weight on the side of righteousness. On the other hand, Hsün Tzu based his philosophy chiefly on the more practical portions of Confucian teaching, such as rites and music. In order to do so, he not only justified his ideas with historical facts, but also gave a new logical basis for his assertions, as noted in the following selections from the works.

The teachings of Hsün Tzu are preserved in the book bearing his name. It originally consisted of three hundred and twenty-two articles, but after being edited and condensed, the number of articles in the standard edition by Yang Ching of the T'ang dynasty is thirty-two. As judged from his writings, Hsün Tzu was not only a master of prose, but also a profound thinker. The following selections from the *Hsun Tzu* are arranged under the following subjects:

> Part One: Heaven and Human Nature
> Part Two: Rites and Music
> Part Three: Education and Knowledge
> Part Four: The Theory of Government

⇜ SELECTIONS FROM THE HSÜN TZU

Part One: Heaven and Human Nature

As we have noted above, the teachings of Hsün Tzu are diametrically opposed to those of Mencius in two ways: (1) To Mencius heaven was personal or ethical; to Hsün Tzu it was naturalistic, a natural phenomenon which had nothing to do with man's activities. Hsün Tzu believed that it was man himself, and not heaven, who was responsbile for his own life. Hence, by rejecting heaven as a supernatural force or ethical principle, Hsün Tzu hastened the process of divorcing religion from philosophy. This was his great contribution to the development of Chinese thought about man and nature. (2) To Mencius human nature was good; Hsün Tzu, noting the unhappy events that were occurring around him, concluded that human nature was evil, and suggested steps to bring about its transformation. The controversy between these two teachers has since been a matter of intense discussion among Chinese scholars.

⇜ ⇝

I. Chapter 17: On Heaven

Heaven operates with constant regularity. It does not exist for the sake of Yao; nor does it cease to exist for the sake of Chieh. Respond to it with good government, and blessings will result. Respond to it with misgovernment, and calamity will result. When food and clothes are sufficiently stored and used economically, Heaven cannot impoverish the country. When the people are adequately sustained and their energies are employed in keeping with the seasons, Heaven cannot afflict the people. When the *Tao* is followed and there are no deviations from it, Heaven cannot send misfortune. Under such circumstances, flood or drought cannot cause a famine, the winter's blast or the summer's heat cannot cause any malady, and devils or demons cannot cause disaster. On the other hand, when food and clothing are not stored and are used lavishly, Heaven cannot make the country rich. When the people lack sustenance and their energies are employed inordinately, Heaven cannot make the people wholesome. When the *Tao* is violated and conduct is absurd, Heaven cannot send blessings. Under such circumstances, even in the absence of flood and drought, there will be famine; even with a mild winter and a moderate summer, there will be maladies; even without devils and demons, there will be disasters. Conformity to the seasons and prosperity are found to be interdependent: catastrophe and prosperity are different in nature. It is of no use to complain against Heaven, for such is the *Tao*. Hence one who understands the distinct functions of Heaven and of man may be called a great man.

To accomplish without acting and to obtain without seeking —this is what is meant by the function of Heaven. Although the *Tao* of Heaven is profound, the great man will not deliberate on it; although it is great, he will not devote his energy to it; although it is meticulous, he will not scrutinize it—this is what is meant by refraining from contesting with Heaven. Heaven has its seasons, earth has its resources, man has his government; in this way man is able to form a triad with Heaven and earth. If man abandons his own part in this Triad and desires to rely on Heaven and earth, he is confounding himself.

The stars make their rounds; the sun and moon alternately shine; the four seasons succeed one another; the *yin* and *yang* go through their mutations; wind and rain are widely distributed. All things acquire harmony and thus grow; each thing obtains its nourishment and thus attains its maturity. We do not see the cause of these occurrences, but we do see their effects—this is what is meant by the potency of spirit. We all know the results of these changes, but we do not know their invisible source—this is what is meant by the work of Heaven. It is only the sage who does not seek to know Heaven. When the function of Heaven is established, and its work is brought to completion, man's body is formed, and his spirit is born, together with loving and hating, delight and anger, sorrow and joy within his own self—this is what is meant by the "Heavenly sentiment." Man has eyes, ears, a nose, a mouth, and limbs; each of them is in relation to the others but not to interchange its function for the others—this is what is meant by the "Heavenly organs." In the center dwells the mind, which, though void, controls the five senses—this is what is meant by the "Heavenly sovereign." The other species are used to sustain human species—this is what is meant by "Heavenly sustenance"; for to sustain human species is what is called "blessings," to famish human species is "calamity"—this is what is meant by the "Heavenly government."

Now, for man to obscure his "Heavenly sovereign," confuse his "Heavenly organs," abandon his "Heavenly sustenance," defy his "Heavenly government," and violate his "Heavenly sentiment" will lead to the loss of his "Heavenly work." This is what is meant by "great misfortune." The sage purifies his "heavenly sovereign," rectifies his "Heavenly organs," provides for his "Heavenly sustenance," complies with his "Heavenly government," and nurtures his "Heavenly sentiment." This course leads to the completion of all his "Heavenly work." Thereupon, he knows what he can and what he cannot do. In this way the sage can rule Heaven and earth and command all things. Thus his conduct is well regulated, his nourishment well adopted, and his life not injured — this is what is meant by knowing Heaven.

Therefore, great dexterity requires no exertion, and great wisdom can be obtained without deliberation. In order to know about Heaven, we must observe its phenomena so as to know its climate. In order to know about earth, we must study the quality of the soil so as to know its crops. In order to know about the four seasons, we must observe their proper functions so as to know the proper time. In order to know about the yin and yang, we must observe their interactions so as to know blessing and calamity.

Since this is so, the man who depends upon Heaven abides by his own way.

Does Heaven decide whether good government or misgovernment will prevail? It was said that the sun and moon, stars and planets were the same to Yü and Chieh, but good government prevailed in the time of Yü and misgovernment in that of Chieh. Hence I say that Heaven does not decide whether good government or misgovernment will prevail. Do seasons decide whether good government or misgovernment will prevail? It was said that spring and summer were the time for husbandry and growth, and that autumn and winter were the time for harvest and storage; these were the same to Yü and Chieh, but good government prevailed in the time of Yü and misgovernment in that of Chieh. Hence I say that seasons do not decide whether good government or misgovernment will prevail. Then does earth decide whether good government or misgovernment will prevail? It was said that where there was land there was life, and that where there was no land there was death; this was the same to Yü and Chieh, but good government prevailed in the time of Yü and misgovernment in that of Chieh. Hence I say that earth does not decide whether good government or misgovernment will prevail. It is said in the *Shih:*

> Heaven made the high hill;
> King T'ai tilled the land—
> 'Twas he who began the work;
> Then King Wen brought it under peace.

This expresses what I mean.

Heaven does not suspend the winter because men dislike cold; nor does the earth reduce its wide space because men dislike distances; nor does the *chün-tzu* change his conduct because common men make a clamour. Heaven has its invariable *Tao;* earth has its invariable size; the *chün-tzu* has his invariable demeanor. The *chün-tzu* conforms to the invariable principle, but the common man makes his claims. It is said in the *Shih:*

> [If a man abides by the *Tao,*]
> Why should he be anxious about others' words?

This expresses what I mean.

The King of Ch'u has a thousand chariots following him— this is not because he is wise. The *chün-tzu* eats porridge and drinks water—this is not because he is foolish. In each case, this is due to the circumstances of the time. However, if a man has his purpose cultivated, his virtuous conduct strengthened, his knowledge and deliberation clarified, living in this age but emulating the ancients, he is doing what is within his power. Therefore the *chün-tzu* is concerned about what is within his power, and does not desire what is from heaven. The *hsiao-jen* [common man] neglects what is within his power and longs for what is from Heaven. Because the *chün-tzu* is concerned about what is within his power and does not desire what comes from Heaven, he progresses every day. Because the *hsiao-jen* neglects what is within his power and longs for what comes from Heaven, he degenerates every day. This is the reason why the *chün-tzu* goes forward and the *hsiao-jen* goes backward. This accounts for the difference between the *chün-tzu* and the *hsiao-jen*.

When stars fall or trees groan, all the people panic and ask, "What is the significance of all this?" I would answer, "There is no special significance." This is simply due to the change of Heaven and earth, and the transformation of the *yin* and *yang* —something which rarely happens. We may wonder at it, but we should not fear it. For there is no age which has not experienced from time to time eclipses of the sun and moon, unreasonable rain and wind, or occasional appearances of strange stars. If the sovereign is enlightened and the government equitable, even though these phenomena should all occur at once, no harm would be done. If the sovereign is ignorant and the government is perilous, although not one of these phenomena should occur, it would still be of no avail. Hence the falling of stars and groaning of trees are due to the change of Heaven and earth and the transformation of the *yin* and *yang* —something which rarely happens. We may wonder at it, but we should not fear it.

Of all occurrences and phenomena, human portents are the most to be feared. To plow improperly so as to injure the crops, to hoe carelessly so as to miss the weeds, to govern recklessly so as to lose the people, to leave the fields uncultivated and to harvest poor crops, to let the price of grain rise high and let the people starve and die on the road side—these are what I mean by human portents. When the ordinances of the government are not enlightened; when the measures of the state are not opportune; when the fundamental tasks are not carried out—these are what I mean by human portents. When rules of *li* and *yi* are not cultivated, the quarters of men and women are not kept apart, and men and women become promiscuous; then father and son distrust each other, the ruler and the ruled are at cross purposes, and invasion and distress arrive at the same time—this is what I mean by human portents. Portents come from disorder, and when these three kinds [of human portents] occur together, there will be no peace in the country. These human portents are easily discernible, but their disasters are far beyond compare. If the people's labors are employed not in accord with seasons, then horses will be turned to oxen and all beasts will become portents. We may wonder at them, but we should not fear them. It is said in the *Chuan* [Records]: "In the *Shu* no strange things are mentioned." There would be no use to discuss them; nor would there be any need to scrutinize them; so it would be better not to be concerned about them. However, righteousness of the sovereign and minister, the affection of father and son, and the distinction between husband and wife should be daily observed, and there should be no deviations from them.

If man prays for rain and then it rains, how is that? I would say: Not strange. It would rain all the same even if no man prayed for rain. When people try to save the sun or moon from being devoured [an eclipse], when they pray for rain in a drought, or when they solicit good omens before making an important decision—this is not because they think in this way they will get what they see, but only to add a touch of ritual. Hence the *chün-tzu* regards it as a matter of ritual, whereas the common people generally take it to be a sign of the supernatural. One who sees it as a matter of ritual will suffer no harm; one who sees it as a sign of the supernatural will suffer harm.

In Heaven there is nothing as brilliant as the sun and moon; on earth nothing as essential as water and fire; among objects nothing as precious as pearls and gems; for man nothing as glorious as the rules of *li* [decorum] and *yi* [righteousness]. When the sun and moon are not high, they will not shine with brilliance. When water and fire are not accumulated, they will not extend far and wide. When pearls and gems are transparent in appearance, they will not be treasured by princes and nobles. When the rules of *li* and *yi* are not complied with in the country, honors and titles will not be esteemed. Therefore, just as the fate of man depends upon Heaven, the destiny of a state depends on the rules of *li*. When the sovereign esteems the rules of *li* and honors men of worth, he will attain the kingly rule. When the sovereign stresses law and loves the people, he will become the leader of the feudal lords. On the other hand, if the sovereign is greedy and crafty, his life will be in peril; if he governs with force and stratagem, his state will be overthrown; all cloaked schemes and oppressive measures will bring about his ruin. Such being the case, since you glorify Heaven and meditate on it, why not domesticate it and regulate it? Since you obey Heaven and praise it, why not control its course and make use of it? Since you look upon seasons with expectation and await them, why not seize the seasonal opportunities and exploit them? Since you rely upon entities multiplying by themselves, why not exercise all your ability in developing them? Since you speculate about what makes them things, why not set them in order so that you do not lose them? Since you will that things grow, why not assist them in their development? Hence, [I say,] if a man neglects his effort and speculates about Heaven, he fails to understand the true nature of things.

That which the kings of all ages have followed without change is sufficient to be the essence of the *Tao* [i.e., *li* or the rules of decorum]. In spite of the dynastic changes, this essence has persisted. When this essence is comprehended, there will be no disorder; when it is ignored, changing circumstances will lead to disorder. This essence has indeed been constant and never ceased to exist. As disorder is born of variations, order should come from detailed provisions. That which the *Tao* stresses is to follow the *mean*, for deviation leads to negligence, and concealment brings about great delusion. For instance, one who wades through water needs a sign to mark its depth; if the sign is not clear, he is in danger of drowning. Similarly, one who governs the people needs a sign to mark the *Tao*; if the sign is not clear, there is disorder. *Li* is the sign. Without *li*, the world is confounded; when the world is confounded, there will be great disorder. Therefore the *Tao* should be clear and distinct, to mark all the distinctions of ranks. When these distinctions are uniform, disasters to the people will come to an end.

The myriad things are single aspects of the *Tao*, and one thing is a single aspect of the myriad things. The stupid person who sees only a single aspect of one thing claims to comprehend the totality of the *Tao*. The *Tao* cannot be comprehended in such a partial way. Shen Tzu[1] had vision regarding following, but no vision regarding leading. Lao Tzu [the

1. Shen Tzu, the author of twelve discussions, studied the arts of *Tao* and *Te* of Huang-ti and Lao Tzu.

supposed author of *Tao-te Ching*] had vision regarding bending but no vision regarding straightening. Mo Tzu had vision regarding uniformity, but no vision regarding individuality. Sung Tzu [a contemporary of Mencius] had vision regarding [the fact that the desires of some men are] few, but no vision regarding [the fact that those of others are] many. Given vision regarding following but no vision regarding leading, the people will be at a loss where to go. Given vision regarding bending but no vision regarding straightening, the high and low will not be distinguished. Given vision regarding uniformity but no vision regarding individuality, the government will not operate. Given vision regarding the few but no vision regarding the many, the people will not be transformed. It is said in the *Shu*:

> Let us have no undue attachments,
> But follow the *Tao* of the kings;
> Let us have no excessive antipathies,
> But follow the path of the kings.

This expresses what I mean.

II. Chapter 23: Human Nature Is Evil

The nature of man is evil; his goodness is acquired. As to his nature, man is born, first, with a desire for gain. If this desire is followed, strife will result and prudence will disappear. Second, man is born with envy and hate. If these tendencies are followed, injury and cruelty will abound; loyalty and good faith will disappear. Third, man is born with the lusts of the ear and eye, leading to the love of sound and beauty. If these lusts are followed, lewdness and disorder will spring up; *li* and *yi*, together with good manners, will disappear. Hence, if man gives rein to his nature and follows his passions, he will strive and grab, leading to a breach of order and confounding of reason, and culminating in violence. Only under the restraint of teachers and laws and the guidance of rules of *li* and *yi*, does man conform to prudence, observe good manners, and yield to order. From all this, it is evident that the nature of man is evil and that his goodness is acquired.

Crooked wood needs to undergo steaming and plumbing; only then can it become straight. Blunt metal needs to undergo grinding and whetting; only then can it become sharp. Now the nature of man is evil; therefore, he needs the teachers and laws so as to be upright; he needs the rules of *li* and *yi* so as to be orderly. Without teachers and laws men are biased, vicious, and unjust; without *li* and *yi* men are rebellious and disorderly. In ancient times the sage-kings recognized that the nature of man was evil and therefore biased, vicious and unjust, rebellious and disorderly. Thereupon they instituted the rules of *li* and *yi* and established laws and ordinances to modify and rectify the nature of man, to transform and guide it. All men are thus made to yield to order and to abide by the *Tao.* At present those who are influenced by teachers and laws, who accumulate the culture of learning, and who follow the rules of *li* and *yi* are the *chün-tzu.* On the other hand, those who give rein to their nature, who indulge in their insolence, and who disregard the rules of *li* and *yi* are the *hsiao-jen.* From all this, it is evident that the nature of man is evil, and that his goodness is acquired.

Mencius said: "The reason why man is educable is that his nature is good." I reply: This is not so. Mencius failed to understand human nature, failed to distinguish between what is congenital and what is acquired. Man's nature as conferred by Heaven cannot be learned and cannot be worked for; whereas the rules of *li* and *yi*, as formulated by sage-kings, can be attained by learning and accomplished by work. What in man cannot be learned and cannot be worked for is man's nature. What in man can be attained by learning and can be accomplished by work is the acquired. This is the distinction between nature and the acquired. Now by the nature of man, the eye has the faculty of seeing and the ear has the faculty of hearing. When man sees, his keenness of sight is not separate from the eye; when he hears, his keenness of hearing is not separate from the ear. It is evident that the keenness of sight and the keenness of hearing cannot be learned.

Mencius said: "The nature of man is good; but because he loses and ruins his original goodness, his nature becomes evil." I reply: In this he is mistaken. As to the nature of man, as soon as he is born, he tends to depart from his congenital quality and depart from his innate disposition; he is bent to lose it and ruin it. From all this, it is evident that the nature of man is evil.

To say that human nature is good means that without departing from his congenital quality, man becomes graceful, and without departing from his innate disposition, he becomes beneficial. To maintain that man's congenital quality and disposition are graceful and that his heart and mind are good is the same as to maintain that the keenness of the faculty of sight is not separate from the eye and the keenness of the faculty of hearing is not separate from the ear. So we say that the eye is keen in seeing and that the ear is keen in hearing. Now as to the nature of man, when he is hungry, he desires to be fed; when he is cold, he desires to be warm; when he is tired, he desires to rest. This is man's instinct and nature. But now a man may be hungry and yet in the presence of elders he dare not be the first to eat. This is because he yields precedence to others. He may be tired and yet he dare not rest; this is because he works for others. Contrary to man's nature and antagonistic to his instinct are actions of a man yielding to his father and a younger brother yielding to his elder brother, or a son working for his father and a younger brother working for his elder brother. However, these are the ways of filial piety and in accordance with the rules of *li* and *yi*. Therefore, if a man follows his nature and instinct, he has no prudence; if he has prudence, he acts contrary to his nature and instinct. From all this, it is evident that the nature of man is evil and that his goodness is acquired.

Someone may ask, "If the nature of man is evil, whence come the rules of *li* and *yi?*" In answer I say: All rules of *li* and *yi* are born of something acquired by the sages, and not of the nature of man. The potter pounds and moulds the clay and so makes vessels, but vessels are born of his acquired skill and not of man's nature. The craftsman hews a piece of wood and so makes a utensil, but the utensil is born of his acquired skill and not of man's nature. The sage gathers ideas and thoughts, and possesses acquired knowledge, so as to bring forth rules of *li* and *yi* and institute laws and regulations. So the rules of *li* and *yi*, laws and regulations, are similarly born of something acquired by the sage, and not of man's nature.

The eye likes color, the ear likes sound, the mouth likes flavors, the heart likes gain, the body likes comfort and ease— all these are born of man's nature and instinct. When stimulated, they come forth of their own accord; they need not be taught before they arise of themselves. If anything, when stimulated, cannot come forth of its own accord, and if it needs to be taught before it comes forth, it is acquired. This shows the distinction between that which arises from nature and that which arises from the acquired. This is why the sage transformed nature and established the acquired. Out of the acquired, the rules of *li* and *yi* were evolved, and laws and regulations were brought forth by the sage. Therefore, the sage is the same as the mass of people; he does not differ from them in their nature, but he differs from them in what has been acquired.

It is man's nature and instinct to desire gain and to seek to attain it. If brothers have property and are to divide it, if they follow their nature and instinct to desire gain and to seek to obtain it, they will strive with each other to seize the property. On the other hand, if they were transformed by the rules of *li* and *yi*, they would yield to outsiders. So by following the nature and instinct, even brothers contend with each other; if they are transformed by *li* and *yi*, they will yield to strangers. For man wishes to be good because his nature is evil. If a man is mediocre, he wishes to be important; if he is ugly, he wishes to be beautiful; if he is niggardly, he wishes to be generous; if he is poor, he wishes to be rich; if he is lowly, he wishes to be honored—whatever he has not within himself he seeks from without. Therefore the rich do not wish for wealth, and the honorable do not wish for position—whatever he has within himself, he does not seek from without. From all this, we see that man wishes to be good because his nature is evil. Now the nature of man is really without *li* and *yi*, so that he strives to learn and seeks to obtain them. By man's nature, he does not know *li* and *yi*, so he thinks and reflects, and seeks to know them—only then are they developed. So man by nature is without *li* and *yi*, nor does he know them. If man is without them, there is disorder; if he does not know them, there is rebellion. Hence *li* and *yi* are instituted; rebellion and disorder are within man himself. From all this it is evident that the nature of man is evil, and that his goodness is acquired.

Mencius said: "The nature of man is good." I reply: This is not so. In the past and in the present what is meant by goodness is true principles and just government; what is meant by evil is perilous injustice and disorderly rebellion. This is the distinction between goodness and evil. Now by his nature does man conform to true principles and just government? If so, what can be the use of the sage-kings? What can be the use of the rules of *li* and *yi?* Although there were sage-kings and rules of *li* and *yi*, how could they enhance true principles and just government?

Now that is not the situation. The nature of man is evil. The ancient sage-kings recognized that man's nature was evil, by which they meant that man was prone to perilous injustice without rectitude, and disorderly rebellion without good government; hence they established the authority of the sovereign to govern the people; they instituted the rules of *li* and *yi* to tranform the people; they set up laws and government to rule the people; and they administered severe punishments to restrain the people—with the result that the world was made to conform to peace and order and to accord with goodness. This was the government of the sage-kings, the transformation brought about by *li* and *yi*.

Now suppose we discard the authority of the sovereign and have no transformation by *li* and *yi*; suppose we discard the control of the laws and government and have no restraint by *li* and *yi*. Let us stand by and watch to see how the people will behave. The strong would injure the weak and rob them; the many would oppress the few and rend them. As a result, the whole world would soon be reduced to a state of disorderly rebellion and, consequently, ruin. From all this it is evident that the nature of man is evil and that his goodness is acquired.

The man who is versed in ancient times must witness its evidence in the present; he who is versed in the way of Heaven must demonstrate their effects on man. He who joins the discussion must make his ideas clear and distinct, supporting them with evidence, so he can make his statements, elaborate his arguments, and carry out his ideas. Mencius said: "The nature of man is good." This is not clear or distinct, and it is without evidence. He made his statement, but he did not elaborate his arguments, nor was he able to carry out his ideas. Is this not extremely erroneous? For if man's nature were good, we could dispense with the sage-kings and shelve the rules of *li* and *yi*. On the other hand, if man's nature is evil, we need to have the sage-kings and must rely on the rules of *li* and *yi*. Because wood is crooked, we produce the carpenter's tools; because things are not straight, we use the plumb-line. Similarly, because man's nature is evil, we establish the sovereign and institute the rules of *li* and *yi*. From all this it is evident that the nature of man is evil and that his goodness is acquired. Straight wood does not require the carpenter's tool to be straight; by nature it is straight. Crooked wood needs to undergo steaming and plumbing by the carpenter's tools, and only then will it be straight; it is not straight by nature. As the nature of man is evil, he needs to be governed by the sage-kings and to be transformed by the rules of *li* and *yi*; only then will order reign and conformity to goodness prevail. From all this it is evident that the nature of man is evil and that his goodness is acquired.

It may be objected, "The accumulation and acquisition of

li and *yi* must be in the nature of man so that the sage could bring them forth." In reply I say: This is not so. Now the potter pounds and moulds the clay and produces earthenware. Are the earthenware and clay in the nature of man? The workman hews a piece of wood and produces a utensil. Are the utensil and wood in the nature of man? So it is with the relation of the sage to *li* and *yi;* he institutes them in the same way as earthenware is produced. Are the accumulation and acquisition of *li* and *yi* in the nature of man? So far as the nature of man is concerned, Yao and Shun were the same as Chieh and Chih; the *chün-tzu* is the same as the *hsiao-jen.* If the accumulation and acquisition of *li* and *yi* were regarded as being in the nature of man, why should Yao and Yü be esteemed and the *chün-tzu* be honored? The reason is that they could transform nature and produce the acquired. From the acquired, they evolved the rules of *li* and *yi.* Thus the sage is to the accumulation and acquisition of *li* and *yi* as the potter is to the production of earthenware. How can the accumulation and acquisition of *li* and *yi* be of man's nature? The reason why Chieh and Chih were mean and the *hsiao-jen* is low is that they followed their nature and acted according to their instinct—they took to sensual enjoyments, with the result that they were greedy for profit and striving for gain. Hence it is evident that the nature of man is evil and that his goodness is acquired.

Heaven was not partial to Tseng, Chien, and Hsiao Yi, nor does Heaven ignore the common multitude. But why are Tseng, Chien, and Hsiao Yi alone praised as being truly filial, and alone have the name of filiality? The reason is that they were in accord with the rules of *li* and *yi.* Heaven was not partial to the people of Ch'i and Lu, nor does Heaven ignore the people of Ch'in. But why are the people of Ch'in not as good in the righteous relation between father and son and in the proper distinction between husband and wife as are the people of Ch'i and Lu in filial piety and reverential respect? The reason is that the people of Ch'in follow their instinct and nature—they take to sensual enjoyments and neglect the rules of *li* and *yi.* How can their nature be different?

There is a saying, "A man in the street can become a Yü." What is its meaning? My answer is that Yü became what he was because he abided by *jen, yi,* laws, and uprightness. However, there are principles by which *jen yi,* laws, and uprightness can be known and practiced. Meanwhile a man in the street has the quality of knowing *jen, yi,* laws, and uprightness, and the ability whereby he can carry out these virtues. Thus it is evident that he can become a Yü. Now are there no principles by which *jen*, *yi*, laws, and uprightness can be known and practiced? If so, even Yü could not know them or practice them. Then is a man in the street without the quality of knowing these virtues and the ability to practice them? If so, then he cannot know, on the one hand, the righteous relation between father and son, and, on the other hand, the correct standard of sovereign and minister. That, however, is not the case. Now every man in the street knows, on the one hand, the righteous relation between father and son, and, on the other hand, the correct standard of sovereign and minister. Thus it is evident that a man in the street has the capacity of knowing and the means to practice these virtues. Now let the man in the street rely on his quality of knowing and his ability of acting in accordance with the principles by which *jen* and *yi* can be known, and the ability whereby these virtues can be practiced; hence it is evident that he can become a Yü.

Now suppose a man in the street pursues knowledge and devotes himself to learning, by concentration of mind and singleness of purpose, thinking, studying, and investigating, day in and day out, with persistence and patience. He accumulates goodness without ceasing, and then may be counted among the divinities, to form a triad with Heaven and earth. Sagehood is a state that any man can achieve by cumulative effort. One may ask, "Why is it possible for the sage and not possible for the mass of people to make accumulations?" My answer is that it is possible for anyone, but the mass does not use it. The *hsiao-jen* can become a *chün-tzu*, but he is not willing; the *chün-tzu* can become a *hsiao-jen*, but he is not willing. It is not impossible for them to exchange places, but they simply do not. This demonstrates that there is possibility, but they do not use it. Thus, it is possible for a man in the street to become a Yü, but it is improbable that he has the ability. Even so, this does not vitiate the possibility. It is possible for a man to travel throughout the world, but he may never have the ability. It is possible for the laborer, the artisan, the farmer, and the merchant to exchange jobs, but they may never have the ability. From all this, it follows that the possibility does not necessarily involve the ability, while the inability does not vitiate the possibility. Hence there is a great difference between ability or inability and possibility or impossibility—evidently it is not possible for men to exchange places.

Yao asked Shun: "How are the sentiment and passion of man?" In reply, Shun said: "The sentiment and passion of man are far from perfect. Why do you ask? When a man has a wife and children, his filial piety to his parents declines; when sensual desires are satisfied, faithfulness between friends declines; when title and emolument are raised, loyalty toward the prince declines. The sentiment and passion of man are such—they are far from perfect! Why do you ask? Only the man of worth will not be so!"

There are those who have the wisdom of the sage, those who have the wisdom of the scholar or *chün-tzu*, those who have the wisdom of the *hsiao-jen*, and those who have the wisdom of the menial. To speak much with refinement and coherence, to discourse for a whole day with various reasonings and different approaches, but to concentrate on one subject—this is the wisdom of the sage. To speak little, but to the point and briefly, and to discourse in accord with rules, as if there were one thread that runs through his speech—this is the wisdom of the scholar or *chün-tzu*. To flatter, to conduct himself imprudently, so that all his actions and doings are regretful—this is the wisdom of the *hsiao-jen*. To respond quickly and act promptly, but without intelligence, to have great skill and wide knowledge, but no usefulness, and to be alert in speech and good in discourse, but not to the point, not caring for right and wrong, not considering error or truth, but with an object to be superior to others—this is the wisdom of the menial.

There is superior courage, mediocre courage, and inferior courage. When the world is in accord with the *Tao*, one dares to stand by oneself; when the *Tao* of the former kings prevails, one dares to follow their instructions. When there is *jen*, one will not consider poverty a distress; when there is no *jen*, one will consider riches an attraction. When the world knows this one, he wishes to rejoice with it; when the world does not know this one, he will stand alone between Heaven and earth, without fear—this is superior courage. To be respectful of the rules of *li* and have few desires; to esteem fidelity and despise wealth; when there is a worthy man, daring to recommend and exalt him; when there is an unworthy man, daring to expel and remove him—this is mediocre courage. To neglect one's personality but treasure wealth; to feel easy about troubles and assert oneself in words; making evasions, caring not for right and wrong, and tolerating one's imprudence, but with an object to be superior to others —this is inferior courage.

Fan-jo and *Chü-shu* were famous bows of antiquity. But if they had not been framed for straightening, they could not have been straight of themselves. The *Ts'ung* of Duke Huan, the *Ch'ueh* of Duke T'ai, the *Lu* of King Wen, the *Fu* of Prince Chuang, Ho-lü's *Kan-chiang, Mo-hsie, Chü-ch'ueh, P'i-lu:* these were famous swords of antiquity. But if they had not been ground, they could not have been sharp; if they had not been labored on, they could not have cut. *Hua, Liu, Ch'i, Chi, Hsien, Li, Lu, Erh:* these were all famous horses of antiquity. But on the one hand they were restrained by the means of a bit and reins, and on the other hand they were urged by the threat of the whip; they were driven with the skill of Ts'ao-fu; only then could they run the thousand *li* in one day. Thus, although a man has good natural qualities with a clear and intelligent mind, he needs to seek a virtuous teacher and serve him as a disciple; he needs to choose good friends and associate with them. When he obtains a virtuous teacher and serves him as a disciple, then what he hears is the *Tao* of Yao, Shun, Yu, and T'ang. When he obtains good friends and associates with them, then what he sees is the conduct relating to loyalty, faithfulness, reverence, and prudence. His person daily advances in *jen* and *yi*, and unconsciously he becomes good by following the sage-kings. Now should a man live with people who are not virtuous, that which he would hear would be cheating, maliciousness, falseness, and hypocrisy. That which he would see would be impurity, imprudence, lust, and avarice. His person would suffer death, and unconsciously he would become evil by following these people. The Chüan says: "If you do not know a person, look at his friends. If you do not know a sovereign, look at his favorites." Such is the way to which we conform! Such is the way to which we conform!

Part Two: Rites and Music

Rites [*Li*] and music are not unique to the teachings of Hsün Tsu. The history of their origin and evolution into transforming influence on man's life is as old as that of the country itself. In Chinese humanism, *li* and music are even more important than gymnastics and music were to Plato's and Aristotle's systems.

There is some difference between the function of *li* and that of music. To Hsün Tzu *li* denotes something very important and fundamental in social life; he considered *li* to be the most effective means of counteracting the evilness of human nature, not, as Mencius conceived them, a mere outgrowth of the inner spirit of *jen*. It was, he believed, only through the influence of rituals that man could transform his evil nature and live properly and harmoniously in a well-ordered society. In Chapter 19 Hsün Tzu stressed that the value of *li*, aside from serving to determine proper limits and thus restraining human desires, lies also in its use to beautify and refine the expression of human emotion. In his elaboration of *li* as the acme of moral perfection, Hsün Tzu rose to the realm of poetry.

Like Confucius, Hsün Tzu also taught that music as an expression of human emotion, was essential to man's life. Together with *li*, music served as "the inner bond of harmony" to form or transform man's character. Early in their lives, the Chou aristocrats were taught the rudiments of the "six arts": charioteering and archery, history and numbers, music and rituals. The Chou *Classic of Music* is lost to posterity, and it is only in the works of Hsün Tzu that we can understand the part played by music as a ritual experience and a communal entertainment in ancient times. He also gave a good description of the various instruments used in ancient China, as we shall note in Chapter 20.

ఇ§ ఏ

III. Chapter 19: On Li

From whence does *li* arise? In reply, I say: Man by birth has desires. When these desires are not satisfied, he cannot but pursue their satisfaction. When the pursuit is carried on without restraint or limit, there cannot but be contention. When there is contention, there is chaos. When there is chaos, there is dissolution. The ancient kings were disgusted by this chaos and instituted *li* and *yi* to limit it, so that man's desires might be nourished and their pursuit gratified. In this way desires would not be frustrated by objects, nor would objects be used by desires; these two would balance each other. This is from whence *li* arises.

Li is to nourish. Meat, grain, and five flavors nourish the mouth; the pepper and the orchid, fragrance and perfume nourish the nose; carved gems and inlaid gold, elegance and refinement nourish the eye; bells and drums, flutes and stone chimes, lutes, lyres, and reed organs nourish the ear; mansions and palaces, furniture and furnishings nourish the body. Thus *li* is to nourish. When the *chün-tzu* obtains its nourishment, he also esteems its distinctions.

What is meant by distinctions? In reply, I say: There are classes of the noble and the common; there is the difference between the senior and the junior; there is that which is appropriate to the poor and the rich; there is that which is termed the unimportant and the important. For this reason, the imperial chariot has a fine mat, to nourish the emperor's body; by his side are carried fragrant flowers, to nourish his nose; in front it has ornamented yokes to nourish his eye. Moreover the chiming of bells, as the *Wu* and *Hsiang*[1] in steps and the Shao[2] and Hu[3] in strides, is to nourish his ear; the dragon banner with nine scallops is to nourish his confidence; the rhinocero-armor, tiger-spear, and alligator-harness, together with silk canopy and dragon-yoke, are to nourish his authority. For this reason, the horses of the imperial chariot must be excellent and well trained, and then only be driven so as to nourish his safety. He has the daring and the loyal to nourish his life; he has the prudent and the frugal to nourish his wealth; he has the respectful and courteous to nourish his security; he has the sagacious and discreet, abiding by *li* and *yi*, refinement and propriety, to nourish his emotion. Hence if a man aims only at pursuing life, he shall certainly die; if he aims only at pursuing profit, he shall certainly meet with disaster; if he is lazy and timid, and leads an easy life, he shall certainly be in danger; if he indulges in sensual pleasures, he shall certainly perish. For if a man is devoted to *li* and *yi*, then he will gain both; if he is devoted to emotion and passion, he will lose both. This is the reason why the Confucian doctrine causes men to gain both, and why the doctrines of Mohists causes men to lose both—this is the difference between Confucianism and Mohism.

Li rests on three bases: Heaven and earth, which are the source of life; forefathers and ancestors, who are the source of the human race; sovereigns and teachers, who are the source of government. Without Heaven and earth, from

1. The music of King Wu.
2. The music of Shun.
3. The music of T'ang.

where would life come? Without forefathers and ancestors, from where would the offspring come? Without sovereigns and teachers, from where would government come: If any of the three were lacking, there would be either no men or men without peace. Therefore, *li* is to serve Heaven above and earth below, to honor forefathers and ancestors, and to exalt sovereigns and teachers. Herein lies the threefold basis of *li*.

Accordingly, the kings made their first ancestor be Heaven's peer; the feudal lords dare not damage their ancestral temples; the ministers have their fixed ancestral shrines. All these are to distinguish their honorable origin; honorable origin is the source of virtue.

The sacrifice to Heaven is limited to the emperor; sacrifices to the spirits of the land belong to the feudal lords down to the ministers and scholars. This is to distinguish the honorable, who serve the honorable deities, from the lowly, who only serve the lowly deities. It is proper that the great should have important deities, and the small, minor deities. Consequently, the emperor of the world has the ancestral temple for the worship of seven generations; the sovereign of a state has the ancestral temple for the worship of five generations; the ministers have the ancestral temples for the worship of three generations; the scholars have ancestral temples for the worship of two generations; the peasants and laborers have no ancestral temples. This is to distinguish those whose accomplishments are great, for those whose accomplishments are great exercise great influence, while those whose accomplishments are small exercise small influence.

At the great sacrifice it is preferable to offer water, raw fish, and the meat soup—this is to honor the origin of food and drink. In the seasonal sacrifice, it is preferable to offer water together with wine and then to serve millet and rice. At the monthly sacrifice the meat soup is tasted, but other viands are eaten—this is to honor the origin and to appreciate the use of food and drink. To honor their origin is called refinement; to appreciate their use is called propriety. When both are in accord, *li* becomes so elegant as to revert to antiquity—this is the excellence of *li*. It is for the same reason that water, raw fish, and meat soup are offered at the sacrifice, after the sacrifice has been completed, its etiquette persists and its vessels remain, but the food is not kept. It is for the same reason that in marriage there is no temple presentation; that in the ancestral temple there is no impersonation; that in death there is no funeral. It is for the same reason that the imperial chariot is not painted; that in the sacrifice to Heaven the emperor wears a sackcloth cap; that in mourning apparel the hemp girdles are worn loose. It is for the same reason that in the three years' mourning the weeping is without mannerism; that as one sings in the imperial temple three others echo; that only one bell is placed there and the *fu* drum is beaten, as in ancient times; that red string passes through the hole in the lute.

In general, the rules of proper conduct begin with primitive practices, attain refinement, and finally achieve beauty and felicity. When *li* is at its best, man's emotion and sense of beauty are both fully expressed. When *li* is at the next level, either the emotion or the sense of beauty overlaps the other. When *li* is at the lowest level, the emotion reverts to the state of simplicity.

Indeed it is through *li* that Heaven and earth are in harmony, that the sun and moon are splendid, that the four seasons succeed each other, that the stars follow their movements, that the rivers and streams maintain their flow, that all things and creatures enjoy prosperity, that love and hatred are tempered, and joy and anger are controlled. *Li* causes the lower orders of society to be obedient, and the higher orders to be illustrious. One who abides by *li* never goes astray amid the multifarious changes; one who deviates from *li* is lost. Is not *li* the greatest of all principles?

When *li* is established with all the proper solemnity, it becomes the guiding principle of all, and nothing in the world can enhance or lessen its value. Its source and aim are in accord with each other; its end and beginning are mutually related. *Li* attains refinement, for it maintains the distinctions; it achieves its comprehensiveness, for it embraces all. When the world follows it, there is good government; when it departs from it, there is anarchy. One who follows it is safe; one who deviates from it is in danger. One who follows it endures; one who deviates from it perishes. But the *hsiao-jen* cannot comprehend this.

Deep indeed is the principle of *li*: it penetrates and permeates "hardness and whiteness" or "likeness and unlikeness." Great indeed is the principle of *li*: it penetrates and eradicates unauthorized laws and depraved doctrines. High indeed is the principle of *li*: it penetrates and overcomes tyranny, insolence, cynicism, and self-importance. Hence, when the plumb-line is truly laid out, one cannot be deceived as to crookedness or straightness; when the balances are truly placed, one cannot be deceived of the weight; when the compass and square are truly applied, one cannot be deceived as to squareness or roundness. Similarly, when the *chün-tzu* is well versed in *li*, he cannot be deceived of what is false. For the plumb-line is the measure of straightness; the balances are the measure of equilibrium; the compass and square are the measure of squareness and roundness; so *li* is the measure of human *Tao*. Moreover, one who neither follows *li* nor maintains *li* is a man without the *Tao*: one who follows *li* and maintains *li* is a man with the *Tao*. To be able to meditate on *li* is to be able to reflect; to be able to persist in keeping *li* is to be firm. One who is able to reflect and to be firm, with a love of *li*, is a sage. Just as Heaven is the extreme of height, earth is the extreme of depth; as the boundless is the extreme of breadth, so the sage is the extreme of *Tao*. Hence one who persists in learning *li* becomes a sage; one who fails to learn *li* is a person without the *Tao*.

Li provides wealth and things for its use, the noble and the low for its adornment, the many and the few for its distinction, and the embellishment and simplification for its occasion. *Li* is embellished when its refinement is elaborate but sparing in its emotion. *Li* is simplified when it is sparing in its refinement but generous in emotion. *Li* secures the mean when its refinement and emotion are related as its external conduct and internal sentiment, which go together and are interrelated to each other. Hence the *chün-tzu* in major ceremonials reaches the embellishment of *li* and in minor ceremonials its simplification; as to ceremonials at large, he secures the mean. While walking and running, riding, and charioteering, he will not depart from *li*—this is the *chün-tzu*'s terrace and his palace. If a man keeps within its boundary, he is a scholar or a *chün-tzu*; if he goes beyond it, he is but an unlearned man. Then, he who conducts himself within the scope of *li* and conforms to its order is a sage. He is honored because he accumulates *li*; he is great because he broadens *li*; he is exalted because he embellishes *li*; he is illustrious because he perfects *li*. The *Shih* says:

> As *li* and *yi* are followed,
> Smiles and words are proper.

This expresses what I mean.

Li requires that life and death be carefully treated. Life is the beginning of man; death is the end of man. When man's end and beginning are both well treated, the *Tao* of humanity is fulfilled. Hence the *chün-tzu* respects the beginning and attends to the end. To treat them alike is the *Tao* of the *chün-tzu* and the refinement of *li* and *yi*. To exalt the living and belittle the dead is to respect one who has consciousness and neglect one who has lost it—this is the way of the evil man, with a rebellious heart. The noble man would consider it shameful to treat a lowly slave with a rebellious heart. How much better he will treat those whom he honors or loves.

Hence the *Tao* of death is this: once dead, one cannot live again. Such being the case, the minister more completely fulfills the honor due to his sovereign, and the son the honor to his parents. For to serve the living without loyalty and sincerity, or without respect and refinement, is what is meant by savagery. To venerate the dead without loyalty and sincerity, or without respect and refinement, is what is meant by shabbiness. The *chün-tzu* despises savageness and is ashamed of shabbiness. Hence for the emperor the coffin has seven thicknesses; for the feudal lords, five thicknesses; for the ministers, three thicknesses; for the scholars, two thicknesses. Then the body in the coffin is dressed in its best robes, and the hearse is ornamented with various adornments, according to the rank of the deceased, so as to serve the living and the dead alike, and to make the end be the same as the beginning. This service fulfills the wishes of man. This is the *Tao* of the ancient kings—herein lies the most important duty of a faithful minister or a filial son.

The funeral of the emperor stirs the whole world and is managed by the feudal lords; the funeral of a feudal lord stirs all friendly states and is managed by the ministers; the funeral of a minister stirs a whole state and is managed by the official-scholars; the funeral of an official-scholar stirs a whole village and is managed by his friends; the funeral of the ordinary man stirs his district and neighborhood and is managed by his clan or neighbors. When a criminal is put to death, his funeral is managed not by his clan or neighbors, but by his wife and son; his coffin can be only three inches thick; his burial clothes can only be three in number; his coffin cannot be ornamented; his funeral cannot be made by day; he should be buried at dusk; and those who go to the burial must wear ordinary clothes. Contrary to other funerals, there should be no token of grief, such as weeping and crying, nor should there be any mourning badge or apparel; the near and distant relatives need not observe the mourning rites—every-

thing is as usual in life. When he is buried, it should be as if
there were no funeral—this is called the greatest disgrace.

Li requires that worship and mourning be carefully treated,
so as not to overlap its proper rules. The floss is put in the
mouth or nose, to detect when the breathing has stopped;
only then can the loyal minister or the filial son know his
loss. But he still cannot bring himself to order the articles
needed for encoffining. He sheds tears and is in fear, but he still
cannot stop hoping that the dead may come back to life; nor
can he cease to treat the dead as living. When death has occurred, then only does he act and make preparations. Hence,
although the whole household is prepared, a day must pass
before the dead man is placed in the coffin; three days, before
the formal mourning starts. After that the messengers who
inform the distant relative set out, and those who make preparations get to work. The funeral should be between fifty and
seventy days after the death. Why is this so? In reply, I say:
The distant may come, everything required may be obtained,
and all matters may be completed. When the loyalty is shown,
when filial duty is done, when all requisites for the funeral
are prepared, then on the first of the month a day is selected
for the funeral, and on the last of the month the sepulcher is
selected—then only should the dead be buried. At this time if
the mourning rites come to end, who would continue them? If
the mourning rites continue, who would stop them? Therefore
the three months' burial is to beautify the dead by the living,
not to comfort the living by retaining the dead. This is the significance of the elaborate mourning rites.

The general principle of funeral rites is this: to beautify
the dead with ornaments, to remove the body further away
at every ritual, and to ease the mourning with the lapse of
time. For the *Tao* of death is thus: if it is not made beautiful,
it becomes ugly; if it is ugly, there is no mourning; if it is
near, it becomes irksome; if irksome, then it becomes distasteful; if distasteful, then it becomes neglected; if neglected,
it lacks reverence. Suppose one day a man should lose his
parents, and those in the funeral should neither mourn nor
be respectful; then he should be loathed by the birds and
beasts. The *chün-tzu* feels shame at this; hence he beautifies
the dead with ornaments and thereby lessens his ugliness;
he removes the body further away at every ritual and thereby
holds it in reverence; he eases the mourning with the lapse
of time and thereby soothes the living. *Li* serves to shorten
that which is too long and lengthen that which is too short;

li serves to diminish that which is too much and augment that which is too little; finally, *li* serves to express the beauty of love and reverence and nourish the elegance of *yi*. Beautiful adornment and coarse sackcloth, music and weeping, happiness and sorrow are all opposites, but *li* equally uses them and alternately brings them into play. For beautiful adornment, music and happiness are appropriate on occasions of felicity; coarse sackcloth, weeping, and sorrow are appropriate on occasions of ill-fortune. Hence *li* provides for adornments which are beautiful, but not to the point of being fascinating; *li* provides for sackcloth which is coarse, but not to the point of being shabby and neglectful; *li* provides for music and happiness, but not to the point of lewdness and indolence; *li* provides for weeping and sorrow, but not to the point of distress and self-injury. The function of *li* is to secure the mean. Hence when one changes in emotion and countenance he should be able, on the one hand, to differentiate between a happy occasion and a sad one and, on the other hand, to make clear whether the dead is noble or low, near or distant—this is all and no more. Anything beyond this is evil. Even though it takes effort to go beyond the proper propriety, yet the *chün-tzu* feels contempt for this. To limit one's food and eat only so much, to demarcate one's necessities and abide by that, to win high praise by making oneself sick and lean—all these are the ways of an evil man without the refinement of *li* and *yi*. All these are not motivated by the genuine emotion of a filial son, but by the desire for fame.

Pleasure and happiness, grief and distress are the expression of sentiments of good or bad fortune, sorrow or joy shown in the countenance. Singing and jesting, weeping and wailing are the expression of sentiments of good or bad fortune, sorrow or joy shown in the voice. Meat and grain, fish and pork, broth and wine—all these are the expressions of sentiments of good or bad fortune, sorrow or joy shown in food and drink. Caps and crowns, embroidered costumes and silk garments; mourning apparel and sackcloth badges, coarse clothes and straw sandals—all these are the expressions of sentiments of good or bad fortune, sorrow or joy shown in clothing. Mansions and temples, elevated beds and fine mattresses, tables and benches; thatched houses and bungalows, firewood for chairs and clods for pillows—all these are the expressions of sentiments of good or bad fortune, sorrow or joy shown in dwellings. These two kinds of sentiments certainly have their origins in human life. However, they may be shortened or lengthened, elaborated or simplified, augmented or reduced, classified or synthesized, and glorified and beautified, to make the source and result be in harmony, the end and beginning be in order, so that they become the pattern for all generations—all these are the functions of *li*.

Without following this pattern for self-cultivation, even though one is a *chün-tzu*, one cannot know how to act. Hence I say: What belongs to nature is the crude material of the original; what belongs to the acquired goodness is refinement and accomplishment brought about by culture and reason. Without original nature there would be nothing to which acquired goodness could be added; without acquired goodness original nature could not become beautiful. Only with the unity of original nature and acquired goodness can a man deserve the name of a sage and merit the reward of the world. Hence it is said: With the unity of Heaven and earth, all things come into being; with the intercourse of the *yin* and *yang*, mutations and changes begin; with the combination of original nature and acquired goodness, good order prevails in the world. Heaven can produce things but cannot distinguish between them; the earth can support men but cannot rule them. In the universe there are various things and different beings, but it is only the sage who places them in their proper order. The *Shih* says:

> He cherishes and presides over all the spirits;
> Even to the spirits of the river and high mountain.

This expresses what I mean.

The funeral rites are for the living to adorn the dead and to send off the dead as if they were living. In this way they are served like the living, the absent like the present, so as to make the end the same as the beginning. Soon after death, bathe the head and body, tie the hands, and put rice in the mouth. If the hair is not washed, then wet it and comb it three times only; if the body is not bathed, then wet the towel and wipe the body three times only. Then fill the ears with floss silk; provide raw rice for food, and put dry bones in the mouth—it is the opposite of what is done at birth. Provide for three suits of underclothing, with an unfastened girdle around. Cover the face, bind up the eyes, and tie up the hair, without a hat or a hairpin. Write his name and put it on his tablet, so that his name is not seen, but only the coffin is visible. Display the sacramental articles and the hat with a

flaring rim, but use no fillet. The wine jars should be empty
and not filled. There should be a fine bamboo mat but no
bed. The wooden articles should not be carved; the potteries
should not be formed into vessels; thin articles should not
be usable. The pipes and organ should be ready for use but
not sound in harmony; the lyre and lute should be displayed
but not be in tune. The carriages should be buried, but the
horses sent away; they are not to be buried. The articles used
in life should be ready to put into the grave, as if the deceased were moving from the house. Only a few articles
should be prepared, not all of them; the articles should be
showy in form, but not elaborately made. The carriages
should be buried in haste, but metal reins and collars are not
to be buried, to show that they are not for use. The articles
are buried as if the deceased were moving from the house,
in order to show that they are not for use. All these sacramental practices are conducted in token of grief. Hence the
articles used in life are adorned but not elaborately made;
the "spiritual articles" for the dead are elegant but not useful.

The *li* used on the occasion of birth is to adorn joy; the *li*
used on the occasion of death is to adorn sorrow; the *li* used
at sacrifice is to adorn reverence; the *li* used on military occasions is to adorn dignity. In this respect the rites of all the
kings are alike, the ancient times and the present age agree;
and no one knows whence they came. Hence the grave and
its tumulus are shaped like a house; the coffin is like a carriage screen and its cover; the pall and the fringe are shaped
like a door curtain or a bed drapery; the matting and framework are shaped like the plaster on thatch and the screen in
front of the door. Therefore the function of funeral rites is
to make clear the meaning of death and life, to send off the
dead with sorrow and reverence; and when the end comes, to
provide for storing the body away. The purpose of burial is to
store the body with reverence. To serve one's spirit with
reverence is to sacrifice; to pass on the name with reverence
is to eulogize. To serve the living is to adorn the beginning
[of their life]; to send off the dead is to adorn their end.
When the end and the beginning are both attended to, the
duty of the filial son is fulfilled, and the *Tao* of the sage is
completed. Slighting the dead and stressing the living is what
is known as Mohism [teachings of Mo Tzu]; slighting the
living and stressing the dead is what is a misconception of *li*.
Killing the living to send off the dead is murder. The pattern
of *li* and *yi* serves to send off the dead with as much respect

as they enjoyed when they were alive, so as to cause both death and life, the end and the beginning, to be properly treated, and to be in accord with goodness. This is the teaching of the Confucian school.

Why are there three years of mourning? In reply, I say: Its rites and ceremonies are instituted in accordance with emotion in order to adorn social relations and to differentiate between the near and the distant, the noble and the low. They cannot be augmented or reduced. Hence it is said that these are the invariable principles which are applicable to all occasions. A bad wound remains for a long time; a severe hurt heals slowly; the three years' mourning arises because its rites and ceremonies are instituted in accordance with emotion. Therefore this is the deepest sorrow. Mourning garments, a rush staff, living in a hovel, eating rice gruel, using firewood for mat and clods for a pillow—these practices are the expression of deepest sorrow. The three years' mourning is finished, and longings are not yet forgotten. This is what has been regulated by *li*. Does it not require that the funeral be terminated and ordinary life be returned at that time? Every living creature who is born between Heaven and earth has the sense of knowing. No living creature who has the sense of knowing does not love his species. Now if one of the large birds or beasts should lose its mate, even after the lapse of a month or a season, it certainly would return to its old haunts. Then it would wander about, howl, trudge, and linger, before it goes away. Then the small ones, such as the greenfinch, will twitter a moment before they fly away. But among the living creatures there is none who is more intelligent than man. Hence man's affection for his parents persists forever, for even after death. Now let us consider a stupid, mean, dissolute, and wicked man; if in the morning there were a death, in the evening he would have forgotten it and returned to his indulgences; he would not be equal to a bird or beast. So how could he live with his neighbors without stirring up trouble? But let us consider a cultivated and refined *chün-tzu:* he would feel that the lapse of his three years' mourning which is completed in twenty-five months as fast as the speed of a team of four horses passing over a crevice; even if the time of mourning were extended, his sorrow would never come to an end. For this reason, the early kings and sages established the mean and regulated the period of mourning to make it long enough to perform a series of appropriate and refined actions; only then is it to be laid aside.

How is the period determined? In reply, I say: There is a break in the mourning for the nearest relatives at a full year. Why is it? I say: Heaven and earth have then already made a complete rotation; the four seasons have then already gone through their changes; all things in the world have begun their processes anew. Hence the early kings, in conformity to this, made the period of mourning a full year. Then why is there the three years' mourning? In reply, I say: They wanted to enhance the affectionate yearning for the dead by doubling the time; hence they made it two full years. And why is there nine months' mourning or even less? I say: They wanted to make it not as much as that for parents. For three years' mourning should be regarded as the solemn mourning; the five or three months' mourning should be regarded as the simple mourning; the year and nine months' mourning should be regarded as the common mourning between these two. There is the pattern of Heaven above and the model of earth below, and between them there is the example of man. It is because of this that men can live together in harmony and unity. For the three years' mourning is the most elegant ritual in the *Tao* of man; it is the greatest exaltation of human conduct. In this respect the rites of all the kings are alike, the ancient times and the present age agree.

Why does the mourning for a prince take three years? In reply, I say: The prince is the lord of rule, the source of customs and regulations, the one toward whom loyalty and respect should be rendered. Cannot all men join together and exalt him to the highest? The *Shih* says:

> The happy and courteous prince,
> The father and mother of the people.

This maintains that the prince is the father and mother of the people. The father can beget us and cannot nourish us: the mother can feed us but cannot instruct us: the prince can both feed us and instruct us. Is the three years' mourning enough? The wet-nurse gives us food and drink, so we mourn three months for her; the foster-mother clothes us, so we mourn nine months for her; the prince does both: is the three years' mourning enough for him? When we have the prince, there is order; when we lose the prince, there is disorder. This is due to his good rendering. When we have the prince, there is peace; when we lose the prince, there is danger. This is due to his affection. When we have enjoyed his goodness and affection, the three years' service for him seems not enough, but there is no proper way to extend it. Instead of the spirits of land and grains, we worship either the god of the soil or the god of agriculture; in the sacrifice of Heaven, all gods, together with High Heaven, are worshipped.

What is the reason for the three months' funeral? In reply, I say: This is to make it great and important. The early kings feared that in taking up and moving the most exalted and dear ones from the house to the graveyard, the performance would not be elegant; therefore they extended the period to make the number of days sufficient for necessary preparation. Hence for the emperor the funeral requires seven months; for feudal lords five months; for the ministers three months—all so that the period will be long enough for handling the business. When the business is well handled, it may be completed; when it is completed, it may be elegant; when it is elegant, it may be perfect. What is perfect is the *Tao*.

Sacrifice is to express man's memories and intention, thoughts and longings, for grief and affliction cannot be kept out of his consciousness all the time. When men are enjoying the pleasure of good company, the loyal minister or the filial son may feel grief. Once such feelings arise, he is greatly moved. If such feelings are not given proper expression, his emotions and memories are disappointed and not satisfied; consequently, the appropriate rules of *li* are lacking. For this reason, the early kings instituted *li,* and since then the principle of expressing honor to the honorable and love to the beloved has been fully observed. Hence I say: Sacrifice is to express man's memories and intentions, thoughts and longings; as to the height of loyalty, faithfulness, love and reverence, the richness of propriety and refinement—all these cannot be fully understood except by the sage. Sacrifice is something that the sage clearly understands, the scholar and *chün-tzu* accordingly perform, officials consider as a duty, and the common people regard as established custom. Among *chün-tzu* it is considered to be the *Tao* of man; among the common people it is considered as having to do with spirits and ghosts.

Hence the bells, drums, pipes, stone chimes, lyres, lutes, reeds and organs, the *shao,* the *hu* of the Hsia dynasty, the *so* of King Wu, the *hsiao-chien-hsiang* of Duke Huan—all these are musical instruments with which the *chün-tzu* may adapt himself to different situations by refining his joy and happiness. Mourning garments, a rush staff, living in a hovel, eating rice gruel, using firewood for a mat, and clods for a pillow—all these are the ways whereby the noble man adapts himself to different situations by refining his sorrow and grief. Armies have their regulations; criminal law has its scales of penalty, all to suit the crime—this is the way the noble man adapts himself to the situation by refining his hatred. To divine and select auspicious days, to fast and clean the temple; to spread out tables and mats, to offer animals and grains, to pray for blessings as if the deceased enjoyed the sacrifice, to select and offer sacrifices as if the deceased would taste them, to offer the goblet without washing it, for the one who sacrifices to have a wine-flask ready as if the deceased would drink from the goblet; for the host to bow to the guests as they leave, then change the mourning clothes, take his position and wail as if the spirit of the departed had left—all these are to express sorrow and reverence by serving the dead as if serving the living, serving the departed as if serving those who were present. What is served has neither substance nor shadow, yet this is the completion of propriety and refinement.

IV. Chapter 20: On Music

Music is the expression of joy, an irrepressible part of human emotion. For man cannot be without joy, and joy invariably emerges in the voice and finds expression in movement and repose. The *Tao* of man is this: His sounds, movements, and pauses are expressive of all the changes in his disposition. Hence man cannot be without joy, and joy invariably has its expression. If this expression does not conform to the *Tao*, riots invariably result. In view of this, the early kings instituted the music of the *Ya* and *Sung* in order to conform to the *Tao*, so that its sounds might express joy but not excite riot, its beauty might be distinct but not limited, and its composition and orchestration might inspire good thoughts and suppress evil notions. This is the manner in which the early kings instituted music. But Mo Tzu was opposed to it; what is to be done now?

For music, when performed in the ancestral temple, inspires reverence in the prince and minister, the ruler and ruled, who hear it together; when performed in the inner apartments, the feeling of affection in father and son, elder and younger brothers, who hear it together; when performed in the village squares, the feeling of amity in the multitude, who hear it together. Music unites to establish harmony, compares to enrich its notes, and orchestrates to create beauty. While leading in one direction, it regulates the myriad of changes. This is the manner in which the early kings instituted music. But Mo Tzu was opposed to it; what is to be done now?

When we hear the music of the *Ya* and *Sung*, our purposes are magnified. When we see the dancers, with shields and axes, move up and down, bend and stretch, our deportment becomes dignified. When they move in groups and accord with the music, they fall into rank, and they advance and retreat in unity. For music may make the dancers step forward as if to make an attack; music may also make them step backward as if to show courtesy. Their meaning is the same: when they step forward to make an attack, none fails to obey; when they step backward to show courtesy, none fails to accord. Hence music is the great unifying force of the world, the inner bond of harmony, the irrepressible part of human emotion. This is the manner in which the early kings instituted music. But Mo Tzu was opposed to it; what is to be done now?

The early kings used music to regulate joy; with armies and halberds they regulate anger. Hence the joy and anger of the early kings were properly expressed: when they were joyous, the world was in harmony; when they were angry, the riotous were in fear. Thus the *Tao* of the early kings is this: They governed with *li* and music. But Mo Tzu was opposed to it. Hence I say: Mo Tzu was to the *Tao* as the blind man is to white and black, or as the deaf man is to fine music and coarse sound, or as a man who goes to the south-state of Ch'u by turning to the north.

Now the sound of music penetrates man's heart deeply and transforms his conduct fast. Hence the early kings carefully regulated it. When it is moderate and even, the people are in harmony and not riotous; when it is reverent and dignified, the people are in unison and not contentious. When the people are in harmony and in unison, the armies are strong, the cities are secure, and the enemy dare not attack. Then the people will be safe in their dwellings and happy in their villages; as a result, they will be satisfied with their sovereign. Thus his reputation will be good, his glory great; all the people of the world will be willing to accept his leadership. This is the beginning of the kingly rule.

If music is delightful and charming, it is dangerous; then

the people will be riotous and negligent, mean and low. If they are riotous and negligent, there will be turmoil; if they are mean and low, there will be contention. If they are in turmoil and in contention, the armies will be weak, the cities will be invaded, and the enemy will come to attack. Then the people will not be safe in their dwellings, nor will they be happy in their villages; and consequently they will not be satisfied with their sovereign. Then *li* and music will be cast aside, and heterodox ditties arise; this is the source of danger and loss of territory, humiliation and disgrace. Therefore the early kings exalted *li* and music, and despised heterodox tunes. In the *Arrangement of Officials*,[1] it is said: "Let the laws and edicts be codified; let the punishments and rewards be reviewed; let the licentious music be suppressed. To make transformations at the proper time, so that the barbarian, and indecent heterodox tunes do not become confused with the Orthodox Odes—this is the business of the Grand Master."

Mo Tzu said: "Music is what the sage-kings were opposed to, and wherein the Confucians err." But the *chün-tzu* thinks otherwise. For music is what the sages enjoyed, and something that stirs up goodness in people's hearts. Its influence on people is profound; it changes their customs and transforms their manners. Hence the early kings guided them by *li* and music, and the people were in harmony and in amity. If the people have the sentiment of love and hatred but lack the proper expression of joy and anger, there will be riot. In view of this, the early kings cultivated their conduct and rectified their music, so that the world was in good order. For mourning clothes and the sound of wailing cause people's hearts to be sad; to wear armor and a helmet and to sing among the ranks makes people's hearts reckless. Pretty and charming appearance and the music of Ch'eng and Wei make people's hearts licentious; with elaborate girdle and bright cap, dancing to the *Shao* and singing the *Wu* make people's hearts dignified. Hence the ear of the *chün-tzu* does not listen to licentious sounds, his eyes do not look at the fair sex, his mouth does not utter evil words; these are the three things of which the *chün-tzu* is wary. Bad music affects man and stirs up evil notions; if these evil notions find expression in action, riots result. On the other hand, good music affects man and inspires good thoughts; if these good thoughts find expression in action, good order begins. Just as the singing

1. This is a section of Chapter 9 in the Works of Hsün Tzu.

and the response correspond with each other, so good and
evil react to one another. Hence the *chün-tzu* is prudent in
his conduct. He makes his purpose conform to the *Tao* by
using the bells and drums; he makes his heart rejoice by
using the lyre and lute; he dances with the shield and axe;
he decks himself with feathers; he moves in time to the stone
chime and flutes. The clarity of music symbolizes Heaven,
and its breadth signifies earth; the lowering and raising of
the head, and the turning around represent the "four seasons." When music is played, the mind is clarified; when *li*
is cultivated, conduct is perfected. Then the ear and eye are
clear and acute, the body and mind are calm and at peace,
customs are changed and manners transformed; only then
can the world enjoy peace and happiness.

It is said, "Music is the expression of joy." The *chün-tzu*
rejoices in attaining his *Tao;* the common man rejoices in
satisfying his desires. When men regulate desire by the *Tao,*
there is joy but no riot. When they give rein to desire and
forget the *Tao,* there is delusion but no joy. "Metal, stone,
silk and bamboo"—all these are the musical instruments used
to cultivate virtue. When music is played, the people turn
toward it. Music is therefore an important means by which
the people are governed. But Mo Tzu was opposed to it.

Moreover, music exemplifies invariable harmony, *li* signifies
an immutable principle. Music establishes union and harmony; *li* maintains difference and distinction. Thus music and
li are united to embrace the human heart. To exhaust the
source and extend changes—this is the nature of music. To
display sincerity and eliminate hypocrisy—this is the essence
of *li*. Mo Tzu was opposed to it, but he almost met with
punishment. The enlightened kings had already passed away,
so no one could rectify him. Those who are stupid enough
to learn his teachings endanger themselves. The virtue of the
chün-tzu is to comprehend the significance of music. But this
is an evil generation, which hates goodness and will not listen
to him. Alas! Nothing has been accomplished! Youth, study
music, and be not deluded!

Sound is the form of music. The drum is the king of the
orchestra; the bells are the perfect rulers; the stone chimes
discriminate and regulate; the reed organs are reverent and
harmonious; the flageolet and flute give volume; the ocarina
and the bamboo flutes are excellent and beautiful. And while
singing represents the perfection of clarity, dancing symbolizes the *Tao* of Heaven. Since the drum is the leader of

music, it is akin to Heaven; the bells are akin to the earth; the stone chimes are akin to water; the organs, flageolet, and flutes are akin to the stars, the sun, and the moon; the hand drums, the wooden clappers, and the bell-frames are akin to myriad things. How do we understand the meaning of dancing? In reply, I say: The dancer's eyes do not look at himself, and his ears do not listen to himself; yet he controls the lowering and raising of his head, the bending and straightening of his body, his advancing and retreating, his slow and rapid movements—everything is thus regulated. He exerts all the strength of his body to keep time with the beat of the drum and sound of the bells, and never for a moment will he dance out of tune or move contrary to the rhythmic measures.

When I observe the village festival, I know that kingly rule is very easy. The host goes to fetch the guests and their attendants, and all the guests follow him. When they arrive at the gate, the host does obeisance to the guests together with their attendants, and then all the guests enter; thus the distinction between the noble and the lowly is determined.

Thrice they bow and come to the steps. After the precedence has been thrice offered and declined, the guests ascend and bow. When wine is offered, there is much ceremony of declining and yielding; but toward the attendants it is simpler. Then the guests ascend and receive the wine. They kneel down and make offerings of worship; they rise and drink it, without toasting the host in return; thus the complexity and simplicity of ceremony are distinguished.

When the chorus enters, ascends, and sings three pieces, the host offers them wine. When the reed organists enter and play three pieces, the host offers them wine. After an intermission the chorus sings three pieces, and then they play three pieces together. After they announce that the music is ended, they leave. Two men raise their horn goblets, and a presiding officer is appointed to see that everything is properly regulated. Thus I know that they rejoice in harmony without riot.

The guests toast the host; the host toasts the attendants; the attendants toast all the guests; the junior and the senior toast each other according to their age; finally, they toast all those in charge of the festival. Thus I know that they show deference to their elders and neglect no one.

After this they descend to take off their shoes and ascend again, to sit down and to drink the wine. The festival of drinking wine, if in the morning, does not use up the morning; if in the evening, it does not use up the evening. When the guests leave, the host bows and escorts them away. All the ceremonials of the festival come to an end. Thus I know that they enjoy the feast without confusion.

The distinction between the noble and the lowly is thus determined; the complexity and simplicity of ceremony are thus distinguished. There is harmony and rejoicing without riot; there is deference to the elders without neglect; there is a merry feast without confusion—these five courses of conduct are enough to rectify one's person and pacify a state. When the state is pacified, the world is at peace. Therefore I say: When I observe the village festival, I know that kingly rule is very easy.

These are the symptoms of the evil world: outlandish clothes, "womanly" manners, licentious habits, selfish purpose, and absurd conduct; the sounds of music don't express joy but excite riot; the writings are ambiguous but beautifully worded; the living are nourished extravagantly, but the dead are sent off poorly; li and yi are but ignored, power and force are exalted. Under such circumstances, if men are poor, they will commit crimes; if they are rich, they will be usurious. Those who govern the world well will do otherwise.

Part Three: Education and Knowledge

Hsün Tzu and Mencius both believed in the importance of education to the individual's development. However, allowing that there were some fundamental differences in their teachings, it must be understood that the philosophers took different views on the theory of education. To Mencius education enhanced the good that is in man, and so the keynote to his theory of education is *extension*—that is, development of man's inherent goodness. Hsün Tzu, on the other hand, insisted that education is to cultivate virtue in the man who has been cleansed of his evil nature; thus his theory of education is *accumulation*. Hsün Tzu pleaded for perseverance, concentration of mind, and singleness of purpose to make education effective. This effort was expected to achieve a cumulative effect. He said:

Unless steps and half steps are accumulated no one can cover a thousand li; unless streams are accumulated no rivers or seas can be forded. (Chapter on Learning)

Hsün Tzu's view of the learning process as one of accumulation brings to mind a whole group of important problems relating to knowledge. To him all knowledge, wisdom, and values had to be implanted in the individual in the process of accumulation. Therefore much of the emphasis is on the logical method. A good deal of the chapter on "The Rectification of Names" deals with the logical principles of theoretical knowledge. The term "the Rectification of Names," as originated by Confucius, was applied purely along ethical lines, but Hsün Tzu's theory contains great logical reasoning![1]

❧ ☙

V. Chapter 1: An Exhortation to Learning

The *chün-tzu* says: There should be no stop to learning. Indigo is extracted from the indigo plant, but it is bluer than the indigo plant; ice is made of water, but it is colder than water. A piece of timber, straight as a plumb-line, can be bent for a wheel, and then its curvature conforms to the compass; when it is wilted and dried, it will not again become straight because the bending has made it so. For wood must undergo the use of plumb-line to be straight; metal must undergo the use of the sandstone to be sharp. Likewise, the *chün-tzu* must pursue broad learning and examine himself daily in order to have his knowledge illuminating and his conduct faultless.

If a person does not ascend a high mountain, he will not know the height of Heaven; if he does not descend into a deep ravine, he will not know the depth of the earth. Likewise, if he never hears the teachings handed down from the early kings, he will not know the magnificence of knowledge. The children of Kan, Yüeh, Yi, and P'o all make the same sounds at birth but follow different customs when grown up; this is because training has made them so. The *Shih* says:

> Ah! Ye Noble Men!
> Do not rest for long;
> Quietly fulfill your official duties;
> Cherish the correct and the upright.
> So shall the spirits hear,
> And bless you with happiness.

No divinity is higher than transforming with the *Tao;* no happiness is greater than being without calamity.

1. Cf. Ch'u Chai: *The Story of Chinese Philosophy* (New York, Washington Square Press, 1961) pp. 175-183.

I have sometimes meditated for a whole day, and the result is not as good as that which one might learn in a moment. I have sometimes stood on tiptoe to watch, and the view is not as good as what one might see from a high place. When a person goes up on a high place and beckons, his arm does not get any longer, and yet it can be seen at a distance. When a person shouts with the wind, his voice does not get any stronger, and yet it can be heard more plainly. When a person employs horse and carriage, he can travel a thousand *li*, even though he cannot walk fast. When a person employs boat and oars, he can cross streams and rivers, even though he cannot swim. The nature of *chün-tzu* is not different from that of other men; the *chün-tzu*, however, is well versed in employing things.

In the south there is a bird called the tailor bird, which uses feathers to make its nest, weaves it with hair, and attaches it to reeds. When the wind blows, the reeds snap, the eggs break, and the birdlets die. The nest is well-made, but the disaster is due to the reeds to which it is attached. In the west there is a plant, called the She-kan [Belamcanda chinensis]. Its stalk is four inches long, but it grows on a high mountain overlooking an abyss of a hundred fathoms. The stalk does not grow any longer, but the location where it stands makes it so. Raspberry vines growing among hemp keep straight without being supported; white sand in black mud becomes black with the mud. The root of the orchid is as fragrant as the plant. But if it is soaked in manure, the *chün-tzu* will not come near it and the commoners will not like it. Its quality is excellent, but that in which it is soaked makes it so. Hence, for his residence, the *chün-tzu* should select a proper community, and on his study travel he should go to good scholars, so as to keep himself away from the heretical and depraved and to place himself in the company of the orthodox and the upright.

The existence of things and species must have its origin; the visitation of honor and humiliation must be due to a man's virtue. Putrid meat produces worms; rotten fish brings forth maggots. When there are indolence and negligence, calamity and disaster invariably result. Overbearance will bring on its own undoing; docility will lead to self-inhibition. Personal impurity makes one the focus of animosity. Over the same lot of firewood, fire inclines toward the dried pieces; over the same patch of flat land, water tends toward the moist areas. Plants and trees grow among their own species; birds and beasts live in flocks. Hence things follow their own kinds. When the target is set up, bows and arrows will come; when the forest becomes luxuriant, axes and hatchets will approach. When trees make shade, numerous birds will rest there; when vinegar turns, gnats will gather. Accordingly, a person's speech can invite misfortune; his actions can invite humiliation. So the *chün-tzu* is careful about his learning.

When enough earth is accumulated to make a mountain, wind and rain arise. When enough water is accumulated to make a stream, crocodiles and dragons appear. When much goodness is accumulated to make virtue, spiritual enlightenment comes of itself, and the sagely heart is attained. Unless steps and half-steps are accumulated, no one can cover a thousand *li;* unless little streams are accumulated, no rivers and seas can be formed. Even a thoroughbred horse cannot cover ten paces at one stride; yet a worn-out nag can cover the distance of a ten-day journey—this is all a matter of perseverance. If one carves spasmodically, even a piece of rotten wood cannot be cut down; if one carves steadfastly, metal and stone can be engraved.

The earthworm has not the sharpness of claws or teeth, nor has it the strength of sinews or bones. Yet it manages to eat dirt above and to drink water below—the worm has a single-purpose mind. Whereas the crab has six legs and two claws and yet finds no refuge except in the burrow of a snake or an eel—the crab has an impetuous mind. Therefore, a man who has not a deep purpose cannot have clear perception; he who has not a steadfast goal will not gain illustrious achievement. He who tries to travel along both forks of a road will never get anywhere; he who tries to serve two masters will never be favored by either. The eye cannot look to two directions and see clearly; the ear cannot listen to two things and hear distinctly. The dragon of the clouds has no feet and yet can fly; the squirrel has five skills and yet is confined in its movements. The *Shih* says:

> The turtle-dove is in the mulberry tree;
> Her little ones are seven.
> The good man, our noble prince—
> He is steadfast in his deportment;
> He is steadfast in his deportment;
> His heart is as a knot.

So the *chün-tzu* is steadfast like a knot.

Formerly, when Hu Pa played the zither, fish would come up to listen; when Po Ya played the lute, the six horses of the imperial chariot would look up from their feed. For there is no sound so small that it is not heard; there is no action so secret that it does not leave traces. If there is jade in the mountain, plants and trees will grow luxuriantly; if there are pearls in the pool, the banks will not be parched. How could a man of good deeds who is opposed to heresy fail to become known?

Where should learning begin, and where should it end? In reply, I say: The process of learning begins with the reciting of the classics and ends with the study of *li*. The purpose of learning aims first at cultivation to be a scholar, and then at the cultivation to be a sage. Accumulated devotion and persistent effort will lead to progress, and learning should proceed until it comes to a stop by death. Hence to the process of learning one may put a stop, but for the purpose of learning one should not cease to persist for a moment. To pursue learning is to be a man; to cease learning is to become like a beast. The *Shu* is a record of political events. The *Shih* is the repository of the standard sounds and tunes. The *li* is the greatest of principles, regulating the distinction and classification of human conduct. For this reason, the process of learning ends with the *li*. This is the acme of virtue. The civility of the *li*, the harmony of the *Yüeh* [*Book of Music*], the magnificence of the *Shih* and the *Shu*, the subtleties of *Ch'un-Ch'iu* [*the Spring and Autumn*]: herein lies the completion of all creation.

This is the manner of the *chün-tzu*'s learning: it goes into his ears, it is taken into his heart, it spreads over his four limbs, and it is manifest in his movements. Mild in speech and gentle in movement—all his ways of acting serve as his code of conduct. This is the manner of the *hsiao-jen*'s learning: it goes into his ears and comes out of his mouth. The distance between mouth and ear is only four inches; how can his seven-foot body be beautified?

The purpose of learning in ancient times was to improve one's self; the purpose of learning at present is to show it to others. The study of the *chün-tzu* is to beautify his person; the study of the *hsiao-jen* is to make him a "bird and calf."[2] To offer instruction without being asked is impetuous; to speak about two things when asked about one is talkative. It

2. Used as items of gifts.

is bad to be impetuous, so is it to be talkative. In speech, the *chün-tzu* is like an echo.

To learn there is no better way than to be near a worthy teacher. The *li* and the *Yüeh* contain principles but give no explanation; The *Shih* and the *Shu* deal with antiquity 'but are not applicable to the present; the *Ch'un-Ch'iu* is suggestive but not articulate. Follow a worthy teacher and practice the teachings of the *chün-tzu*, and one will ennoble his character and broaden his knowledge, so as to be able to deal with any situation in the world. Hence it is said, "To learn there is no better way than to be near a worthy teacher."

The most expeditious way of learning is to be near a worthy teacher, and next to it, to exalt *li*. If a person is neither able to be a worthy teacher nor to exalt *li*, then all he will be learning will be miscellaneous teachings and commentaries on the *Shih* and the *Shu*. To the end of his days, he will not be more than an absurd scholar. If a man inquires back to the early kings and is true to *jen* and *yi*, then *li* will regulate his ways of action. This is like holding a fur coat by the collar and stroking it with his fingers; innumerable hairs will be in their places. If a man does not follow *li* as his pattern but merely acts according to the *Shih* and the *Shu*, it is like sounding a river with the fingers, pounding millet with a spear, or eating from a pot with an awl; it simply will be of no avail. Therefore, a man who exalts *li*, though he may not be distinguished, will be a learned scholar. On the other hand, he who does not exalt *li*, though he may be keen and acute, will be a negligent scholar.

Do not inform a man who asks about evil; do not ask questions of a man who speaks about evil; do not listen to a man who speaks evil; and do not discuss anything with a man who seeks to quarrel. When someone comes to you in accord with the *Tao*, only then should he be received; otherwise, he should be rejected. Only when he observes *li* may he be told the method of the *Tao*; only when his speech accords with *li* may he be told the principles of the *Tao*; only when his demeanor conforms to *li* may he be informed about the attainment of the *Tao*. To talk to those who may not be talked to is impetuous; not to talk to those who may be talked to is secretive; to talk to a person without observing his mood and expression is to be blind. The *chün-tzu* is not impetuous, secretive, or blind; he is careful to adapt himself to the situation. The *Shih* says:

> They associate without being remiss,
> They are rewarded by the Son of Heaven.

This expresses what I mean.

If a person misses once in a hundred shots, he is still not an expert marksman; if his team fails to go the last half step in a thousand *li*, he is not an expert driver; if he fails to understand the underlying principles of human relationships and distinctions, and fails to comply with the virtues of *jen* and *yi*, he is still not a well-learned scholar. Learning is the one and all-inclusive principle. If a person follows one principle at home and another principle abroad, he belongs with the men on the street. If he has little good and much evil, he belongs with evil men such as Chieh, Chou, and Robber Chih. Learning should be applied all-inclusively and exhaustively.

Knowing that anything which is not perfect and pure may not be regarded as beautiful, the *chün-tzu* recites and expounds the classics in order to have a full grasp of them; he thinks and reflects on them in order to understand them thoroughly. Then he conducts himself in accordance with them in order to make them a part of his habit; and he eliminates all evil influences in order to nurture the good that may come from them. Thus, he disciplines his eyes not to see what is improper, disciplines his ears not to hear what is improper, disciplines his mouth not to speak what is improper, disciplines his heart not to think what is improper. When he achieves what he desires, his eyes will delight in the five colors, his ears will delight in the five sounds, his mouth will delight in the five tastes, and his heart will delight in the possession of the world. For this reason, power and gain cannot overturn him, mobs and multitudes cannot sway him, the whole world cannot move him. By this great principle he will live, by this great principle he will die; this is moral integrity. With moral integrity, there is firmness; with firmness, there is flexibility. With firmness and flexibility, one may be said to be a perfect man. Heaven is exalted for its brilliance; the earth is exalted for its vastness; the *chün-tzu* is exalted for his perfection.

VI. Chapter 22: On the Ratification of Names

When the later kings formed the terminology, they certainly followed the penal names of the Shang dynasty, the noble titles of the Chou dynasty, and the ceremonial terms of the *Li*. As to the miscellaneous names given to things, they would follow the traditional terms and customary designations of the *Hsia* people [the Chinese]. Because of these names, they could communicate with the people of distant districts with different customs.

In the adoption of these miscellaneous names by the people, that which at birth is so is called the "nature." That which is produced by the harmony of life, accords with essence, and reacts naturally and spontaneously, without being trained— this is called "natural disposition." The like and dislike, joy and anger, sorrow and pleasure of this nature—all these are called the "emotions." When the heart [mind] is moved by the emotions and makes a selection, this is called "reflection." When the heart reflects and acts accordingly, this is called "the acquired." When reflection is accumulated and abilities are trained, there results completion—this is called "the acquired character." To be engaged in righteous gain is a proper occupation; to act in accordance with righteousness is good conduct. That in man by which he knows is called [the faculty of] "knowing"; that in [the faculty of] knowing which corresponds to external things is called "knowledge." That in man by which he can acquire knowledge is called "ability." That in ability which corresponds to what can be done is called "competence." What injures the nature is called "defect"; what happens by chance is called "destiny." These are the miscellaneous names as used by the people; these are the names as formed by the later kings.

The kings regulated names, for when names were fixed, actualities were distinguished; when the *Tao* was carried out, their will was made manifest. Then they would be careful to lead the people toward unity.

To make unauthorized names, thus confusing the correct nomenclature, would cause the people to be in doubt and bring about much litigation; therefore this was called "great wickedness." It was a crime like that of using false credentials or false measures. For this reason, their people did not dare to depend on making strange terms in order to confuse the correct nomenclature. Hence their people were honest. Being honest, they could be easily ruled. Being easily ruled, they achieved results.

Since the people did not dare to depend on making strange terms in order to confuse the correct nomenclature, they were united in the *Tao* and law-abiding and respectful in obeying orders. In this way their example [i.e., that of the kings] spread. Their example spread, and results were achieved;

such was the acme of good government. This was the benefit of being careful in preserving the names which had been agreed upon.

Now that the sage-kings are no more, the preserving of names has become lax, strange terms have arisen, and names and actualities have become confused. As the standards of right and wrong are indistinct, even officials who maintain the law and scholars who study by themselves and teach others are likewise in a state of confusion. Should some king arise, he would certainly follow the old names and create new ones. Then it is imperative for him to investigate the reason for having names, the conditions under which similarities and differences are distinguished, and the fundamental principles for instituting names.

Different forms as received by the mind are intermixed, different things are entangled, when names and their actualities are intertwined; noble and base are not differentiated; similarities and differences are not distinguished. In this situation, there would certainly be the danger of the people's ideas not being understood and their affairs being hindered and forsaken. Therefore, the wise man separates what is different and institutes names in order to denote actualities— on the one hand, to differentiate noble and base and, on the other hand, to distinguish similarities and differences. When noble and base are differentiated, and similarities and differences are distinguished, the danger of people's ideas not being understood or of their affairs being hindered and forsaken will no longer exist. This is the reason names are given.

What, then, are the conditions under which similarities and differences arise? In reply, I say: They are the natural senses. All [creatures] that are of the same kind and have the same emotions have the same natural senses with which to perceive things. Therefore things are compared, and those which are found to be approximately alike are grouped together. In this way they share the same name and claim each other. The eye distinguishes between forms and bodies, colors and designs. The ear distinguishes between "clear" voice and "confused" sound, musical notes and strange noises. The mouth distinguishes between sweet and bitter, salty and fresh, peppery and sour, and other tastes. The nose distinguishes between perfumes and smells, fragrance and stench, the smell of fresh meat and fetid smells, the smell of the mole-cricket and the smell of decayed wood, and other smells. The body distinguishes between pain and itching, cold and heat, smoothness and roughness, lightness and heaviness. The mind distinguishes between happiness and gloom, joy and anger, sorrow and pleasure, love and hatred, as well as desires.

The mind has the faculty of knowing. By this faculty it is possible to know sound through the ear and to know forms through the eye. However, the faculty of knowing depends on objects first being noted and classified by the natural senses. When the five senses note something but cannot classify it, and the mind tries to identify it but fails to give it designation, one can only say that there is no knowledge. These are the conditions under which similarities and differences arise.

Then, accordingly, names are given to things. Those which are similar are given the same names; those which are differentiated are given different names. A simple name is given to what is simple; if the simple name is not applicable, a compound name is used. And, again, if the simple name and the compound name do not conflict, a general name is used; although it is a general name, there is no harm in using it. Knowing that different actualities have different names, one should never refer to different actualities other than by different names; thus there can be no confusion. Likewise, one who refers to the same actualities should use the same names.

Moreover, although there are myriad things there are times when we wish to generalize, and call them "things"—the term "things" is the Great General Name. We press on and generalize; we generalize and generalize still more, until we reach that than which there is nothing more general; only then do we stop. There are times when we wish to specify things which we call "birds and beasts"—the term "birds and beasts" is the Great Specific Name. We press on and specify them; we specify and specify them still more, until we reach that which there is nothing more specific; only then do we stop.

There are no names necessarily appropriate of themselves. It is by agreement that things are named. Once agreed upon, the name becomes customary, and then this is called an "appropriate designation." That which does not conform to the agreement is called an "inappropriate designation." Names have no actualities necessarily corresponding to them. It is by agreement that things are named. Once agreed upon, these names become customary and then these are called "names appropriate to actualities." But some names are inherently felicitous. When a name is simple and direct, easily understood, and not contradictory, this is called a "felicitous name."

There are things which have the same appearance but are in different places; there are things which have different appearances but are in the same place. Distinctions can be made between them. Things which have the same appearance but are in different places, although they may be classified together, are called "two actualities." When the appearance changes but the actuality remains the same, though it looks different, this is called "transformation." When there is transformation but no differentiation, this is called "one actuality." By this method actualities are investigated and their number is determined. These are the fundamental principles for instituting names. It is imperative for one to investigate the way in which the later kings fixed names.

"To receive insult is no disgrace"; "the sage does not love himself"; "to kill robbers is not to kill men": these are fallacies in the usage of names, which confuse them. Investigate the reason for having names, observe of what kind the names are, and then you will be able to stop this confusion.

"Mountains and abysses are on the same level"; "the desires seek to be few"; "domestic animals do not contribute to good eating, nor does the great bell contribute to pleasure": these are fallacies in the usage of actualities which confuse names. Investigate the conditions under which similarities and differences arise, observe what is appropriate to the actuality, and then you will be able to stop this confusion.

". . .[1] and a white horse are not a horse": these are fallacies in the usage of names which confuse the actualities. Investigate the agreements among names, take what is agreed upon and reject what is refused, and then you will be able to stop this confusion.

All heretical doctrines and heinous teachings which deviate from the *Tao* and which are impudently fabricated can be classed among these three fallacies. Hence the wise sovereign, knowing to which class they belong, does not dispute about them. Thus the people can be easily united in the *Tao*, although they cannot be given all the reasons for things. Hence the wise sovereign deals with the people by authority and guides them to the *Tao;* he orders things by decrees, illustrates things by maxims, and restrains them by punishments. Hence the people are turned into the *Tao* as by magic. Why should he use dialectic?

Now the sage-kings are no more, so that the world is in dis-

1. The meaning of the first sentences is not clear and hence is omitted.

order, wicked doctrines have arisen, but the sovereign has no power to govern the people, and no punishments to restrain them; so there is need for dialectic. When an actuality is not understood, its name is given; when its name is not understood, it is designated; when the designation is not understood, then it is explained; when the explanation is not understood, then dialectic comes into use. Hence the name, designation, explanation, and dialectic are the great refinements of human activity and the beginnings of the kingly rule.

The object of a name is to know the actuality when one hears the name. The beauty of names lies in stringing them together to make expressions. When both the object and beauty of terms are secured, that is called "knowing these names." Names are that whereby we define various actualities. Statements are the combinations of names of different actualities which express one idea. Dialectic and explanation refer only to one actuality and its name, so as to understand the *Tao* of their different aspects. Designation and naming are the object of dialectic and explanation. Dialectic and explanation are that whereby the mind delineates the *Tao*. The mind is the master-artisan of the *Tao*, and the *Tao* is the natural and invariable principle of order and good government.

When a person's mind accords with the *Tao*, when his explanation accords with his mind, when his statements accord with his explanation, when he rectifies names and so designates actualities, when names are based on actualities and so are understood, when he discriminates differences without making mistakes, when he classifies things without making errors, then he can listen to discussions and tell if they accord with refinement; he can argue and exhaust all possible reasoning; by means of the *Tao* he can distinguish wickedness, just as with the plumb-line one may determine the crooked and the straight. For this reason, unorthodox doctrines cannot confuse him; all the schools of philosophy cannot evade him.

To have the wisdom of having heard everything without the manner of being impetuous and proud; to be honest and tolerant without the air of boasting his virtue; when his teachings are carried out, the world is rectified; when his teachings are not carried out he still abides by the *Tao*, but retires into private life—this is the dialectic of the sage. The *Shih* says:

> O graceful and grand,
> Like jade sceptre, like jade tablet,

> With good fame and great hope,
> My joyous and pleasant prince—
> You are the guide of the world.

This expresses what I mean.

He has the virtue of prudence and conforms to the principle of the elder and younger; he does not speak of what is shunned or forbidden, nor does he utter curses; he talks with a *jen*-heart; he listens with a receptive mind; he argues in a fair spirit. He is not moved by the condemnation or praise of the multitude, nor does he pervert the ears and eyes of the onlookers; he does not bribe the power of the nobility, nor does he rejoice at the words of the depraved. Hence he is able to abide by the *Tao* and never deviate; he may offer his opinion but cannot be forced; he may be in accord with others but cannot be coerced; he respects fairness and uprightness but despises indecency and contention—this is the dialectic of the scholar and *chün-tzu*. The *Shih* says:

> As the long night is endless,
> So is my thought forever nimble.
> As the ancients are not ignored,
> So *li* and *yi* are not evaded.
> What then care I for the people's talk?

This expresses what I mean.

The speech of the *chün-tzu* is profound and yet refined, being readily understood and yet systematic, making distinctions and yet having unity. He rectifies the names and makes his words appropriate, so that his meaning and intention can be clarified. The names and words are the messengers of his meaning and intention. When they are fully expressed and understood, he stops. To use them improperly is wickedness. Hence when the names fully designate the actualities, and when his words make his ideas manifest, he stops. Beyond this, he is considered to be slow of speech. This is what the *chün-tzu* rejects and the stupid man considers as his treasure. For the speech of the stupid man is hasty and coarse, boisterous and unsystematic, babbling and bubbling. He sophisticates the names and mystifies his words, without making any sense of them. Hence he goes far, but there is no destination; he works hard but there is no result; he covets fame, but none is acquired. Reflect on the words of the wise man, and you will easily understand them; practice his words, and you will be easily at peace; hold to his words, and you will be easily established; bring his words to perfection, and you will certainly obtain what you like and not meet with what you hate. However, the stupid man does just the opposite of this. The *Shih* says:

> Were you a spectre or a demon,
>   Then you would be beyond my reach;
> But looking at you face to face,
>   One cannot refrain from seeing you.
> I have made this good song
>   To show how very shifty you are.

This expresses what I mean.

Every doctrine of order which depends on the elimination of desires cannot submit desires to the *Tao* and is hampered by the presence of desires. Every doctrine of order which relies on the lessening of desires cannot curb desires and is hampered by the great number of desires. The distinction between the presence of desire and its absence is like that between life and death; this is not the result of order and disorder. The distinction between many desires and few desires is due to the response of emotion; this is not the result of order and disorder. Desire does not depend on whether satisfaction is possible, but its gratification seeks what is possible. That desire does not depend on whether satisfaction is possible is something conferred by Heaven; that its gratification seeks what is possible is something brought about by the mind. Hence desires are conferred by Heaven, but they are regulated and restrained by the mind. What man desires most is life, and what he dislikes most is death. Yet there are men who cling to life and find death, not because they do not desire life and do desire death, but because they cannot live and can only die. Therefore if a person's action stops short of his desires, it is the mind which has arrested it. If what the mind permits is in accord with reason, although the desires are many, what harm are they to order? If a person's desires are weak, while his actions go beyond them, it is the mind which has caused this. If what the mind permits deviates from reason, although the desires are few, how would that prevent disorder? Therefore order and disorder depend on the permission given by the mind, not on the desires as related to the instinctive disposition. If a person does not seek for that which order depends upon, and instead seeks for that which it does not depend upon, although he says, "I have it," he has lost it.

Human nature is the product of Heaven. Emotions are the essence of human nature. Desires are the reactions of the emotions. The emotions can never avoid assuming that what is desired can be sought and obtained. The starting point of knowledge is to consider that desires are permissible and so to guide them. Hence, although a person be a doorkeeper, his desires cannot be eliminated. If he tries to satisfy all natural desires, even if he is the emperor, these desires cannot be completely fulfilled. Although desires cannot be completely fulfilled, their gratification can be nearly satisfied; although desires cannot be eliminated, their pursuit can be restrained. Although that which a person desires cannot be completely fulfilled, what he seeks to be gratified can be nearly satisfied; although desires cannot be eliminated, if what he wants cannot be obtained, he will certainly wish to restrain his pursuit. If the man who abides by the *Tao* advances, he can come near to satisfying all his desires; if he retires he can restrain his pursuit—there is nothing else in the world that is better than this!

Men never fail to follow what they deem possible and reject what they deem impossible—there is nothing better than this in knowing the *Tao*. None of those who do not abide by the *Tao* can do this. Suppose there were a man who liked the south: although much had been taken out of it, yet he desired it; and he disliked the north: although little had been taken out of it, yet he disliked it. Could it be that because he could not have all of the south, he would leave the south and go north? What people of today desire is much, but they still desire it; what they dislike is little, but they still dislike it. Can it be that because they cannot have all they desire, they will act contrary to the *Tao* to satisfy their desires by taking what they dislike? Therefore, let us follow what accords with the *Tao;* how can we disregard this for the sake of loss and disorder? Let us reject what is contrary to the *Tao;* how can this be disregarded for the sake of gain and order? Hence a wise man is only concerned about the *Tao*. Then that which the heterodox schools of learning wished for in their much prized theories will be of no avail.

Men never obtain what they desire without being adulterated; nor do they reject what they dislike without being mixed. Hence men's action should always correspond to the standard. When the balance is held improperly, a heavy article suspended from it will swing up high, and people will think it is light; a light thing will hang down low, and people will think it is heavy. In this way people are misled about weights. When the standard is not right, calamity is mixed with what is desirable and people think it is happiness, or happiness is mixed with what is disliked and people think it is calamity. And so in this way people are misled about calamity and happiness. The *Tao* was the correct standard in ancient times as it is in the present. If a man deviates from the *Tao* and chooses his own inner standard, he will not know whether calamity or happiness will befall him.

If a trader barters one item for another, people say, "He has neither loss nor gain." If he barters one item for two, people say, "There is no loss, but a gain." If he barters two items for one, people say, "There is no gain, but a loss." The schemer gets as much as he can, while the plotter follows what he deems possible. No one will barter two for one because he knows the art of counting. To follow the *Tao* is like bartering one for two; how can there be a loss? To deviate from the *Tao* and instead choose one's own inner standards is like bartering two for one; how can there be any gain? Such a man will barter the time-honored desire for the momentary dislike, because he does not know the art of counting.

Moreover, the person who has tried to see man's hidden traits and been deep in his investigation finds that there is no one who intends to despise moral principles and not to value material goods; that there is no one who values external material goods and does not make any internal disturbance; that there is no one whose conduct deviates from moral principles and whose life is not in danger; that there is no one whose life is in danger and whose mind feels no fears. When his mind is anxious and fearful, even though his mouth holds meat, he will not know the flavor of it; though his ears hear bells and drums, he will not know the sound of them; though his eyes behold elaborate embroidery, he will not know the design of it; though he is wearing light and warm clothes, and sitting on a fine bamboo mat, his body will not know the comfort of it. For though he may enjoy the beauty of all things, yet he cannot be content. If he manages to be content, he still cannot be free from anxiety and fears. Hence, though he enjoys the beauty of all things, yet he is full of anxieties; though he absorbs the benefit of all things, yet he suffers injury. Such being the case, does he seek those things which he admires? Or, does he nourish his life? Or does he wish for a long life? As a result, he desires to foster his desires, but he indulges his emotions; he desires to foster his nature, but he endangers his body; he desires to foster his enjoyment, but he attacks his mind; he desires to foster his fame, but he deranges his actions. Under these circumstances, although this sort of man may be made a marquis and called a prince, he will be no different from a mere fellow in crimes; although he may ride in a coach and wear a crown, he will be no different from a footless cripple. Then he can well be called one who makes himself the servant of those things he admires.

When the heart is calm and contented, the colors, though not too bright, can nourish the eyes; the sounds, though not too vibrant, can nourish the ears; coarse food and vegetable soup can nourish the mouth; coarse cotton clothes and coarse hemp sandals can nourish the body; a straw hut for a house, reed screens for doors, straw beds, and out-of-date stands and mats can nourish the form. Therefore, a person, though he may not have the beauty of all things, can foster his enjoyment; though he may not have a position of nobility, he can foster his fame. If such a man were given the world, it would mean much for the world, but it would mean little for his contentment and enjoyment. Then he can well be called one who makes himself the master of things. The noble man is cautious about unverified statements, obscure actions, and disguised schemes.

Part Four: The Theory of Government

Hsün Tzu was also interested in the problems of government and maintained, as a necessary corollary to his theory of desires, that good government could be achieved by making evident the distinction between the superior and the inferior as well as between the sovereign and the minister. He was consistent with his theory in maintaining that the purpose of politics was to regulate men's desires in order to keep them at their appointed station. Hence he advanced a theory that implies a demarcation of social classes. On the one hand, there was the higher group, including "the superior, senior, learned, and competent"—in general, all the upper strata in society. On the other hand, the lower stratum consisted of the great mass of "the inferior, junior, unlearned, and incompetent." These social distinctions served as the basis of society and the state.

Stemming from his view of man's evil nature was his de-

scription of the primitive state as one of "beasts and birds"—
that is, "a state of strife." For this reason, he said it had been
necessary to have teachers to guide and laws to correct man's
evil nature. By means of education and legal measures, the
spirit of mutual respect is fostered, refinement of life cultivated, and an ordered state of society brought about. This
is why we have government and social institutions. However
Hsün Tzu remained true to the Confucian tradition in attach-
ing the highest importance to the people and lesser weight
to the sovereign. Thus, when he exalted the sovereign, he
only meant to say that the sovereign possessed the *Tao* for
attaining to good government.

᭓᭐

VII. Chapter 9: On Kingly Government

Please speak of government. In reply, I said: Advance the
worthy and capable without regard to seniority; dismiss the
incompetent and incapable without delay; put incorrigible
criminals to death without trying to reform them; transform
the common people without resorting to coercive methods.
When social distinctions are not established, there is difference in senior and junior. The descendants of kings, dukes,
and ministers, if they do not abide by the rules of *li* and *yi*,
are certainly relegated to the common people; the descendants of the common people, if they are versed in literature,
upright in conduct, and abide by the rules of *li* and *yi*, are
certainly elevated to be prime ministers and ministers. But
lewd people, scandal-mongers, evil-doers, scoundrels, rioters,
and other mischief-makers should be confined to take trade-
training and given time for reformation. Encourage them by
rewards and warn them by punishments. If they are willing
to work, then keep them; if they are not willing to work, then
deport them. The five defectives [i.e., the dumb, the deaf,
the crippled, the lame, and the disabled] should be received
and cared for; if they have ability, they should be employed.
The authorities should make use of them, and clothe and feed
them; they all should be cared for with no exception. But
those who are incorrigible should be put to death with no
mercy. This is what is called "heavenly virtue"; this is the
government of a true king.

The great distinctions to be made in administration are as
follows: Treat those who are good with *li;* treat those who

are not good with punishment. When those two kinds of people are distinguished, the worthy and the unworthy will not be mixed; right and wrong will not be confused. When the worthy and the unworthy are not mixed, then heroes will come; when right and wrong are not confused, then the state will be well governed. In such a situation, the reputation will become well known, and the world will be willing to submit to the rule and obey the injunctions; then the duties of a true king will have been completely performed.

When in administration the ruler is severe and harsh, and never listens to others, then his subordinates fear him and are not close to him; they all remain silent and do not keep him informed. Such being the case, important matters are slackened, while minor matters are ruined. If he is amiable and complaisant, too fond of listening to others, and has no sense of where to stop, then malicious doctrines will be presented to him, and all kinds of dubious proposals will bristle around him. Such being the case, he will have to listen too much and become tired; this also will ruin his government. Moreover, if he governs by law without regard to its general applicability, then cases not covered by the law are left undecided. If men are appointed to offices without regard to their ability, then matters beyond their abilities are neglected. Therefore law must be applicable and men in office must have abilities. There are no disguised schemes, no good men are neglected, and all matters proceed without error. Only the *chün-tzu* is capable of such administration. Hence fairness is the standard of making appointments; moderation is the measure of administration. When there is law, one acts according to the law, but when there is no law, one acts according to the analogies of the case; this is one's doing the utmost possible in administration. But one who is a biased partisan and has no principles of action is the worst of all in administration. Therefore, there has been bad government under good laws; but from ancient times to the present there has never been a bad government under the *chün-tzu*. The *Chüan* says:

> Good government comes of the *chün-tzu*,
> Whereas bad government comes of the *hsiao-jen*.

This expresses what I mean.

When division is equal, there is no distinction; when power is equal, there is no unity; when the multitude is equal, there is no order. When Heaven and earth exist, there is a

distinction between the high and the low. When the enlightened king arises, the state is governed by different institutions. For two superiors cannot serve each other, two inferiors cannot order each other; this is a law of Heaven. When
people's power and position are equal, so their likes and dislikes are the same, things will not be sufficient to satisfy them,
and hence strife will invariably result. When there is strife,
there must be riot; when there is riot, there must be poverty.
In view of this, the early kings instituted *li* and *yi* for social
distinctions, in order to have the classes of poor and rich,
superior and inferior, so that each would be under another's
control; these are the fundamentals of nourishing the world.
The *Shu* says:

> They are only equal in that they are not equal.

This expresses what I mean.

When the horse is afraid of the carriage, the prince is not
secure in his carriage. When the common people are afraid
of the government, the prince is not secure in his position.
When the horse is afraid of the carriage, there is no better
way than quieting it; when the common people are afraid of
the government, there is no better way than treating them
kindly. Choose men of worth and merit, advance those who
are sincere and reverent, and encourage filial piety and
brotherly reverence; shelter the orphan and the widow, and
help those who are poor and in need; then the common people will be satisfied with the government. Only when the
common people are satisfied with the government is the prince
secure in his position. It is said:

> The prince is like the boat;
> The people, like the water.
> Water can support the boat,
> But it also sinks it.

This expresses what I mean.

Hence if the prince wishes to be secure, there is nothing as
good as a just government and love for the people. If he
wishes to have glory, there is nothing better than exalting
li and respecting the scholars. If he wishes to have achievement and fame, there is nothing as good as honoring men of
worth and employing those who are capable. These are the
great guiding principles of the prince. When these three prin-

ciples are followed, then all else will certainly be achieved. Confucius once said: "One who is right in both major and minor matters is a prince of the superior class; one who is right in major matters but sometimes right and sometimes wrong in minor ones, is a prince of the middle class; if one is wrong in major matters, even though one may be right in minor ones, I have never seen that one to achieve anything."

Marquis Ch'eng and Duke Sze of Wei were princes well versed in levying taxes and scheming extortion, but they failed to win the allegiance of the people. Tze Ch'an [prime minister of Ch'eng] was one who won the allegiance of the people but failed in his administration. Kuan Chung [prime minister of Ch'i] was well versed in administration, but failed to cultivate *li*. One who cultivates *li* can be a true king; one who is well versed in administration can be powerful; one who wins the allegiance of the people can be secure; one who levies taxes will be ruined. Hence the prince who governs as a true king will enrich the people; he who governs as a leader of the feudal lords will enrich his soldiers; he who only retains his state will enrich his ministers; he who loses his state will enrich his coffers and fill his treasury. When the coffers are enriched and the treasury is filled, but the people are poor, this is what is meant by the saying, "The prince has superabundance but the people are in want." Such being the case, within its territory the state will not be able to defend itself; beyond its borders the state will not be able to fight. One needs only to see that it will not take long for such a state to totter and fall. Hence I accumulate wealth and so am ruined, but the enemy obtains it and becomes strong. The prince who only levies taxes invites marauders and benefits the enemy; this is the *Tao* which will destroy his country and endanger his person. Therefore the enlightened king does not tread this path.

The prince who governs as a true king gains men of worth; he who governs as a leader of feudal lords gains allies; he who governs as a powerful feudal lord gains territories. He who gains men of worth will make feudal lords his ministers; he who gains allies will make friends of the feudal lords; he who gains territories will make enemies of the feudal lords. He who makes the feudal lords his ministers will attain kingly rule; he who makes friends of feudal lords will win the leadership; he who makes enemies of feudal lords will be in danger. If the prince depends on the use of force, the cities of other states will be guarded and their people will be belligerent; if we overcome them by force, then we will certainly injure their people greatly. If we injure their people greatly, then they will certainly dislike us greatly; if so, they will be more anxious to fight against us. When their cities are guarded and the people are belligerent, if we overcome them by force, we will certainly injure our own people greatly. If we injure our own people greatly, they will certainly dislike us greatly; if so, they will be less willing to fight for us. If their people are more anxious to fight against us and our own people are less willing to fight for us, a strong prince will become weak. If our territory increases and our population decreases, then we shall have much trouble but little gain. If that which is guarded is enhanced, but the number of guards is reduced, a great state will become small. Then the feudal lords will certainly make allies, nurse hatred, and never forget their enemies; they will wait for the weakness of the powerful and great state and take advantage of its defeat. This is the time of danger for the state which is great through force.

The prince who knows how to be powerful and great will not depend on the use of force. He will ponder the use of kingly rules; he will preserve his power; he will consolidate his virtues. When his power is preserved, the feudal lords cannot weaken him; when his virtue is consolidated, the feudal lords cannot degrade him. If the world is without a king in control, such a powerful prince will always prevail. This is the *Tao* of the prince who knows how to be powerful and great.

But the leader of feudal lords acts differently. He opens up new lands; he fills granaries and storehouses; he provides implements for use; he carefully recruits officers of ability and talents. Then he offers rewards in order to encourage them to progress; he makes severe punishments in order to restrain them. He preserves those who have lost their country and sustains those whose posterity has come to an end. He protects the weak and restrains the oppressive, but he has no intention of acquiring territory; only then will the feudal lords be friendly with him. This is his *Tao:* whether they be friends or enemies, he treats the feudal lords with respect; only then will the feudal lords be pleased. They want to be friendly with him because he does not seek territory; if he seeks territory, they will turn away from him. They are pleased with him because he treats enemies as friends; if he wants to make them his subordinates, they will turn away

from him. Hence he makes it understood that he has no intention of acquiring territory; he makes them believe in his
Tao of treating enemies as friends. If the world is without a
true king, such a leader of feudal lords will invariably prevail. This is the *Tao* of the prince who knows how to be the
leader of the feudal lords.

King Min of Ch'i was ruined by the five states; Duke Huan
of Ch'i was captured by Chuang of Lu. It was for no other
reason than that they sought to attain the kingly rule, but did
not follow the *Tao*.

The true king acts differently. His humanity spreads over
the world; his righteousness permeates the world; his authority dominates the world. His humanity spreads over the
world, and there is no one in the world who does not love
him; his righteousness permeates the world, and there is no
one in the world who does not honor him; his authority dominates the world, and there is no one in the world who dares
to oppose him. He carries out the *Tao* of humanity with his
unassailable authority and wins without fighting; he conquers
without attacking; he subdues the world without effort. This
is what is known as the "kingly rule." On the basis of these
three guiding principles, if he wishes to become a king, he
can become one; if he wishes to be the leader of the feudal
lords, he can succeed; if he wishes to be strong, he can become strong.

The assistants of a king should refine their conduct by the
code of *li* and *yi;* they should listen to reports and make de-
cisions in accordance with proper principles; they should
attend to their work with prudence. In their actions they
should adapt themselves to various circumstances and never
be at a loss. These are the fundamentals in conformity with
which they can be the assistants of a king.

The *Tao* of the kingly government should not depart from
that of the three dynasties, nor should its methods differ from
those of the later kings. The *Tao* that departs from that of
the three dynasties is immoral; the methods that differ from
those of later kings are uncouth. There are regulations for
costumes, there are rules for buildings, there are standards
of grading officials and soldiers. Mourning rites and sacrifices,
as well as their appropriate utensils, all have their proper
gradations. All music which is not conventional should be
eliminated. All colors which do not conform to established
patterns should be prohibited. All utensils which are not of
ancient types should be destroyed. This is what is meant by

"conforming to the ancients." This is the kingly government.

The general principles of a true king are as follows: He does not honor those who are without virtue; he does not make officials those men who have no ability; he does not reward those who have no merit; he does not punish those who commit no crime. In his court there are no positions for opportunists; among the people there are no parasites. He promotes the worthy and employs the capable, so that all are fit for their positions. He recognizes the good people and restrains the ruthless, so that his punishments are not severe. All the people who are observant understand that one who is good at home will receive reward at the court; one who is evil in secret will receive punishment in public. This is what is meant by having unvarying principles. These are the general principles of a true king.

The administration of a true king is as follows: He grades taxation and makes regulations, so that all things are regulated for the purpose of nourishing the people. He levies a tithe on the land. At the frontier passes and markets, he inspects travelers but levies no tolls. He prohibits or permits forestry or fishing in accordance with the season, but he levies no duties on its produce. He appraises the land and assesses the tax. He regulates the tribute in accordance with the distance of the place. Hence money and goods, corn and rice, should be circulated without restriction so that they may be mutually supplied. Such being the case, all within the four seas will be like one family. Then those who are near will not hide their ability, and those who are far away will not worry about their efforts. There will be no distant and secluded country which fails to serve and rejoice in him. He is a teacher of men. This is the law of a true king.

On the North Sea there are swift horses and large dogs, but China can obtain and raise them for service. On the South Sea there are feathers, ivory, furs, and minerals, but China can obtain them and thus be enriched. On the Eastern Sea there are indigo plants, shells, fish, and salt, but China can obtain them for ornaments and food. On the Western Sea there are furs and painted weaves, but China can obtain them for use. Hence the people who live on the coast can have a sufficient supply of wood, while those who live on the mountain can have a sufficient supply of fish. Farmers who do not chop the wood, make the pottery, or melt the metal can have sufficient vessels and implements, while laborers and merchants who do not till and plough the land can have

sufficient pulse and millet. Though the tiger and leopard are
fierce, yet the prince can have them skinned and use them.
Therefore what Heaven covers and the earth produces will
yield up all its goodness and be brought for his use. On the
one hand, he will exalt men of worth and virtue, and, on the
other, he will nourish the people and pacify them. This is
what is called the great divine king. The *Shih* says:

> Heaven made the hill,
> King T'ai tilled the land;
> 'Twas he who began the work;
> Then King Wen brought it under peace.

This expresses what I mean.

Variations can be classified; myriad things can be unified.
From the beginning to the end, and vice versa; like a ring,
there is neither beginning nor end. Whatever deviates from
this principle will invariably result in ruin.

Heaven and earth are the beginning of life. *Li* and *yi* are
the beginning of good government. The *chün-tzu* is the beginning of *li* and *yi*. To practice *li* and *yi*, to carry them out,
to accumulate them, and to love them—all these are the beginning of being a *chün-tzu*. Hence Heaven and earth give
birth to him; he brings Heaven and earth into order; he
forms a triad with Heaven and earth. Hence he is the ruler
of all things and the parent of the people. Without him
Heaven and earth are not ordered, *li* and *yi* are not regulated.
As a result, on the one hand, there is no sovereign and no
teacher; on the other there is no distinction between father
and son.[1] This is the greatest disorder. The sovereign and
minister, the father and son, the older and younger brothers,
the husband and wife—here all have defined the beginning
and the end, or the end and beginning; this social structure
exhibits the same principle as Heaven and earth; it is of the
same permanence as the universe.[2] This is the "great foundation." Hence mourning rites, sacrifices, court ceremonies, and
etiquettes are governed by the same principle.[3] Promotion
and degradation, death and life, rewards and punishments are
governed by the same principle. The sovereign as sovereign,
the minister as minister, the father as father, the son as son,
the elder brother as elder brother, the younger brother as

1. No social order.
2. Lit., "myriad things."
3. The kingly government is founded on the distinctions of ordered society.

younger brother—this social structure is governed by the same principle. The farmer as farmer, the scholar as scholar, the laborer as laborer, the merchant as merchant—this social structure is governed by the same principle.

Water and fire possess force but are without life; grass and trees have life but no knowledge; birds and beasts have knowledge but no sense of *yi*. Man has force, life, knowledge, and also a sense of *yi*. Hence he is the highest being on earth. His strength is not equal to that of the ox; his running is not equal to that of the horse; and yet the ox and horse are used by him. How is this? In reply, I say: Men are able to form social organizations, whereas the ox and horse are unable.

How is it that men are able to form social organizations? Because of their social distinctions. How is it that these social distinctions can be made? By the reason of *yi*. Thus when there is *yi* in distinctions, there is harmony. When there is harmony, there is unity. When there is unity, there is strength. When there is strength, there is power. With power, men can overcome obstacles. Hence men can have magnificent buildings and chambers for habitation. Hence men can adjust their actions according to the four seasons, control all things, and enjoy all the benefits in the world. This is due to no other reason than the fact that they have social distinctions and the sense of *yi*.

Therefore, if men are to live, they cannot get along without a social organization. If they form a social organization but have no social distinctions, they will strive; if they strive, there will be disorder; if there is disorder, they will disintegrate. When they disintegrate, they will become weak; when they are weak, they will be unable to overcome obstacles. Hence they will not have magnificent buildings and chambers for habitation. This is to prove that men cannot abandon *li* and *yi* for an instant.

One who is able thereby to serve his parents is said to have filial piety; one who is able thereby to serve his older brother is said to have brotherly respect; one who is able to serve his superior is said to be dutiful; one who is able to direct his inferiors is said to be a sovereign. A sovereign is one who is good at social organization.

If the *Tao* of social organization is properly carried out, then all things will fulfill their appropriate functions; the six domestic animals will prosper; all living beings will meet their destiny. When they are nourished and sustained at the proper

season, the six animals will grow; when the ground is weeded
and tilled at the proper season, shrubs and trees will thrive.
Likewise, when government decrees are timely, the people
will be united; men of worth and virtue will serve the sovereign. This is the administration of the sage-king. When shrubs
and trees are in bloom and leaf, the axe must not be brought
to the forest, so as not to cut short their life and stop their
growth. When tortoises, fish, turtles, and eels are full of roe
or have spawned, nets and poison must not be allowed in the
pools and lakes, so as not to cut short their life and stop their
growth. The spring ploughing, the summer weeding, the
autumn harvesting, and the winter storing—these four things
must not be out of season. Hence the five grains will not fail
to flourish, and the people will have more food than can be
consumed. Ponds, pools, lakes, and streams must be closed
at the proper time; hence fish and turtles will be abundant,
and the people will have a surplus for use. The cutting down
and growth of the forest must not be at the wrong season;
the mountains and forest will not become gaunt and bare, and
the people will have more timber than is required. This is the
way the sage-king utilizes the natural resources. He observes what happens in Heaven and cultivates what is produced on the earth. He fills up what is lacking in Heaven
and earth and diffuses it to all things. He enlightens what is
obscure; he lengthens what is short; and he broadens what
is narrow. He is divine and magnificent and yet he is simple
and pure. Hence it is said, "By one principle he unified the
whole." The man who acts in accord with this principle is
called "the sage."

The arrangement of official duties is as follows: The Master
of Ceremonies should know the number of stables for sacrificial animals for the entertainment of guests and for sacrifices. The Minister of the Interior should know the number
of all clans, cities, and suburbs, and the current utensils. The
Minister of War should know the number of regiments, bat-
talions, armor, soldiers, and chariots. The Grand Master
should attend to the codification of laws and edicts, the examination of odes and songs, and prohibitions of licentious
music. All these things should attentively be done at the
proper time, so that barbarian ditties and vulgar tunes will
not be confused with the orthodox music. The business of the
Minister of Works is to build embarkments and bridges, to
clean the ditches and canals, to drain off the accumulated
water, and to make the reservoirs secure so as to meet timely

emergencies. When all these things are done, even in the famine years caused by flood or drought, the people will have some land for weeding and ploughing. The business of the Minister of Agriculture is to survey the high and low lands and inspect fertile and poor soils for the cultivation of the five grains, to watch the industry of the farmers and carefully to store up the grain. All these things should be done attentively at the proper time, so that the farmer may simplify his efforts and make fewer activities. The business of the Warden of Mountains and Lakes is to codify the laws for regulating the fire,[4] to protect the hills and forests, the marshes, trees, fish, turtles, and all vegetables, so as to close or open the season at the proper time; then the country shall have abundant supply of things to use and its wealth never be exhausted. The District Governor should keep the countryside in harmony, regulate the households and residences, rear the six domestic animals, supervise the cultivation of mulberry trees and other plants, encourage moral teachings, and urge filial piety and brotherly reverence. All these things should be done at the proper time, so that the people will obey the order and be happy to live in the village. The Superintendent of Artisans should supervise the artisans, attend to the seasons and activities of the people, distinguish the fine articles from the rough ones, and praise the well-made and useful goods, so that the people will not make their carved and painted goods at home. The business of the Mayor of the Municipality is to observe the *yin* and *yang*, to tell the future by natural phenomena, to scorch the tortoise-shell and arrange divining stalks, to pray for averting evil and to select the five omens,[5] so as to know good or bad fortune, as well as ominous or auspicious signs and also to remove the refuse and repair the roads, to suppress robbers and thieves, and to pacify hotels and lodges. All these things should be done at the proper time, so that travelers and visitors will be safe and goods and valuables will be protected. The Minister of Crimes should suppress the risky and restrain the ferocious, guard against the wicked and eliminate the evil, and execute them according to the five penalties; then the risky and ferocious may be transformed, and wicked and evil actions may be avoided.

The Prime Minister should attend to the admonition of administration and rectify the laws and regulations, hold

4. I.e., burning the mountainsides and marshes for fertilizer.
5. The five omens are rain, clear sky, fogs, mist, and variations.

court and inspect the officers so as to evaluate their merits
and consider their rewards. All these things should be attentively done, so that all the officers will be devoted to their
duties and all the common people will not be slovenly. The
Prince should elaborate *li* and *yao* [music], rectify personal
conduct, extend culture, and beautify customs, so as to transform them and harmonize them. The Heavenly Emperor will
bring morals to perfection, be the pattern of exalted greatness and of cultivated refinement, unify the world, and urge
the lowest, so that no one will fail to obey and submit to his
rule. Hence if the government is in confusion, this is the
crime of the Prime Minister. If the state deteriorates in
morality, this is the fault of the Prince. If the world is not
unified and the feudal lords are in revolt, the Heavenly Emperor is not the right man.

Among all these officers, some have reigned as true king,
while others have become leaders of feudal lords; among all
these officers, some have been preserved, while others have
been ruined. Whether a state of ten thousand chariots will
establish its majesty and strength, beautify its fame, subdue
its enemies, and make the country secure or dangerous, good
or bad, depends entirely on the ruler, not on others. Whether
the king of men or the leader of feudal lords will be stable
and secure or in danger and be destroyed depends wholly
on the ruler, not on others.

When the majesty and strength of a state is not sufficient
to threaten a neighboring enemy, and when its fame is not
sufficient to dominate the world, such a state cannot be inde-
pendent. How can it avoid being suddenly overwhelmed?
When the world is coerced by one aggressive state and [I,
as a ruler of another state] side with the aggressor, doing
what I do not want to do, and so I am daily helping a Ch'ie
[a wicked king], this fact does not prevent me from being a
sage-king. But this is not the way to the establishment of my
merit and fame; nor is this the cause for the existence of my
rule or its ruin, its safety, or its danger. The establishment
of merit and fame, as well as the conditions of determining
existence or ruin, safety, or danger of a prince, will certainly
rely on the prince's sincerity when he contents himself with
his prosperity. When the prince acts sincerely as a true king,
he will certainly become a true king. When the prince acts to
endanger or destroy his state, he will certainly accomplish it.
Accordingly, I as a sovereign should be neutral and impartial, and where there are various alliances or leagues of

states, I should calmly curb his troops and not mobilize them, so as to watch the aggressive states strive with each other. Then I should pacify my government and moderate my administration and, at the same time, train and indoctrinate my people. While I carry out these measures, my troops will become the strongest in the world. Accordingly, I should cultivate *jen* and *yi;* I should exalt the highest principles and rectify the laws; I should choose men of worth and virtue and nourish the people. While I carry out these measures, my fame will become the greatest in the world. As a result, my authority will make me important, my army will make me powerful, and my fame will make me great. Then Yao and Shun, who unified the world, could not find anything to add to such a ruler.

Under these circumstances, those who seek gain and subvert others will be out of the government, but those who are worthy and virtuous, with the knowledge of the sage, will come forward to offer their services. Punishments and government will be fair and just, the people will be in accord and harmony, and the customs of the state will be regulated; consequently, the army will be strong, cities will be impregnable, and enemy states will submit of their own will. Accordingly, I should attend to the essentials of life and accumulate wealth. I should not loaf about and waste; then all the officers and the people will follow usages and regulations, wealth will be accumulated, and the state will become rich of its own accord. When these three things are carried out in this way, the world will submit, and the sovereign of any aggressive state will not be able to use his army against me. How is this? He will have no one to send against me. Those whom he will send must be his people, but his people will have been attached to me and will rejoice in me as in the fragrant orchid. Then they will turn and regard their own superior as a frightful whale, or as an enemy to themselves. That is human nature. Even though a man were a Chieh or a Chih, how could he do what he dislikes, or injure what he loves? An evil ruler will be destroyed!

Hence, in ancient times a man could win the whole world by his single state, not because of conquests, but because he cultivated his government to transform it. He could penalize an aggressor and restrain an invader. When the Duke of Chou sent expeditionary forces to the south, the northern states complained, "Why does he not come to us?" When he sent expeditionary forces to the east, the western states complained, "Why does he come to us last of all?" Who could fight with such a ruler? This is the way whereby a ruler can advance from his own state to be Emperor. In times of prosperity, he works for peace in order to pacify his army and to rest his people. He loves his people, opens up new fields, fills his granaries and storehouses, and provides good implements. Then he selects men of skill and capacity, encouraging them with rewards and restraining them by penalties. As a result, officers who are thus selected are well versed in their duties and coordinate in their positions, wealth is stored and developed, and so there is an abundance of things for use.

The militarist [i.e., the man of soldiers, armors, and weapons] will daily expose and destroy his soldiers, armors, and weapons in the central domain of his country. Now I should train them, comfort them, and shelter them. He will daily procrastinate and waste the wealth of his treasury and grain in the midst of wilderness. Now I should accumulate and gather it in granaries and storehouses. He will daily injure and exhaust his skilled and brave officers in fighting against his enemies. Now I should summon them, inspect them, and train them in court. In this manner, he will daily accumulate defeat, while I shall daily accumulate success; he will daily accumulate poverty, while I shall daily accumulate riches; he will daily accumulate toil, while I shall daily accumulate ease. In the relation of sovereign and minister, ruler and ruled, he will be cursed, and their relations will daily become more distant and spiteful; but I shall be revered, and our relations will daily become closer and more amiable. In this way I shall await his collapse, and be sure of gaining his country.

Suppose there is a man who, in his personal conduct, follows the ordinary customs; who, in his administration, follows the ordinary precedents; who, in making appointments or promotions, advances the ordinary officials; who, in dealing with his inferiors and his people, is generous and kind. Such a man will be merely secure in his position. Next, suppose there is a man who, in his personal conduct, is discourteous and undignified; who, in his administration, is suspicious and has no faith in others; who, in making appointments and promotions, advances those who are flattering and cunning; who, in dealing with his inferiors and his people, likes to encroach on and plunder them. Such a man will certainly endanger his position. And, again, suppose there is a man who, in his personal conduct, is proud and aggressive; who, in his administration, is subversive and injurious; who, in making appointments and promotions, advances those who are deceitful and treacherous; who, in dealing with his inferiors and his people, likes to use his power and is heedless of his reputation; who likes to levy heavy taxes and forgets his basic duties. Such a man will certainly ruin his position.

Of the classes of men [as mentioned above], a sovereign should make a good choice, for such a choice is the means of determining whether he be a true king or a leader of the feudal lords; secure, in danger, or ruined. He who makes a good choice will rule others; he who does not make a good choice will be ruled by others. He who makes a good choice will be a true king; he who does not make a good choice will be ruined. The difference between the man who is a true king and the one who is ruined is the difference between the man who rules others and the one who is ruled by others. The difference between the two kinds of sovereigns is very great.

CONTENTS

⤳ FOUR: TA HSÜEH (THE GREAT LEARNING) ⤶

⤳ INTRODUCTION

In the *Han Fei Tzu*, there is a passage about the later Confucians:

> . . . Since the death of Confucius, there have appeared the schools of Tzu-chang, Tzu-ssu, the Yen Clan, the Meng Clan, the Ch'i-tiao Clan, the Chung Liang Clan, the Sun Clan, and the Yo-cheng Clan . . . (Chapter L).[1]

These eight comprised the Confucian schools of the later part of the Warring States period. The writings of these men and those of the early Han dynasty were compiled by Tai Te into a single work of eighty-five sections, which was reduced by Tai Sheng, the nephew of Tai Te, to forty-six sections. This later compilation comprises what is now known as the *Li Chi*, or The Book of Rites. Two important sections of the *Li Chi* (secs. 39 and 40) have exerted a great influence on later Chinese philosophy. They are the *Ta Hsüeh* (Great Learning) and *Chung Yung* (Doctrine of the Mean), which, together with the *Lun Yu* and the *Mencius*, comprise the *Four Books*, the basis of Confucian education.

The *Ta Hsüeh* was traditionally attributed to Tseng Ts'an, one of the chief disciples of Confucius. Modern scholars, however, discredit his share in the book because of several passages which are definitely of a much later origin. But, whoever its author may be, the book represents the genuine interpretation of the Confucian political and ethical views.

A unique feature of the *Ta Hsüeh* is the connected logical reasoning it applies to a general thesis which has come to be called the three "main cords" and eight "minor wires." This central thesis is self-cultivation. The steps preceding self-cultivation, such as investigation, extension of knowledge, and so forth, are the ways and means for cultivating the self, while the steps following self-cultivation, such as regulation of the family and so forth, are the ways and means for culti-

---

1. The classification, as made by Han Fei, a legalist philosopher of the third century B.C., was both confusing and arbitrary.

vating the self to its highest perfection, which is the same as the manifestation of illustrious virtue—that is, the *Tao* of the Great Learning. Here we note the unity of ethics and politics, which is characteristic in Chinese Humanism. It was the goal of every man from the Son of Heaven down to the common people; a well-cultivated individual, a well-regulated family, a well-governed state, and a peaceful and harmonious world.

The *Ta Hsüeh* is a brief treatise of some 1,750 words. It originally constituted one section of the *Li Chi* and later became a separate book, during the Sung dynasty. There are at least nine different editions, and the texts vary in the arrangement of paragraphs and in the number of chapters. However, we have tried to rearrange the entire text into two parts.

✌§ THE TA HSÜEH

Part One: The General Statement

The General Statement of the *Ta Hsüeh* consists of the Three Guiding Principles, or the three "main cords," and the Eight Ethical-Political Items, or the eight "minor wires." The Three Guiding Principles are (1) "manifestation of illustrious virtue," (2) "loving the people," and (3) "rest in the highest good." The Eight Ethical-Political Items are (1) "investigation of things," (2) "extension of knowledge," (3) "sincerity in one's thoughts," (4) "rectification of one's heart," (5) "cultivation of one's person," (6) "regulation of one's family," (7) "the governing of one's state," and (8) "insurance of world peace."

✌§ ৪∾

Chapter I. The Three Guiding Principles

1. The *Tao* of the Great Learning is to manifest illustrious virtue, to love the people, and to rest in the highest good.

2. Only when one knows where one is to rest can one have a fixed purpose. Only with a fixed purpose can one achieve calmness of mind. Only with calmness of mind can one attain a tranquil repose. Only in a tranquil repose can one devote oneself to careful deliberation. Only through careful deliberation can one attain to the highest good.

Chapter II. The Eight Ethical-Political Items

3. Everything has its roots and branches. Affairs have their end and beginning. To know what comes first and what comes last is to be near to the *Tao*.

4. The ancients who wished clearly to manifest illustrious virtue throughout the world would first govern their own states well. Wishing to govern their states well, they would first regulate their families. Wishing to regulate their families, they would first cultivate their own persons. Wishing to cultivate their own persons, they would first rectify their hearts. Wishing to rectify their hearts, they would first seek sincerity in their thoughts. Wishing for sincerity in their thoughts, they would first extend their knowledge. The extension of knowledge lay in the investigation of things.

5. Only when many things are investigated is knowledge extended; only when knowledge is extended are thoughts sincere; only when thoughts are sincere are hearts rectified; only when hearts are rectified are our persons cultivated; only when our persons are cultivated are our families regulated; only when our families are regulated are states well governed; only when states are well governed can the world be at peace.

6. From the Son of Heaven down to the common people, all must consider the cultivation of the person as the root. When the root is in disorder, the branches cannot grow in order. To treat the important as unimportant and to treat the unimportant as important—this should never be.

7. This is called knowing the root; this is called the perfection of knowledge.

Part Two: The Detailed Elaborations

In Part One, we have noted the main ideas of the *Ta Hsüeh*, consisting of the Three Guiding Principles and the Eight Ethical-Political Items by which one attains these principles. Most of the ideas will be further elaborated in the following passages, but the two phrases, "extension of knowledge" (*chih chih*) and "investigation of things" (*ko wu*), which are not clearly explained in the text, have given rise to the most important controversy between the two divergent schools of Neo-Confucianism[1] over the question whether the

1. See Ch'u Chai, "Neo-Confucianism of the Sung-Ming Periods," *Social Research*, Vol. XVIII, No. 3, 1951.

phrase "*ko wu*" should be interpreted as "to investigate things" or "to rectify the mind." That is, the choice is between objective study and intuitive knowledge.

⋖§ ⪾⋗

Chapter III. Elaboration of the Three Guiding Principles

8. In the *Announcement to K'ang,* it is said, "He could manifest his illustrious virtue." In the *T'ai Chia,* it is said, "He contemplated and studied the illustrious mandates of Heaven." In the *Canon of Emperor Yao* it is said, "He could manifest his glorious virtue." These passages all show how the ancients made themselves illustrious.

9. On the bathtub of Emperor T'ang the following inscription was engraved: "Be sincere in renewing yourself every day, and do so day after day. Yes, let yourself be renewed always!" In the *Announcement to K'ang,* it is said, "To urge the people to renew themselves." In the *Shih,* it is said:

> Though Chou is an old state,
> Heaven's mandate is new.

Therefore, the *chün-tzu* does his utmost to attain the highest good.

10. In the *Shih* it is said:

> The imperial domain was
> of a thousand *li;*
> Herein the people would
> rest in peace.

And again:

> Twitters the yellow bird
> And rests on a corner of the mound.

The Master said: "When it rests, it knows where to rest. Is it possible that a man snould not be equal to this bird?"

11. In the *Shih* it is said:

> Dignified and profound was King Wen,
> Ever bright and reverent in his resting place!

As a sovereign, he rested in *jen;* as a minister, he rested in reverence; as a son, he rested in filial piety; as a father, he rested in kindness; in intercourse with his people, he rested in good faith.

12. In the *Shih* it is said:

> Look at the banks of the Ch'i,
> How luxuriant are the green bamboos!
> Elegant is our lord—
> He is as if cut and filed;
> He is as if chiselled and polished.
> How grave and dignified is he!
> How majestic and distinguished is he!
> Elegant is our lord!
> Never can we forget him!

"As if cut and filed" signifies the way of learning. "As if chiselled and polished" signifies the way of self-cultivation. "How grave and dignified is he" signifies his cautious reverence. "How majestic and distinguished is he" signifies his inspiring appearance. "Elegant is our lord! Never can we forget him" signifies the perfection of virtue and the attainment of the highest good, so that the people cannot forget him.

13. In the *Shih* it is said, "Oh, the former kings are never forgotten!" For the future, the princes will exalt what they exalted, and love what they loved. The common people will enjoy what they enjoyed and be benefited by their good work. On this account, the former kings are never forgotten after they have died.

Chapter IV. Elaboration of the Eight Ethical-Political Items

14. The Master said: "In hearing litigations, I am like other men. It is necessary to prevent the people from having litigations." Hence those devoid of truth will be unable to pour out their words and a great awe would prevail in the people's mind. This is called "knowing the root."

15. What is meant by the phrase "making the thoughts sincere" is allowing no self-deception. For example, when we dislike a bad odor or like a beautiful color, this is called "being true to one's self." Therefore, a *chün-tzu* must watch over himself when he is alone.

16. When the common man is alone, he will concede to any sort of evils; but when he sees a *chün-tzu,* he will try to disguise himself, concealing his evil and displaying what is

good. The other beholds him as if he saw his lungs and liver; of what use is his disguise? This is the meaning of the saying, "What sincerity is within will be manifested without." Therefore the *chün-tzu* must watch over himself when he is alone.

17. Tseng Tzu said: "Ten eyes behold it. Ten hands point to it. Is this not serious?"

18. As riches adorn a house, so virtues adorn the person. When the mind becomes broad, the body appears at ease. Therefore the *chün-tzu* must make his thoughts sincere.

18. "The cultivation of the person depends on the rectification of the heart" means this: When a man is under the influence of anger, of terror, of fond regard, and of sorrow and distress, he will not be correct in his conduct. When the mind is not present, we look but do not see; we listen but do not hear; we eat but do not know the taste. This is what is meant by saying that the cultivation of the person depends on the rectification of the heart.

19. "The regulation of one's family depends on the cultivation of one's person" means this: Men are partial to those whom they hold dear and love; those whom they despise and dislike; those whom they stand in awe of and reverence; those toward whom they feel pity and compassion and those whom they ignore and neglect. Hence there are few men in the world who know the shortcomings of those whom they love or know the good in those whom they dislike. So there is a maxim: "A good man does not know the wickedness of his son; nor does he recognize the richness of his growing corn." This is what is meant by saying that if a man fails to cultivate his person, he cannot regulate his family.

20. "In order to govern his state well, he must first regulate his family" means this: There is no man who cannot teach his own family and yet can teach others. Therefore, the *chün-tzu*, without going beyond his family, may complete his instructions to the state. There is filial piety, with which the sovereign should be served; brotherly reverence, with which elders should be served; parental kindness, with which the multitude should be treated.

In the *Announcement to K'ang* it is said, "Act as if you were watching over an infant." If the heart be really sincere in its seeking, though it may not meet its wants, it will not be far from its goal. There has never been a woman who learned first to bring up a child and then marry afterwards.

21. When one family practices *jen*, the whole state will abide by *jen*. When one family is prudent, the whole state

will become prudent. On the other hand, when one man is avaricious and perverse, the whole state will be thrown into confusion. Such is the contagion of man's moral character. This is what is meant by the saying, "A single word may ruin an enterprise, and a single man may pacify the state."

Yao and Shun led the world with *jen,* and the people followed them; Chieh and Chou with oppression, and the people followed them. When the orders of a ruler are contrary to what he himself likes, the people do not follow these orders. Therefore the *chün-tzu* requires from others only the virtue that he himself has and blames others for the fault of which he himself has not. Never has there been a man who could teach others without having cherished altruism in his own person. Therefore the government of the state depends upon the regulation of the family.

22. In the *Shih* it is said:

> How fresh and fair are the peach blossoms!
> How luxuriant and green are the leaves!
> This young lady goes to her new home,
> And will order well her house-people.

One must be able to order well the people of his family before he can teach the people of the state.

In the *Shih* it is said, "He sets an example to his brothers!" One must be able to set an example to his brothers before he can teach the people of the state.

In the *Shih* it is said:

> His fine demeanor is without fault;
> He rectifies the whole state.

When the ruler, as a father, a son, an elder brother, or a younger brother, is a model, then the people follow his example. This is what is meant by the saying, "The government of his state depends on his regulation of the family."

23. "The establishment of peace in the world depends on the government of the state" means this: When the superiors nourish their aged, the people will be inspired to become filial; when they reverence their elders, the people will be inspired to learn brotherly respect; when the superiors are compassionate to the orphaned, the people will not do otherwise. Thus the *chün-tzu* has a guiding principle by which, as with a measuring-square, he may regulate his conduct.

24. What a man dislikes in his superiors, let him not display in his treatment of his inferiors; and what he dislikes in his inferiors, let him not display in his service to his superiors. What a man dislikes in those before him, let him not set before those who are behind him; what he dislikes in those behind him, let him not set behind those who are before him. What a man dislikes in those on his right, let him not display to those on his left; what he dislikes in those on his left, let him not display to those on his right. This is called the principle by which, as with a measuring-square, one may regulate one's conduct.

25. In the *Shih* it is said:

> Happy be the lord—
> He is the parent of the people.

When the sovereign loves what the people love and hates what the people hate, then he is called the parent of the people.

26. In the *Shih* it is said:

> Oh lofty is that southern mountain!
> Its rocks are massed high!
> Greatly distinguished are thou Master Yin;
> The people all look up to thee!

Thus those who govern the states may not fail to be prudent. If they deviate from this guiding principle, the people of the world will inflict punishment on them.

27. In the *Shih* it is said:

> Ere Yin lost the multitudes,
> It could be a counterpart to Shang Ti
> Take warning from the House of Yin!
> It is not easy to keep Heaven's decree.

This shows that by gaining the people, the state is secured, and by losing the people, the state is lost.

28. Therefore, the sovereign will first take care of his own virtue. When he has virtue, he will have the people; when he has the people, he will have the territory; when he has the territory, he will have wealth; when he has wealth, he will have resources for use. Hence, virtue is the root; wealth is the branch. If he makes the root secondary and the branches primary, he will only quarrel with the people and teach them

to scramble for private gain. Hence when the sovereign accumulates wealth, he will scatter the people; when he distributes wealth among the people, he will unite them. Hence, if one's words are improper, one will be affronted in retort. Similarly, if one gains wealth by improper means, so one will lose it by the same means.

29. In the *Announcement to K'ang* it is said, "Indeed Heaven's decree is not irrevocable." That is to say: the virtuous will obtain the decree, and the corrupt will lose it.

In the *Book of Ch'u* it is said, "The State of Ch'u does not consider anything as its treasure. Its treasures are the good men."

Tzu Fan [uncle of Duke Wen of Tsin] said: "Our fugitive prince has no treasures. The affection due to his parent is his treasure."

30. In the *Declaration of Ch'in* [in the *Shu Ching*], it is said: "Let me have one minister who is faithful and sincere, who does not pretend to other abilities, who has an upright and tolerant heart; who, seeing abilities in other men, values them as if they were his own, and, hearing sagacious wisdom from other men, loves it as though it were from his own mouth, showing that he is open-minded. Such a minister would be able to protect my descendants and my people, and also to help my country profit. On the other hand, if my minister be one who, seeing abilities in other men, envies and dislikes them, and, hearing sagacious wisdom from other men, obstructs and prevents their advancement, thereby showing that he is narrow-minded; such a minister cannot protect my descendants and my people, and, moreover, I should say that he is dangerous to my country!"

31. Only the humane man can send away such a minister and banish him from the Imperial Domain to live among the Yi people [barbarians]. This is what is said: "Only the humane man knows how to love and how to dislike others."

32. To see men of worth and not to raise them to office or to raise them to office but not to do so promptly is negligence. To see bad men and not to remove them or to remove them but not to a distance is a mistake.

To love those whom men dislike and to dislike those whom men love is detrimental to human nature. Calamities will certainly come down to him who does so.

33. There is a great principle for the sovereign: Only through loyalty and sincerity can he win the world, and through self-indulgence and pride will he lose it.

There is also a great principle for the production of wealth: Let the producers be many and consumers few; let them be industrious in production and frugal in expenditure; then the wealth will always be sufficient.

34. The man of *jen* distinguishes himself by means of wealth. The man devoid of *jen* accumulates wealth at the expense of his life.

Never has there been a case where the sovereign loved *jen* and his people did not love *yi*. Never has there been a case where the people loved *yi* and yet the affairs of the sovereign could not be successfully accomplished. And never has there been a case where the state collected wealth in its treasury and yet its wealth could not be in the sovereign's possession.

35. Meng Hsien-tzu once said: "He who is entitled to keep horses and a carriage should not look after fowls and pigs. He who is entitled to use ice in his family funeral service should not rear cattle and sheep. So the house which is entitled to possess a hundred chariots should not keep a minister to levy tolls and duties on the people. I would rather have one who should rob me of my revenues than to have such a minister." This is what is said: "The state will not get benefit from its wealth, but its benefit will be found in *yi*."

36. If the man who governs the state is devoted to the accumulation of wealth, he has no choice but to employ the *hsiao-jen*. He may consider this man to be worthy, but as long as the *hsiao-jen* is employed in the government, disasters and injuries will befall the state. Even though a good man may take his place, he will not be able to perform well. This is again what is said: "The state will not get benefit from its wealth, but its benefit will be found in *yi*."

FIVE: CHUNG YUNG (THE DOCTRINE OF THE MEAN)

CONTENTS

◅§ INTRODUCTION

The *Chung Yung*, like the *Ta Hsüeh*, is included in the *Li Chi*, and forms one of the *Four Books*. As to authorship, there is strong and commonly accepted testimony that the *Chung Yung* was the work of K'ung Chi, or K'ung Tzu-ssu, the grandson of Confucius. The *Shih Chi* of Ssu-ma Chien, in its biography of Confucius, states that "Tzu Ssu composed the *Chung Yung*." However, there is suspicion that some of its passages on such philosophical concepts as *ming* (fate), *hsing* (man's nature), and *ch'eng* (sincerity), which seem to be developments of Mencius' doctrines, might be interpolations by a follower of Tzu Ssu.

This treatise, as shown by its title, is a systematic exposition of the mean (*chung*) and normality (*yung*).[1] To secure the mean and normality is not merely to pursue a middle course; it means rather to be in harmony with the universe. Thus the way of *chung yung* involves a sense of justice and fairness, a spirit of tolerance, a state of harmony, and a doctrine of equality. It is a way of action which avoids going to extremes; or a state of mind in which human reasoning and feeling reach a perfect harmony. In other words, the doctrine of the mean serves as a guide for human emotions and actions.

There is another important concept in this book: *ch'eng* (sincerity). In one sense, *ch'eng* means perfect virtue, corresponding to Confucius' *jen; ch'eng* the way of Heaven, which transcends and develops man's nature.

It is obvious that the main purpose of this book is to search for a *Tao* by which an individual can become a genuine or real man. Such a man has the virtue of the Sage, "who can make the warp and woof of the great fabric of society, who can establish the great foundation of the world, and who can understand the transforming and nurturing processes of Heaven and earth." The book stresses that such a *Tao* can only be found in man's *ch'eng* to himself as well as in the doctrine of *chung yung*. On the basis of this central thesis,

---

1. These concepts of *chung* and *yung* are expressed in Confucius' *Lun Yü*: "Perfect indeed is the virtue which is in accord with the mean. . . ."

it discourses brilliantly on the character and duties of the
chün-tzu, the moral responsibilities of the sovereign, the performance of social obligations, and the ideal institutions of
the sage-kings.

We have followed the text as it is included in the Li Chi
but have rearranged it into the following six chapters: General
Statement; The Doctrine of Chung Yung; The Exposition of
the Tao; The Attainment of Sincerity [Ch'eng]; The Moral
Influence of the Sage; Conclusion.

✒ THE CHUNG YUNG

Chapter I. General Statement

Like the Ta Hsüeh, the book begins with a chapter stating
the general theme, supposedly handed down by Confucius.

✒ ફે᷎

1. That which Heaven confers is called "man's nature";
the development of this nature is called the Tao; the cultivation of the Tao is called "culture."

The Tao cannot be disregarded even for a moment. If it
may be disregarded, it is not the Tao. Hence the chün-tzu is
ever cautious regarding matter not yet seen and stands in awe
of things not yet heard. There is nothing more evident than
that which is hidden; there is nothing more manifest than
what is minute. Therefore the chün-tzu is watchful even when
he is alone.

2. To have none of the passions, such as pleasure and
anger, sorrow and joy, surging up, is called being in a state
of equilibrium [chung]. To have these passions surging up,
but all in due time, is called being in a state of harmony.
This state of equilibrium is the supreme root of the great universe, and this state of harmony is its far-reaching Tao. Once
equilibrium and harmony are achieved, Heaven and earth
shall maintain their proper positions and all things receive
their full nourishment.

Chapter II. The Doctrine of Chung Yung

3. Chung-ni [i.e., Confucius] said: "The chün-tzu lives in
accordance with the mean while the hsiao-jen lives contrary

to it; the *chün-tzu* lives in accordance with the mean because he is the noble man and holds the timely mean; the *hsiao-jen* [lives contrary to] the mean because he is the common man, and knows no restraint."

4. The Master said: "Perfect indeed is the mean! For long people seldom had the capacity for it."

5. The Master said: "I know now why the *Tao* is not observed. The wise overlook it, and the foolish fall short of it. I know now why the *Tao* is not understood. Men of worth overlook it, and the unworthy fall short of it. There is no one who does not eat or drink, but there are few who can distinguish flavors."

6. The Master said: "How is the *Tao* neglected?"

7. The Master said: "Shun indeed was profoundly wise! He was fond of making inquiries and studying casual remarks of men. Then he withheld what was bad and displayed what was good. When he was confronted with two extremes, he held to the mean in dealing with the people. It was by acting this way that he was Shun!"

8. The Master said: "Men all say, 'I am wise,' but when driven and taken in a net, a trap, or a pitfall, they know not how to escape. Men all say, 'I am wise,' but when they choose the mean, they can hardly hold to it for a round month."

9. The Master said: "Hui [Confucius' disciple] was a man who chose to abide by the mean. When he found something good, he would hold to it firmly and never lose it."

10. The Master said: "The world, state, and family may be well governed; honors and emoluments may be declined; naked weapons may be trampled; but the mean can hardly be attained to."

11. Tzu Lu [Confucius' disciple] asked about courage.

The Master said: "Do you mean the courage of the southern people or the courage of the northern people? Or do you mean the courage [one should cultivate]? of the brave man? To be patient and gentle in teaching others and not to revenge an injustice is the courage of the southern people. This is what the *chün-tzu* abides by. To take up arms and meet death without regret is the courage of the northern people. This is what the brave man abides by.

"Therefore, the *chün-tzu* accords with others without being coerced. How firm is he in his courage! He maintains his mean position without throwing his weight to either side. How firm is he in his courage! When the *Tao* prevails in the country, he does not deviate from the principles he maintained in retirement. How firm is he in his courage! When the *Tao* fails to prevail in the country, he holds fast to his principle even if it means death. How firm is he in his courage!"

12. The Master said: "There are men who pursue what is abstruse and practice what is eccentric, so that they may be known to posterity. This is what I do not do.

"Again, there are men who try to pursue the *Tao* but abandon it halfway. This is what I cannot do.

"But the *chün-tzu* accords with the mean. Though he may be unknown and neglected by the world, he feels no regret. Indeed, only the sage was able enough for this."

Chapter III. The Exposition of the Tao

13. The *Tao* of the *chün-tzu* is pervading and yet is concealed. Common men and women, however ignorant, may know it; yet in its ultimate development there is something which even the sage does not know. Common men and women, however worthless, may practice it; yet in its ultimate development there is something which even the sage cannot practice. Vast as Heaven and earth are, men still find something therein to disparage. Hence, when the *chün-tzu* speaks of the *Tao* in greatness, the world cannot embrace it; when he speaks of it in its minuteness, the world cannot split it.

In the *Shih* it is said:

> Up to the heaven flies the hawk;
> Fishes leap in the deep.

This is to say that the *Tao* operates high up in the Heaven and down below on the earth. The *Tao* of the *chün-tzu* begins with the relationship of common men and women, but in its ultimate development it pervades Heaven and earth.

1. THE SUBSTANCE OF THE TAO

14. The Master said: "The *Tao* is not far from man. When men try to pursue a *Tao* which is far from man, it is not the *Tao*. In the *Shih* it is said:

> In hewing an ax-shaft, in hewing an ax-shaft,
> The pattern is not far off.

"We grasp one ax-handle to hew the other; but if we look from one to the other, we still consider them as apart. Therefore the *chün-tzu* governs men by men; and as soon as they change [what is wrong], he stops.

"*Chung* [conscientiousness to others] and *shu* [altruism] are not far from the *Tao*. What you do not like done to yourself, do not do to others.

"In the *Tao* of the *chün-tzu* there are four things, none of which I have attained to. To serve my father as I would have my son serve me; I am not yet able to do that. To serve my sovereign as I would have my minister serve me; I am not yet able to do that. To serve my elder brother as I would have my younger brother serve me; I am not yet able to do that. To set an example in behaving to a friend as I would have him behave to me; I am not yet able to do that. The *chün-tzu* practices the ordinary virtues and pays attention to ordinary words. When there is deficiency, he never fails to make further efforts; when there is excess, he dares not go to the limit. His words must conform to his actions, and his actions must conform to his words. Is not the *chün-tzu* characterized by being cautious and earnest?"

15. The *chün-tzu* acts in accord with his station in life and does not desire what is beyond it. If he is wealthy and honorable, he acts like one wealthy and honorable; if poor and lowly, he acts like one poor and lowly. If he is among the barbarians, he does what one does among the barbarians; if he is in trouble or danger, he does what one does in trouble or danger. There is no situation in which the *chün-tzu* is not at ease with himself.

In a superior position he does not abuse his inferiors; in an inferior position he does not lean on his superiors. He rectifies himself and seeks nothing from others, and so he has no complaint. He does not complain against Heaven, nor does he grumble against men.

Thus the *chün-tzu* lives at ease and calmly awaits the Fate, whereas the *hsiao-jen* walks in danger and looks for lucky occurrences.

The Master said: "In the archer there is something like the *chün-tzu*. When he misses the target, he turns inward to look for the cause of his failure."

16. The *Tao* of the *chün-tzu* may be compared to that by which one goes to a distance by proceeding from the space that is near or that by which one ascends to a height by climbing from the low ground. In the *Shih* it is said:

> When wife and children live in concord,
> 'Tis like harps and lutes playing in chord;
> When brothers live in accord and peace,
> Their harmony and joy never cease.
> May your chamber and room be bright,
> And give your children and wife delight.

The Master said: "In such a state, the parents are indeed happy and contented!"

17. The Master said: "How profound is the power of the ghosts and spirits! We gaze but never see them, we listen but never hear them; yet they form the substance of things, and there is nothing without them.

"They cause all the people of the world to fast and purify themselves, and array themselves in the finest costumes, in order to attend the annual sacrifices. Like the rushing water, they seem to dominate the people from high and to take hold of them on their right and left." In the *Shih* it is said:

> The approach of spirits
> Can never be calculated;
> How can they not be reverenced?

Such is the manifestation of the subtle. Such is the impossibility of the real [ch'eng].

2. THE FUNCTION OF THE TAO

18. The Master said: "The filiality of Shun, how great it was! His virtue came up to that of the sage; his dignity entitled him to be the emperor; his riches embraced all within the four seas. He was worshipped at the Imperial Temple, and his descendants preserved this worship. Therefore, having such great virtue, he would certainly win the throne, those riches, the fame, and longevity. Thus Heaven, in production of all creatures, is sure to be bountiful in its blessings to them, according to their own merits. For example, the tree that flourishes Heaven will foster and sustain, while that which decays Heaven will overthrow and destroy.

"In the *Shih* it is said:

> Admirable and amiable is our prince;
> Illustrious is his good virtue.
> He orders well all the people,

From Heaven he receives blessings.
Heaven protects and decrees him the throne
Whose grant Heaven often renews.

Therefore he who possesses great virtue will certainly receive Heaven's decree."

19. The Master said: "Only King Wen had no cause for grief! He had a father like King Chi and a son like King Wu. His father commenced the work, and his son transmitted it.

"King Wu continued the work of King T'ai, King Chi, and King Wen. When he put on his armor and joined the wary, he gained possession of the world. Meanwhile he did not lose his great fame throughout the world. His dignity entitled him to be emperor; his riches embraced all within the four seas. He was worshipped in the Imperial Temple, and his descendants preserved this worship.

"In his old age, King Wu received Heaven's decree to the throne, and the Duke of Chou consolidated the royal sway of Wen and Wu. Then he conferred the imperial title to King T'ai and King Chi and accorded all ancestors at the sacrifice with the imperial ceremonies.

"This ceremonial code has been extended to the feudal princes, ministers, scholars, and common people. In the case where the father is a minister and the son is a scholar, the burial is accorded with the ceremonies due to a minister, and the sacrifice is accorded with the ceremonies due to a scholar. In the case where the father is a scholar and the son is a minister, the burial is accorded with the ceremonies due to a scholar, and the sacrifice is accorded with ceremonies due to a minister. The one year's mourning for kindred is extended to the ministers, but the three years' mourning for the parents is extended to the Son of Heaven. In the mourning for the parents, no distinction is made between the noble and the low."

20. The Master said: "The filiality of King Wu and the Duke of Chou, how far-reaching it was! Filiality is the force which continues the purposes of our ancestors and transmits their achievements. In spring and autumn they repaired the ancestral temple, set forth the ceremonial vessels and costumes, and presented the offerings for the season.

"The ceremonies of the ancestral temple served to symbolize, by their arrangement, the order of descent. By recognizing ranks of nobility, the high and the low are distinguished. By the order of the various services, they made a distinction of talents and worth. In drinking pledges, the inferiors served their superiors, and thus the service reached to the lowest. At the banquet for the aged, the order recognized the distinctions of age.

"Thus we stand in the same place where our forefathers stood, perform the same ceremonies which they performed, play the same music which they played, pay respect to those whom they honored, and love those who were dear to them. In short, we should serve the dead as if they were living and the departed as if they were present. This is the perfect expression of filial piety.

"Men serve gods by the ceremonies of sacrifices to Heaven and earth, and they serve their forefathers by the ceremonies of the ancestral temple. He who understands the ceremonies of sacrifices to Heaven and earth and the significance of the various sacrifices to ancestors will find the government of the state as easy as looking into his own palm!"

21. Duke Ai of Lu asked about government, and the Master said: "The government of Wen and Wu is set forth in the historical records on wood and bamboo. When right men are in office, the government prospers; when right men are out of office, the government collapses. The *Tao* of man is keen in matters of government, as that of the earth is keen in the growth of trees. Indeed, government is like a growing reed.

"Therefore the administration of government depends upon the right men. The choice of the right men is made by means of one's own personality. One cultivates one's personality by means of the *Tao*. And one learns the *Tao* through the practice of *jen*. *Jen* is what is attributed to man, and loving one's relatives is the most important expression of *jen*. *Yi* is what is right and proper, and honoring the worthy is the most important expression of *yi*. The degree to which one loves one's various relatives and the grades to which one honors various worthy men are regulated by the rules of *li*.

"Therefore the *chün-tzu* may not neglect the cultivation of his personality. Wishing to cultivate his personality, he may not neglect to serve his parent. In order to serve his parent, he may not neglect to understand men. In order to understand men, he may not neglect to understand Heaven.

"The universal *Tao* of the world is fivefold, and that by which the *Tao* can be fulfilled is threefold. There are the relations of ruler and subject, of father and son, of husband and wife, of elder and younger brother, and between friends; these five constitute the universal *Tao* of the world. *Chih* [wisdom], *jen,* and *yung* [fortitude]; these three are universal virtues of the world and that by which the virtues are practiced is one [i.e., sincerity].

"There are some who possess knowledge of these virtues by birth, others who study to attain it, and others who gain it by bitter experience. But if they all attain knowledge, they are one and the same.

"There are some who practice these virtues with natural ease, others who practice them with a view to their advantages, and others who practice them with strenuous effort. But since they make achievements, they are one and the same."

21. The Master said: "To be fond of learning is to be near to wisdom; to be earnest in practice is to be near to *jen;* to know to be ashamed is to be near to fortitude. He who knows these three things knows how to cultivate his own person. Knowing how to cultivate his own person, he knows how to govern other men. Knowing how to govern other men, he knows how to rule the world and state.

"For the government of the world, state, and family, there are nine cardinal principles:

1) The cultivation of one's own person
2) The honoring of men of worth
3) Loving one's parents and relatives
4) Showing respect to great ministers
5) Being considerate to all officials
6) Treating the common people as children
7) Encouraging the artisans
8) Lodging the strangers
9) Taking interest in the welfare of the feudal princes.

"By cultivating one's own person, the *Tao* of life is established. By honoring men of worth, one is not led in bewilderment. By loving one's parents and relatives, there is no resentment among the members of the family. By showing respect to great ministers, one is free from faults. By being considerate to all officials, all the scholars are grateful and loyal to the sovereign. By treating the common people as children, they exhort one another to do good. By encouraging the artisans, wealth is sufficient for use. By lodging strangers, people from all over the world flock to him. If one takes an interest in the welfare of the feudal princes, the whole world will stand in awe.

"To attend to the purity of his person and adjustment of his dress and to regulate his actions in conformity with the rules of propriety; this is the way for the sovereign to cultivate his own person. To discard flatterers and keep away from sensuous beauty and to slight wealth and value virtue; this is the way for the sovereign to encourage men of worth. To give them places of honor and endow them with large emolument and to share with them in their likes and dislikes; this is the way for the sovereign to inspire love among his kindred. To let them have subordinates to discharge their orders and commissions; this is the way for the sovereign to encourage the great ministers. To have confidence in them and make their emolument large; this is the way for the sovereign to encourage the scholars. To employ them only in the proper seasons and reduce the heavy taxation; this is the way for the sovereign to encourage the common people. To inspect them daily and examine them monthly and to make their rations in accordance with their labors; this is the way for the sovereign to encourage artisans. To escort them on their departure and meet them on their coming and to commend what is good in them and show compassion for the incompetent; this is the way for the sovereign to lodge the strangers. To restore the families whose line of succession has been broken, revive the states that have been ruined, bring order out of chaos and support those who are in peril, fix a regular schedule for court attendance, give their envoys liberal gifts and receive them with small tributes; this is the way for the sovereign to show interest in the welfare of the feudal princes. These are the nine cardinal principles for the government of the world, state, and family; that by which these principles are practiced is one [i.e., sincerity].

"In all things, that which is previously prepared succeeds; that which is not prepared fails. When words are previously determined, there will be no stumbling. When affairs are previously determined, there will be no difficulty with them. When actions are previously determined, there will be no regrets. When the *Tao* of life is previously determined, there will be no obstruction to practicing it.

"When those in inferior positions fail to win the confidence of their superiors, they cannot succeed in governing the people. There is a way to win the confidence of superiors. If a man is not trusted by his friends, he cannot win the confidence of his superiors. There is a way to obtain the trust of one's friends. If a man is not filially obedient to his parents, he cannot obtain the trust of his friends. There is a way to show filial obedience to one's parents. If a man is not sincere to himself, he cannot be filially obedient to his parents. There is a way to be sincere to oneself. If a man fails to comprehend what is good, he cannot be sincere to himself."

Chapter IV. The Attainment of Sincerity [Ch'eng]

22. [The Master said:] "Sincerity is the *Tao* of Heaven; its attainment is the *Tao* of man. He who possesses sincerity achieves what is right without effort, understands without thinking, and naturally and easily embodies the *Tao*. He is indeed a sage. He who attains to sincerity chooses the good and holds fast to it. This involves the extensive study of it, close inquiry into it, careful deliberation of it, clear distinction of it, and earnest practice of it. If there is anything which has not been studied or, being studied, has not been mastered, it should not be set aside. If there is anything which has not been questioned or, being questioned, has not been known, it should not be put aside. If there is anything which has not been thought about or, being thought about, has not been understood, it should not be set aside. If there is anything that has not been distinguished or, being distinguished, has not been made clear, it should not be put aside. If there is anything which has not been practiced or, being practiced, has not been undertaken with earnestness, it should not be put aside. If other men put forth one effort, he will put forth one hundred efforts; if other men put forth ten efforts, he will put forth a thousand. Let a man proceed in accordance with the *Tao*, and, though dull, he will surely become intelligent; though weak, he will surely become strong."

23. Enlightenment [*ming*], which comes out of sincerity, is to be ascribed to man's nature. Sincerity, which comes of enlightenment, is to be ascribed to culture. Where there is sincerity, there is enlightenment; where there is enlightenment, there is sincerity.

24. It is only the individual possessed of supreme sincerity who can give full development to his nature. Able to give full development to his nature, he can give full development to the nature of all men. Able to give full development to the nature of all men, he can give full development to the nature of all things. Able to give full development to the nature of all things, he can assist the transforming and nurturing pro-

cesses of Heaven and earth. Able to assist the transforming and nurturing processes of Heaven and earth, he may, with Heaven and earth, form a triad.

25. Next to the above is the individual who can develop some of the goodness in him to its utmost; thus he is possessed of sincerity. His sincerity is sure to be expressed in overt acts. What is expressed in overt acts is sure to be manifest. That which is manifest is enlightened. Being enlightened, he can move other men. When he moves other men, they are all changed. When he changes them, they are all transformed. It is only the individual possessed of supreme sincerity who can stimulate transformation.

26. This is the *Tao* of supreme sincerity—to be able to know beforehand. When a state is about to prosper, there are certainly suspicious signs. When a state is about to perish, there are certainly bad omens. These forebodings manifest themselves in the milfoil and tortoise, as well as in the movements of the four limbs. When calamity or happiness is about to come, it can be known beforehand. Therefore, the individual possessed of supreme sincerity is like a divinity.

27. Sincerity is self-completing, and the *Tao* of it is self-directing. Sincerity is the beginning and end of things; without sincerity, nothing can come into being. Therefore the *chün-tzu* considers sincerity as the most valuable of all attainments. Sincerity does not consist simply in the completion of one's self. It is that whereby all other things are completed. The completion of one's self leads to *jen;* the completion of other things leads to wisdom. Herein lies the virtue inherent in man's nature. This is the way whereby the inner and outer are united. Hence with sincerity all things are right and proper.

28. Therefore, supreme sincerity is unceasing. Being unceasing, it is everlasting. Being everlasting, it manifests itself. Manifesting itself, it is extensive. Being extensive, it is broad and deep. Being broad and deep, it is lofty and glorious. By being broad and deep, it supports all things. By being lofty and glorious, it embraces all things. By being far-reaching and everlasting, it completes all things. In its breadth and depth, it matches earth. In its loftiness and glory, it matches Heaven. Far-reaching and everlasting, it is infinite. Such being the nature of supreme sincerity, it manifests itself without display, transforms itself without motion, and completes itself without action.

The *Tao* of Heaven and earth may be summed up in one

sentence: "It exists of itself without duality, and it produces things inexhaustibly." The *Tao* of Heaven and earth is broad and deep, lofty and glorious, far-reaching and everlasting. Heaven is but a small bright spot; yet in its vast extent, the sun, the moon, and all the constellations are suspended, and myriad things are embraced by it. The earth is but a handful of soil, yet in its breadth and thickness it upholds the Mountains Hua and Yo without feeling their weight, holds the rivers and seas without their overflowing, and supports myriad things. The mountain is but a mass of rock, yet in its vastness the grass and trees grow, birds and beasts dwell, and all the treasures are found. The water is but a ladleful; yet in its depth, the largest tortoises, dragons, fishes, and turtles are produced and sources of wealth abound.

In the *Shih* it is said:

> The Decree of Heaven,
> Oh, profound and never-ending!

This expresses why Heaven is Heaven. And, again:

> Oh, illustrious and pure,
> The virtue of King Wen!

This expresses why King Wen was called *Wen* [culture]. His purity is never-ending.

Chapter V. The Moral Influence of the Sage

29. Great is the *Tao* of the sage! Like overflowing water, it sustains and nourishes all things; so its magnificence reaches Heaven.

Splendid is its greatness! It embraces the three hundred codes of ritual and the three thousand rules of conduct, awaiting the proper man to put them into practice.

Hence it is said, "Only by perfect virtue can the supreme *Tao* be accomplished."

Therefore the *chün-tzu*, while esteeming his virtuous nature, maintains inquiry and study; while seeking to pursue his studies extensively, he neglects none of the more exquisite and minute points; though he attains the highest understanding, yet he still abides by the doctrine of the mean. He ponders over what he has learned and acquires new knowledge. He is earnest and reverent and observes all the rules of *li*.

Thus when he is in a superior position, he is not proud; in an inferior position, he is not disobedient. When the *Tao* prevails, his words bring prosperity to the country; when the *Tao* fails to prevail, his silence commands forbearance to himself. In the *Shih* it is said:

> He is enlightened and prudent,
> And so he guards his life and fame!

Does this express what I mean?

30. The Master said: "Let a man who is ignorant be fond of being self-assertive; let a man who is in a low position be fond of being self-willed; let a man who lives in the present age go back to the ways of antiquity; if he behaves in this manner, calamities will certainly befall this person.

"Only the Son of Heaven is in a position to institute *li*, to regulate legal measures, and to determine the written script. Now, over the world, carriages have wheels of the same size, writing is with the same script, and human conduct is governed by the same rules. One may occupy the throne, but if one possesses no proper virtue, one should not institute *li* and music. Neither should one do so if one possesses only the proper virtue but does not occupy the throne."

31. The Master said: "I can describe the *li* of Hsia, but the State of Ch'ih offers no adequate evidence. I have studied the *li* of Yin, and in the State of Sung it still continues. I have studied the *li* of Chou, which is now used, and I will follow Chou."

32. He who attains to the kingly rule over the world has three weighty matters and so he is seldom at fault.[1]

However excellent might be the institutions of the ancients, if these institutions cannot be attested to, they cannot command credence. That which cannot command credence will not be observed by the people. However excellent might be the institutions initiated by men in low positions, they will not be honored. Without being honored, these institutions cannot command credence. That which cannot command credence will not be observed by the people.

Therefore the *Tao* of the *chün-tzu* is rooted in his own person and attested to by the multitude of the people. Then he examines it by comparison with those of the Three Dy-

---

1. Chu Hsi (1130-1200) identified "the three weighty matters [*san chung*]" as "to order the ceremonies, to fix the measures, and to determine the written script."

nasties and finds it without mistake; he sets it up before
Heaven and earth and finds nothing in it absurd; finally, he
makes inquiry about it to the ghosts and spirits, and no
doubts arise; he is prepared for the rise of a sage a hundred
generations later, and no flaws will be shown in it. That he
makes inquiries about it to the ghosts and spirits without
doubts shows that he knows Heaven. That he is prepared
for the rise of a sage a hundred generations later, without
flaws, shows that he knows man.

Such being the case, every movement the *chün-tzu* makes
constitutes the *Tao*, every action he performs constitutes the
pattern, every word he utters constitutes the law, for ages to
the world. Those who are far off long for him, and those who
are near never weary of him.

In the *Shih* it is said:

> There, nothing to dislike;
> Here, nothing to loathe.
> May they, day and night,
> Perpetuate their praise!

Never has there been a *chün-tzu* who obtained an early re-
nown throughout the world without answering this description.

33. Chung-ni ascribed his doctrines to Yao and Shun and
patterned them after the laws and institutions of Wen and
Wu. His doctrines conformed to the laws of nature and were
in harmony with the physical environment. His doctrines were
like Heaven and earth, which embrace and support all things.
His doctrines were also like the successions of seasons and
alternations of the sun and the moon. All things are nourished
together without injuring one another; all courses are pursued
without collision. In minor matters virtue evolves like river
currents; in major matters virtue manifests itself in mighty
transformation. It is this which makes Heaven and earth so
great.

34. Only the greatest sage is possessed of perspicacity, discernment, wisdom, and prudence; so is he fitted for the rule
of the world; magnanimity, generosity, benignity, and mild-
ness; so is he fitted for the display of forbearance; initiative,
energy, fortitude, and determination; so is he fitted for the
exercise of leadership; sincerity, dignity, moderation, and
rectitude; so is he fitted for the command of respect; learning, reasoning, accuracy, and discretion; so is he fitted for the
exercise of judgment.

Like the deep and overflowing spring, these qualities are gushing unceasingly. Such a sage may be comparable to Heaven in its vastness and to the spring in its depth. His appearance evokes the reverence of the people, his words command their confidence, his actions rejoice their hearts.

Therefore his fame spreads over the extent of China and up to the barbarian tribes. Wherever reachable by ships and carriages, wherever penetrable by human efforts, wherever the sun and the moon shine, wherever frosts and dews fall, all beings who have blood and breath honor and love him. Hence it is said, "He is a peer to Heaven."

Only a man possessed of supreme sincerity can make the warp and woof of the great fabric of society, establish the great foundation of the world, and understand the transforming and nurturing processes of Heaven and earth. Can there be anything beyond himself on which he depends? His *jen*, how pervading! His depth, how unfathomable! His heavenliness, how overwhelming! Who can comprehend this unless he possess superior intelligence and sagely wisdom, unless he reaches out to the spiritual power of Heaven.

Chapter VI. Conclusion

35. In the *Shih* it is said:

> Over her brocade robe,
> She puts on a plain garment.

This is to show her dislike of the display of magnificence and colors. Hence the *Tao* of the *chün-tzu* is hidden and yet daily becomes illustrious, whereas the *Tao* of the *hsiao-jen* is ostentatious and yet daily falls into decay. The *Tao* of the *chün-tzu* seems to be inattentive and yet never to be repugnant, simple and yet elegant, gracious and yet discriminating. He knows how to distinguish what is distant and what is near, what is general and what is special, what is manifest and what is minute. Such a man can attain to virtue.

36. In the *Shih* it is said:

> Though the fish lie deep in water,
> They can still be clearly perceived.

Therefore the *chün-tzu* examines himself to see that his heart feels no regret and entertains no evil. That part of him that cannot be equaled lies in what other men cannot see.

37. In the *Shih* it is said:

> Be cautious in your own chamber;
> May you be shameless in seclusion!

Therefore the *chün-tzu* is respected when he does nothing; he is trusted when he is silent.

38. In the *Shih* it is said:

> In the ceremony, silence prevails—
> With no contention, but one concord.

Therefore the *chün-tzu* uses no rewards, and yet the people are encouraged to do good; he does not anger, and yet the people are awed as if they were threatened with hatchets and axes.

39. In the *Shih* it is said:

> Let him make no display of virtue,
> And the princes will follow him.

Therefore when the *chün-tzu* is sincere and reverential, the world will be at peace.

40. In the *Shih* it is said:

> I cherish your illustrious virtue,
> That has neither sound nor display.

The Master said: "Among the ways of transforming the people, sounds and displays are the least effective."

41. In the *Shih* it is said: "Virtue is as light as a hair." A hair, however, is comparable. And, again:

> The operation of Heaven
> Cannot be heard or smelled.

Such is the perfect virtue.

CONTENTS

◄§ INTRODUCTION

The *Hsiao Ching* is another important Confucian work. It has been traditionally ascribed to Tseng Tzu a paragon of filial piety, who was a disciple of Confucius. However, it was apparently a later compilation, though its content might have been gathered from the teachings of the Confucian school. During the Han period this brief work gained great popularity among the educated class and became an elementary text-book for all subsequent generations.

The book is in the form of a colloquy between Tseng Tzu and the Master. Confucius expounds the view that "filial piety is the basis of virtue and the source of culture." "The body and the limbs, the hair and the skin are given one by one's parents," said the Master, "and to them no injury should come. This is where filial piety begins. To maintain oneself and to practice the *Tao* is to immortalize one's name and thereby to glorify one's parents. This is where filial piety ends" [ch. 1].

An example of how Tseng Tzu tried to preserve his own body intact is illustrated in the *Lun Yü*: "When Tseng Tzu was very ill, he sent for his disciples and said: 'Uncover my feet, uncover my hands.' The *Odes* say:

> In fear and trembling,
> With caution and care,
> As if standing by a deep abyss,
> As if treading on thin ice.

My pupils, from now on I know I shall be free from injury to my person." However, Confucian teachings stress moral cultivation rather than the observance of ritual as the basis of filial piety. Hence filial piety, during the lifetime of one's parents, consists not only of giving them physical care, but also nourishing their wills; after their death, it consists not only of offering sacrifices to them and thinking about them, but also perpetuating their activities and carrying on their unfinished purposes. Thus filial piety becomes a living faith, awakening and kindling in men the sentiment necessary to make them follow the activities and purposes of their parents. This sentiment so permeated mourning and sacrificial rites [*li*] that the two were really one and operated together in the transmission of accumulated culture from one generation to another.*

Moreover, according to Confucius filial piety is not merely a domestic virtue; it diffuses its influence through all actions of life, whether moral, political, or social. It originates with the bonds of a common parentage and extends to other relationships until it reaches the stage of *jen*, love due to men. On the development of *jen*, Confucius said:

> A youth should be filial at home, and fraternal when abroad. He should be earnest and sincere, feeling an affection for all and a disposition toward *jen*.

The basic principles of filial piety are beautifully elaborated in this little book, which had great influence during the Han dynasty, as well as in the later ages, when all who were filial in the service of their parents were especially favored by the government.

~§ ఠ~

~§ THE HSIAO CHING

Chapter I: The General Theme

Chung-ni[1] was at leisure, and Tseng Tzu attended him. The Master said: "The early kings possessed the supreme virtue and the basic *Tao* for the regulation of the world. On account of this, the people lived in peace and harmony; neither superiors nor inferiors had any complaints. Do you know this?"

Tseng Tzu rose from his seat and said: "How can Sheng,[2] dull of intelligence, know this?"

The Master said: "Filial piety is the basis of virtue and the source of culture. Sit down again, and I will explain it to you. The body and the limbs, the hair and the skin, are given to

* See Ch'u Chai and Winberg Chai, *Changing Society of China* (New York, The New American Library, 1962), pp. 78-80.
1. I.e., Confucius' name, see p. 1.
2. I.e., Tseng Tzu's name: this was a courteous way of addressing seniors.

one by one's parents, and to them no injury should come; this is where filial piety begins. To establish oneself and practice the *Tao* is to immortalize one's name and thereby to glorify one's parents; this is where filial piety ends. Thus, filial piety commences with service to parents; it proceeds with service to the sovereign; it is completed by the establishment of one's own personality.

"In the *Shih* it is said:

> May you think of your ancestors,
> And so cultivate their virtues!"

Chapter II: The Son of Heaven

The Master said: "One who loves one's parents does not dare to hate others. One who reveres one's parents does not dare to spurn others. When love and reverence are thus cherished in the service of one's parents, one's moral influence transforms the people, and one becomes a pattern to all within the four seas. This is the filial piety of the Son of Heaven.

"In the *Fu Code*,[1] it is said:

> When the One Man has blessings,
> The millions of people rely on him."

Chapter III: The Feudal Princes

When the prince is not proud and arrogant, he will be secure in his position, however high it may be. When the prince is frugal and prudent, he will keep his wealth, however abundant it may be. When he secures himself in his high position, he will remain unimpaired in his dignity; when he keeps his abundant wealth, he will remain rich. And thus, preserving his wealth and dignity, he will be able to protect his country and pacify his people. This is the filial piety of feudal princes.

In the *Shih* it is said:

> In fear and trembling,
> With caution and care,
> As if standing by a deep abyss,
> As if treading on thin ice.

1. I.e., the Fu Code; see the *Shu Ching* [Book of History], Book VI, Part III, Section VIII.

Chapter IV: The High Officers

They do not presume to be in costume not prescribed by the early kings; they do not presume to use words not sanctioned by the early kings; they do not presume to act contrary to the virtuous conduct of the early kings. Thus, none of their words are contrary to sanctions, and none of their actions are not in accordance with the *Tao*. Their words are not improper; nor are their actions indecent. Their words spread over the world, and yet no fault is found in them. Their actions spread over the world, and yet no complaint is caused by them. When these three things are properly observed, they will be able to preserve their ancestral temples. This is the filial piety of high officers.

In the *Shih* it is said:

> Day and night, never slacken
> In the service of the One Man.

Chapter V: The Scholars

One serves one's mother in the same manner in which one serves one's father, and the love toward them is the same. One serves one's prince in the same manner in which one serves one's father, and the reverence toward them is the same. Thus, to the mother one shows love and to the prince one shows reverence, but to the father one shows both love and reverence. Therefore, to serve the prince with filial piety is to show loyalty; to serve the senior with reverence is to show obedience. Not failing in loyalty and obedience in the service of one's superiors, one will be able to preserve one's emolument and position and to carry on one's family sacrifices. This is the filial piety of scholars.

In the *Shih* it is said:

> Rise early and go to sleep late;
> Never disgrace those who bore you.

Chapter VI: The Common People

In order to support their parents, they follow the *Tao* of Heaven; they utilize the earth in accordance with the quality of its soil, and they are prudent and frugal in their expenditure. This is the filial piety of the common people.

Therefore, from the Son of Heaven down to the common

people, there has never been one on whom, if filial piety was not pursued from the beginning to end, disasters did not befall.

Chapter VII: The Trinity—Heaven, Earth, and Man

Tseng Tzu said: "How great is filial piety!" The Master said: "Filial piety is the basic principle of Heaven, the ultimate standard of earth, and the norm of conduct for the people. Men ought to abide by the guiding principle of Heaven and earth as the pattern of their lives, so that by the brightness of Heaven and the benefits of earth they would be able to keep all in the world in harmony and in unison. On this account, their teachings, though not stringent, are followed, and their government, though not rigorous, is well ordered. The early kings, knowing that their teachings could transform the people, made themselves an example of practicing all-embracing love; thereby the people did not neglect their parents. They expounded the virtuous and righteous conduct, and the people enthusiastically complied. They made of themselves an example of respectful and prudent behavior, and the people were not contentious. They guided themselves with *li* and music, and the people lived in concord. They verified the distinction between good and evil, and the people knew restraint.

"In the *Shih* it is said:

Oh, majestic Master Yin,
The people all look up to thee!"

Chapter VIII: Government by Filial Piety

The Master said: "Formerly the enlightened kings governed the world by filial piety. They did not dare to neglect the ministers of small states—to say nothing of the dukes, marquises, earls, viscounts, and barons! They thereby gained the good will of all the states to serve their early kings.

"Those who governed the states did not dare to ignore the w dows and widowers—to say nothing of scholars and the people! They thereby gained the good will of all the subjects to serve their former princes.

"Those who regulated their families did not dare to mistreat their servants and concubines—to say nothing of their wives and children! They thereby gained the good will of others who served their parents.

"Accordingly, while living, the parents enjoyed comfort; after their death, sacrifices were offered to their spirits. In this way the world was kept in peace; disasters did not arise, nor did riots occur. Such was the way in which the early enlightened governed the world by filial piety.

"In the *Shih* it is said:

> Glorious was his virtuous conduct,
> And all states submitted themselves."

Chapter IX: Government by the Sage

Tseng Tzu said: "I venture to ask whether in the virtue of the sage there is anything that surpasses filial piety."

The Master said: "It is the nature of Heaven and earth that man is the most honorable of all beings. Of all human conduct none is greater than filial piety. In filial piety nothing is greater than to revere one's father. In revering one's father, nothing is greater than making him a peer of Heaven. The Duke of Chou did this. Formerly the Duke of Chou sacrificed to Hou Chi[1] in the suburbs as the peer of Heaven. He sacrificed to King Wen [his father] at the Ming T'ang [Bright Temple] as the peer of Shang Ti [Supreme Being]. Therefore, all the feudal princes within the four seas came, each with his tribute, to join in the sacrifices. How can there be anything in the virtue of the sage that surpasses filial piety?

"Affection is fostered by parents during childhood, and from there springs the child's reverence, which grows daily, while sustaining his parents. The sage was to follow this innate development by teaching reverence and to follow this innate feeling of affection by teaching love. Thus, the teachings of the sage, though not stringent, were followed, and his government, though not rigorous, was well ordered. All this was brought about because of this innate disposition.

"The *Tao* of father and son is rooted in the Heaven-endowed nature, and develops into the equity between sovereign and ministers. Parents give one life; no bond is stronger. They bring up and care for their child; no kindness is greater. Therefore, one who does not love one's parents, but others, acts to the detriment of virtue. One who does not revere one's parents, but others, acts to. the detriment of *li*. Should the rules of conduct be modeled on such perversity, the people would have no true norm by which to abide. Therein is found

1. Hou Chi, reputed to have been a minister under Emperor Shun, was adopted by the House of Chou as its first ancestor.

no goodness but only evil. Although such a person may gain a high position, the *chün-tzu* will not esteem him.

"The *chün-tzu* is not like this. His speech is consistent with the *Tao*, his action with what is good. His virtuous equity is respected; his administration is commendable; his demeanor is pleasing; his movements are proper. In this way he governs the people, and therefore they look upon him with awe and love—make him their model and follow him. Thus he is able to realize his virtuous teachings and to carry out his edicts and orders.

"In the *Shih* it is said:

> The *chün-tzu* our princely lord—
> His fine demeanor is without fault."

Chapter X: The Practice of Filial Piety

The Master said: "In serving his parents, a filial son reveres them in daily life; he makes them happy while he nourishes them; he takes anxious care of them in sickness; he shows great sorrow over their death; and he sacrifices to them with solemnity. When he has performed these five duties, he has truly served his parents.

"He who really serves his parents will not be proud in a high position; he will not be rebellious in an inferior position; among the multitude he will not be contentious. To be proud in a high position is to be ruined; to be rebellious in an inferior position is to incur punishment; to be contentious among the multitude is to bring about violence. As long as these three evils are not discarded, a son cannot be called filial, even though he treats his parents daily with the three kinds of meat."[1]

Chapter XI: The Five Punishments

The Master said: "There are five punishments for three thousand offenses, and of these offenses there is no greater crime than lack of filial piety. To intimidate the sovereign is to defy a superior; to denounce the sage is to disregard the law; to decry filial piety is to not acknowledge parents. This is the way to great chaos."

Chapter XII: Illustration of the Basic Tao

The Master said: "There is nothing better than filial piety to teach the people love for one another. There is nothing

1. I.e., beef, lamb, and pork.

better than brotherly deference to teach the people propriety and prudence. There is nothing better than music to transform their manners and to change customs. There is nothing better than *li* to safeguard the sovereign and to govern the people.

"*Li* is but reverence. When the parents are revered, the son is pleased; when the elder brother is revered, the younger brother is pleased; when the sovereign is revered, the ministers are pleased; when the One Man is revered, the millions of men are pleased. Thus, those who are revered are few, but those who are pleased are many. This is said to be the 'basic *Tao*.' "

Chapter XIII: Illustration of the Supreme Virtue

The Master said: "The *chün-tzu* in teaching filial piety need not go daily to visit the families. He need only teach filial piety and he will show reverence due to all the fathers of the world. He need only teach brotherly deference and thereby show reverence due to all the elder brothers of the world. He need only teach the duties of ministers and thereby show reverence due to all the sovereigns of the world.

"In the *Shih* it is said:

> The princely man, cheerful and pleasant,
> Is the father and mother of the people!

"Without possessing the supreme virtue how can he keep the people in such harmony?"

Chapter XIV: Illustration of Perpetuating the Name

The Master said: "The *chün-tzu* serves his parents with filial piety; thus his loyalty can be transferred to his sovereign. He serves his elder brother with brotherly deference; thus his respect can be transferred to his superiors. He orders his family well; thus his good order can be transferred to his public administration.

"Therefore, when one cultivates one's conduct within oneself, one's name will be perpetuated for future generations."

Chapter XV: The Duty of Admonition

Tseng Tzu said: "I have heard about parental love, loving respect, cherishing care for parents, and making their name known. I venture to ask whether a son, by obeying every command of his father, can be called filial?"

The Master said: "What are you talking about? What are you talking about? In the old days, the Son of Heaven, who had seven ministers to admonish him, would not have lost his world, even if he were devoid of virtue. A state prince, who had five officers to admonish him, would not have lost his state, even if he were devoid of virtue. A minister, who had three assistants to admonish him, would not have lost his family, even if he were devoid of virtue.

"Thus, if a scholar has a friend to admonish him, he will not deviate from his good name. If a father has a son to admonish him, he will not commit gross wrong. In case of gross wrong, the son should never fail to admonish his father against it; nor should the minister fail to admonish his sovereign. Hence when there is gross wrong, there should be admonition. How can a son, by obeying the command of his father, be called filial?"

Chapter XVI: Influence and Effect

The Master said: "Formerly the enlightened kings were filial in the service of their fathers and thereby became enlightened in the service of Heaven. They were filial in the service of their mothers and thereby became discreet in the service of earth. When the young deferred to the elders, superiors governed inferiors well. When they were enlightened and discreet in the service of Heaven and earth, the blessings of spirits were manifest.

"Hence, even the Son of Heaven has someone to honor—his father. He has someone to respect—his elder brothers. He sacrifices at the ancestral temple, lest he forget his parents. He cultivates his person and acts with prudence, lest he disgrace his elders. He pays reverence, at the ancestral temples, to the spirits and ghosts, so as to enjoy their blessings. When his filial piety and brotherly deference reach perfection, he is endowed with divine enlightenment. His virtuous influence illuminates the four seas and penetrates far and wide.

"In the Shih it is said:

> From the west to the east,
> From the south to the north,
> None thought of not submitting."

Chapter XVII: Serving the Sovereign

The Master said: "In serving his sovereign, the *chün-tzu* endeavors to be utterly loyal when he is in office; he contemplates, in retirement, to remedy his shortcomings. Then he tries to conform to what is good in the sovereign, and to rectify what is wrong in him. In this way a mutual affection will be fostered between superiors and inferiors.

"In the *Shih* it is said:

> In my heart I love him,
> Why should I not tell it?
> I keep him in my heart,
> When shall I forget him?"

Chapter XVIII: Mourning for Parents

The Master said: "In mourning for his parents, a filial son weeps without wailing, he observes funeral rites without heeding his personal appearance, he speaks without regard for eloquence, he finds no comfort in fine clothing, he feels no joy on hearing music, he has no appetite for good food; all this is the innate expression of grief and sorrow. After three days, he breaks his fast, so as to teach the people that the dead should not hurt the living and that disfigurement should not destroy life; this is the rule of the sages. Mourning only extends to the period of three years, so as to show the people that sorrow comes to an end.

"The body, dressed in fine robes, is placed in the encased coffin. The sacrificial vessels are set out with grief and sorrow. Beating the breasts and stamping the feet, weeping and wailing, the mourners escort the coffin to the resting-place selected by divination. A shrine is built, and there offerings are made to the spirits. Spring and autumn sacrificial rites are performed, for the purpose of thinking about them at the proper season.

"When parents are alive, they are served with love and reverence; when they are dead, they are mourned with grief and sorrow. This is the performance of man's supreme duty, fulfillment of the mutual affection between the living and the dead, and the accomplishment of the filial son's service to his parents."

SEVEN: LI CHI (THE BOOK OF RITES)

CONTENTS

INTRODUCTION

Religion, politics, and ethics are the three stages in the development of ancient Chinese culture. Long before Confucius' time there already existed in China an unwritten code of rituals and etiquette, known as *li*, that governed the moral, social, and religious activities of the entire aristocratic world. During the Chou dynasty there were some *li* books, but they are now lost. There must have been many discrepancies between the written *li* of the Chou period and the unwritten *li* of past ages and also between the traditional *li* of different feudal states. During the course of time some reports were lost and some were incomplete. In view of this, Confucius made a study of the ancient *li* and discovered its real meaning, upholding it against some of the illegal practices of the time. Moreover, he brought the ancient *li* to the common people, one of his greatest contributions to Chinese civilization.

The *Li Chi* was one of three prominent treatises on the subject of *li* in ancient times; the other two were the *Chou Li*[1] and the *I Li*.[2] The *Li Chi* was compiled by Tai Te and his nephew Tai Sheng at the end of the last century B.C. Those sections in the *Li Chi* which deal with *li* and music are a definite development of Hsün Tzu's view, and if not actually taken from the *Hsün Tzu*, were probably written by the followers of Hsün Tzu at a later period. Its section entitled *Li-Yün* (Evolution of *Li*), dealing with the Confucian political and social philosophy, was definitely tinged with Taoist teachings. The *Li Chi* is divided into a large number of sections, the number varying with different editions. The number in the standard edition by Ch'eng Hao (1032-1085) is forty-nine, and much of its material is of post-Chou composition.

1. The *Chou Li*, or Book of Chou Ceremonies, dealing with the institutions of the Eastern Chou period, was written about the end of the Age of Warring States.
2. The *I Li*, or Book of Etiquette and Ceremony, is a factual record of the procedure of ceremonies as practiced in the early times, written after the time of Confucius.

⋖﹩ Selections from the *Li Chi*

Chapter I: Li-Yün (*The Evolution of* Li)

The ideal which Confucian scholars held highest was the Grand Unity (Ta-t'ung), as illustrated in this chapter of the *Li Chi*. According to this ideal, the world passes through three ages or stages of progress. The first stage is a world of disorder, the second is that of Minor Peace [*Hsiao-K'ang*], and the third that of "Grand Unity" based on the golden ages of antiquity, when sage-kings like Yao, Shun, Yü, and T'ang reigned. This ideal is indeed a beautiful vision, and has been of special importance in modern China. Both K'ang Yu-wei[1] and Sun Yat-sen[2] advocated this ideal, although they differed in their interpretation.

⋖﹩ ﹩⋗

Once Chung-ni [i.e., Confucius] took part in the winter sacrifice. After the ceremony was over, he strolled on the top of the city gate and sighed. He sighed for the State of Lu.

Yen Yen [i.e., Tzu You], by his side, said: "Why should the *chün-tzu* sigh?"

Confucius said: "The practice of the Great *Tao* and the eminent men of the Three Dynasties—this I have never seen in person, and yet I have a mind to follow them. When the Great *Tao* prevailed, the world was a commonwealth; men of talent and virtue were selected, mutual confidence was emphasized, and brotherhood was cultivated. Therefore, men did not regard as parents only their own parents, nor did they treat as sons only their own sons. Old people were able to enjoy their old age; young men were able to employ their talents; juniors respected their elders; helpless widows, orphans, and cripples were well cared for. Men had their respective occupations, and women their homes. They hated to see wealth lying about in waste, and they did not hoard it for their own use. They hated not to use their energies, and

1. See Ch'u Chai and Winberg Chai, *The Changing Society of China* (New York, The New American Library, 1962), ch. XVI.
2. See *ibid.*, ch. XVII. See also K'ang Yu-wei's *Ta T'ung Shu* (*The One-World Philosophy*), translated by Laurence G. Thompson (London, George Allen & Unwin, Ltd., 1958).

they used their energies not for their own benefit. Thus evil schemings were repressed, and robbers, thieves, and traitors no longer appeared, so that the front door remained open. This was called *Ta-tung* [Grand Unity].

"Now the Great *Tao* has fallen into obscurity, and the world is in the possession of families. Each regards as parents only his own parents and treats as sons only his own sons; wealth and labor are employed for selfish purpose. The sovereigns take it as the proper *li* that their states should be hereditary; they endeavor to make their cities and suburbs strong, their ditches and moats secure. *Li* and *yi* are used as the norms to regulate the relationship between ruler and subject, to insure affection between father and son, harmony between brothers, and concord between husband and wife; to set up institutions, organize farms and hamlets, honor the brave and the wise, and bring merit to the individual. Hence schemes and plottings come about, and men take up arms.

"It was in this way that Emperor Yü, Kings T'ang, Wen, Wu, Ch'eng, and the Duke of Chou achieved eminence: all these six noble men paid attention to *li*, and made manifest their *yi* and acted in good faith. They exposed their errors, made *jen* their law and prudence their practice, thus showing the people wherein they should constantly abide. If there were any who did not follow these principles, he would lose power and position and be regarded by the multitude as dangerous. This is called *Hsiao-K'ang* [Minor Peace]."

This theory of historical progress, as set forth in terms of the Three Ages, is also found in the Kung-yang commentary on the *Ch'un-Ch'iu* (*Spring and Autumn Annals*) and in the writings of the Han scholars, particularly Tung Chung-shu (cf. 8). The modern scholar K'ang Yu-wei (1858-1927), the leader of the notable reform movement of 1898, revived this theory, interpreting it to mean that "Confucius was born in the Age of Disorder. Now communications extend throughout the earth, and changes have taken place in Europe and America; this is to show that the world is evolving toward the Age of Approaching Peace. . . . There will be no national barriers, no racial distinctions, and basic customs will be everywhere the same. With this uniformity will come the Age of Great Peace. Confucius knew all these things beforehand." See his *Lun-yü Chu*, or *Commentary to the Analects, Chüan* 2.

Chapter II: Rites (Li) and Music (Yüeh)

It was earlier learned that in Chinese humanism, *li* and music are very important institutions for the regulation of man's conduct and emotion. The following passages are taken from Chapter XIX *Yüeh Chi* (Record of Music) of the *Li Chi*, to illustrate the theory of music and ritual as developed in the *Hsün Tzu*.

కోఁ ఏఁ

Musical tones arise from the heart when it is moved by external things. The heart, being moved by external things, finds expression in movements and breaks out in sound. These sounds respond to each other and produce various modulations. These modulations are composed and become tones. When these tones are played on instruments and accompanied by the dance, either with the shields and axes or with the feathers and pennants, they are music.

Music is produced by tones and based on the response of the heart to external things. Hence when the heart is moved to sorrow, the sound is sharp and fading away; when to happiness, it is broad and slow; when to joy, it is exultant and unrestrained; when to anger, it is coarse and fierce; when to reverence, it is direct and austere; when to love, it is harmonious and soft. These six types of sounds are not of man's nature but are produced by the response to external things. Therefore the early kings were careful about that which might affect the heart. They instituted *li* to guide the mind and music to harmonize the sound, the government to unify the actions, and penalties to restrain the evils. Thus *li*, music, government, and penalties are instituted in accordance with the same ultimate principle, and they are in accord with man's heart and act as regulators.

Tones arise from the heart, and the heart, being affected, breaks out into sound. When the sound is composed, it becomes music. The music of a well-governed state is peaceful and joyous, and its government is in harmony; the music of an ill-governed state is full of resentment and anger, and its government is in confusion; the music of a decaying state is mournful and retrospective, and its people are in distress. The ways of music and of government are closely related. . . .

Tones arise from man's heart, and music is related to man's morality. Those who know only sound but not its tones are birds and beasts; those who know the tone but not its music are the multitude. It is only the *chün-tzu* who can know music. On this account, to examine the sound is to know its tones, to examine the tone is to know its music, and to examine its music is to know the government; thereby can the way of government become complete. Thus one who does not know the sound cannot speak of the tone, nor can one who does not know the tone speak of music. To know music is to be versed in *li*. One who knows music and is versed in *li* is said to possess virtue; virtue is but music and *li*. . . .

Therefore, the early kings, when they instituted *li* and music, did not do so to gain full satisfaction for the desires of the mouth, stomach, ears, and eyes. They intended to teach the people to moderate their likes and dislikes, and thus to turn them back to the norm of humanity.

Man is still at birth; this is his nature given by Heaven. He is active when acted upon by external things; this is the desire of his nature. He comes to know external things, and likes and dislikes arise. If these likes and dislikes are not regulated within himself and his undertaking is allured by the external world, then he cannot return to his true self, and thereby his Heavenly reason will be extinguished. When man is acted upon by external things without limit, and there is no regulation of his likes and dislikes, he will be transformed by contact with external objects. When he is thus transformed, he will extinguish his Heavenly reason and give utmost indulgence to human desires. As a result, his heart will turn to revolt and deception, and his actions will become dissolute and rebellious. Then the strong will coerce the weak; the many will oppress the few. The wise will deceive the ignorant; the brave will tyrannize the timid. The sick will be untended; the aged and the young, the orphaned and the solitary will find no place. This is the way to great disorder.

Therefore the early kings instituted *li* and music to regulate man's conduct. The ritual of wearing sackcloth and wailing is the means by which mourning can be regulated; bells and drums and dances with shields and axes are the means by which ease and joy can be moderated; the ritual of marriage and capping is the means by which male and female can be distinguished; the ritual of the archery contest and the feast is the means by which social intercourse can be rectified. *Li* is to regulate man's heart; music is to harmonize man's sound; government is to carry this out; penalties are to guard against its violation. When *li*, music, government, and penalties are practiced without irregularity and collision, the kingly rule is complete.

Music leads to common union; *li* leads to distinction. From common union comes mutual affection; from distinction, mutual respect. When music predominates, there is weak coalescence; where *li* predominates, a tendency to separation. It is the business of both—*li* and music—to harmonize man's feelings and give elegance to his outward manifestations. When *li* and *yi* are established, there is a distinction between the noble and the mean. When music and elegance are united, there is harmony between the superior and the inferior. When good and evil are distinguished, there is a difference between the worthy and the unworthy. When outlaws are restrained by penalties and men of worth are promoted to high ranks, then the government will be fair and just. To love the people with *jen,* and to rectify them with *yi;* thereby can the government by the people prevail.

Music comes from within, and *li* acts from without. Music, coming from within, produces the serenity [of the mind], while *li*, acting from without, produces the elegance [of manner]. Great music must be easy; great *li* must be simple. When music attains its full result, there will be no resentment; when *li* attains its full result, there will be no contention. When the world is governed by bowing and courtesy, it is, in fact, governed by *li* and music. Lawless people do not appear; feudal lords are courteously submissive; arms and armors are not practiced; the five penalties are not used. On this account, the effects of music are realized. The affections of father and son are harmonized; the ranks between seniors and juniors are distinguished; then reverence prevails within the four seas. On this account, the Son of Heaven practices *li*.

Great music accords with the harmony of Heaven and earth; great *li* accords with their regulation. Through harmony all things are in order; through regulation, sacrifice to Heaven and worship of earth is performed. When there is distinction, *li* and music exist; when there is obscurity, there are ghosts and spirits. This being so, both reverence and love prevail within the four seas. *Li*, though varied, accords with reverence; music, though varied in elegance, accords with love. Since *li* and music are the same in expression, the enlightened kings institute *li* in accordance with occasions, and music in accordance with achievements.

.   .   .

Music is the harmony of Heaven and earth; *li* is the order of Heaven and earth. Through harmony all things are transformed; through order all things are distinguished. Music arises from Heaven; *li* is patterned after earth. That which overlaps its pattern is in confusion; that which is overdone is violent. When one understands the functions of Heaven and earth, then only can one institute *li* and music.

.   .   .

High in Heaven and below on the earth all things are scattered and diverse. In accordance with this pattern, *li* is instituted. Things flow forth unceasingly; they act in unison and yet are transformed. In accordance with this principle, music arises. In spring all things burst forth, and in summer all things grow; this is *jen*. In autumn all things consummate, and in winter all things repose; this is *yi*. *Jen* is akin to music, and *yi* is akin to *li*. Music establishes union and harmony, and so it accords with *Shen* [Spirits][1] and follows the pattern of Heaven. *Li* maintains difference and distinction, and so it accords with *Kuei* [Ghosts][2] and follows the pattern of earth. Therefore the sage creates music in response to Heaven and institutes *li* to match earth. When *li* and music are distinct and complete, Heaven and earth function in perfect order.

Heaven is honorable, earth is lowly; so are the positions of the sovereign and subjects fixed. Just as the depths and heights are manifest, so the noble and low positions are determined. Just as movement and repose are constantly regulated, so the small and the big are differentiated. The border peoples are grouped according to their tribes, and things are classified according to their kinds. Their innate nature and qualities are not the same. In Heaven they take natural forms, and on earth they acquire physical bodies. Thus, *li* maintains the distinction between Heaven and earth.

The *ch'i*[3] of the earth ascends on high, and that of Heaven descends below. The *yin* and the *yang* act upon one another;

1. According to metaphysical speculation, man is composed of two primary elements: *Yin* (Negative) from which he derives *Ch'i Po* (the seven Emotions), and *Yang* (Positive) from which he derives *San Hun* (the Three Spiritual Energies). The *Ch'i P'o*, on his death, descends to the earth and becomes his *Kuei* (ghost), while the *San Hun* on his death ascends to heaven and becomes his *Shen* (spirit).

2. *Ibid.*

3. The word *ch'i*, which may be translated as vital force, plays an important part in Chinese cosmological and metaphysical thought. Here it may mean the air or ether.

Heaven and earth agitate each other. They are drummed by thunder and lightning; they are animated by wind and rain; they are moved by the four seasons; and they are warmed by the sun and moon. In this way, all transformations are brought about. Since this is so, music maintains the harmony of Heaven and earth.

Transformations that are not timely do not operate, and no distinction between male and female results in riot; this is the nature of Heaven and earth.

When we think how *li* and music reach the height of Heaven and embrace the earth, how they prevail in the *yin* and the *yang*, and how they come into contact with spirits and ghosts, we must admit their height as the highest, their distance as the farthest, their depth as the deepest, and their breadth as the broadest. Music manifests Heaven and so knows the Grand Beginning. *Li* prevails on earth and so brings about accomplishments. Heaven manifests itself without ceasing; earth is what manifests itself without moving. Thus what happens in Heaven and on earth is but the interaction of movement and stillness. Hence the sage says: "*Li* and music are interrelated."

Chapter III: Theory of Education

There is a wealth of educational doctrine in the Chinese humanistic writings which deserves to be better known and understood by Occidental students. The following passages taken from the *Hsüeh Chi* (Record of Learning), which forms Section XVIII of the *Li Chi*, offer a good illustration, particularly with regard to high ideals or the worth of learning.

If one devotes oneself to conforming to legal measures and seeks the righteous and the virtuous, one will gain some reputation, but it will not be sufficient to move the multitude. If one seeks the company of the worthy and has concern for those who are not relatives, one's reputation will be sufficient to move the multitude, but not sufficient to transform the people. If the *chün-tzu* wishes to transform the people and perfect their manners, must he not begin with learning?

If jade is not cut it cannot become an article. If a man does not study he cannot know the *Tao*. The ancient kings, in order to build up the country and govern the people, first stressed teaching and learning. In the *Mandates* of Yüeh III [Section XIV of the *Shu Ching*] it is said:

> Remember the end and aim of learning,
> While you are constantly engaged in it.

This is what is meant here.

Although there is good food, if one does not eat, one will not know its flavor. Although there is a supreme *Tao*, if one does not learn it, one will not know its goodness. After learning, one knows one's deficiencies; after teaching, one knows its difficulties. When one knows one's deficiencies, one will strive to learn by oneself. When one knows the difficulties of teaching, one will exert oneself to overcome them. Therefore it is said, "Teaching and learning develop together." In the *Mandates* of Yüeh III, it is said, "Teaching and learning are each half." This expresses what is meant here.

In the ancient [system of] education, there were *shuo* [schools] for those at home, *hsiang* [academies] in villages, *hsü* [colleges] in counties, and a *hsüeh* [university] in the capital.[1] Every year there were youths who entered the imperial institution [*hsüeh*], and every other year they would be examined; in the first year to test whether they could read the classics and clarify their minds; in the third year, whether they were diligent in their studies and friendly to others; in the fifth year, whether they studied extensively and felt affection for their teachers; and in the seventh year, whether they obtained profound learning and made a good choice of friends; all these were called the "preliminary accomplishments." In the ninth year, they were well versed in their learning and very firm in their purposes; this was called the "great accomplishment."

Only having made this great accomplishment, can one be expected to transform the people and perfect their manners, so that those who are near are pleased, and those who are far away are cherished; this is the *Tao* of *Ta-hsüeh* ["great learning"; i.e., the imperial institution]. In the *Record*, it is said, "A tiny insect is constantly learning." Does this express what is meant here?

When the youths begin to receive their *Ta-hsüeh*, the Chan-

---

1. The terms *shuo, hsiang, hsü,* and *hsüeh* used for different educational institutions were common in the Chou period. For these terms we find no better names than "school," "academy," "college," and "university." But in fact the use of these modern names seem somewhat questionable in discussing the educational institutions in the Chou period.

cellor, dressed in a fur-lined costume, leads them to worship the early teachers, in order to teach them respect. During the worship, they will sing the festal odes, in order to acquaint themselves with official etiquette. On their coming, the Grand Master beats the drum and opens up their bookcases, in order to orient them to their studies. The discipline-rods are exhibited, in order to restrain their arrogance. Before they see the Grand Sacrifice, they do not study its rituals, in order not to constrain their purposes. They observe the seasonal sacrifices without speaking, in order to preserve their minds. The juniors listen without asking questions, in order not to overlap their studies. All these seven items are the great principles of teaching. In the *Record*, it is said, "In education, one learns to fulfill one's duties as an official, and to cherish one's purpose as a scholar." Does this express what is meant here?

This is the *Ta-hsüeh* education: instruction given during the four seasons must accord with their proper occupations; studies must continue in retirement. If one does not study every kind of lute, one cannot play its strings with ease. If one does not study all subjects, one cannot write poetry with ease. If one does not study all types of costumes, one cannot practice one's rituals with ease. If one is not interested in these arts, one cannot love one's studies. Hence the *chün-tzu's* studies continue in his retirement, in his self-cultivation, in his recreation, and in his exercise. Having done so, he is satisfied with his studies and feels affection for his teacher. He is fond of his friend and has faith in his *Tao*. Although he is not guided by his teacher, he will not act contrary to him. In the *Mandates* of Yüeh III, it is said:

> Be studious and constantly exert yourself,
> And accomplishment will come to you.

Does this express what is meant here?

But the teachers nowadays mutter over the simple lessons, ask too many questions, and talk too much; without regard to the ability of the students, they push them forward. They do not have enough sincerity to direct the students, nor do they give their efforts to teach them. What they teach is absurd; what the students seek is detrimental to themselves. They avoid their studies and hate their teachers. Their bitter efforts are not rewarded with advantage. Although they finish their education, what they have learned soon fades away. Is this the reason why teaching does not bring about any result?

The *Ta-Hsüeh* method is as follows: to suppress what has not yet emerged is called "prevention"; to present what is opportune is called "timeliness"; not to transgress what is proper is called "conformity"; to observe each other and follow what is good is called "imitation." These four methods are accountable for the success of teaching.

On the other hand, to suppress what has broken out will arouse opposition which cannot be overcome; to study what is not opportune calls for bitter efforts which do not bring about any result; to teach what is improper will result in confusion not cultivation; to study alone and have no companions will cause one to lead a solitary life with little learning; to feast friends in defiance of teachers and to associate with evil companions is to the detriment of study. These six things are accountable for the failure of teaching.

The *chün-tzu*, when he knows the causes of the success of teaching, as well as the causes of its failure, is suitable to be a teacher. In his teaching he leads without coercion; he develops without suppression, he opens the way without interference. Leading without coercion produces harmony. Developing without suppression produces ease. Opening the way without interference produces contemplation. Harmony, ease, and contemplation characterize good teaching.

In learning there are four causes of failure, which a teacher should know: men's learning may fail because of learning too much or because of learning too little; it may fail because the study is too easy or because it is too difficult. In these four respects, men's minds are not alike. If the teacher knows men's minds he will be able to remedy their failures. Teaching is to develop what is good in men and to remedy their failures.

The good singer makes others follow his voice. The good teacher makes the students follow his will. His words are simple but expressive, low but firm, with few examples but instructive. In this way he makes the students follow his will.

When the *chün-tzu* knows what is difficult in learning and what is easy, when he knows what is beautiful and what is ugly, he is then able to teach with comprehensive illustrations. When he can teach in this manner, he is qualified to be a teacher. After he has become a teacher, he is qualified to be an official. After he has become an official, he is qualified to be a sovereign. Thus, from teaching one learns how to become a sovereign. For this reason care must be exercised in selecting teachers. In the *Record* it is said: "The good rule of the Three Kings and Four Dynasties was due to their teachers." Does this express what is meant here?

In the *Tao* of learning a strict teacher is hard to secure. If the teacher is strict, the *Tao* will be honored. If the *Tao* is honored, then the people will respect learning. For this reason there are two cases in which the sovereign will not treat his ministers as ministers. When one impersonates one's ancestor in worshipping,[2] one will not be treated as a minister. When one serves as the imperial teacher, one will not be treated as a minister. Thus when he is received in audience by the emperor, he does not stand facing the throne [as is required of ministers]. This is the way in which the teacher is honored.

In the case of the good student, the teacher's task is easy and the results are doubled. The student proceeds to elaborating his learning. In the case of the dull student, although the teacher exerts himself, the results are halved. Moreover, the student makes complaints. The good teacher who asks questions is like one working with hard wood. He first works on easy parts and then turns to the knotty sections. After a time, the teacher and the student discuss and explain together. The teacher who is not good at asking questions is the opposite of this. The good teacher who answers questions is like one striking a bell. If it is struck with a light blow, the tone is small; if it is struck with a heavy blow, the tone is large. So the teacher waits till he is asked to answer questions. He who is not good at asking questions is the opposite of this. This is the *Tao* of learning which makes progress.

He who merely asks questions from memory is not qualified to be a teacher. Should he wait for the students' questions? Yes, but if the students have no questions to ask, then he will explain. After he has explained and the students are still not able to understand, then he may drop the matter. The son of a good founder must learn to become a furrier; the son of a good bow-maker must learn to become a basket-weaver; when a horse is first harnessed to a cart, the cart is reversely placed in front of the horse. The *chün-tzu* takes note of these three instances, and then he may devote himself to learning.

The students of ancient times compared things and traced their resemblances. For instance, the drum does not sound the five notes, but without the drum those five notes cannot be synchronized. Water has none of the five colors, but without

---

2. The ancient cult of ancestor worship required that one of the sons impersonate the deceased, so that when they worshipped the dead he would seem to see the dead in the place. Later the spirit tablet or portrait was used.

water those five colors cannot be displayed. Learning does not belong to the five senses, but without learning those five senses cannot be controlled. The teacher is not included in the five relationships, but without the teacher, those five relationships cannot be affiliated with affection.

The *chün-tzu* says: "The great virtue is fitted not merely to one position. The great *Tao* is practiced not merely in one place. The great faith is carried out not merely at the last moment. The great season does not prevail uniformly throughout the year. One who takes note of these four things may devote himself to the fundamentals."

In offering sacrifices to the water-god, the Three Kings went first to the river and then to the sea, for the river is the source of the sea and the sea is formed of rivers. This expresses that which is called devoting oneself to the fundamentals.

CONTENTS

CONTENTS

చ్రీ **INTRODUCTION**

During the Ch'in-Han period (about the 3rd century B.C.), Chinese philosophy, particularly Humanism (Confucianism), suffered a decline in vitality and appeal. In a sense, this period, with its stress on unity both in the intellectual and political spheres, was an inevitable reaction to the wide freedom of the late Chou period, as characterized by the "hundred schools." And it was in the spirit of this reaction that the Ch'in emperor, Shih Huang Ti, sought to control thought by the notorious decree for burning all writings of the "hundred schools," with the exception of works on medicine, divination, and agriculture.

While agreeing with the Ch'in dynasty's basic goal of homogeneity, the succeeding Han dynasty (206 B.C.-A.D. 220) disapproved of harsh measures such as those exercised by Shih Huang Ti. In the year 136 B.C., Tung Chung-shu (c. 179-104 B.C.), the greatest of the early Han scholars, proposed to the emperor Hsiao-ching (156-141 B.C.) that unity be sought by new means—by the elevation of Confucianism at the expense of the other schools of thought. As soon as the other philosophers were expelled from the Board of Eruditi, the Confucian scholars, under the leadership of Tung Chung-shu, reorganized it into five faculties, each specializing in one of the five Confucian classics: namely, the *Shu Ching*, the *Shih Ching*, the *Yi Ching* (Book of Change), the *Li Chi*, and the *Ch'un-Ch'iu* (Spring and Autumn Annal). Another important measure in promoting the teachings of Confucius was the introduction of an examination system based on the Five Classics.

But the Confucianism expounded by Tung Chung-shu and adopted by the early Han period was something quite different from that originally set forth by the Sage and his immediate followers. Han Confucianism was tinged by ideas of the rival schools, especially Taoism (Naturalism). Mohism (teachings of Mo Tzu) had not survived the "Ch'in fire," and Legalism, as typified by the writings of Han Fei, had fallen into disgrace, even though elements of its political theory lingered on in the thinking of the ruling class. Taoism, however, had become influential in government circles to the extent that the *wu wei* doctrine, which is essentially a laissez-faire theory, was adopted as state policy and that Taoist occultism became an often-held personal creed. This fact determined the general character of Han Confucianism.

The writings of Tung Chung-shu as set forth in his *Ch'un Ch'iu Fan-lu* or *The Copious Dew in Spring and Autumn*[1] show a distinct leaning toward the supernatural ideas of the Yin-yang School.[2] For instance, in his work he gave a fantastic interpretation of Confucius' *Ch'un Ch'iu*, in accordance with the prevalent doctrines of the Kung-yang School.[3] In the interpretation of these doctrines, he made an ingenious discovery of a formula—"to subject the people to the ruler, and the ruler to Heaven"—that acted wonderfully as a check on the absolute sway of the monarch.

Here we should note that since the death of Confucius, Confucianism has undergone several stages of theoretical development. The first stage was reached shortly before the Ch'in dynasty, when Mencius and Hsün Tzu established two rival schools of thought and developed Confucius' teaching in two directions.[4] The second stage culminated with Tung Chung-shu and other Kung-yang scholars. And the third stage was brought about by the Neo-Confucianists of the Sung dynasty,[5] when the elements of Taoism and Buddhism were appropriated to give Confucianism a philosophical refinement hitherto unknown. Because of the limitation of space, the

1. His biography in *Ch'ien Han Shu* or *History of the Early Han Dynasty* reads: ". . . Chung-shu's writings all served to elucidate the meaning of the classics. His writings, in the form of petitions to the emperor, totaled about 123 sections. Moreover, his exposition about the success and failure of the events as recorded in the *Ch'un Ch'iu*, . . . amounted to several additional tens of sections, consisting of more than 100,000 words. These were all transmitted to later generations."
2. The Yin-yang school, an offshoot of the Taoist, was so called because its members believed in the existence of *yin* (female) and *yang* (male) as two cosmic principles, in whose reactions all creations were produced. It was also called the Five-Elements School, because it taught the fantastic theory that each period of history was dominated by one of the five elements —namely, earth, wood, metal, fire, and water.
3. Within the ranks of the Han scholars there raged a bitter controversy over the interpretation of the classics and the three commentaries of *Ch'un Ch'iu* by Kung-yang Kao, Ku-laing Ch'ih, and Tso Ch'iu-ming, all products of the Warring States period. Among the three, the Kung-yang Commentary, in particular, interprets the *Ch'un Ch'iu* in agreement with the theories of Tung Chung-shu.
4. Hsün Tzu attached importance to legal institutions and the royal authority as means to attain human purposes, whereas Mencius championed the cause of the people.
5. Neo-Confucianism began in the eighth century, flourished vigorously in the eleventh and twelfth centuries, and produced notable interpreters and critics down to recent times.

writings of Neo-Confucianists will not be included in this volume.

The following passages taken from Tung's *Ch'un Ch'iu Fan-lu* are selected to show his theory of human nature, his philosophy of history, and his "science of catastrophes and anomalies."

✎ SELECTIONS FROM THE CH'UN CH'IU FAN-LU

Chapter I. Human Nature

The opening sentence of the *Chung-Yung* offers a good illustration of the broad meaning of the term "nature" (*hsing*):

That which Heaven confers is called man's nature. Much controversy arose in the past among the Confucians as to the moral quality of human nature. Mencius was the first who distinctly propounded the doctrine that the nature of man inclines him to goodness and kindness as surely as the nature of water compels it to flow downward. In direct opposition to Mencius was Hsün Tzu, who took the position that man is born with a nature inclined toward evil. Tung Chung-shu seemed to suggest an ethical criteria based on a compromise between the views of Mencius and Hsün Tzu. He agreed with Mencius that man's "innate quality" contains the beginnings of goodness, but he thought that these "beginnings" are not, in themselves, sufficient evidence that man's nature itself is good, for man's "innate quality" contains not merely his nature, but also his feelings. Thus he argued:

If one says that man's nature is good, then what about man's feelings?

He compared man's nature and feelings with the *yin* and *yang* of Heaven. "To speak of man's 'innate quality' and exclude from this his feelings is like speaking of Heaven's *yang* while excluding its *yin*."

From *Ch'un Ch'iu Fan-lu*, Section 35

✎ ❧

In this age the people are quite ignorant about the nature of man; they fail to agree. Why do they not go back to the word *hsing* itself? Does not the word *hsing* mean *sheng* [birth]?[1] The qualities endowed spontaneously at birth are called man's nature. *Hsing* constitutes man's "innate quality" [chih]. Now can the word "good" be applied to the "innate quality" in man's nature? No, it cannot. How is it possible to speak of the "innate quality" as good? *Hsing* cannot differ from the "innate quality." If it did, it would not be man's nature. This should be clearly understood. The *Ch'un Ch'iu* examines the principles of things and rectifies their names. It applies names to things as they are without making mistakes. . . . It is for the Sage to rectify the names. [As Confucius said:] "*Chün-tzu*, in what he says, leaves nothing that is remiss." . . .

Now that which confines all the evils within and prevents them from being revealed is the mind. Therefore, the mind is known as the confiner. Unless there are evils that touch man's innate quality, what need is there for the mind to act as a confiner? The word "mind" may be regarded as expressing a real feature in man. Truly, there exists in man both *jen* and *t'an* [covetousness], each of which lies within the "self" which he receives from Heaven. As Heaven has its dual manifestations of the *yin* and the *yang*, the "self" has the dual qualities of *t'an* and *jen*. As Heaven has restraints for the *yin* and the *yang*, the "self" has its confiner of feelings and desires; in this sense, man is at one with the course of Heaven. In the same sense, the *yin* in its operation should concern itself with spring and summer, and the moon, when it is full, will always be obscured by the sun's light, sometimes completely and sometimes partially. Such is the way in which Heaven restrains the *yin*. Since this is so, why should one not diminish one's desires and check one's feelings, in order thus to conform with Heaven? The self restrains what Heaven wishes to be restrained. This is what is meant by saying that man's self is Heaven, so that it restrains what Heaven wishes to be restrained and does not run counter to Heaven. It must be noted that if man's nature from Heaven does not undergo training, it shall never be able to act as a confiner. If we examine actuality to give names, when there has been no training, on what ground can man's nature be so identified [as good]?

· · ·

Therefore man's nature may be compared to growing grain, and goodness to its kernel. Though the kernel is produced

---

1. The *hsing* ideograph is composed of *sheng* [birth] and *hsin* [heart].

from the grain, yet all growing grain does not necessarily produce kernels. Similarly, though goodness comes from man's nature, yet man's nature does not necessarily become good. Both the kernel and goodness are brought to completion when man continues Heaven's work in its external sphere; they are not actually existent in what Heaven itself has produced. Heaven does produce to a certain degree and then stops. What has been produced thus far is "heavenly nature"; what is beyond this point is "man's work." Man's work is outside man's nature, and yet man's nature is inevitably brought to the practice of virtue. . . .

Man's nature may be compared to the eyes. In sleep the eyes are shut and there is darkness; they wait for awakening before they can see. So long as awakening has not come, it may be said that the eyes have the innate disposition to see, but it cannot be said that they actually see. Now take the nature of all people into consideration, . . . and what is to be made of it? Some say that man's nature contains the beginnings of goodness, and the mind contains the innate quality of goodness. If this is so, how can the nature itself be not good? I reply that this is not so. The silk cocoon contains silk fibers, but it is not silk. The egg contains the chick, but it is not a chick. These analogies leave no more doubts. Heaven gives life to man in accordance with its great principle, and those who speak of man's nature should not differ from each other. Yet there are some who say that it is good, and others who say it is not good. This is because when they thus speak of goodness, they each mean something different by it. Inasmuch as nature contains the beginnings of goodness, the child's love for its parents is superior to that of the birds and beasts and may be called goodness. This is what Mencius means by it. However, it may also be defined as conformity to the Three Bonds and Five Laws,[2] comprehension of the Eight Beginnings,[3] and the practice of loyalty and good faith, all-embracing love, generosity, and love of *li*. These comprise the goodness of the sages, and so Confucius said: "It is not for me to see a good man." "Could I see a man of constant purpose I would be content."

2. The Three Bonds are those relating to the relationships between ruler and subject, father and son, husband and wife. The Five Laws have not been defined.
3. The Eight Beginnings are not very clear, and Mencius speaks only of four beginnings—the feelings of compassion, shame, modesty, and discrimination between right and wrong.

In fact, what the Sage called goodness is not easy to match. It is not the sort of goodness that may be called goodness merely because we are better than the birds and beasts. . . . Just as being better than the birds and beasts is not considered goodness, so too, being wiser than the plants and trees cannot be regarded as wisdom. Man's nature is better than that of birds and beasts, but may not be regarded as good. The word "wisdom" is derived from the word "sageness." What the Sage commanded is accepted by the world as correct. Just as the course of day and night depends on the polar star, so the solution of doubts and suspicions depends upon the Sage. According to the Sage, the age without a king and men without training are not equal to goodness. Such is the difficulty of matching goodness. It is too much to say that the nature of all people is equal to goodness. If compared with the nature of birds and beasts, man's nature is indeed good; but if compared with the goodness of his *Tao*, it certainly falls short. We may grant that his nature is better than that of birds and beasts, but not that which the Sage speaks of as his goodness. The innate quality which I maintain to be his nature is different from that of Mencius. Mencius thinks of the innate lowliness of the doings of birds and beasts, and therefore he says that man's nature is good. I think of the innate nobility of the doings of the sages, and therefore I say that man's nature is not good. Goodness transcends man's nature, just as the Sage transcends goodness. The *Ch'un Ch'iu* is concerned with the great origin. Hence it is careful in the rectification of names. If a name does not come from its proper origin, how can we say whether man's nature is good or evil?

. . .

What Heaven and earth confer at birth is called man's nature and his feelings: the two together constitute the whole. . . . If one says that man's nature is good, then what about his feelings? Man's self has the nature and the feelings, just as Heaven has the *yin* and the *yang*. To speak of man's "innate quality" and exclude his feelings is like speaking of Heaven's *yang* while excluding its *yin*, but there is no time for an elaborate discussion of that. That which is called man's nature does not refer to that of the highest level or that of the lowest level, but is that of the average man. The nature [of the average man] is like a silk cocoon or an egg. An egg, awaiting the change, can become the chick; a silk cocoon, awaiting the winding, can become silk thread. Man's nature, awaiting instruction and precept, can become good.

Chapter II. Philosophy of History

Tung Chung-shu modified the theory of the Five Elements School[1] by maintaining that the succession of dynasties does not accord with the movements of the Five Elements, but with a sequence of what he called the "Three Reigns" (San T'ung), also known as the "Three Beginnings" (San Cheng): the Black, White, and Red Reigns. Each had its own system of government and each dynasty represented one Reign. On the basis of the theory of the "Three Reigns," Tung Chung-shu interpreted the *Ch'un Ch'iu* to illustrate the "three ages of social progress."

From *Ch'un Ch'iu Fan-lu*, Sections 1 and 23

ৰ্জ্ঞ ৡৢ

1. THE THREE REIGNS

Of the Three Reigns, the Black Reign comes first. On the first day of the first moon, the sun and new moon stand in the constellation of the *Ying-Shih* [Barracks] and the *Tou* Star [Big Dipper] stands in the *yin* point of time [third of the twelve "earthly branches"]. Heaven's vital energy then first begins to permeate and generate all things; buds of growth appear in black color. Hence the court costumes worn on the first day of the moon are black, as are pendants on official caps, the imperial chariots, and their horses. The cords attached to the great seals are black, as are their headdresses, the banners, the great precious jades, and animals used in the suburban sacrifices. The horns of these animals are egg-shaped. The capping ritual is performed at the eastern steps; in the marriage ritual, the groom fetches the bride in the courtyard [of her home], and in the funeral ritual, the deceased is encoffined above the eastern steps. . . .

In the White Reign, the sun and new moon, on the first day of the first moon stand in the *Hsu* [Hollow], and the *Tou* Star stands in the *ch'ou* point of time [the second of the twelve "earthly branches"]. Heaven's vital energy then first

1. Tsou Yen, of the fourth century B.C., maintained the theory that the changes of dynasties in history are dominated by the movements of the Five Elements.

begins to permeate and generate all things; buds of growth appear in white color. Hence the court costume worn on the first day of the moon are white, as are the pendants on official caps, the imperial chariots, and their horses. The cords attached to the great seals are white, as are their headdresses, the banners, the great precious jades, and animals used in the suburban sacrifices. The horns of these animals are shaped like silk cocoons. The capping ritual is performed at the main hall; in the marriage ritual, the groom fetches the bride at the main hall [of her home]; in the funeral ritual, the deceased is encoffined between the columns. . . .

In the Red Reign, the sun and new moon, on the first day of the first moon, stand in the *Ch'ien Niu* [Cowherd], and the *Tou* Star stands in the *Tzu* point of time [the first of the twelve "earthly branches"]. Heaven's vital energy then first begins to permeate and generate all things; buds of growth appear in red color. Hence the court costumes worn on the first day of the moon are red, as are the pendants on official caps, the imperial chariots, and their horses. The cords attached to the great seals are red, as are their headdresses, the banners, the great precious jades, and the animals used in the suburban sacrifices. The horns of these animals are shaped like a chestnut. The capping ritual is performed in the side chamber; in the marriage ritual, the groom fetches the bride at the gate [of her home]; in the funeral ritual, the deceased is encoffined above the western steps.

The significance of these changes in beginnings arose in homage to Heaven. The ancient kings, after receiving the mandate and becoming kings, changed the institutions, titles, and beginning of the year. At the sacrifices they announced their accession to Heaven and earth, the multitude of spirits, and their distant and near ancestors. Then they proclaimed the change throughout the world. The feudal lords having received this proclamation in their ancestral temples announced it to the spirits of the land and grain, to the ancestors, and the spirits of mountains and rivers. By the influence of these measures, there was a single rule. As a result of the Three Reigns, murders ceased among the near tribes and distant lands. This was only in the Middle Kingdom that there were three dynasties with their institutions.

The reason why these reigns are known as the "Three Beginnings" is that "Beginning" means "what is rectified." These reigns bring the [*yin* and *yang*] elements into operation, to which all things respond and are thus rectified with the result that, when the reigns are rectified, everything else is also rectified. That which is essential for the year is its first moon. The way to take that which is rectified as a pattern is to rectify what is basic, with the result that what follows will respond, rectify what is internal, with the result that what is external will respond. Then, as movements begin and end, everything follows in its transformations. This is known as "taking that which is rectified as a pattern. . . ."

Therefore, for the kings there are certain measures in which they should not change; certain measures in which they should return after two dynasties; certain measures in which they should return after three; certain measures in which they should return after four; certain measures in which they should return after five and certain measures in which they should return after nine. . . .

The institutions of these kings are those of *Shang* and *Hsia*, as well as those of *Chih* [Simplicity] and *Wen* [Refinement]. Those of *Shang* and of *Chih* take Heaven as their guiding principle; those of *Hsia* and of *Wen* take earth as their guiding principle; those of the *Ch'un Ch'iu* take man as their guiding principle. . . .

The *Tao* of the king, who takes Heaven as his guiding principle and models himself on *Shang*, is that of the *yang* in all its fullness. It emphasizes family relations and exalts love and simplicity. Hence the succession [to the throne] passes to the son, while generosity is shown to [the king's] younger brothers, who are born of the same mother. . . . The *Tao* of the king, who takes earth as his guiding principle and models himself on *Hsia*, is that of the growing *yin*. It emphasizes the honoring of superiors and exalts the regulations governing the proper relationships. Hence the succession [to the throne] passes to the grandson, while generosity is shown to the heir apparent. . . . The *Tao* of the king, who takes Heaven as his guiding principle and models himself on *Chih*, is that of the *yang* in all its fullness. It emphasizes family relations and exalts simplicity and affection. Hence the succession [to the throne] passes to the son, while generosity is shown to [the king's] younger brother who is born of the same mother. . . . The *Tao* of the king, who takes earth as his guiding principle and models himself on *Wen*, is that of the growing *yin*. It emphasizes the honoring of superiors and exalts propriety and refinement. Hence the succession [to the throne] passes to the grandson, while generosity is shown to the heir apparent. . . . These four administrations [*Shang*,

Hsia, Chih, and *Wen*] are like four seasons. When their cycle is completed, it starts again; when it reaches its end, it returns to its beginning.[1] [Sec. 23]

I now say that the king must change his institutions, but this does not mean that he changes his course or alters his principles. He, having received the Mandate of Heaven, rules under a different family name, and he reigns as a new king rather than as the direct successor of the preceding kings. If he continued the early institutions and practiced ancient ways without making any changes, he would not be distinguishable from the direct successor of the preceding kings. When a king receives the Mandate of Heaven, this is the manifestation of Heaven's will. Let one serve a father and one will carry out the father's ideas; let one serve a ruler and one will exemplify the ruler's purpose. Similarly, let the ruler serve Heaven and he will manifest Heaven's will. But if Heaven manifests itself to someone, and yet all things are perpetuated without changes, then no proper manifestation has been made; this is not in accord with the will of Heaven.

Therefore the new king must shift his place of residence, assume a new title, change the beginning of the year, and alter the color of clothes, because he dares not but obey the will of Heaven and make clear its manifestation to him. However, the bonds of human relationships, morality, government, instruction, customs, and meanings of words all remain as they were before. Why should these things be changed? Thus, the king changes his institutions, but he does not alter his basic principles. Confucius said: "To have done nothing and yet have the state well-governed—Shun was the one!" By this he meant that Shun did nothing more than take the principles of Yao [his predecessor] as a pattern. Is this not the good result of avoiding changes?[2] [Sec. I]

1. Tung Chung-shu's biography in the *Chien Han Shu* (History of the Early Han Dynasty) quotes him as saying:

Therefore the king might change the institutions, but he would not alter the basic principle. Thus the *Hsia* exalted *chung* [loyalty], the *Yin* [i.e., *Shang*] *ching* [reverence], and the *Chou wen* [refinement]. He who follows these dynasties, to sustain himself, must adopt these three teachings. Confucius said: "We know how the *Yin* modified the code of *li* when they followed upon the Hsia. We know how the Chou modified the code of *li* when they followed upon the *Yin.* And hence we can know the code of *li* as modified by the successors of the Chou even after one hundred ages." By this he meant the practice of these three teachings by the kings of one hundred succeeding generations.

2. In his biography in the *Chien Han Shu,* Tung Chung-shu is noted as having said: "The great source of the *Tao* [right principles] derives from Heaven; Heaven does not change, nor does the *Tao.*"

2. THE THREE AGES

The *Ch'un Ch'iu* is divided into twelve generations, which may be classified as follows: those that Confucius witnessed, those of which he heard, and those about which he learned [from transmitted records]. Three of these twelve generations were witnessed, four were known, and five were learned. The reigns of Ai, Ting, and Chao were those that the *chün-tzu* [Confucius] witnessed; those of Hsiang, Ch'eng, Wen, and Hsüen were the ones of which he heard; and those of Hsi, Min, Chuang, Huan, and Yin were the ones about which he learned. Those that were witnessed comprise 61 years [541-480 B.C.]; those that were heard of comprise 85 years [626-542 B.C.]; and those about which he learned comprise 96 years [722-627 B.C.].

He makes allusions to events he witnessed; he expresses sorrow for disasters of which he heard; but as to what he learned he sets aside his passions. This is the way in which sentiments are expressed in accordance with the situation.

For instance, when Chi was expelled, he simply said, "The rain ceremony is restored"; this is the way in which he made allusions. And when Tzu-Ch'ih was assassinated, he could bear to record the date; this is the way in which he expressed his sorrow for the disaster. But when Tzu-pan was assassinated, he recorded the date of *yi-wei;* this is the way in which he set aside his compassion.

His purpose, sometimes extensive and sometimes restricted, and his texts, sometimes detailed and sometimes sketchy, are both in conformity with these principles. Thereby I can understand how he treats that which is near with close attention and what is remote with less attention, what is dear to him with affection and what is less dear with less affection. I also understand how he values what is precious and despises what is cruel, how he stresses what is important and disregards what is trivial. In the same way, I understand how he treats substantially what is substantial and indifferently what is indifferent, how he praises what is good and condemns what is evil. Moreover, I understand how he considers the *yang* as the *yang*, and the *yin* as the *yin;* how he regards the white as the white, and the black as the black.[1] [Sec. I]

1. This theory of Three Ages is further elaborated by Ho Hsiu (129-182 B.C.) in his commentary on *Kung-yang Chuan*. According to him, the *Ch'un Ch'iu* was a record of the process through which Confucius transformed the Age of Disorder, through the Age of Approaching Peace, into the Age of Universal Peace. He called the age of which Confucius heard through trans-

Chapter III. The "Science of Catastrophes and Anomalies"

As early as the time of Mencius, there was already a tendency among Confucius' followers to take an interest in supernaturalism. It was for this reason that Hsün-tzu raised a strong protest against it insisting that the pursuit of knowledge be restricted to human affairs.[1] This tendency, however, persisted in Han times when members of the New-Text school showed a strong inclination toward cosmic speculations. Tung Chung-shu's "Science of Catastrophes and Anomalies" was in line with the prevalent beliefs of the time. The central idea of his system may be summarized briefly as follows: Because of the close relation between man and nature and the great similarity in the social and cosmic orders, human actions would affect the universal course of Heaven and earth and manifest themselves in the natural phenomena. Man's wicked deeds, for instance, would culminate in catastrophes such as fire, flood, drought, and earthquake, and in anomalies such as comets, eclipses, and weird animals. As he wrote: "All things avoid that from which they differ and cleave to that to which they are similar"; hence, "a beautiful thing will call to itself another beautiful thing of the same kind, whereas an ugly thing will call to itself another ugly thing of the same kind."[2] By applying this doctrine of "response of Nature to man," he wrote further: "When an emperor or a king is about to arise, auspicious omens first appear, whereas when he is about to be destroyed, evil auguries likewise first appear."[3]

These pseudo-scientific beliefs, which Tung Chung-shu called the "Science of Catastrophes and Anomalies," had a tremendous influence upon the Han political thought, for this ingenious theory acted wonderfully as a useful weapon with which to combat misgovernment on the part of the monarch; for even though the emperor's powers were unlimited, he would at least be subject to the judgments of Heaven as manifested in the abnormalities of nature. In this connection

---

mitted records, the "Age of Disorder," when the Sage devoted himself to his own state of Lu as the center of reform. The age of which Confucius heard through oral testimony was called the "Age of Approaching Peace," when the Sage extended his reform to all other Chinese states within the Middle Kingdom. Finally, the age which Confucius personally witnessed was called the "Age of Universal Peace," when "the whole world, far and near, large and small, was like one."

1. *Hsün Tzu*, Ch. XVII, *"T'ien-lun"* (On Heaven).
2. *Ch'un-ch'iu Fan-lu*, Sec. 57.
3. *Ibid*.

Tung emphasized that the principal object of *Ch'un-ch'iu* was to "subject the people to the ruler, and the ruler to Heaven."[4] That the device was in some measure successful is attested by the imperial edicts recorded in the *Ch'ien Han Shu* (*the History of the Former Han Dynasty*), in which the emperor requested the ministers and people to remonstrate with him on his misdeeds whenever anything of ill omen occurred.

From *Ch'un Ch'iu Fan-lu*, Sections 30 and 56

৵৵ ঽ৶

1. Interpretation of "Catastrophes and Anomalies"

According to a rough classification, when the creatures of Heaven and earth display unusual changes, these are called "anomalies"; lesser ones are called "catastrophes." The catastrophes always appear first and are then followed by anomalies. Catastrophes are the warnings of Heaven; anomalies are its threats. Heaven first sends warnings, and if [man, being thus warned] fails to understand, then he is made to feel awe through such anomalies. This is what is meant in the *Shih* when it says: "Stand in awe of the swaying power of Heaven."[1] The genesis of all such catastrophes and anomalies is the direct result of errors that exist within the nation. When the first indications of error begin to appear in the nation, Heaven sends forth fearful catastrophes to warn men. If, being thus warned, [man] fails to understand [the reason for] these manifestations, then ominous anomalies appear to terrify him. And if, being thus terrified, he still does not understand [the cause for] his fear, only then do misfortunes and calamities visit him. From this we may see that Heaven's will is benevolent, for it has no desire to bring ruin upon man.

If we examine these catastrophes and anomalies carefully, we may discern Heaven's will, which wishes us to do certain things and not to do others. As to that which Heaven wishes and does not wish, if a man searches within himself, he will surely find its warnings in his own heart, and if he looks about him at daily affairs, he will find verification of these warnings in the nation. Thus we can discern Heaven's will in these catastrophes and anomalies. We should not hate these signs, but stand in awe of them, considering that Heaven wishes

4. *Op. cit.*, Sec. 23.
1. Bk. IV, Sec. 1, Ode 7.

to rectify our faults and save us from our errors. Hence this
is the way in which Heaven warns us. [Sec. 30]

2. The Correspondence of Man with Heaven

Heaven is noted for the power to create things, earth is
noted for the power to transform, and man is noted for moral
principles. The *ch'i* [vital force] of Heaven is above, that of
earth below, and that of man in between. Spring produces
and summer grows, and all things flourish. Autumn destroys
and winter stores, and all things are preserved. Therefore
there is nothing more subtle than *ch'i*, richer than earth, or
more divine than Heaven. Of the essence of Heaven and earth
whereby the creatures were born, none is more exalted than
man. Man receives the Decree of Heaven, and therefore is
superior to other creatures. Other creatures suffer troubles and
distress, and are unable to practice *jen* and *yi;* man alone is
capable of practicing them. Other creatures suffer trouble and
distress, and are unable to match Heaven and earth; man
alone is capable of matching them.

Man has three hundred and sixty joints, which match the
number of Heaven; his body, with its bones and flesh, matches
the thickness of earth. He has ears and eyes above, with their
keen sense of hearing and seeing, which symbolize the sun
and moon. His body has its orifices and veins, which symbolize rivers and valleys. His heart has feelings of sorrow, joy,
pleasure, and anger, which are analogous to divine feelings
[of Heaven]. When we look at man's body, how much
superior he is to other creatures, and he is indeed the same
as Heaven! Other creatures derive their life from Heaven's
yin and *yang* in a recumbent way, but man brilliantly bears
his markings. Thus as to the physical form of other creatures,
they all move about in a recumbent way; man alone, with
head erect and upright posture, looks straight forward. And
so, those who receive less from Heaven and earth are recumbent, while those who receive more from Heaven and earth
are erect. This shows man in his superiority to other creatures
and in his forming a trinity with Heaven and earth.

Therefore, in the body of man, his head rises up and is
round, like Heaven's form. His hair is like the stars and constellations. His ears and eyes, keen in their senses, are like the
sun and moon. The breathing of his nostrils and mouth is like
the wind. The penetrating wisdom of his mind is like the
divine intelligence [of Heaven]. His abdomen and womb,

now full and now empty, are like the myriad things. The myriad things are nearest to the earth. The portion of the body below the waist corresponds to earth. As the body like Heaven and earth, the waist serves as a sash. That which is above the neck is noble and majestic in spirit, to manifest the feature of Heaven and its kind. That which is below the neck is full and humble, comparable to the soil. The feet are square and spreading out, like the form of the earth. Therefore when a man wears ceremonial sash and girdle, his neck must be erect to distinguish it from the heart. That which is above the sash is all *yang*, and that which is below sash is all *yin*, each with its own function. The *yang* is the *ch'i* of Heaven, and the *yin* is the *ch'i* of the earth. When *yin* and *yang* become operative and cause man to have ailment in the foot or numbness in the throat, the *ch'i* of the earth rises to become clouds and rain. Thus there is resemblance in the correspondence. The symbols of Heaven and earth, as well as the correspondence between *yin* and *yang*, are ever found complete in the human body. The body is like Heaven, and its numerical categories are interwoven with those of Heaven, so that their lives are linked together. With the number of days in the year, Heaven gives form to man's body. As a result, in the body there are three hundred and sixty-six small component parts, making the sum total of the days in the year, and twelve major parts, making the sum total of the months in the year. Within, there are five viscera, making the sum total of the five elements. Without, there are four limbs, making the sum total of the four seasons. At one time [man's eyes] open and at another time [they] close, thus corresponding to day and night. At one time [man] asserts and at another time [he] yields, thus corresponding to summer and autumn. At one time [he feels] sorrow and at another time [he feels] joy, thus corresponding to the *yin* and *yang*. The mind has [the power of] calculation and deliberation, which corresponds to [Heaven's] numerical categories. Man's conduct follows the principles of human relationships, which correspond to [the relationship of] Heaven and earth. All this, appearing in body, is born with man. With what can be numbered, there is correspondence in number; with what cannot be numbered, there is correspondence in category. In both cases, man is identical with and corresponds to Heaven. [Sec. 56]

Ai (愛): Love or affection.

Chan Kuo (戰 國): Warring States.

Chèng Ming (正 名): The rectification names—a Confucian doctrine holding that names would correspond to actualities.

Ch'ēng (誠): Honesty; sincerity; truthfulness; being one's true self.

Ch'i (氣): Life breath; vital force; spirit. Used in connection with the Neo-Confucianist li (理, eternal principle), the *ch'i* means matter-energy; i.e., whatever is within the realm of matter.

Chih (知): Wisdom or knowledge.

Chih chih (致 知): Extension of knowledge.

Chiao (教): Teaching, cultivation, civilization, religion, or organization having these as their purpose; a compound of "filiality" and "supporting," stressing the virtue of filial piety.

Chien ai (兼 愛): Love for all, equally and without discrimination; universal love (Mohist concept).

Ch'in ai (親 愛): to cherish or love warmly.

Ch'ing ta fu (卿 大 夫): Noble great officers.

Chu hou (諸 侯): Prince or rulers of states; feudal lords.

Chün-tzu (君 子): Lord's son; princely man; originally, noble over-lord—later, perfect gentleman or superior man.

Ch'un Ch'iu (春 秋): Spring and Autumn.

Chung (忠): Faithfulness or loyalty to one's self; conscientiousness.

Chung Yung (中 庸): Doctrine of the golden mean as illustrated in the *Book of Chung Yung.*

Fa (法): Law or regulation; one of the Legalist concepts.

Fa Chia (法 家): School of the Legalist; Legalism.

Fo Chiao (佛 教): Buddhist religion; Buddhism as a religion.

Fo Hsüeh (佛 學): Buddhist learning; Buddhism as a philosophy.

Hao ch'i (浩 氣): All-embracing force; the Great Morale; the vital spirit; the "Ch'i of Supreme Greatness."

Hao jan chih ch'i (浩 然 之 氣): same as "Hao ch'i."

Ho (和): Harmony.

Hsiao (孝): Filial or filiality—the character depicting a son bearing an old man; *hsiao* was esteemed as the foundation of virtue.

Hsiao-jen (小人): "Small man" or common man, opposite of chün-tzu; originally a peasant—later, a mean, despicable person.

Hsiao k'ang (小康): Minor peace.

Hsin (心): Mind; heart.

Hsin (信): Good faith; sincerity.

Hsing (性): Nature conferred heaven on man.

   (形): Physical form.

   (刑): Code of punishment used for law in general, especially criminal law.

Hsüan hsüeh (玄學): System of profound and mysterious doctrines advocated by Neo-Taoists of the third and fourth centuries A.D.

Jen (仁): Humanity; human-heartedness; true manhood; a compound of "two" and "man," stressing the relationship between man and his fellow men; love; benevolence; kindness; charity. *Jen* is the essence of Confucius' ethical teachings.

Ju (儒): Literati; scholars who were versed in the six arts (*Liu I*): charioting and archery, history and numbers, music and rituals.

Ju Chia (儒家): School of Literati, chiefly based on the teachings of Confucius and the Confucian classics, or commonly known as Confucianism.

Ju Chiao (儒教): Confucian teachings or religion.

Ko wu (格物): Investigation of things.

Li (禮): Ceremonies or rituals; propriety or code of proper conduct; rules of social conduct. *Li* and *yueh* (music) are two important institutions in Confucianism.

   (理): Reason; eternal principle; truth; a basic concept of modern Chinese philosophy. *Li* and *ch'i* are the dualistic principles of Neo-Confucianism.

   (利): Profit; gain; benefit; opposite of *yi* (righteousness).

Li Chi (禮記): Book of Rites.

Liang chih (良知): Intuitive knowledge.

Liang neng (良能): Intuitive ability.

Liang hsin (良心): goodness of mind; conscience.

Li Hsüeh (理學): Learning or Study of Principle; Li-ism or commonly known as Neo-Confucianism.

Li-yün (禮運): "Evolution of Rites"—a section in *Li Chi*.

Ming (命): Fate; destiny; decree of Heaven.

(名): Name (See Cheng Ming)

(明): Enlightenment.

Ming ch'i (明 器): Spiritual utensils.

Ming Chia (名 家): School of Names; Sophists, logicians, or dialecticians who dealt with problems of relation between *ming* (name)
and *shih* (actuality).

Ming chiao (名 教): Religion of Names.

Ming fen (名 分): Nominal status; social status—*fen* means "duty."
Hence a name is a title that gives a man his definite place in society
and defines his relationships with others.

Ming t'ang (明 堂). "Bright Hall"—the palace where open court was
held.

Mo Chia (墨 家): Mohist School, under the leadership of Mo Tzu;
Mohism.

Pa (霸): Tyrant or Lord-Protector, who "employs scheming and
force."

Pa kua (八 卦): Eight trigrams as represented by an arrangement of
certain mystic symbols consisting of triplet combinations of straight
line and divided line. These were later combined until there were
sixty-four hexagrams.

Pa tao (霸 道): The Way of the Lord-Protector.

Pien che (辯 者): Dialecticians.

San ts'ai (三 才): Three powers; together with heaven and earth,
which are considered two powers, man is included to make the three
powers, referred as:

T'ien ching (天 經): first principle of heaven;

Ti yi (地 義): ultimate standard of earth;

Jen hsing (人 行): norm of conduct for man.

Shang Ti (上 帝): Supreme Emperor; i.e., Supreme Being.

Shê chi (社 稷): "Land and Grain" represented an altar erected to
the deity of the soil and the god of grain.

Shêng (聖): "Sage," designating an integral humanist development of
mind and once capable of wisely directing human affairs.

Shêng chih (聖 治): Government by the sage.

Shêng jen (聖 人): A sagely man, the wise man; the ideal ruler.

Shêng wang (聖 王): A Sage-king.

Shih (士): The warring, ruling class—the military officers and government officials; later, *shih* denotes scholars as a class, standing at

the head of the fourfold designation of the classes in society: *shih,*
nung (farmers), *kung* (laborers), *shang* (merchants).

(詩) or Shih Ching (詩 經): *Odes* or *Book of Odes.*

Shih chung (時 中): timely mean.

Shu (書) or Shu Ching (書 經): *History* or *Book of History.*

Shu (恕): Consideration or sympathy for the feeling of others; i.e.,
altruism.

Shu jen (庶 人): The multitude, the common people of the empire.

Shu ming (庶 民): Same as *shu jen.*

Ssŭ hai (四 海): The "four seas"—the surrounding nations.

Ssŭ kuo (四 國): "Four nations" standing for the four quarters of the
state.

Ssŭ tuan (四 端): The four beginnings or four essentials—*jen, yi, li,*
and *chih* (wisdom).

Ssŭ yü (私 欲): Selfish desires.

Ta Hsüeh (大 學): *The Great Learning;* the university.

Ta Tao (大 道): The Great Course; Great Tao.

Ta t'ung (大 同): Great Commonwealth; Great Union; Great Harmony; One World; the Confucian Utopia.

Tai chi (太 極): Great Ultimate or Terminus.

Tai I (太 一): Great Oneness.

Tao (道): Way; principle; truth; cosmic order. Confucian Tao is
ethical in sense and deals with the way of life, while the Tao of the
Taoists is essentially metaphysical and can be taken as an all-embracing first principle for the universe.

Tao Chia (道 家): The Taoist School; the system based on the teachings of Lao Tzu, known as Taoism.

Tao Chiao (道 教): Taoism as a religion.

Te (德): Virtue; power, both in the moral and nonmoral sense.

Ti (帝): same as Shang Ti; emperor, who employs kindliness and
good faith.

(地): Earth.

T'i (悌): Brotherliness or brotherly respect; fraternal love.

T'ien (天): Heaven or sky—both in the physical and supernatural
sense.

T'ien hsia (天 下): All under Heaven—the world.

T'ien kuan (天 官): Natural senses.

T'ien li (天 理): Heavenly reason; divine law; the moral principle
of Heaven.

T'ien ming (天命): Heavenly order or mandate by authority of which a ruler reigns.

T'ien Tao (天道): Way of Heaven.

T'ien ti (天地): Heaven and earth; the universe; the origin of life.

T'ien tzu (天子): Son of Heaven; i.e., the emperor.

Wang (王): King, who "employs justice and correctness."

Wang tao (王道): Kingly way that embodies virtuous government; opposite of *pa tao*.

Wu Chiao (五教): Five doctrines or maxims, teaching "fathers to be righteous, mothers to be kind, elder brothers to be friendly, younger brothers to be reverent, and sons to be filial."

Wu Ching (五經): Five Classics—*Shu Ching, Shih Ching, Yi Ching* (Book of Change), *Li Chi*, and *Ch'un Ch'iu*.

Wu chang (五常): Five Constant Virtues—*jen, yi, li, chih, hsin*.

Wu hsing (五行): Five Elements—water, fire, wood, metal, earth.

(五刑): Five Punishments—*mo* (branding), *i* (cutting off the nose), *yueh* (cutting off feet), *kung* (castration), *ta p'i* (death).

Wu lun (五倫): Five Relationships: between king and subjects, between father and son, between husband and wife, between brothers, and between friends.

Wu wei (無爲): Inaction; inactivity; nonassertion; noninterference.

Yi (義): Righteousness; what one ought to do as opposed to what one would like to do for profit (*li*).

(易): Change; in the *Yi Ching, yi* is often used interchangeably with Tao.

Yin Yang (陰陽): Passive and active principles of the universe; the female, negative force and the male, positive force, always contrasting but complementary.

Yin-yang Chia (陰陽家): Yin-yang School, believing in the two cosmic principles of *yin* and *yang* whose reactions supposedly created all things.

Yü (欲): Desire.

Yü Wu (有無): The corporeal and the incorporeal; existence and nonexistence; being and nonbeing.

Yüeh (樂): Music.

Yung (庸): Normality; common and ordinary.

INDEX

Library of the Mystic Arts

A LIBRARY OF ANCIENT AND MODERN CLASSICS

BARTON, R. F. Autobiographies of Three Pagans in the Philippines. intro. by Dr. Nancy Oestreich Lurie. ill. index bibliog. 320 pp. 5½" x 8¼" 62-19195. $7.50   ANTHROP
"It is difficult to realize that the people in these autobiographies, two men and a woman live on the same planet that we do. Head-hunting and spearing your enemy are everyday occurrences. Anyone who knows your kin is an enemy, unless he is your kin. It is the savage eye for an eye and tooth for a tooth of Biblical times, even though coming of the Americans has discouraged some of the practices. R. F. Barton was among the Ifugaos long enough to select three representatives of the tribe. In the autobiographies he gives their life history before marriage, including many of their ceremonies and customs. It is an interesting and informative anthropological study." — WICHITA EAGLE & BEACON

BERNHEIM, H. Hypnosis and Suggestion in Psychotherapy: The Nature and Uses of Hypnotism. intro. by Ernest R. Hilgard. index. 428 pp. 6⅛" x 9¼" 63-22664. $10.00   PSYCH
Hypnosis has had a checkered career over a period of centuries, going through cycle after cycle of general approval and total eclipse. The fate of this book indicates how fragile the reputation of hypnosis has been; written almost eighty years ago, and translated into English a few years later, it has always been acknowledged as a great classic. Yet it has been out of print for some seventy years. It was not obsolete; nor was it suppressed. It has simply been neglected — as has hypnotism itself. It was the Second World War that reintroduced hypnosis in psychotherapy, and the widespread contemporary interest dates from that time. Today its potential is recognized by practically all medical societies over the world, and courses in hypnotism are appearing in medical school curricula and in training programs for psychiatric residents. Numerous psychologists are also turning to hypnosis as a fertile field for research and therapy.

BULLOUGH, Vern L. The History of Prostitution. index. 320 pp. 6⅛" x 9¼" 64-16619. $7.50   HIST
Prostitution, like the weather, has often been talked about, but very rarely has any scholar bothered to do any research on the topic. Few serious studies on prostitution have been undertaken by social scientists over the past fifty years. Although an occasional sociologist, psychologist, psychiatrist, or anthropologist has concerned himself, the historian has totally neglected the subject. As a result this book is the first attempt at a serious history of prostitution in English in this century.
The author, Dr. Vern L. Bullough, is a historian who has specialized in the history of medicine and science. He has published numerous articles, primarily on medical history, in various learned journals. He was assisted in his researches by his wife, Bonnie L. Bullough.

COOMARASWAMY, Ananda Kentish. Buddha and the Gospel of Buddhism. intro. by John C. Wilson. ill. index. bibliog. glossary. 370 pp. 6⅛" x 9¼" 64-16160. $10.00   REL
A classic introduction to Buddhism, Coomaraswamy's book was originally published in England in 1916. It was reprinted without change in 1927, and it is now finally available in its original form in an American edition. The author was revered both in the East and the West for his unique contributions to art

and philosophy as well as religion. An ardent Indian nationalist, his life work became the preservation of India's heritage and the monumental task of teaching the West to respect and revere the great civilization of India.

When Coomaraswamy died, Aldous Huxley spoke of his "unique importance as a mediator between East and West."

The author was fond of calling himself a traditionalist and often emphasized the virtues of orthodoxy. He was always suspicious of the Western fashionable interest in Buddhism and frequently spoke with considerable irony of the contemporary offbeat Zen enthusiasts. "The suspicious popularity of 'Buddhism' in Europe," he wrote in 1938, "has rested upon a very thorough misunderstanding of what Buddhism really means. The essential doctrines of Buddhism, like those of all orthodox relgions, are in radical opposition to our modern individualism."

The book continues to be a solid exposition of Buddhistic thought and its reissue should be timely in view of current rapprochment between the West and Eastern religious systems. Some twenty plates add interest and value.—VIRGINIA KIRKUS SERVICE.

FEILDING, Everard. Sittings with Eusapia Palladino and other Studies. intro. by E. J. Dingwall. 324 pp. 6⅛" x 9¼" 63-18682. $10.00   PARAPSYCH

"The author, well known as an objective observer of psychical phenomena, presents primarily a detailed report of 13 seances with the noted Italian medium of the 20th Century. There are included accounts of other mediums and of the stigmata of a French abbe. Facts are given; conclusions are left for the reader." — JOURNAL OF THE AMERICAN MEDICAL ASSOCIATION

"William James deplored the cheating and the vulgarity connected with the mediumship of Eusapia Palladino, but he believed that there was a residuum of phenomena in her performances which could not be explained. So did Everard Feilding of the Society for Psychic Research. He put her through the most rigid tests possible early in this century and concluded that she possessed some inexplicable power which caused tables to levitate, bells to ring, and lights to flash. In this most interesting collection of Feilding's writings we find that although he was a serious researcher, he always retained a sense of humor and a healthy skepticism. Eric Dingwall, who was his friend, has contributed a witty and appreciative introduction which reinforces the impression one gets from these papers that Feilding was a "most acute and well-balanced investigator" of ESP. Recommended for all libraries interested in this field of research." — LIBRARY JOURNAL

GUIGNEBERT, Charles. Jesus fwd. by Joel Carmichael. index. bibliog. xv + 560 pp. 6⅛" x 9¼" 56-7837. $10.00   REL

This historical study of the life of Jesus and the origins of Christianity has received the highest possible praise from biblical scholars of the status of Niebuhr, Barth and Pfeiffer. Its author, Charles Guignebert, is generally considered one of the finest examples of European scholarship. He spent a lifetime of research into the genesis of all forms of religious belief; toward the end of his life he held the chair of the History of Christianity at the Sorbonne.

REINHOLD NIEBUHR: "The virtue of Professor Guignebert's venture lies in his comprehensive analysis of the scholarship of the past decades in this field. The specialists are ãcquainted with all the evidence which he analyzes. But there is no book of recent years which will give the interested layman a more comprehensive account of what has been written and said about the life of Jesus and a fairer estimate of conflicting evidence. Naturally the author has a position of his own to maintain, but the reader is permitted to see how he arrived at it, and with what cogency and plausibility he defends it against contrasting views."

ROBERT H. PFEIFFER: "Aside from Guignebert's JESUS, only Goguel's LIFE may be regarded as a serious attempt to write a critical and objective historical work.

Guignebert furnishes an excellent introduction to the subject, a reliable guide to beginners, and an informing manual for scholars. We need to be reminded again by Guignebert of the strict and sober discipline required of the true historian."

JAFFE, Aniela. Apparitions and Precognitions: A study from the Point of View of C. G. Jung's Analytical Psychology. intro. by C. G. Jung. index. 224 pp. 6⅛" x 9¼". 63-19744. $7.50   PSYCH
The author, well known for her valuable contributions to the literature of analytical psychology, was specifically selected by Dr. Jung to write this book. The book represents a psychological evaluation of more than 1500 personal accounts elicited in response to a series of articles by Dr. Jung, dealing with prophetic dreams, coincidences, premonitions, apparitions. The articles appeared in the popular Swiss magazine, *Schweizerische Beobachter,* and the astonishing response to it came from all social classes — farmers, workmen, tradesmen, office employees and various professions.
One of the notable things to come to light in Dr. Jaffe's book is the fact that among the Swiss, who are commonly regarded as stolid, unimaginative, rationalistic and materialistic, there are just as many ghost stories and strange tales as is likely to be found in any other land; bewitching, sorcery, magic spells, as practiced in the Middle Ages and remoter times have by no means died out, but presently flourish among the Swiss as rampantly as they did centuries ago.
The author leaves aside the questioner of ultimate truth; instead she tries to inquire into the psychological questions: Exactly who is it that sees a ghost? Under what psychic conditions does he see it? What does a ghost signify when examined for its content as a symbol?

KING, C. Daly. The States of Human Consciousness. fwd. by Roy Finch. index. v-xiii + 176 pp. 6⅛" x 9¼" 63-10385. $7.50   PSYCH
The crucial thesis of this book is that in addition to the forms of consciousness known to all human beings (Sleep and Waking) there exist two further forms not yet widely known (Awakeness and Objective Consciousness).

What led such an extremely skeptical man as Dr. King to accept the unorthodox idea that additional states of human consciousness are possible? There were four main lines of evidence which convinced him: These were: 1) the neurological and physiological teachings of the Guardjieff Institute; 2) his personal psychological experiments and experiences; 3) his historical studies of ancient civilizations; 4) his studies in behavioral patterns.

LEARY, Timothy; ALPERT, Richard; Metzner, Ralph. A Guide to Psychedelic Experience. 150 pp. 8" x 9" 64-19705. $5.00   PSYCH
During the past few years newspapers and magazines have poured out unrestrained criticism on the subject of psychedelic drugs. Meanwhile certain technical journals have simultaneously dealt out unrestrained praise. Whom are we to believe?
Perhaps the most objective evidence available on these important new drugs comes from recent studies made by four scientific research groups, which administered LSD and psilocybin to 462 persons — among them physicians, lawyers, writers, ministers, psychologists, artists, musicians, engineers and housewives. The percentage of these persons reporting it was a pleasant experience was 73%; the percentage reporting they wished to try it again was 82%; a total of 67% reported the experience brought them greater regard for other human beings; 67% felt a sense of relaxation and freedom from anxiety and tension; 65% felt it was of lasting benefit; 38% said it increased their interest in nature, art, music; and 64% felt the experience had changed their lives.
Drs. Leary, Alpert and Metzner have for years been among the most prominent names in the research of psychedelics. They were engaged in a program of experiments with the drugs at Harvard University, until sensational national

publicity, unfairly concentrating on student interest in the drugs, led to the suspension of the experiments. Since then, the authors have continued their work without academic auspices.

Like other scientists involved with psychedelic research, the authors maintain that the drug is only one component of the psychedelic session. Equally important is the mental and spiritual preparation, both before and in the course of taking the drug. The authors find no need to invent new mental and spiritual materials for this purpose. The great literature of meditation lends itself very well to this use. This particular guide uses preparation material from THE TIBETAN BOOK OF THE DEAD.

LEGMAN, G. The Horn Book; Studies in Erotic Folklore and Bibliography. index. bibliog. 565 pp. 6⅛" x 9¼" 63-19743. $12.50   REF

The author is probably the most learned and most controversial figure in the field of American folklore. He is also the principal living specialist in erotic folklore. A former bibliographer for the Kinsey Institute, he enjoys repute as a lecturer and as the editor of *Neurotica* magazine. He is also the author of *Love and Death: A Study in Censorship,* now in its second edition. In his present work, the author's intention is to give the real facts about erotic literature and folklore. Eloquently, he attacks the substitution of fakelore for folklore in the mass communications media of America today. After establishing the value of unfettered folk-art, Mr. Legman analyzes with penetrating psychological discernment the displacement of sexual symbolism in our society and makes a strong case for authentic, unexpurgated collections. He attacks the patently illogical and insensible idea that sex must be expunged — while allowing the sadistic programs, books and plays an uncriticized place in our society. Murder, torture, cannibalism freely appear in our mass media, while the healthy normality of sexual intercourse between man and woman is deprecated or silently omitted. And the author points a serious warning: "The substitution of allowed sadism for prohibited sexuality in folk literature and mass communications can only result in the most sinister abnormalization of the whole psychic structure of future generations."

The book's table of contents follows:

I. STUDIES IN EROTIC BIBLIOGRAPHY
    1. The Bibliography of Prohibited Books: Pisanus Fraxi
    2. The Horn Book, and Other Bibiliographical Problems
    3. Great Collectors of Erotica

II. THE REDISCOVERY OF BURNS' MERRY MUSES OF CALEDONIA
    4. The Cunningham Manuscript
    5. *The Merry Muses* as Folklore

III. PROBLEMS OF EROTIC FOLKLORE
    6. Folklore and Fakelore
    7. Misconceptions in Erotic Folklore
    8. The Bawdy Song...In Fact and In Print
    9. The Limerick: A History and Critique
    10. Toward a Motif-Index of Erotic Humor
    11. Folksongs, Fakelore, Folkniks and Cash
    12. Who Owns Folklore?

MARTIN, Eva. Reincarnation: The Ring of Return. index. bibliog. v-xi + 306 pp. 5½" x 8¼" 63-18492. $5.00   REL

The idea of reincarnation has always appealed powerfully to man's innate sense of justice, to his yearning for eternal progress. Yet, strangely enough, there are not many books to be found in English on the subject. Nor are any of them likely to be, as the present volume is, an anthology of the great writings on reincarnation.

"This first American edition of what is regarded as a standard work in its field, is comprehensive in that it covers the pre-Christian era, the early Christian era and other writings of the first five centuries. Miscellaneous sources are drawn upon and material from the first three decades of the Twentieth Century is also included. Almost exclusively, the author in her quotations, turns to the poets. Such a book as this, as the publisher remarks, 'whatever its shortcomings is not likely to become dull reading.' " — CHRISTIAN HERALD

PODMORE, Frank. From Mesmer to Christian Science: A Short History of Mental Healing; intro. By E. J. Dingwall. index. xxi + 306 pp. 6⅛″ x 9¼″ 63-21599. $10.00 PSYCH
"This short history of mental healing covers broadly and impressively just about everything from Mesmer to Christian Science. Certainly, spiritual healing has become an important part of our everyday life. In medicine there are psychoanalysts and an entire new school of therapy along with the use of hypnosis as an anesthesia; and in religion, not only Christian Science and New Thought, but many movements within the established churches and synagogues. More and more it brings into sharp focus the 'miraculous therapy' of Jesus. In these pages one follows the steady march of mental healing from quackery and chicanery to respectability, with something added." — *Dr. Daniel A. Poling,* CHRISTIAN HERALD

"Since the first appearance of this book in 1909, no publication has superseded Podmore's critical and detailed study. An outstanding member of the British Society for Psychical Research, he traced the subject from the hectic days of pre-Revolutionary Paris to the beginning of the 20th Century. Obsessed with the idea of fraud, the medical profession obstinately rejected all evidence of the validity of these investigations, abandoning the field to amateurs and fanatics. Eventually the phenomena which Mesmer attributed solely to a material fluid came to be explained as a purely spiritual process. The progeny of Mesmerism therefore include not only hypnotism and aspects of experimental psychology, but also Spiritualism, New Thought, and Mental Healing, of which Christian Science is most prominent. Recommended for most psychology collections." — LIBRARY JOURNAL

PRINCE, Walter Franklin. The Case of Patience Worth. intro. by John C. Wilson. 509 pp. 6⅛″ x 9¼″ 63-23268. $10.00 PARAPSYCH
The author, a renowned psychologist and a pioneer in scientific psychic research, regards the case of Patience Worth as one of the most fascinating and enigmatic psychic manifestations of all time. In the conclusion of his book, Dr. Prince states that he could offer no rational explanation to the riddle of Patience Worth, despite years of impartial scientific investigation.
Patience Worth identified herself as a spirit from 17th Century England and she communicated through a medium, Mrs. Pearl Curran, an unlettered Missouri housewife. Over a period of five years, Patience created and communicated through Mrs. Curran an enormous quantity of poetry and prose of astonishing quality. Her literary creations displayed original genius, enormous erudition, familiarity with classic literature and history, piercing wit and penetrating wisdom; in brief, creations which could not conceivably have come from the simple, unlettered Mrs. Curran, who had never been out of the Mid-West and who had managed to complete a grammar school education only after considerable difficulty.

ROSSMAN, Joseph. Industrial Creativity: The Psychology of the Inventor. intro. by Gardner Murphy. index. bibliog. 288 pp. 6⅛″ x 9¼″ 64-16161. $7.50 PSYCH
In this scholarly and painstaking study of the mental processes of creativity, Dr. Rossman, long associated with the U.S. Patent Office, presents many startling conclusions developed after a long and careful analysis of source material obtained from 700 active and important inventors. Dr. Rossman, a chemical engineer, a member of the bar practicing before both the U.S. Supreme Court and the Court of Customs and Patent Appeals, a famous patent attorney, and a doctor of psychology, is perhaps the only man who could have undertaken such a study.

Popular fantasy pictures the inventor as a wild-eyed, impractical dreamer. But the cumulative portrait that emerges in this book reveals an ability for keen analysis, a mind strikingly original and observant, an astonishing perseverance in the face of apparently insurmountable obstacles.

Dr. Rossman's book was first published primarily to help inventors understand all the implications of the inventive process. That was thirty years ago. Today it is published anew, with new material by Dr. Rossman. This time he addresses his book to all those interested in the nature of creativity. For those more specifically interested in scientific invention, there is a considerable body of original information.

SMITH, Susy. The Mediumship of Mrs. Leonard, photographs. bibliog. 256 pp. 6⅛″ x 9¼″ 64-17317. $7.50
PARAPSYCH

This is the first comprehensive study taking in the entire life work of Mrs. Leonard, the last of the great trance mediums of the golden age. She is now well into her eighties. This important new work is destined to endure as a classic in the search for psychic truth; it presents the strongest evidence ever obtained of the survival of the human spirit — of earthly memories abiding beyond the grave.

The scientific evidence in the case of Mrs. Leonard is the most documented in psychic history. No trance medium has ever been more thoroughly investigated and researched. Most of her career was spent not as a private medium but under the exclusive control of the Society of Psychical Research. The Society established a framework of painstaking supervision and kept exact records of everything said at Mrs. Leonard's sittings.

This book continues the series from University Books dealing with the great mediums. The two outstanding physical mediums, D. D. Home and Eusapia Palladino, are already represented. Of the three great trance mediums, Mrs. Piper was introduced in *William James On Psychic Research* and Helene Smith in Flournoy's *From India To The Planet Mars.* The third trance medium is Gladys Osborne Leonard.

APOCRYPHA. Introduction by Morton Enslin, Professor of Biblical Languages and Literature, St. Lawrence University. Bound in white and gold, 3-color slipcase. xv + 239 pp. 7¼″ x 11″ 62-12335. $15.00
REL

"In 1924 the Nonesuch edition of the Apocrypha appeared, limited to 1325 copies. This new edition is an almost exact facsimile of that very beautiful work, bound in a most attractive cover with stamped gilt design, and boxed. Most marked of its changes from the original, and one that enhances the value of the work considerably, is an Introduction by the editor of this Journal, Dr. Morton S. Enslin, who in brief, concise paragraphs provides excellent prefaces to the work as a whole and to each of the books individually. He places the Apocrypha in its proper context in biblical literature, indicates the inappropriateness of the name when applied to the books as a whole, and shows how it was that Luther split off these writings and placed them in the limbo between the Old Testament and the New.' The individual introductions serve to provide the backgrounds, probable datings, and general contents of each of the fourteen pieces. This is a valuable work for both the biblical scholar and the lover of fine books." — *J. Calvin Keene,* JOURNAL OF BIBLICAL LITERATURE

BIRREN, Faber. Color: A Survey in Words and Pictures: From Ancient Mysticism to Modern Science. ill. index. 250 pp. 7⅝″ x 10½″ 62-18889. $15.00
PSYCH

"This book is a compilation of information concerning color, from the physiology of the eye and theories of color vision to the ancients' belief in magical qualities of color, and even current theories of color and personality. The author has written several books on color and color psychology, particularly relating color to commercial purposes." — LIBRARY JOURNAL

"An introduction to the history of color, both ancient and modern, and to its various uses. This book is highly recommended." — PSYCHIATRIC QUARTERLY "All in all, an absorbing book in an uncrowded field, and one which does credit to the author's erudition and intuition." — ST. LOUIS POST-DISPATCH

BIRREN, Faber. Color Psychology and Color Therapy: A Factual Study of the Influence of Color on Human Life. intro. by Felix Morrow. ill. photogs. index. biblio. xv + 302 pp. 6⅛" x 9¼" 61-14266. $7.50   PSYCH
"Faber Birren is a consultant on the use of color in industrial and other applications, and perhaps without peer in this field. The book, however, goes much farther than the mere applications and their psychology. There is fascinating detail from historical, medical, occult, physiological sources as well — fascinating and documented ... Recommended." — LIBRARY JOURNAL

THE BOOK OF THE DEAD: the Hieroglyphic Transcript of the Papyrus of ANI. tr. and intro. by E. A. Wallis Budge. ill. appendixes. xiv + 704 pp. 6⅛" x 9¼" 60-12165. $12.50   REL
This is the collection of texts which the ancient Egyptian scribes composed for the benefit of the dead. A book-length introduction by Sir Wallis Budge, late Keeper of the Egyptian and Assyrian Antiquities in the British Museum, gives us its history and theology. This is an exact reproduction of the famous Medici Society edition of 1911 except that the original two volumes are here bound as one.

BUCKE, Richard Maurice, M.D. Cosmic Consciousness; A Study in the Evolution of the Human Mind. bibliog. xvii + 326 pp. 7¼" x 9¾" 61-11100. $5.95   PSYCH
One of the great classics of mystical experience, this work was first published in 1901. The author saw the emergence of a new faculty, the natural outgrowth of our present level of consciousness to a level as far above it as it is above the simple consciousness of animals. William James read the work when it appeared and wrote to the author: "I believe that you have brought this kind of consciousness 'home' to the attention of students of human nature in a way so definite and inescapable that it will be impossible henceforward to overlook it or ignore it ... But my total reaction on your book, my dear Sir, is that it is an addition to psychology of first rate importance, and that you are a benefactor of us all."

BUDGE, E. A. Wallis. Amulets and Talismans. ill. b/w 22 plates, 300 ill. index. xxxix + 543 pp. 6⅛" x 9¼" 61-7163. $10.00   REL/ARCHEOL
"This encyclopedic volume represents years of research and an extensive knowledge of ancient civilizations. The author, as teacher at Cambridge University and curator of the British Museum, has accumulated a wealth of data dealing with demonology, divination, astrology, numerology and the belief in the prophylactic properties of the gems prevalent among the people of the ancient civilizations of Sumer, Babylon, Persia, Egypt and others. The author throws new light on many passages in early biblical writings which will give the student of the Old Testament often a clearer meaning of the archaic sense of the text. 'Amulets and Talismans' is a reliable reference book of lasting value." — THE LUTHERAN

BUDGE, E. A. Wallis. Osiris; the Egyptian Religion of Resurrection; 2 vs. bound in one; intro. by Jane Harrison. ill. 14 b/w plates, 212 line cuts. index. appendix. xliii + 440 pp. 6⅛" x 9¼" 61-10531. $15.00   REL
"In this full-length study, Dr. Wallis Budge, the late Keeper of the Egyptian and Assyrian Antiquities in the British Museum, interprets Osiris as a year-god who dies and lives again. In contradistinction to Frazer, he dwells on the native African origins of this ancient Egyptian cult and avoids the obvious parallels with the Mid-Eastern gods Attis and Adonis ... His work will be read with profit and enjoyment by all students of comparative religion." — LIBRARY JOURNAL

CHANG, Garma C. C. The Teachings of Tibetan Yoga. intro. by John C. Wilson. 128 pp. 6⅛″ x 9¼″ 62-22082. $5.00   YOGA
"One has always to be careful with books claiming to bring to light the occult tradition or the Tantric practices of the yogis in Tibet. Mostly they are based on second-hand information embellished with a liberal coating of fancy and fiction. But the works of Garma Chang are clearly not of this dubious variety. A scholar in Chinese, he has practised the Tibetan Yoga under traditional Gurus in that land of the Lamas and whatever he writes he does with a high sense of responsibility and imparts a genuine touch which only a person with direct acquaintance with the subject could give...A profound work to be read and re-read by all serious students of Yoga." — *M. P. Pandit*, THE VEDANTA KESARI

DAVID-NEEL, Alexandra. Magic and Mystery in Tibet. intro. by Aaron Sussman. photogs. xiv + 320 pp. 6⅛″ x 9¼″ 56-13013. $7.50   OCCULT
"Precisely the person to explore Tibet...absolutely fearless. Her accounts of Tibetan religious ceremonies and beliefs are the fullest and best we have." — THE NEW YORKER

DINGWALL, Eric J. Some Human Oddities: Studies in the Queer, the Uncanny and the Fanatical. ill. bibliog. appendixes. 198 pp. 6⅛″ x 9¼″ 62-14948. $6.00   PSYCH
DINGWALL, Eric J. Very Peculiar People: Portrait Studies in the Queer, the Abnormal, and the Uncanny. ill. index. bibliog. appendixes. 224 pp. 6⅛″ x 9¼″ 62-14949. $6.00   PSYCH
"These reissues of two fascinating books, originally written in 1946 and 1951 respectively, will be welcomed by all lovers of true tales of the weird, strange and abnormal. Here are stories, scholarly written and scientifically analyzed, of visionary mystics like Emanuel Swedenborg, masochistic saints like St. Mary Magdalene de Pazzi, flying friars like Joseph of Copertino, mediums *extraordinaires* like D. D. Home and Eusapia Palladino, pornographers de luxe like Hadrian Beverland, transvestites like James Allen, and many others."—M. D. PUBLICATIONS
"Dr. Dingwall recounts some real-life stories that rival fiction for strangeness. He views and interprets the lives of these queer folk through the eyes of a psychic researcher — one of great note, indeed, and one with a sound academic background. The author has combined his talents as historian, psychologist and psychic researcher to produce a work for the scholarly with a taste for the macabre." — MEDICAL JOURNAL OF AUSTRALIA

FLOURNOY, Theodore. From India to the Planet Mars. intro. and final chap. by C. T. K. Chari. xxxvi + 469 pp. 5½″ x 8½″ 63-16228. $10.00   PARAPSYCH
Recent research into extra-sensory perception and the problems of survival and reincarnation has given a new and decisive importance to this classic. The author, who was professor of psychology at the University of Geneva, has consistently received the highest praise for his critical and objective study of that remarkable medium, Helene Smith. Eulogistic estimates of his work have been made even by such eminent scientists as F. W. H. Myers, William McDougall and William James.

FOX, Oliver. Astral Projection: A Record of Out-of-the-Body Experiences. fwd. by John C. Wilson. xiii + 160 pp. 5½″ x 8½″ 62-19195. $5.00   OCCULT
The noted psychic researcher, Dr. Hereward Carrington, reports in one of his works: "The only detailed, scientific and first-hand account of a series of conscious and voluntarily controlled astral projections which I have ever come across is that by Mr. Oliver Fox, published in the *Occult Review* for 1920." The articles were expanded into a book. This is its first publication in the United States.

FRAXI, Pisanus (pseudonym of **ASHBEE, Henry Spencer**). 3 vols. Each indexed. v. 1. Index Liborum Prohibitorium. intro. by G. Legman. 51 + lxxvi + 543 pp. v. 2. Centuria Liborum Absconditorum. lx + 587 pp. v. 3. Catena Liborum Tacendorum. lvii + 591 pp. All bound in buckram and boxed 5¼" x 7¼" 63-13985. $35.00 per set   BIBLIOG
"The random bibliographical articles of which the present volumes are composed, sampling and describing at length the more difficult but elusive masterpieces of erotic literature in various languages" is the most important work of its kind in English. A 50-page introduction by G. Legman, whose name will be familiar to many librarians as a great bibliographer in his own right, makes clear the importance of this work, originally privately published a volume at a time. The present imprint in these volumes is that of Jack Brussel, publisher, but the edition has been taken over by University Books, Inc.

GRILLOT DE GIVRY, Emile. The Picture Museum of Sorcery, Magic and Alchemy. intro. by Cynthia Magriel. 376 ills. index. 395 pp. 7" x 9½" slipcased. 63-11177. $17.50   OCCULT
"Containing almost 400 illustrations, with descriptions and commentary woven into a smoothly reading text, this work studies the iconography of mysticism and the occult.... The entire volume forms a valuable contribution to our understanding of the 15th, 16th and 17th century thought. Medical historians and all interested in the history of ideas and of culture will welcome this book as a presentation of unusual and worthwhile pictorial documents. The translator and publishers are to be congratulated." — JOURNAL OF THE AMERICAN MEDICAL ASSN.
"Picture Museum of Sorcery, Magic and Alchemy is considered to be the best and most representative volume of illustrations on the subject. The roster of writers and works included is a roll-call of occult literature." — KANSAS CITY STAR

GUIGNEBERT, Charles. The Jewish World in the Time of Jesus. fwd. by Charles Francis Potter. index. bibliog. xiii + 288 pp. 5½" x 8¼" 59-14528. $6.00   REL
The Old Testament closes hundreds of years before Jesus; the New is written long after his death. What, then, do most of us know about his Jewish world? Most of us do not know that world — its Essenes, gnostics, magicians, angels and demons, hermetic books and Messiahs, none of them to be found in the Old Testament.
"It is only by ignoring the work of men like Guignebert that orthodox Christianity can maintain its claim to divine sanction and authority. Eventually it must succumb, and return to a sound historical base. This is a book which liberal ministers should regard as a 'must,' and which laymen will read with fascination and enlightenment." — *Donald S. Harrington,* COMMUNITY CHURCH BULLETIN

HARRISON, Jane Ellen. Epilegomena to the Study of Greek Religion (and) Themis: A Study of the Social Origins of Greek Religion. 152 ills. index. lvi + 600 pp. 6⅛" x 9¼" 62-16379. $10.00 REL
"Jane Harrison (1850-1928) symbolizes the meeting between the more traditional classical studies and the disciplines of cultural anthropology and psychoanalytical psychology. She was a contemporary of Sir James Frazer, Sigmund Freud, and C. G. Jung and one of the first classical scholars to identify and discuss the primitive bases of the Greek religious tradition...." — LIBRARY JOURNAL
"A book that changed my life — there are times when I think it is the most revolutionary book of the 20th century — has just been reissued, marking the 50th anniversary of its publication. It is *Themis....* Jane Harrison is truly what Edith Hamilton is popularly taken to be, the great lady who found Greece marble and left it living flesh." — *Stanley Edgar Hyman,* THE NEW LEADER

HUYSMANS, Joris-Karl La Bas: Down There: A Study in Satanism. intro. by Robert Baldick. xxviii + 317 pp. 5″ x 7¾″ 56-13015. $5.00   OCCULT

"It is generally believed that *La Bas* is a reasonably faithful picture of occult practice in medieval and 19th century France. It is worth remembering that Huysmans occupies a position in the direct line from Balzac to the modern psychological novel." — PSYCHIATRIC QUARTERLY

JAMES, William. The Varieties of Religious Experience: A Study in Human Nature. Enlarged Edition with Appendixes and Introduction by Joseph Ratner. index. bibliog. 672 pp. 6⅛″ x 9¼″ 63-14505. $10.00   REL

"A new edition of a highly respected and widely used classic now appears to make available to a new generation the early original insights of William James.... Prof. Ratner has included a critical essay on James as an introduction, in which he shows that legitimatizing of religious faith was the central theme of all his work. He also compares and contrasts James with Freud, Dewey and Jung. Thus a valuable almost indispensable volume is made available once again to all modern students of religion and psychology. It is a reference book all college and church libraries must add to their lists." — VIRGINIA KIRKUS SERVICE

"James, who taught philosophy at Harvard for most of his career, was impatient with his fellow academicians and their endless hair-splitting over matters that had no relation to life. A vibrant, generous person, he hoped to show that religious emotions, even those of the deranged, were crucial to human life. The great virtue of *The Varieties*, as noted by Pragmatist Philosopher Charles Pierce, is its 'penetration into the hearts of people.' " — TIME

"Just as interesting as when it first came out, the book seems scarcely at all dated." — JOURNAL OF THE AMERICAN MEDICAL ASSOCIATION

JUNOD, Henri A. The life of a South African Tribe. 2 vols. intro. by Keith Irvine, Research Officer of the Ghana Mission. 150 ills. photos. index. glossary. 1230 pp. 6⅛″ x 9¼″ 62-18890. Slipcased. $20.00   AFRICA

"This is the first American edition of a classic anthropological study of an African tribe written by a Swiss missionary and first published in Europe as long ago as 1912. Henri Junod came to what is now Mozambique in 1889, and lived for many years in the interior among the Bathonga people. On his return to Europe he wrote this monumental monograph, surprisingly enough in English when his own language was French.... The book examines in great detail the daily lives of the Bathongas as individuals and as members of the tribe, their religion, culture, and social life. It is a massive and masterly performance, all the more valuable now since it represents a way of life that has virtually vanished.... The two volumes are illustrated with photographs, maps and diagrams, and come boxed." — *John Barkham,* SATURDAY REVIEW SYNDICATE

"The finest monograph on any African tribe." — AFRICA, JOURNAL OF ANTHRO-POLOGY

LELAND, Charles Godfrey. Etruscan Magic and Occult Remedies. intro. by Margery Silver. ills. index. xxxiii + 385 pp. 6⅛″ x 9¼″ 63-18491. $10.00   ANTHROP

"This book tells the story of a people who, like the Mayas of Yucatan, disappeared without leaving a written language...There are numerous illustrations and an index of papers and authorities. If the reader is looking for something out of the ordinary, here is a most interesting volume." DETROIT MEDICAL NEWS

"This book, a reprint of an expensive edition of 50 years ago, is a delightful accounting of the (Etruscan) magic spells, curses and invocations..." — BERKELEY DAILY GAZETTE

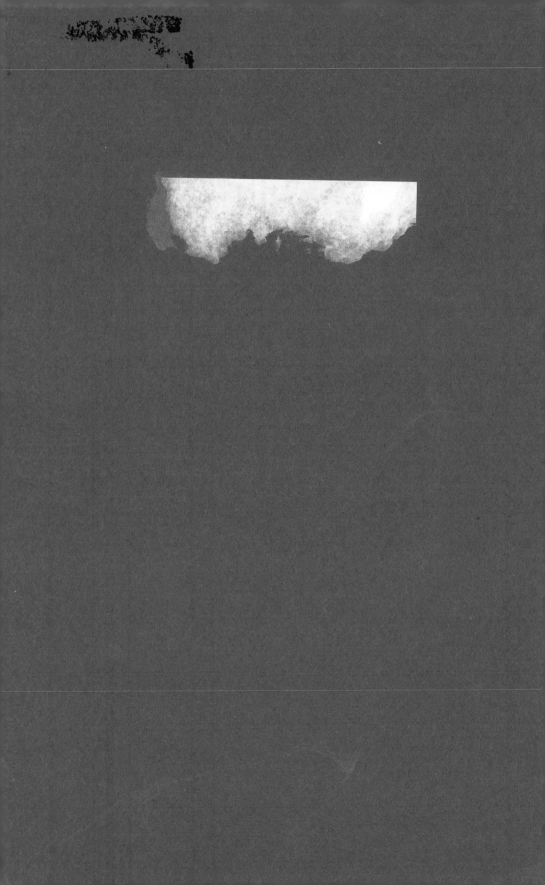